Checklist of Writings About John Dewey

1887-1973

Jo Ann Boydston

Kathleen Poulos

SOUTHERN ILLINOIS UNIVERSITY PRESS
Carbondale and Edwardsville

Feffer & Simons, Inc.
London and Amsterdam

Library of Congress Cataloging in Publication Data

Boydston, Jo Ann, 1924-
    Checklist of writings about John Dewey, 1887-1973.

    1. Dewey, John, 1859-1952 — Bibliography.
I. Poulos, Kathleen, 1944-   joint author.
II. Title.
Z8228.B59   016.37'01'0924   74-5236
ISBN 0-8093-0670-0

CONTENTS

PREFACE

This Checklist is lagniappe from the process of
planning and publishing the collected works of John
Dewey. As we gathered Dewey's writings, our primary
effort starting in 1961, we gradually amassed detailed
information on works about Dewey as well as about his
writings--materials and references important as background for editing Dewey's own work. Increasing interest in and demand for a list of this kind provided
impetus for searching and organizing the materials in
a systematic way. Leads to the items in this Checklist came from standard references, indexes, bibliog-
raphies, and librarians. The basic first list came
from the indispensable starting point in Dewey bibliography, M. H. Thomas's *JOHN DEWEY: A CENTENNIAL BIB-
LIOGRAPHY* (Chicago: University of Chicago Press, 1962).
Most of the information about unpublished materials
came from reference librarians throughout the country
who responded to our queries promptly, thoroughly, and
graciously. An unexpected source of leads and precise
information was found in the readers of *The Dewey News-
letter*. From their questions and the bibliographical
data they volunteered, we have been able to achieve a
degree of completeness that would not have been possible without their help.

As the title of this work indicates, the Checklist includes all works we have been able to locate
about John Dewey in English from 1887 through 1972.
We have also included as many items published in 1973
as our deadline would permit. We have seen and examined the published items; we have not seen many of
the unpublished materials. We make the traditional
and necessary disclaimer of completeness; we have attempted to be exhaustive, but as is well known to bib-
liographers, publication constitutes a stage in the
movement toward completeness, a more or less "complete" starting point for further work. We urgently
solicit the help of those who use this Checklist in
the months and years ahead: please continue to send
us materials, leads, information.

Among items we decided to exclude are *WHO'S WHO*
entries and encyclopedia articles about John Dewey.
Newspaper and news magazine articles are listed only

from those sources with readily available indexes and should be considered suggestive of the wealth of material appearing in such publications. So also with local and student publications from the several locations in which Dewey spent a number of years; a few such items have come to hand and are included but no attempt has been made to list these systematically.

The four main sections of the Checklist are:

1. Published works about Dewey, listed alphabetically by author's name. Complete information about collective and edited volumes appears under the author's or editor's name; individual entries are made under contributors' names, where only the article and book titles appear.

2. Unpublished works about Dewey, listed alphabetically by author's name.

3. Reviews of Dewey's works, grouped under the name of the work reviewed. The Dewey titles are arranged alphabetically.

4. Reviews of works about Dewey, listed alphabetically by author's name.

We want to acknowledge with real gratitude the help given us by Halsey Thomas, Dennis Rohatyn, Aldona Johnson, Karen Milligan, Alan Cohn, Tom Kilpatrick, scores of reference librarians and local librarians, and the many Dewey scholars who have thoughtfully sent offprints, references, dissertations, and queries. We acknowledge with special thanks a grant from the American Council of Learned Societies.

The items making up this Checklist span a period of just over eighty-five years: from G. Stanley Hall's review of *PSYCHOLOGY*, published in 1887--the first work in English about Dewey or about his writings--up through the latest, last-minute addition in 1973. Without making a year-by-year count, a task we hope will be undertaken by an interested Checklist user, our subjective impression is that interest in John Dewey is accelerating rather than diminishing. The John Dewey Essay Project, now being undertaken by the John Dewey Foundation and the Center for Dewey Studies, will contribute to this acceleration in the years immediately ahead.

The writings listed here show that after eighty-five years, Dewey's ideas are constantly being examined in new ways, in new contexts, using new resources uncovered by investigations in a variety of fields; this Checklist provides continuing proof that Dewey's work is still found fresh and exciting by successive generations of scholars.

--Jo Ann Boydston
Kathleen Poulos

CHECKLIST OF WRITINGS

ABOUT JOHN DEWEY

1887-1973

PUBLISHED WORKS ABOUT DEWEY

Abel, Reuben. *THE PRAGMATIC HUMANISM OF F. C. S. SCHILLER.* New York: King's Crown Press, 1955. [Dewey, passim.]

---. "Pragmatism and the Outlook of Modern Science." *Philosophy and Phenomenological Research* 27 (1966): 45-54.

Adams, Elie Maynard. *ETHICAL NATURALISM AND THE MODERN WORLD-VIEW.* Chapel Hill: University of North Carolina Press, 1960. [Dewey, passim.]

Addams, Jane. *TWENTY YEARS AT HULL HOUSE.* New York: Macmillan Co., 1920. [Dewey, passim.]

---. "Toast to John Dewey." *Survey* 63 (1929): 203-4.

---. "John Dewey and Social Welfare." In *JOHN DEWEY: THE MAN AND HIS PHILOSOPHY.* Addresses Delivered in New York in Celebration of His Seventieth Birthday, pp. 140-51. Cambridge: Harvard University Press, 1930.

Adler, Mortimer Jerome. *PROBLEMS FOR THOMISTS: THE PROBLEM OF SPECIES.* New York: Sheed and Ward, 1940. [Dewey, pp. 268, 271-72.]

---. "The Chicago School." *Harper's Magazine*, September 1941, pp. 377-88.

---. *THE IDEA OF FREEDOM: A DIALECTICAL EXAMINATION OF THE CONCEPTIONS OF FREEDOM.* Garden City, N.Y.: Doubleday and Co., 1958. [Dewey, passim.]

---, and Mayer, Milton. *THE REVOLUTION IN EDUCATION.*

Chicago: University of Chicago Press, 1958. [Dewey, passim.]

Advocate. [Retail Clerks Union.] "Dewey is Second Unionist Honored on U.S. Stamp." *Advocate* 72 (1969): 31.

Aiken, Henry David. Introduction to *PHILOSOPHY IN THE TWENTIETH CENTURY, AN ANTHOLOGY*, edited by William Barrett and Henry David Aiken. New York: Random House, 1962.

---. "Reflections on Dewey's Questions about Value." In *VALUE: A COOPERATIVE INQUIRY*, edited by Ray Lepley, pp. 15-42.

---. "Definitions of Value and the Moral Ideal." *Journal of Philosophy* 42 (1945): 337-52. [Dewey, pp. 340-43.]

---. "A Pluralistic Analysis of the Ethical 'Ought'." *Journal of Philosophy* 48 (1951): 497-505.

---. *REASON AND CONDUCT: NEW BEARINGS IN MORAL PHILOSOPHY*. New York: Alfred A. Knopf, 1962. [Dewey, passim.]

---. "Sidney Hook As Philosopher." *Commentary* 33 (1962): 143-51.

---. "American Pragmatism Reconsidered, III: John Dewey." *Commentary* 34 (1962): 334-44.

---, and Lepley, Ray. "Criticisms by Aiken, Rejoinder by Lepley." In *VALUE: A COOPERATIVE INQUIRY*, edited by Ray Lepley, pp. 293-301.

Alberty, Harold Bernard. "An Appraisal of Dewey's Aphorism, 'Education is Life'." National Education Association, Department of Superintendence, *Official Report*, 1930, p. 152.

---. "The Direction of Learning on the Elementary School Level." *Educational Outlook* 8 (1933-34): 10-20.

Aldrich, Virgil Charles. "John Dewey's Use of Language." *Journal of Philosophy* 41 (1944): 261-71.

Alger, George William. "Recollections of John Dewey." *Saturday Review*, 19 December 1959, p. 21.

Alilunas, Leo J. "John Dewey's Pragmatic Ideas about School History and Their Early Application." *Social Studies* 41 (1950): 111-14.

---. "The Problem of Children's Historical Mindedness." *Social Studies* 56 (1965): 251-54.

Aliotta, Antonio. "Dewey's Instrumental Logic." In his *THE IDEALISTIC REACTION AGAINST SCIENCE*, pp. 174-79. Translated by Agnes McCaskill. London: Macmillan and Co., 1914.

Allen, Carleton Kemp. "Excursus A: Custom as Law." In his *LAW IN THE MAKING*, 5th ed., pp. 145-49. Oxford: Clarendon Press, 1951. [Response to Dewey's review of *LAW IN THE MAKING* (1927) in *Columbia Law Review* 28 (1928): 832-33.]

Allen, Devere. "Education in Action." In his *ADVENTUROUS AMERICANS*, pp. 130-40. New York: Farrar and Rinehart, 1932.

Allport, Gordon Willard. "Dewey's Individual and Social Psychology." In *THE PHILOSOPHY OF JOHN DEWEY*, edited by Paul Schilpp, pp. 263-90.

---. "Psychology and the Fourth R." *New Republic*, 17 October 1949, pp. 23-26.

Allsopp, A. H. *THE ESSENTIALS OF PSYCHOLOGY FOR STUDENT TEACHERS*. London: J. M. Dent and Sons, 1936. [Dewey, passim.]

Altman, Jules, and Ratner, Sidney, eds. *JOHN DEWEY AND ARTHUR F. BENTLEY: A PHILOSOPHICAL CORRESPONDENCE, 1932-1951*. New Brunswick, N.J.: Rutgers University Press, 1964.

American Teacher Magazine. "Our Most Honored Member." *American Teacher Magazine* 44 (1960): 2.

---. "John Dewey Honored with New U.S. Stamp." *American Teacher Magazine* 53 (1968): 19.

Ames, Edward Scribner. *BEYOND THEOLOGY: THE AUTOBIOGRAPHY OF EDWARD SCRIBNER AMES*. Edited by Van Meter Ames. Chicago: University of Chicago Press, 1959. [Dewey, passim.]

Ames, Van Meter. "John Dewey as Aesthetician." *Journal of Aesthetics and Art Criticism* 12 (1953): 145-68.

---. "Aesthetic Values in East and West." In *PHILOSOPHY AND CULTURE--EAST AND WEST*, edited by Charles A. Moore, pp. 342-61.

---, ed. *BEYOND THEOLOGY: THE AUTOBIOGRAPHY OF EDWARD SCRIBNER AMES.* [Dewey, passim.]

Anderson, Archibald W. "The Task of Educational Theory." *Educational Theory* 1 (1951): 9-21.

---. "Milestones of Educational Progress: Horace Mann, 1796-1859; John Dewey, 1859-1952." *Educational Theory* 10 (1960): 1-8.

Anderson, Frederick M. "Dewey's Experiment with Greek Philosophy." *International Philosophical Quarterly* 7 (1967): 86-100.

Anderson, Harold A. "John Dewey." *School Review* 60 (1952): 320-22.

Anderson, Paul Russell, and Fisch, Max Harold, eds. *PHILOSOPHY IN AMERICA: FROM THE PURITANS TO JAMES.* New York: D. Appleton-Century Co., 1939. [Dewey, passim.]

Anderson, W. "On a Fragment from Dewey." *Australasian Journal of Psychology and Philosophy* 8 (1930): 168-75.

Anderson, Walter A. "Implementing Dewey's Philosophy." *Educational Trends* 7 (November-December 1949): 31-32. [Review of *THE PROGRESSIVE ELEMENTARY SCHOOL* by Robert H. Lane. New York: Houghton Mifflin Co., 1938.]

Angell, James Rowland. "The Toastmaster's Words." In *JOHN DEWEY: THE MAN AND HIS PHILOSOPHY*, Addresses Delivered in New York in Celebration of His Seventieth Birthday, pp. 136-39. Cambridge: Harvard University Press, 1930.

Angier, Roswell P. "The Conflict Theory of Emotion." *American Journal of Psychology* 39 (1927): 390-401.

Anton, John Peter. "John Dewey's Place in American Thought and Life." *Humanist* 23 (1963): 138-39.

---. "John Dewey and Ancient Philosophies." *Philosophy and Phenomenological Research* 25 (1965): 477-99. [Abstracted in *Journal of Philosophy* 56 (1959): 963-65.]

---, ed. *NATURALISM AND HISTORICAL UNDERSTANDING: ESSAYS ON THE PHILOSOPHY OF JOHN HERMAN RANDALL, JR.* Albany: State University of New York Press, 1967. [Dewey, passim.]

Archambault, Reginald D. "The Philosophical Bases of the Experience Curriculum." *Harvard Educational Review* 26 (1956): 263-75. [Reprinted in *DEWEY ON EDUCATION: APPRAISALS*, edited by Reginald D. Archambault, pp. 160-84.]

---. Introduction to *JOHN DEWEY ON EDUCATION, SELECTED WRITINGS*, edited by Reginald D. Archambault. New York: Modern Library, 1964.

---. Introduction to *JOHN DEWEY: LECTURES IN THE PHILOSOPHY OF EDUCATION, 1899*, edited by Reginald D. Archambault. New York: Random House, 1966.

---. Introduction to *DEWEY ON EDUCATION: APPRAISALS*, edited by Reginald D. Archambault. New York: Random House, 1966.

Armentrout, Winfield Dockery. "The Optimism in Dewey's Philosophy of Education." *Journal of Educational Method* 6 (1927): 236-39.

Arndt, Ruth Spence. *JOHN DEWEY'S PHILOSOPHY OF EDUCATION*. Pretoria, S.A.: J. L. van Schaik, 1929.

Arnett, Willard Eugene. "Critique of Dewey's Anticlerical Religious Philosophy." *Journal of Religion* 34 (1954): 256-66.

Arrowood, Charles Flinn, and Eby, Frederick. *THE DEVELOPMENT OF MODERN EDUCATION*. New York: Prentice-Hall, 1947. [Dewey, pp. 855-79.]

Arscott, John Robert. "Two Philosophies of Freedom." *School and Society* 74 (1951): 276-79. [William Torrey Harris's Hegelianism and John Dewey's instrumentalism.]

Atherton, Margaret, and Schwartz, Robert. "Practice, Purpose, and Pedagogy." *Studies in Philosophy and Education* 7 (1970): 158-61.

Aubrey, Edwin Ewart. "Is John Dewey a Theist?" *Chris-*

tian Century 51 (1934): 1550. [Letter in response
to "John Dewey's Common Faith," by Henry Nelson Wieman. Ibid.: 1450-52. Wieman's reply to Aubrey,
ibid.: 1550-51. Dewey's response, ibid.: 1551-52.
Wieman's reply, ibid.: 1552-53.]

Austin, Ernest H., Jr. "Dewey's Consistent Attitude toward History." *Educational Theory* 15 (1965): 198-204.

Axelson, John A. "1884-1894, Decade of Ferment for
Young Michigan Teacher John Dewey." *Michigan Educational Journal* 43 (May 1966): 13-14.

Axtelle, George E. "A Personal Appreciation of John
Dewey." *Hawaii Educational Review* 18 (1929): 33-34,
41-43, 45-46.

---. "John Dewey and the Concept of Democracy." *Educational Trends* 7 (November-December 1939): 6-14.

---. "Philosophy in American Education." *Harvard Educational Review* 26 (1956): 184-89.

---. "William Heard Kilpatrick: An Interpretation."
Progressive Education 34 (1957): 35-37, 63.

---. "Philosophy in American Education." *Education
Synopsis* 3 (1957-58): 4-5, 15. [Dewey, passim.]

---. "Dewey's Impact on American Education." In *University of Colorado Studies*, Series in Philosophy,
no. 2, pp. 35-51. Boulder: University of Colorado
Press, 1961.

---. "John Dewey's Concept of 'The Religious'; Basis
for Religious Humanism?" *Religious Humanism* 1
(1967): 65-68.

---. "John Dewey and the Genius of American Civilization." In *JOHN DEWEY AND THE WORLD VIEW*, edited by
Douglas Lawson and Arthur Lean, pp. 35-63.

---, and Burnett, Joe R. "Dewey on Education and
Schooling." In *GUIDE TO THE WORKS OF JOHN DEWEY*,
edited by Jo Ann Boydston, pp. 257-305.

Ayers, Robert Hyman. "Cryptotheologies and Educational
Theories." *Educational Theory* 15 (1965): 282-92.

---. "The New Theology and Educational Theory." *Educational Theory* 18 (1968): 169-77.

Ayres, Clarence Edwin. "John Dewey, Naturalist." *New Republic*, 4 April 1923, pp. 158-60.

---. "The Gospel of Technology." In *AMERICAN PHILOS-OPHY TODAY AND TOMORROW*, edited by Horace M. Kallen and Sidney Hook, pp. 25-42.

---. "Dewey: Master of the Commonplace." *New Republic*, 18 January 1939, pp. 303-6. [Reprinted, with minor revisions, with the title, "Dewey and His 'Studies in Logical Theory'," in *BOOKS THAT CHANGED OUR MINDS*, edited by Malcolm Cowley and Bernard Smith, pp. 111-26. New York: Doubleday, Doran and Co., 1939.]

---. "Instrumental Economics." *New Republic*, 17 October 1949, pp. 18-20.

---. "The Value Economy." In *VALUE: A COOPERATIVE IN-QUIRY*, edited by Ray Lepley, pp. 43-63.

---, and Lee, Harold N. "Criticisms by Ayres; Rejoinder by Lee." In *VALUE: A COOPERATIVE INQUIRY*, edited by Ray Lepley, pp. 302-11.

Babić, Ivan. "Dewey's Interpretation of Democracy," *Politička misao* 4 (1967): 493; "Fundamental Determinants of Dewey's Approach to the Methodology of Political Theory," ibid. 3-4 (1970): 363. [Abstracts.]

Bagley, William Chandler. "John Dewey, Vigorous at Age 85, Defends Progressive Education." *School and Society* 60 (1944): 292.

Bahm, Archie J. *PHILOSOPHY, AN INTRODUCTION*. New York: John Wiley and Sons, 1953. [Dewey, pp. 159-63, and passim.]

Bain, A. E. "John Dewey and the Peculiar Traits of American Thought." *Contemporary Issues*, nos. 1 and 2 (1948): 47-80, 127-60. [Copy in the British Museum.]

Baker, Melvin Charles. *FOUNDATIONS OF JOHN DEWEY'S EDUCATIONAL THEORY*. New York: King's Crown Press, 1955. [Paperback reprint, New York: Atherton Press, 1966.]

Bakewell, Charles Montague. "An Open Letter to Professor Dewey concerning Immediate Empiricism." *Journal of Philosophy* 2 (1905): 520-22. [In response to Dewey's "The Postulate of Immediate Empiricism." Ibid.: 393-99.]

---. "The Issue between Idealism and Immediate Empiricism." *Journal of Philosophy* 2 (1905): 687-91. [Reply to Dewey's "Immediate Empiricism." Ibid.: 597-99.]

Baldwin, James Mark. "Social Interpretations: A Reply." *Philosophical Review* 7 (1898): 621-28 [*Early Works of John Dewey* 5: lxxxvi-xciv.] [Response to Dewey's review of Baldwin's *SOCIAL AND ETHICAL INTERPRETATIONS IN MENTAL DEVELOPMENT.* *Philosophical Review* 7 (1898): 398-409 (*Early Works* 5: 385-99.)] [Dewey's rejoinder, *Philosophical Review* 7 (1898): 629-30 (*Early Works* 5: 399-401.)]

---. "The Limits of Pragmatism." *Psychological Review* 11 (1904): 30-60.

Ballard, Edward G. "An Estimate of Dewey's *ART AS EXPERIENCE.*" *Tulane Studies in Philosophy*, vol. 4, pp. 5-18. New Orleans: Tulane University, 1955.

Ballinger, Stanley E. "John Dewey: Man Ahead of His Times." *Indiana Teacher* 104 (1959): 10-11, 33. [Abstracted in *Education Digest* 25 (November 1959): 9-11.]

Baltimore Sun. "Dr. Dewey's Articles." *Baltimore Sun,* 15 November 1921.

Balz, Albert George Adam. "A Letter to Mr. Dewey concerning John Dewey's Doctrine of Possibility." *Journal of Philosophy* 46 (1949): 313-29. [Followed by Dewey's reply, ibid.: 329-42.]

Bandman, Bertram. *THE PLACE OF REASON IN EDUCATION.* Studies in Educational Theory of the John Dewey Society, no. 4. Columbus: Ohio State University Press, 1967. [Dewey, passim.]

Banerjee, Gour Mohan. *THE THEORY OF DEMOCRATIC EDUCATION: A CRITICAL EXPOSITION OF JOHN DEWEY'S PHILOSOPHY OF EDUCATION.* Calcutta: New Book Stall, n.d.

Bantock, G. H. "John Dewey on Education." *Cambridge Journal* 5 (1951-52): 531-32.

Barnes, Albert Coombs. "Method in Aesthetics." In *THE PHILOSOPHER OF THE COMMON MAN,* edited by Sidney Ratner, pp. 87-105.

---. "Art as Experience." In *The Educational Frontier*,
    Progressive Education Booklet, no. 13, pp. 13-25.
    Columbus, Ohio: Progressive Education Association,
    1939.

---. "Dewey and Art." *New Leader*, 22 October 1949,
    S-4.

---. "The Educational Philosophy of John Dewey."
    Humanist 5 (1946): 160-62. [Adapted from the
    author's pamphlet, *The Case of Bertrand Russell
    versus Democracy and Education*. Merion, Pa.: Barnes
    Foundation, n.d.]

Barnes, Harry Elmer. "John Dewey--Plato's King." In
    "Some Popular Appraisals of John Dewey," edited by
    Clyde R. Miller. *Teachers College Record* 31 (1929):
    213-14.

---. *AN INTELLECTUAL AND CULTURAL HISTORY OF THE
    WESTERN WORLD*. 3d rev. ed. Vol. 3: From the Nine-
    teenth Century to the Present Day. New York: Dover
    Publications, 1965. [Dewey, passim.]

Barrett, William. "John Dewey in His Eightieth Year."
    Southern Review 5 (1939-40): 700-710.

---. "On Dewey's Logic." *Philosophical Review* 50
    (1941): 305-15.

Barron, Joseph T. "Professor Dewey and Truth." *Cath-
    olic World* 116 (1922): 212-21.

Barrows, Alice. "Some Results of Dewey's Philosophy."
    Platoon School 3 (1929-30): 150-51.

Barry, Robert M. "Direction of American Philosophy: A
    Bibliographical View." *American Benedictine Review*
    15 (1964): 215-36.

---, and Fearon, John D. "John Dewey and American
    Thomism." *American Benedictine Review* 10 (1959):
    219-28; 11 (1960): 262-70.

Barton, George Estes, Jr. "John Dewey: Too Soon a
    Period Piece." *School Review* 67 (1959): 128-38.

Bates, Ernest Sutherland. "John Dewey, America's

Philosophic Engineer." *Modern Monthly* 7 (1933): 387-96, 404.

Battle, John J. *THE METAPHYSICAL PRESUPPOSITIONS OF THE PHILOSOPHY OF JOHN DEWEY*. Privately printed, U.S., 1951. [Doctoral dissertation, Fribourg, Switz.]

Baumgarten, Eduard. "John Dewey and His Influence." *Sammlung* 7 (1952): 465-74.

Bawden, Henry Heath. "What Is Pragmatism?" *Journal of Philosophy* 1 (1904): 421-27.

---. "The New Philosophy Called Pragmatism." *Popular Science Monthly*, July 1908, pp. 61-72.

---. *THE PRINCIPLES OF PRAGMATISM: A PHILOSOPHICAL INTERPRETATION OF EXPERIENCE*. Boston: Houghton Mifflin Co., 1910. [Dewey, passim.]

Bay, Christian. *THE STRUCTURE OF FREEDOM*. Stanford, Cal.: Stanford University Press, 1958. [Dewey, pp. 8, 9, 10n., 355n.]

Bay, James Campbell. "Our Public Schools: Are They Failing?" *Nation*, 26 June 1954, pp. 539-41. [Reply by Paul Woodring, "A Pragmatic Point." Ibid., 31 July 1954, p. 99.]

Bayles, Ernest E. "Deweyism and Doctor [Frederick Stephen] Breed's New Realism." *Educational Administration and Supervision* 25 (1939): 561-68.

---. "A Relativistic Religion." *Phi Delta Kappan* 40 (1958): 33-36.

---. "Are Values Verifiable?" *Educational Theory* 10 (1960): 71-77.

---. "John Dewey and Educational Permissivism." University of Kansas *Bulletin of Education* 14 (1960): 42-48.

---. *PRAGMATISM IN EDUCATION*. New York: Harper and Row, 1966. [Dewey, passim.]

---. "On Morals and Values: the Axiology of John

Dewey." *Teachers College Record* 68 (1967): 654-59.

---. "Did Dewey Flub One?" *Educational Theory* 21
(1971): 455-57. [In response to C. M. Smith, "The
Aesthetics of John Dewey and Aesthetic Education."
Ibid.: 131-45. Reply by Smith, ibid.: 458.]

---, and Hood, Bruce L. *GROWTH OF AMERICAN EDUCATIONAL
THOUGHT AND PRACTICE*. New York: Harper and Row,
1966. [Dewey, pp. 249-95, and passim.]

Beach, Joseph Warren. "Incoherence in the Philosopher:
Mr. John Dewey." In his *THE OUTLOOK FOR AMERICAN
PROSE*, pp. 41-52. Chicago: University of Chicago
Press, 1926.

---. "Unripe Fruits." In *READINGS IN PRESENT-DAY
WRITERS*, edited by Raymond Woodbury Pence, pp. 76-
91. New York: Macmillan and Co., 1933.

Beach, Walter Greenwood. "John Dewey: Sociology and
Social Education United." In his *THE GROWTH OF
SOCIAL THOUGHT*, pp. 200-206. New York: Charles
Scribner's Sons, 1939.

Beard, Charles Austin. "America in Mid-Passage." In
John Dewey and the Promise of America, Progressive
Education Booklet, no. 14, pp. 18-25. Columbus,
Ohio: Progressive Education Association, 1939.

---, and Mary R. *THE RISE OF AMERICAN CIVILIZATION*.
New ed., 2 vols. in 1, rev. and enl. New York: Macmillan Co., 1934. [Dewey, passim.]

---. *AMERICA IN MID-PASSAGE*. New York: Macmillan Co.,
1939. [Dewey, pp. 766, 905-6, 910.]

Beard, Mary Ritter, and Charles A. *THE RISE OF AMERICAN
CIVILIZATION*.

---. *AMERICA IN MID-PASSAGE*.

Beardsley, Monroe C. "Intrinsic Value." *Philosophy and
Phenomenological Research* 26 (1965): 1-17.

---. *AESTHETICS FROM CLASSICAL GREECE TO THE PRESENT*.
New York: Macmillan Co., 1966. [Dewey, pp. 332-42,
and passim.]

Beath, Paul Robert. "John Dewey: Pragmatist." *Daily Illini* [University of Illinois], 26 February 1928.

Beck, Carlton E., and Kersey, Shirley J. "Dewey's Aesthetics: Implications for Teachers." *Journal of Thought* 5 (1970): 92-100.

Beck, Robert Holmes. "Educational Leadership, 1906-1956." *Phi Delta Kappan* 37 (1956): 161.

---. "Progressive Education and American Progressivism: Felix Adler." *Teachers College Record* 60 (1958): 77-89.

---. "Progressive Education and American Progressivism: Caroline Pratt." *Teachers College Record* 60 (1958): 129-37.

---. "Progressive Education and American Progressivism: Margaret Naumburg." *Teachers College Record* 60 (1959): 198-208.

Belford, Elizabeth, and Jackson, Philip W. "Educational Objectives and the Joys of Teaching." *School Review* 73 (1965): 267-91.

Belth, Marc. "Concerning Dewey's Contribution to a Philosophy of Education." In *EDUCATION IN TRANSITION*, edited by Frederick Charles Gruber, pp. 260-64. Philadelphia: University of Pennsylvania Press, 1960.

---. *EDUCATION AS A DISCIPLINE*. Boston: Allyn and Bacon, 1965. [Dewey, passim.]

Benedict, Agnes E. "Parker and Dewey: Prophets of a New Educational Order." In her *PROGRESS TO FREEDOM*, pp. 217-44. New York: G. P. Putnam's Sons, 1942.

Ben-Horin, Meir. "John Dewey and Jewish Education." *Religious Education* 55 (1960): 201-2.

Benjamin, Harold R. W. "John Dewey's Influence on Educational Practice." In *JOHN DEWEY AND THE WORLD VIEW*, edited by Douglas Lawson and Arthur Lean, pp. 15-25.

---, ed. *DEMOCRACY IN THE ADMINISTRATION OF HIGHER EDUCATION*. Tenth Yearbook of the John Dewey Society. New York: Harper and Brothers, 1950. [Dewey, passim.]

Benne, Kenneth Dean. "The Human Individual: John Dewey." *University* [of Kansas City] *Review* 7 (1940): 48-56.

---. "John Dewey and Adult Education." *Adult Education Bulletin* 14 (1949): 7-12. [Reprinted in *Essays for John Dewey's Ninetieth Birthday*, pp. 74-81.]

---. "On Celebrating John Dewey's Birthday." *Progressive Education* 27 (1949): 25-26. [Reprinted in *Essays for John Dewey's Ninetieth Birthday*, pp. 5-8.]

---, and Stanley, William O., eds. *Essays for John Dewey's Ninetieth Birthday*. Urbana: Bureau of Research and Service, College of Education, University of Illinois, 1950.

Bennett, Charles Alpheus. "John Dewey and Industrial Education." *Industrial Education Magazine* 32 (1930): 146-47.

Bentley, Arthur Fisher. "Mind-Language Reconstructions: Dewey, Madison Bentley." In his *BEHAVIOR KNOWLEDGE FACT*, pp. 74-81. Bloomington, Ind.: Principia Press, 1935. [Also passim.]

---. "Situational Treatments of Behavior." *Journal of Philosophy* 36 (1939): 309-23.

---. Comment on Dewey's *LOGIC*. In his "Postulation for Behavioral Inquiry." *Journal of Philosophy* 36 (1939): 405-13. [Dewey, p. 413.]

---. "Decrassifying Dewey." *Philosophy of Science* 8 (1941): 147-56.

---. "As Through a Glass Darkly." *Journal of Philosophy* 39 (1942): 432-39.

---. "Logicians' Underlying Postulations." *Philosophy of Science* 13 (1946): 3-19.

---. *INQUIRY INTO INQUIRIES: ESSAYS IN SOCIAL THEORY*. Edited with introd. by Sidney Ratner. Boston: Beacon Press, 1954. [Dewey, passim.]

---. "Dewey's Logic Compactly Presented." In *JOHN DEWEY AND ARTHUR F. BENTLEY: A PHILOSOPHICAL CORRESPONDENCE, 1932-1951*, edited by Sidney Ratner and

Jules Altman, pp. 478-81. [Memo by Bentley sent to Dewey, 5 October 1945.]

Berger, Morris Isaiah. "John Dewey and Progressive Education Today." *School and Society* 87 (1959): 140-42. [Reprinted in *JOHN DEWEY: MASTER EDUCATOR*, edited by William W. Brickman and Stanley Lehrer, 2d ed., pp. 126-31.] [Also reprinted in *DEWEY ON EDUCATION: APPRAISALS*, edited by Reginald D. Archambault, pp. 185-91.]

Beringause, Arthur F. "The Double Martyrdom of Randolph Bourne." *Journal of the History of Ideas* 18 (1957): 594-603. [Dewey, passim.]

Berkson, Isaac Baer. *THE IDEAL AND THE COMMUNITY: A PHILOSOPHY OF EDUCATION*. New York: Harper and Brothers, 1958.

---. "Science, Ethics, and Education in the Deweyan Experimentalist Philosophy." *School and Society* 87 (1959): 387-91. [Reprinted in *JOHN DEWEY: MASTER EDUCATOR*, edited by William W. Brickman and Stanley Lehrer, 2d ed., pp. 101-14.]

---. "Community Belief Versus Individual Experience as Basis for Education." *Educational Theory* 10 (1960): 66-70.

Bernard, Eunice. "Study Row Stirred by 'Essentialists'." *New York Times*, 2 March 1938, p. 8.

Bernstein, Richard Jacob. "Knowledge, Value and Freedom." In *JOHN DEWEY AND THE EXPERIMENTAL SPIRIT IN PHILOSOPHY*, edited by Charles W. Hendel, pp. 63-92.

---. "Dewey's Naturalism." *Review of Metaphysics* 13 (1959): 340-53. [Reply to John Edwin Smith, "John Dewey: Philosopher of Experience." Ibid.: 60-78.]

---. "John Dewey's Metaphysics of Experience." *Journal of Philosophy* 58 (1961): 5-14. [Abstracted in ibid. 56 (1959): 961-62, with the title, "John Dewey's Theory of Quality."] [Gail Kennedy, "Comments on Professor Bernstein's Paper." Ibid. 58 (1961): 14-21.]

---. *JOHN DEWEY*. New York: Washington Square Press, 1966.

---. Introduction to *DEWEY ON EXPERIENCE, NATURE, AND FREEDOM*, edited by Richard J. Bernstein. New York: Liberal Arts Press, 1960.

---. "Action, Conduct, and Inquiry: Peirce and Dewey." In his *PRAXIS AND ACTION*, pp. 165-229. Philadelphia: University of Pennsylvania Press, 1971. [Also passim.]

Berry, Thomas. "Dewey's Influence in China." In *JOHN DEWEY: HIS THOUGHT AND INFLUENCE*, edited by John Blewett, pp. 199-232.

Bestor, Arthur Eugene, Jr. "John Dewey and American Liberalism." *New Republic*, 29 August 1955, pp. 18-19. [Reply by Vernon F. Haubricht, "Pragmatism and Liberalism." Ibid., 12 September 1955, p. 23.]

Betz, William. "Looking Again at the Mathematical Situation." *Mathematics Teacher* 41 (1948): 372-81.

Bewig, Carl, and Wirth, Arthur G. "John Dewey on School Architecture." *Journal of Aesthetic Education* 2 (1968): 79-86.

Bhattacharyya, Nirmal C. "The Role of the Teacher in John Dewey's Educational Theory." *Alberta Journal of Educational Research* 13 (1967): 33-42.

---. "John Dewey's Instrumentalism, Democratic Ideal and Education." *Educational Theory* 18 (1968): 60-72.

---. "The Concept of 'Intelligence' in John Dewey's Philosophy and Educational Theory." *Educational Theory* 19 (1969): 185-95.

Bierstedt, Robert. "John Dewey at Eighty." *Saturday Review of Literature*, 11 November 1939, pp. 12-13.

Bingham, Walter Van Dyke. Discussion of Dewey's reflex arc concept. In *A HISTORY OF PSYCHOLOGY IN AUTOBIOGRAPHY*, edited by Herbert S. Langfeld, Heinz Werner, and Robert M. Yerkes, vol. 4, pp. 6-7. Worcester, Mass.: Clark University Press, 1930.

Bishop, William Warner. "College Days [University of Michigan]: 1889-1893. Fragments of Autobiography." *Michigan Alumnus, Quarterly Review* 54 (1948):

340-52. [Dewey, p. 348.]

Bixler, Julius Seelye. "Professor Dewey Discusses Religion." *Harvard Theological Review* 23 (1930):
213-33.

---. "The Patriot and the Pragmatist." *Journal of
Religion* 14 (1934): 253-64.

---. "Dewey and the Social Good." In his *RELIGION FOR
FREE MINDS*, pp. 117-27. New York: Harper and
Brothers, 1939. [Also passim.]

Black, Dora Winifred. "American Policy in China." *New
Republic*, 2 November 1921, p. 297. [In response to
Dewey's "Hinterlands in China." Ibid., 6 July 1921,
pp. 162-65. Dewey's rejoinder. Ibid., 2 November
1921, p. 297.]

Black, Hugh C. "A Way Out of Educational Confusion."
Educational Theory 4 (1954): 113-19.

---. "A Four-Fold Classification of Educational Theories." *Educational Theory* 16 (1966): 281-91.

Black, Max. "Dewey's Philosophy of Language." *Journal
of Philosophy* 59 (1962): 505-23. [Reprinted in his
MARGINS OF PRECISION: ESSAYS IN LOGIC AND LANGUAGE,
pp. 222-45. Ithaca, N.Y.: Cornell University Press,
1970.]

Blackhurst, James Herbert. "Does the World-View of
John Dewey Support Creative Education?" *Educational
Theory* 5 (1955): 193-202, 248; "Part 2: Higher
Mental Processes." Ibid. 6 (1956): 1-9, 34; "Part 3:
Nature of Truth and Values." Ibid.: 65-73.

Blake, Joseph F. "A Mid-Century Appraisal of *RECON-
STRUCTION IN PHILOSOPHY*." *Educational Theory* 2
(1952): 72-79.

Blake, Nelson Manfred. *A HISTORY OF AMERICAN LIFE AND
THOUGHT*. 2d rev. ed. New York: McGraw-Hill Book
Co., 1972. [Dewey, pp. 417, 419, 440-43, 633-34.]

Blake, Ralph Mason. "Why Not Hedonism: A Protest."
International Journal of Ethics 37 (1926-27): 1-18.

Blanshard, Brand. "Unraveling an Idea." *Saturday Re-*

view, 22 October 1949, p. 15. [Review of *EVOLUTION AND THE FOUNDERS OF PRAGMATISM* by Philip P. Wiener. Cambridge: Harvard University Press, 1949.]

———. "Can the Philosopher Influence Social Change?" *Journal of Philosophy* 51 (1954): 741-53. [Reply by John L. Childs. Ibid.: 753-63.]

———. "Philosopher through the Fog." *Saturday Review*, 13 August 1955, p. 9.

———. "Pragmatism and Thought." In his *THE NATURE OF THOUGHT*, vol. 1, pp. 341-93. New York: Macmillan Co., 1955.

———. "Instrumentalism." In his *REASON AND GOODNESS*, pp. 161-93. New York: Macmillan Co., 1961.

———; Ducasse, Curt J.; Hendel, Charles W.; Murphy, Arthur E.; and Otto, Max C. *PHILOSOPHY IN AMERICAN EDUCATION.* New York: Harper and Brothers, 1945. [Dewey, passim.]

Blau, Joseph Leon. "Darwin, Dewey and Beyond." *Christian Register* 128 (November 1949): 19-21, 39.

———. "Experimental Naturalism: John Dewey." In his *MEN AND MOVEMENTS IN AMERICAN PHILOSOPHY*, pp. 343-55. New York: Prentice-Hall, 1952. [Also passim.]

———. "John Dewey and American Social Thought." *Teachers College Record* 61 (1959): 121-27. [Condensed in *Education Digest* 25 (March 1960): 28-31.]

———. "John Dewey's Theory of History." *Journal of Philosophy* 57 (1960): 89-100.

Blewett, John. "John Dewey, Salvationist." *Social Order* 9 (1959): 442-51.

———. "John Dewey's Case against Religion." *Catholic World* 189 (1959): 16-21.

———. "Democracy as Religion: Unity in Human Relations." In *JOHN DEWEY: HIS THOUGHT AND INFLUENCE*, edited by John Blewett, pp. 33-58. Orestes Brownson Series on Contemporary Thought and Affairs, no. 2. New York: Fordham University Press, 1960.

Bliven, Bruce. "Farewell to John Dewey." *New Republic*, 16 June 1952, p. 9.

---. *FIVE MILLION WORDS LATER: AN AUTOBIOGRAPHY*. New York: John Day Co., 1970. [Dewey, passim.]

Block, Irving. "The Desired and the Desirable in Dewey's Ethics." *Dialogue* 2 (1963): 170-81.

Bluhm, William T. *THEORIES OF THE POLITICAL SYSTEM*. 2d ed. Englewood Cliffs, N.J.: Prentice-Hall, 1971. [Dewey, passim.]

Blumenfield, Samuel M. "John Dewey and Jewish Education." *Chicago Jewish Forum* 8 (1950): 169-76. [Reprinted in *JUDAISM AND THE JEWISH SCHOOL*, edited by Judah Pilch and Meir Ben-Horin. New York: Bloch Publishing Co., 1966. Later reprinted in *Religious Education* 67 (1972): 163-69.]

Boas, George. "The Literature of Diversity." *New Republic*, 17 October 1949, pp. 26-29.

---. "Instrumentalism and the History of Philosophy." In *JOHN DEWEY: PHILOSOPHER OF SCIENCE AND FREEDOM*, edited by Sidney Hook, pp. 66-87.

---. "Communication in Dewey's Aesthetics." *Journal of Aesthetics and Art Criticism* 12 (1953): 177-83.

---. "John Dewey." In his *DOMINANT THEMES OF MODERN PHILOSOPHY*, pp. 598-602. New York: Ronald Press Co., 1957.

Bode, Boyd Henry. "Cognitive Experience and Its Object." *Journal of Philosophy* 2 (1905): 658-63. [In response to Dewey's "The Postulate of Immediate Empiricism." Ibid.: 393-99.]

---. *FUNDAMENTALS OF EDUCATION*. Modern Teachers' Series, edited by William C. Bagley. New York: Macmillan Co., 1921. [Dewey, passim.]

---. *MODERN EDUCATIONAL THEORIES*. Modern Teachers' Series, edited by William C. Bagley. New York: Macmillan Co., 1927. [Dewey, pp. 25-32, and passim.]

---. "John Dewey." *Educational Research Bulletin* 8

(1929): 342-43.

---. "The New Education Ten Years after, I: Apprenticeship or Freedom?" *New Republic*, 4 June 1930,
pp. 61-64. [See Joseph K. Hart, "Judging Our Progressive Schools." Ibid., 11 June 1930, pp. 93-96,
for second article in series.]

---. *PROGRESSIVE EDUCATION AT THE CROSSROADS*. New
York: Newson, 1938. [Dewey, passim.]

---. "Dewey's Doctrine of the Learning Process." In
Freedom and Education, Progressive Education Booklet,
no. 12, pp. 16-23. Columbus, Ohio: Progressive Education Association, 1939.

---. "Pragmatism in Education." *New Republic*, 17 October 1949, pp. 15-18. [Reprinted in *Education Digest* 15 (February 1950): 5-8.]

---. "John Dewey, Philosopher of Science and Democracy."
Progressive Education 30 (1952): 2-5. [Condensed in
Education Digest 18 (December 1952): 13-15.]

Bogoslovsky, Boris Basil. *THE TECHNIQUE OF CONTROVERSY:
PRINCIPLES OF DYNAMIC LOGIC*. International Library
of Psychology, Philosophy and Scientific Method. New
York: Harcourt, Brace and Co., 1928. [Dewey, pp. 84-
97, and passim.] [Doctoral dissertation, Columbia
University.]

Bookman. "Philosophical Egg Peddler." *Bookman* 66
(1927): 47-48.

Borchers, Gladys L. "John Dewey and Speech Education."
Western Speech 32 (1968): 127-37. [Symposium entitled "The Influence of John Dewey upon Speech,"
with Don M. Burks and R. Victor Harnack.]

Bordeau, Edward J. "Dewey's Ideas about the Great Depression." *Journal of the History of Ideas* 32
(1971): 67-84.

Boring, Edwin G. *A HISTORY OF EXPERIMENTAL PSYCHOLOGY*.
New York: Appleton-Century-Crofts, 1950. [Dewey,
passim.]

---. "John Dewey: 1859-1952." *American Journal of
Psychology* 66 (1953): 145-47.

Bourdeaux, Robert M. "John Dewey's Concept of a Functional Self." *Educational Theory* 22 (1972): 344-43.

Bourne, Randolph Silliman. "John Dewey's Philosophy." *New Republic*, 13 March 1915, pp. 154-56.

---. "Conscience and Intelligence in War." *Dial* 63 (1917): 193-95. [Reprinted in his *THE HISTORY OF A LITERARY RADICAL AND OTHER PAPERS*, pp. 197-204. New York: S. A. Russell, 1956.]

---. "Twilight of Idols." *Seven Arts Magazine* 2 (1917): 688-702. [Reprinted in his *UNTIMELY PAPERS*, edited by James Oppenheim, pp. 114-39. New York: B. W. Huebsch, 1919; and in his *THE HISTORY OF A LITERARY RADICAL AND OTHER PAPERS*, pp. 241-59.]

---. "Making Over the Body." *New Republic*, 4 May 1918, pp. 28-29. [Review of *MAN'S SUPREME INHERITANCE* by Frederick Matthias Alexander. New York: E. P. Dutton and Co., 1918.] [Answer by Dewey, "Reply to a Reviewer." Ibid., 11 May 1918, p. 55, and rejoinder by Bourne, "Other Messiahs." Ibid., 25 May 1918, p. 117.]

Bower, Gordon H., and Hilgard, Ernest R. *THEORIES OF LEARNING*. 3d ed. New York: Appleton-Century-Crofts, 1966. [Dewey, pp. 298-300.]

Bowers, C. A. *THE PROGRESSIVE EDUCATOR AND THE DEPRESSION: THE RADICAL YEARS*. New York: Random House, 1969. [Dewey, passim.]

---, and Sylwester, Robert. "John Dewey: Our Man in Chicago and Woodstock." *Instructor* 80 (1970): 83-85.

Bowers, David Frederick. "Hegel, Darwin, and the American Tradition." In *FOREIGN INFLUENCES IN AMERICAN LIFE*, edited by David Frederick Bowers, pp. 146-71. Princeton Studies in American Civilization. Princeton: Princeton University Press, 1944. [Dewey, pp. 164-71.] [Reprinted, New York: Peter Smith, 1952.]

Bowers, Fredson. "Textual Principles and Procedures." In *The Early Works of John Dewey, 1882-1898*, edited by Jo Ann Boydston, vol. 2, 1967, pp. ix-xix; vol. 1, 1969, pp. ix-xix; vol. 3, 1969, pp. 1-lx; vol. 4, 1971, pp. xli-li; vol. 5, 1972, pp, cxviii-cxxix.

Boyd, William. *THE HISTORY OF WESTERN EDUCATION*. Rev. and enl. ed. by Edmund J. King. London: Adam and Charles Black, 1966. [Dewey, pp. 398-407.]

Boydston, Jo Ann. "Textual Criticism in John Dewey's Writings." In *PHILOSOPHY OF EDUCATION, 1967: Proceedings of the Twenty-third Annual Meeting of the Philosophy of Education Society*, pp. 291-300. Edwardsville, Ill.: Studies in Philosophy and Education, 1967.

---. "A Note on the Text." In *PSYCHOLOGY*. *The Early Works of John Dewey, 1882-1898*, vol. 2, pp. xlix-liv. Edited by Jo Ann Boydston. Carbondale: Southern Illinois University Press, 1967.

---. "The John Dewey Bibliography." *Papers of the Bibliographical Society of America* 62 (1968): 67-75.

---. "Terror in Cuba in 1933." *School and Society* 96 (1968): 444-45. [Introduction to her translation of Dewey's *La terreur à Cuba*.]

---. "The Writings of John Dewey, 1968." *Studies in Philosophy and Education* 6 (1968): 116-22.

---. "Checklist of Works Cited in *LEIBNIZ'S NEW ESSAYS CONCERNING THE HUMAN UNDERSTANDING*." In *EARLY ESSAYS AND LEIBNIZ'S NEW ESSAYS*. *The Early Works of John Dewey, 1882-1898*, vol. 1, pp. lx-lxvii. Edited by Jo Ann Boydston. Carbondale: Southern Illinois University Press, 1969.

---. "A Note on the Texts." In *The Early Works*, vol. 1, pp. lxx-lxxxi.

---. "A Note on *APPLIED PSYCHOLOGY*." In *ESSAYS AND OUTLINES OF A CRITICAL THEORY OF ETHICS*. *The Early Works of John Dewey, 1882-1898*, vol. 3, pp. xiii-xix. Edited by Jo Ann Boydston. Carbondale: Southern Illinois University Press, 1969.

---. "A Note on the Texts." In *The Early Works*, vol. 3, pp. lxi-lxxi.

---. "John Dewey and the Journals." *History of Education Quarterly* 10 (1970): 72-77.

---. "A Note on the Texts." In *EARLY ESSAYS AND THE STUDY OF ETHICS. The Early Works of John Dewey, 1882-1898*, vol. 4, pp. lii-lix. Edited by Jo Ann Boydston. Carbondale: Southern Illinois University Press, 1971.

---. "A Note on the Texts." In *EARLY ESSAYS. The Early Works of John Dewey, 1882-1898*, vol. 5, pp. cxxx-cxxxix. Edited by Jo Ann Boydston. Carbondale: Southern Illinois University Press, 1972.

---. "The Status of Dewey Studies." *Humanist* 32 (November-December 1972): 33-34.

---, and Burnett, Joe R. "The Dewey Project." *Educational Forum* 35 (1971): 177-83.

Boydston, Jo Ann, ed. *GUIDE TO THE WORKS OF JOHN DEWEY.* Carbondale: Southern Illinois University Press, 1970.

---, ed., with Robert L. Andresen. *JOHN DEWEY, A CHECKLIST OF TRANSLATIONS, 1900-1967.* Carbondale: Southern Illinois University Press, 1969.

Boyer, Minor Waller. "An Expansion of Dewey's Groundwork for a General Theory of Value." *Journal of Aesthetics and Art Criticism* 15 (1956): 100-105.

Boyle, W. E. "The Philosophical Background of John Dewey, Educator." *Catholic Educational Review* 37 (1939): 385-92.

Bradley, Ritamary. "Analysis of a Symposium for John Dewey." *Catholic Educator* 23 (1953): 383-85. [Symposium in *Progressive Education* 30 (1952): 1-18.]

Bradshaw, Marion John. "A Comment on Van Dusen's Dismissal of Dewey." *Review of Religion* 3 (1938): 97-100. [In response to Henry Pitney Van Dusen, "The Faith of John Dewey." *Religion in Life* 4 (1935): 123-32.]

Brameld, Theodore. "American Education and the Social Struggle." *Science and Society* 1 (1936): 1-17. [In reply to Dewey's "Class Struggle and the Democratic Way." *Social Frontier* 2 (1936): 241-42.]

---. "Dialectical Materialism." *Marxist Quarterly* 1

(1937): 144-48. [Review of *INTRODUCTION TO DIALEC-
TICAL MATERIALISM, THE MARXIST WORLD VIEW* by August
Thalheimer. New York: Covici-Friede, 1936. Discussion by George Simpson, *Marxist Quarterly* 1
(1937): 148-50.]

---. *EDUCATION FOR THE EMERGING AGE*. New York: Harper
and Brothers, 1950. [Reprinted, 1961.] [Dewey,
passim.]

---. *PATTERNS OF EDUCATIONAL PHILOSOPHY*. Yonkers-on-
Hudson, N.Y.: World Book Co., 1950. [Dewey, pp.
195-202, and passim.]

---. *PHILOSOPHIES OF EDUCATION IN CULTURAL PERSPECTIVE*.
New York: Dryden Press, 1955. [Dewey, pp. 183-97,
and passim.]

---. *TOWARD A RECONSTRUCTED PHILOSOPHY OF EDUCATION*.
New York: Dryden Press, 1956. [Dewey, passim.]

---. *CULTURAL FOUNDATIONS OF EDUCATION: AN INTERDISCI-
PLINARY EXPLORATION*. New York: Harper and Brothers,
1957. [Dewey, passim.]

---. *EDUCATION AS POWER*. New York: Holt, Rinehart
and Winston, 1965. [Dewey, pp. 34, 53, 77, 97.]

---. *THE CLIMACTIC DECADES: MANDATE TO EDUCATION*. New
York: Praeger Publishers, 1970. [Dewey, pp. 156-60,
177-78, and passim.]

---, ed. *WORKERS' EDUCATION IN THE UNITED STATES*.
Fifth Yearbook of the John Dewey Society. New York:
Harper and Brothers, 1941. [Dewey, passim.]

Bratton, Fred Gladstone. *THE LEGACY OF THE LIBERAL
SPIRIT: MEN AND MOVEMENTS IN THE MAKING OF MODERN
THOUGHT*. New York: Charles Scribner's Sons, 1943.
[Dewey, pp. 257-74.]

Brauner, Charles J. *AMERICAN EDUCATIONAL THEORY*. Englewood Cliffs, N.J.: Prentice-Hall, 1964. [Dewey,
passim.]

Brecht, Arnold. *POLITICAL THEORY: THE FOUNDATIONS OF
TWENTIETH-CENTURY POLITICAL THOUGHT*. Princeton,
N.J.: Princeton University Press, 1959. [Dewey,
passim.]

Breed, Frederick S. "Progressive Education." *School and Society* 37 (1933): 544-48. [Reply by William F. Bruce, "Comment upon Breed's Criticism of Dewey." Ibid.: 812-14.]

---. *EDUCATION AND THE NEW REALISM.* New York: Macmillan Co., 1939. [Dewey, passim.]

Breisach, Ernst. "Benedetto Croce, John Dewey, and the Traditional Concept of Liberty." *Papers of the Michigan Academy of Science, Arts and Letters* 44 (1959): 335-44.

Brett, George Sidney. *A HISTORY OF PSYCHOLOGY.* 3 vols. London: George Allen and Unwin; New York: Macmillan Co., 1912-1921. [Dewey, vol. 3, pp. 259-61.]

---. "Ideals That Work." *Canadian Forum* 10 (1930): 214-16.

Brickman, William W. "John Dewey's Foreign Reputation as an Educator." *School and Society* 70 (1949): 257-65. [Revised version, "John Dewey: Educator of Nations," in *JOHN DEWEY: MASTER EDUCATOR*, edited by William W. Brickman and Stanley Lehrer, 2d ed., pp. 132-43.]

---. "The Dewey Centenary." *School and Society* 80 (1959): 373.

---. "John Dewey's Life and Work in Outline." *School and Society* 80 (1959): 400-402. [Reprinted in *JOHN DEWEY: MASTER EDUCATOR*, 2d ed., pp. 149-53.]

---. "Dewey and Russia." In *JOHN DEWEY: MASTER EDUCATOR*, 2d ed., pp. 144-47.

---. "John Dewey in Russia." *Educational Theory* 10 (1960): 83-86.

---. "Soviet Attitudes toward John Dewey as an Educator." In *JOHN DEWEY AND THE WORLD VIEW*, edited by Douglas Lawson and Arthur Lean, pp. 64-149.

---. "John Dewey and Overseas Education: An Introduction." In *JOHN DEWEY'S IMPRESSIONS OF SOVIET RUSSIA AND THE REVOLUTIONARY WORLD, MEXICO--CHINA--TURKEY, 1929*, edited by William W. Brickman, pp. 1-31. New

York: Bureau of Publications, Teachers College, Columbia University, 1964.

---. "Dewey's Social and Political Commentary." In *GUIDE TO THE WORKS OF JOHN DEWEY*, edited by Jo Ann Boydston, pp. 218-56.

---, and Lehrer, Stanley, eds. *JOHN DEWEY: MASTER EDU-CATOR*. New York: Society for the Advancement of Education, 1959. [The John Dewey Centennial special issue of *School and Society*, 10 October 1959, re-printed in book form, with additions.] [2d ed., New York, 1961, adds "Chicago in the 1890's," by Franklin Parker, pp. 25-30; and Robert L. McCaul, "Dewey, Har-per, and the University of Chicago, July 1894. . .-June 1904," pp. 31-74.] [Reprinted, New York: Atherton Press, 1966.]

Brightman, Edgar Sheffield. *THE PROBLEM OF GOD*. New York: Abingdon Press, 1930. [Dewey, passim.]

Brinkley, S. G. "John Dewey's Universal." *Educational Theory* 1 (1951): 131-33.

Brodbeck, May. "The Emergence of American Philosophy." *American Quarterly* 2 (1950): 39-52.

---. "The New Rationalism: Dewey's Theory of Induc-tion." *Journal of Philosophy* 46 (1949): 780-91. [Reply by Milton Mayeroff, "The Nature of Proposi-tions in John Dewey's 'Logic'." Ibid. 47 (1950): 353-58.]

---. "John Dewey." In *AMERICAN NON-FICTION 1900-1950*, edited by May Brodbeck, James Gray, and Walter Metz-ger, pp. 40-57. Chicago: Henry Regnery Co., 1952.

---. "The Philosophy of John Dewey." *Indian Journal of Philosophy* 3 (1961): 69-101. [Reprinted in *ESSAYS IN ONTOLOGY*, Iowa Publications in Philosophy, vol. 1, pp. 188-215. Iowa City: University of Iowa, 1963.]

Brodsky, Garry M. "Dewey on Experience and Nature." *Monist* 48 (1964): 366-81.

---. "Absolute Idealism and John Dewey's Instrumental-ism." *Transactions of the Charles S. Peirce Society* 5 (1969): 44-62.

---. "The Pragmatic Movement." *Review of Metaphysics* 25 (1971): 262-91.

Brotherston, Bruce Wallace. "The Wider Setting of 'Felt Transition'." *Journal of Philosophy* 39 (1942): 97-104.

---. "The Genius of Pragmatic Empiricism." *Journal of Philosophy* 40 (1943): 14-21, 29-39.

---. "Sensuous and Non-Sensuous Perception in Empirical Philosophy." *Journal of Philosophy* 40 (1943): 589-97. [In reply to Dewey's "Valuation Judgment and Immediate Quality." Ibid.: 309-17.]

Broudy, Harry Samuel. "Realism and the Philosophy of Education." In *THE RETURN TO REASON: ESSAYS IN REAL-ISTIC PHILOSOPHY*, edited by John Daniel Wild, pp. 293-312. Chicago: Henry Regnery Co., 1953.

---. "Democracy and Education as a Pedagogical Problem." *Educational Theory* 10 (1960): 40-49.

---. "Dewey's Analysis of the Act of Thought." In *John Dewey in Perspective: Three Papers in Honor of John Dewey*, edited by A. Stafford Clayton, pp. 15-26.

Broun, Heywood. "Dr. Dewey Finds Communists in the C.I.O." *New Republic*, 12 January 1938, pp. 280-81.

Brown, Bob Burton. "Congruity of Student Teachers' Beliefs and Practices with Dewey's Philosophy." *Educational Forum* 33 (1969): 163-68.

Brown, George P. "Dr. John Dewey's Educational Experiment." *Public School Journal* 16 (1897): 533-37.

---. "The University [of Chicago] Elementary School." *School and Home Education* 18 (1899): 98-99.

Brown, James Nisbet. *EDUCATIONAL IMPLICATIONS OF FOUR CONCEPTIONS OF HUMAN-NATURE: A COMPARATIVE STUDY*. Washington, D.C.: Catholic University of America, 1940. [Doctoral dissertation on John Dewey, William Chandler Bagby, Herman Harrell Horne, and the Catholic viewpoint.]

Brown, Marcus. "Concerning the Abandonment of a Certain 'Deweyan' Conception of Metaphysics." *Educational Theory* 7 (1957): 19-27, 75.

---. "Another Note on 'The Metaphysical Development of John Dewey'." *Educational Theory* 8 (1958): 284-85.

Brown, Richard J. "John Dewey and the League for Independent Political Action." *Social Studies* 59 (1968): 156-61.

Brownell, Baker. (As reported by Thomas A. Leahy.) "John Dewey's Influence on American Life and Thought." *Educational Trends* 7 (November-December 1939): 26-29.

Brubacher, John S. *A HISTORY OF THE PROBLEMS OF EDUCATION*. New York: McGraw-Hill, 1947. [Dewey, passim.]

---. "Ten Misunderstandings of Dewey's Educational Philosophy." In *John Dewey in Perspective: Three Papers in Honor of John Dewey*, edited by A. Stafford Clayton, pp. 27-44.

---. Foreword to *JOHN DEWEY: HIS THOUGHT AND INFLUENCE*, edited by John Blewett.

Bruce, William F. "The Relation of Experimentalism to Democracy in Education." *Educational Administration and Supervision* 18 (1932): 241-49.

---. "Comment upon Breed's Criticism of Dewey." *School and Society* 37 (1933): 812-14. [Frederick S. Breed, "Progressive Education." Ibid.: 544-48.]

---. "A Study of Wider Sources in Education Theory." *Educational Theory* 10 (1960): 87-88.

Brumbaugh, Robert S., and Lawrence, Nathaniel M. "Dewey: The Educational Experience." In their *PHILOSOPHERS ON EDUCATION: SIX ESSAYS ON THE FOUNDATIONS OF WESTERN THOUGHT*, pp. 124-53. Boston: Houghton Mifflin Co., 1963. [Also passim.]

Bruner, Jerome S. "After John Dewey, What?" *Saturday Review*, 17 June 1961, pp. 58-59, 76-78. [Reprinted in *DEWEY ON EDUCATION: APPRAISALS*, edited by Reginald D. Archambault, pp. 211-27.]

Brunstetter, Max R., ed. "Conference on Philosophy of
    Education." *Teachers College Record* 49 (1947-48):
    263-90.

Brush, Francis W. "Our Changing World-Views. An Anal-
    ysis of Smuts' 'Holism' and a Comparison of His
    World-View with Those of Plato and Dewey." *Akten des
    XIV. Internationalen Kongresses für Philosophie* 2
    (1968): 348-59.

Buchanan, Scott. "John Dewey." *Nation*, 23 October 1929,
    pp. 458-59. [Reprinted in part in "Some Popular
    Appraisals of John Dewey," edited by Clyde R. Miller,
    p. 222.]

Buchholz, Heinrich Ewald. "Dewey Mocked by the N.E.A."
    Educational Administration and Supervision 18 (1932):
    413-21.

Buchler, Justus. *TOWARD A GENERAL THEORY OF HUMAN JUDG-
    MENT*. New York: Columbia University Press, 1951.
    [Dewey, pp. 25, 80, 106, 141.]

---. *THE CONCEPT OF METHOD*. New York: Columbia Univer-
    sity Press, 1961. [Dewey, pp. 145-54, and passim.]

---, and Randall, John Herman, Jr. *PHILOSOPHY: AN INTRO-
    DUCTION*. New York: Barnes and Noble, 1942. [Dewey,
    pp. 130-32, 287-90, and passim.]

Buckham, John Wright. "God and the Ideal: Professor
    Dewey Reinterprets Religion." *Journal of Religion* 15
    (1935): 1-9.

---. "Religious Experience and Personality." *Journal
    of Religion* 15 (1935): 309-15. [Reply to Henry
    Nelson Wieman, "Dewey and Buckham on Religion."
    Ibid.: 310-21.]

Buermeyer, Laurence. "Professor Dewey's Analysis of
    Thought." *Journal of Philosophy* 17 (1920): 673-81.

Burke, Kenneth. *THE PHILOSOPHY OF LITERARY FORM:
    STUDIES IN SYMBOLIC ACTION*. Baton Rouge: Louisiana
    State University Press, 1941. [Dewey, pp. 382-91.]

Burkhard, Samuel. *A WORK BOOK IN THE PHILOSOPHY OF
    EDUCATION*. Based on Dewey's *DEMOCRACY AND EDUCATION*.

Dubuque, Iowa: W. C. Brown, 1950.

Burkhardt, Frederick. Statement on Dewey. In "The Literature of Diversity," by George Boas. *New Republic*, 17 October 1949, p. 28.

---, ed. THE CLEAVAGE IN OUR CULTURE: STUDIES IN SCIENTIFIC HUMANISM IN HONOR OF MAX OTTO. Boston: Beacon Press, 1952. [Dewey, passim.]

Burks, Don M. "John Dewey and Rhetorical Theory." *Western Speech* 32 (1968): 118-26. [Symposium entitled "The Influence of John Dewey upon Speech," with Gladys Borchers and R. Victor Harnack.]

Burlington Daily News. "John Dewey Acclaimed at UVM 'Family Gathering'." *Burlington Daily News*, 27 October 1949.

Burlington Free Press. "Dewey's Entire Life an Inquiry, says Dr. Schneider." *Burlington Free Press*, 27 October 1949.

---. "Try to Find Meaning of What Goes on around, says Philosopher John Dewey." *Burlington Free Press*, 27 October 1949.

---. "UVM May Have Dewey Memorial; Plan Includes Bringing His Ashes to Campus." *Burlington Free Press*, 5 June 1952.

Burnett, Joe R., and Axtelle, George E. "Dewey on Education and Schooling." In *GUIDE TO THE WORKS OF JOHN DEWEY*, edited by Jo Ann Boydston, pp. 257-305.

Burnett, Joe R., and Boydston, Jo Ann. "The Dewey Project." *Educational Forum* 35 (1971): 177-83.

Burns, Edward McNall. *IDEAS IN CONFLICT: THE POLITICAL THEORIES OF THE CONTEMPORARY WORLD*. New York: W. W. Norton and Co., 1960. [Dewey, pp. 94-97, and passim.]

Burns, James MacGregor. *ROOSEVELT: THE SOLDIER OF FREEDOM*. New York: Harcourt Brace Jovanovich, 1970. [Dewey, pp. 171-72, and passim.]

Burston, Wyndham H. "The Influence of John Dewey in

English Official Reports." *International Review of Education* 7 (1961): 311-25.

Burtt, Edwin Arthur. "A Discussion of the Theory of International Relations." *Journal of Philosophy* 42 (1945): 477-97. [A discussion by several philosophers of two paragraphs of Dewey's Introduction to Jane Addams, *PEACE AND BREAD IN TIME OF WAR*. New York: King's Crown Press, 1945.] [Burtt, pp. 486-91. Other philosophers: Joseph P. Chamberlain, William Ernest Hocking, Sidney Hook, Arthur O. Lovejoy, Glenn R. Morrow, Jerome Nathanson, and Thomas V. Smith.]

---. "Analysis of a Typical Case of Reasoning." In his *RIGHT THINKING: A STUDY OF ITS PRINCIPLES AND METHODS*, pp. 17-30. 3d rev. ed. New York: Harper and Brothers, 1946.

---. *TYPES OF RELIGIOUS PHILOSOPHY*. New York: Harper and Brothers, 1939. [Dewey, pp. 399-408, and passim.]

---. "The Core of Dewey's Way of Thinking." *Journal of Philosophy* 57 (1960): 401-19. [Comments by Gail Kennedy and John Allan Irving. Ibid.: 436-50.]

Bush, Wendell T. "Constructive Intelligence." *Journal of Philosophy* 14 (1917): 505-20.

---. "Value and Causality." *Journal of Philosophy* 15 (1918): 85-96. [Reply by Dewey, "The Objects of Valuation." Ibid.: 253-58.]

---. "The Background of Instrumentalism." *Journal of Philosophy* 20 (1923): 701-14.

Buswell, James Oliver, Jr. *THE PHILOSOPHIES OF F. R. TENNANT AND JOHN DEWEY*. New York: Philosophical Library, 1950. [From his doctoral dissertation, "The Empirical Method of F. R. Tennant." New York University, 1949.]

Butts, R. Freeman. "Centenary of John Dewey." *Teachers College Record* 61 (1959): 117-20.

---, and Cremin, Lawrence A. *A HISTORY OF EDUCATION IN AMERICAN CULTURE*. New York: Henry Holt and Co., 1953. [Dewey, pp. 339-47, and passim.]

Byrns, Ruth Katherine. "John Dewey on Russia: A Leading American Philosopher has been Cool to the Soviets." *Commonweal*, 18 September 1942, pp. 511-13.

---, and O'Meara, William. "Concerning Mr. Hutchins:

Three Philosophies of Education--Dewey, Hutchins, and a Catholic View." *Commonweal*, 31 May 1940, pp. 114-16.

Cahill, Holger. "American Resources in the Arts." In *Resources for Building America*, Progressive Education Booklet, no. 15, pp. 41-57. Columbus, Ohio: Progressive Education Association, 1939.

Cahn, Steven M. *A NEW INTRODUCTION TO PHILOSOPHY*. New York: Harper and Row, 1971. [Dewey, passim.]

Caldwell, William. *PRAGMATISM AND IDEALISM*. London: Adam and Charles Black, 1913. [Dewey, pp. 16-17, 173-75, and passim.]

Callahan, Ronan. "Common Sense in the Tool Shed--John Dewey and His Topsy-Turvy Influence." *Weekly Bulletin* [of the Hour of the Crucified Radio Program], 10 May 1964, pp. 6-8.

Campbell, Harry M. "John Dewey's 'Copernican Revolution in Philosophy'." *Journal of Thought* 3 (1968): 177-90.

---. "Dewey's *ART AS EXPERIENCE*: The Transformation of the World through Art." *Southern Humanities Review* 3 (1969): 86-100.

---. *JOHN DEWEY*. New York: Twayne Publishers, 1971.

Campbell, Paul E. "Fundamental Fallacies in Education." *Homiletic and Pastoral Review* 32 (1932): 1287-95.

Cantril, Hadley. "Some Requirements for a Political Psychology." In *PERSPECTIVES IN THE STUDY OF POLITICS*, edited by Malcolm B. Parsons, pp. 124-26. Chicago: Rand McNally and Co., 1968.

Cargill, Oscar. "John Dewey: The Neglected Philosopher." In *FROM IRVING TO STEINBECK*, edited by Motley Deakin and Peter Lisca, pp. 85-94. Gainesville: University of Florida Press, 1972.

Carmichael, Leonard. Introduction to John Dewey's *THE CHILD AND THE CURRICULUM* and *SCHOOL AND SOCIETY*. Chicago: University of Chicago Press, Phoenix Books, 1956.

Carnap, Rudolf. "Meaning, Assertion, and Proposal." *Philosophy of Science* 1 (1934): 359-60. [In reply to Dewey's "Meaning, Assertion, and Proposal." Ibid.: 237-38.]

Cary, C. P. "John Dewey's Educational Ideas." *Wisconsin Journal of Education* 64 (1932): 333-34, 390-91.

Caswell, Hollis Leland. "Influence of John Dewey on the Curriculum of American Schools." *Teachers College Record* 51 (1949): 144-46.

Cavell, Stanley, and Sesonske, Alexander. "Logical Empiricism and Pragmatism in Ethics." *Journal of Philosophy* 48 (1951): 5-17. [Reprinted in *PRAGMATIC PHILOSOPHY*, edited by Amelie Rorty, pp. 382-95.]

Cawelti, John G. "Individual Success and the Community: John Dewey's Philosophy of Success." In his *APOSTLES OF THE SELF-MADE MAN*, pp. 238-48. Chicago: University of Chicago Press, 1965.

Chadbourne, Richard McClain. "Two Organizers of Divinity, Ernest Renan and John Dewey." *Thought* [Fordham University Quarterly.] 24 (1949): 430-48.

Chamberlain, Joseph P. "A Discussion of the Theory of International Relations." *Journal of Philosophy* 42 (1945): 477-97. [A discussion by several philosophers of two paragraphs of Dewey's Introduction to Jane Addams, *PEACE AND BREAD IN TIME OF WAR*. New York: King's Crown Press, 1945.] [Chamberlain, pp. 482-84. Other philosophers: E. A. Burtt, William Ernest Hocking, Sidney Hook, Arthur O. Lovejoy, Glenn R. Morrow, Jerome Nathanson, and Thomas V. Smith.]

Chambliss, J. J. *BOYD H. BODE'S PHILOSOPHY OF EDUCATION*. Studies in Educational Theory of the John Dewey Society, no. 2. Columbus: Ohio State University Press, 1963. [Dewey, passim.]

Champlin, Nathaniel Lewis. "John Dewey: Beyond the Centennial." *Educational Leadership* 18 (1960): 33-35, 38-42.

---. "Education and Aesthetic Method." *Journal of Aesthetic Education* 4 (1970): 65-85.

---, and Villemain, Francis. "Frontiers for an Experimentalist Philosophy of Education." *Antioch Review* 19 (1959): 345-59.

---, eds. "Dewey and Creative Education." *Saturday Review*, 21 November 1959, pp. 19-25. [Manifesto signed by Joe Burnett, Hobert W. Burns, Nathaniel Champlin, Otto Krash, Frederick C. Neff, and Francis T. Villemain.]

Chapman, J. Crosby, and Counts, George S. *PRINCIPLES OF EDUCATION*. Boston: Houghton Mifflin Co., 1924. [Dewey, passim.]

Chapman, Robert A. "Thinking with John Dewey." In *Some Interpretations of John Dewey's Educational Philosophy*, Bulletin of Florida Southern College, vol. 67, pp. 13-18. Lakeland: Florida Southern College, 1951.

Chase, Daniel. Letter on Dewey-Matthew Woll exchange. *New Republic*, 13 March 1929, p. 73.

Chassell, Clara Frances, and Laura M. "A Restatement of Important Educational Conceptions of Dewey in the Terminology of Thorndike." *Journal of Educational Method* 3 (1924): 286-98.

Chassell, Laura Merrill, and Clara F. "A Restatement. . ." *Journal of Educational Method* 3 (1924): 286-98.

Chennakesavan, Sarasvati. "The Philosophy of John Dewey--as an Indian Sees It." *Philosophical Quarterly* [India.] 33 (1960-61): 267-71.

Chicago Tribune (Paris). "Dewey Declares America Foregoes Faith in Prosperity." *Chicago Tribune* (Paris), 6 November 1930.

Child, Arthur Henry. *Making and Knowing in Hobbes, Vico, and Dewey*. University of California Publications in Philosophy, vol. 16, pp. 271-310. Berkeley: University of California Press, 1953.

Child, H. A. T., ed. *THE INDEPENDENT PROGRESSIVE SCHOOL*. London: Hutchinson, 1962. [Dewey, passim.]

Childs, John Lawrence. *EDUCATION AND THE PHILOSOPHY OF EXPERIMENTALISM*. Century Studies in Education. New York: Century Co., 1931. [Doctoral dissertation on Peirce, James, and Dewey. Columbia University, 1931.]

---. "Democracy, Education, and the Class Struggle."
Social Frontier 2 (1936): 274-78. [In reply to
Dewey's "Class Struggle and the Democratic Way."
Ibid.: 241-42.]

---. "The Educational Philosophy of John Dewey." In
THE PHILOSOPHY OF JOHN DEWEY, edited by Paul Schilpp,
pp. 417-43. [Reprinted in *JOHN DEWEY AS EDUCATOR* by
John L. Childs and William H. Kilpatrick, pp. 419-
43.]

---. "John Dewey and the Educational Frontier." In
The Educational Frontier, Progressive Education
Booklet, no. 13, pp. 5-12. Columbus, Ohio: Progres-
sive Education Association, 1939.

---. "Comments by John L. Childs on John Dewey's Letter." *Frontiers of Democracy* 8 (1942): 181-82. [In
reply to Dewey's "Can We Work with Russia?" Ibid.:
179-80. Dewey's response and Childs's rejoinder,
ibid.: 194.] [Dewey's letter reprinted from *New
York Times*, 11 January 1942, p. 7.]

---. "Cultural Factors in Dewey's Philosophy of Education." *Teachers College Record* 51 (1949): 130-32.

---. "Laboratory for 'Personhood'." *Saturday Review
of Literature*, 22 October 1949, pp. 11-12, 36-38.

---. "John Dewey and Education." In *JOHN DEWEY: PHI-
LOSOPHER OF SCIENCE AND FREEDOM*, edited by Sidney
Hook, pp. 153-63.

---. "John Dewey's Philosophy of Education." *Philippine Educator* 5 (August 1950): 9-13.

---. "Boyd H. Bode and the Experimentalists."
Teachers College Record 55 (1953): 1-9.

---. "John Dewey." *Educational Theory* 4 (1954):
183-86.

---. "Can the Philosopher Influence Social Change?"
Journal of Philosophy 51 (1954): 753-63. [Reply to
Brand Blanshard, ibid.: 741-53.]

---. *AMERICAN PRAGMATISM AND EDUCATION: AN INTERPRETA-
TION AND CRITICISM*. New York: Henry Holt and Co.,

1956. [Dewey, passim.]

---. "John Dewey and American Education." *Teachers College Record* 61 (1959): 128-33.

---. "Enduring Elements in the Educational Thought of John Dewey." *University of Michigan School of Education Bulletin* 31 (November 1959): 17-26.

---. "The Civilizational Functions of Philosophy and Education." In *JOHN DEWEY AND THE WORLD VIEW*, edited by Douglas Lawson and Arthur Lean, pp. 3-14.

---, and Kilpatrick, William Heard. *JOHN DEWEY AS EDUCATOR*. New York: Progressive Education Association, 1940. ["The Educational Philosophy of John Dewey," and "Dewey's Influence on Education," by William H. Kilpatrick, with a separate preface by Professors Childs and Kilpatrick, and the complete table of contents of *THE PHILOSOPHY OF JOHN DEWEY*. Reprinted from *THE PHILOSOPHY OF JOHN DEWEY*, edited by Paul Schilpp.]

Chow Tse-tsung. *THE MAY FOURTH MOVEMENT: INTELLECTUAL REVOLUTION IN MODERN CHINA*. Cambridge: Harvard University Press, 1960. [Dewey, passim.]

Christian Century. "The Philosopher and God." *Christian Century* 51 (1934): 1582-84. [Editorial comment on Wieman, Dewey, and Aubrey exchange in ibid.: 1450-52, 1550, 1550-51, 1551-52, 1552-53.]

---. "John Dewey." [Editorial.] *Christian Century* 69 (1952): 717-19. [Followed by letters from readers. Ibid.: 805-6, and communication from Charles Clayton Morrison. Ibid.: 854.]

Chronicle. [University of Michigan.] "John Dewey, Ph.D." *Chronicle* 21 (1890): 327-28.

Churchman, Charles West, and Cowan, Thomas Anthony. "A Discussion of Dewey's and Bentley's 'Postulations'." *Journal of Philosophy* 43 (1946): 217-19. [On Dewey and A. F. Bentley, "Postulations." Ibid. 42 (1945): 645-62.]

Clapp, Elsie Ripley. *THE USE OF RESOURCES IN EDUCATION*. A Publication of the John Dewey Society. New York: Harper and Brothers, 1952.

Clarenbach, Fred A. "John Dewey's Philosophy of Social
Economy." In *IN HONOR OF JOHN DEWEY ON HIS NINE-
TIETH BIRTHDAY*, pp. 31-33. Madison: University of
Wisconsin, 1951.

Clark, Gordon Haddon. *THALES TO DEWEY: A HISTORY OF
PHILOSOPHY*. Boston: Houghton Mifflin Co., 1957.
[Dewey, pp. 517-33.]

---. *DEWEY*. International Library of Philosophy and
Theology, Modern Thinkers Series. Philadelphia:
Presbyterian and Reformed Publishing Co., 1960.

Clayton, Alfred Stafford. "Dewey's Theory of Language
with Some Implications for Educational Theory." In
Essays for John Dewey's Ninetieth Birthday, edited
by Kenneth D. Benne and William O. Stanley, pp.
37-46.

---. "The Educational Philosophy of John Dewey in Perspective." *Phi Delta Kappan* 41 (1959): 10-13.

---. "Philosophy of Education." *Review of Educational
Research* 31 (1961): 21-37. ["Interpretations of Dewey's Educational Thought," p. 32. Also Dewey, passim.]

---. Preface to *John Dewey in Perspective: Three
Papers in Honor of John Dewey*, edited by A. Stafford
Clayton. Indiana University, Bulletin of the School
of Education, vol. 36. Bloomington: Division of
Research and Field Services, 1960. [Papers by Harry
S. Broudy, John S. Brubacher, and Harold Rugg.]

Clift, Virgil A. "Does the Dewey Philosophy Have Implications for Desegregating the Schools?" *Journal
of Negro Education* 29 (1960): 145-54.

---; Anderson, Archibald W.; and Hullfish, H. Gordon.
*NEGRO EDUCATION IN AMERICA. ITS ADEQUACY, PROBLEMS,
AND NEEDS*. Sixteenth Yearbook of the John Dewey
Society. New York: Harper and Brothers, 1962.
[Dewey, passim.]

Clohesy, William W. "F. H. Bradley and John Dewey on
Subject-Predicate Propositions." *Kinesis* 2 (1969):
43-51.

Cobb, Stanwood. *THE NEW LEAVEN: PROGRESSIVE EDUCATION*

AND ITS EFFECTS UPON THE CHILD AND SOCIETY. New
York: John Day Co., 1928. [Dewey, passim.]

Cohen, Morris Raphael. "On American Philosophy III:
John Dewey and the Chicago School." *New Republic*,
17 March 1920, pp. 82-86.

---. "Later Philosophy." In *THE CAMBRIDGE HISTORY OF
AMERICAN LITERATURE*, edited by William Peterfield
Trent; John Erskine; Stuart P. Sherman; and Carl Van
Doren, vol. 3, pp. 254-57. New York: G. P. Putnam's
Sons, 1921. [Also passim.]

---. "The Intellectual Love of God." *Menorah Journal*
11 (1925): 332-41. ["The Spinozistic Ideal in Contemporary Thinkers. . . Dewey," p. 340.]

---. "Reason, Nature and Professor Dewey." *New Republic*, 17 June 1931, pp. 126-27. [In response to
Dewey's "A Philosophy of Scientific Method." Ibid.,
29 April 1931, pp. 306-7. Rejoinder by Dewey, ibid.,
17 June 1931, p. 127.]

---. "Some Difficulties in Dewey's Anthropocentric
Naturalism." *Philosophical Review* 49 (1940): 196-
228. [Dewey's reply, "Nature in Experience."
Ibid.: 244-58.] [Cohen's article reprinted in his
STUDIES IN PHILOSOPHY AND SCIENCE, pp. 139-75. New
York: Henry Holt and Co., 1949.]

---. "John Dewey and His School." In his *AMERICAN
THOUGHT: A CRITICAL SKETCH*, pp. 290-303. Glencoe,
Ill.: Free Press, 1954. [Also passim.] [Paperback
reprint, Collier Books, 1962.]

Coleman, George W. "Dr. Dewey's Astuteness." Letter
in *New Republic*, 15 April 1931, p. 238. [On Dewey's
"The Need for a New Party." Ibid., 18 March 1931,
pp. 115-17; 25 March 1931, pp. 150-52; 1 April 1931,
pp. 177-79; 8 April 1931, pp. 202-5.]

Collins, James. "Marxist and Secular Humanism." *Social Order* 3 (1953): 207-32. [Reprinted with
slight revisions in his *CROSSROADS IN PHILOSOPHY*,
pp. 220-51. Chicago: Henry Regnery Co., 1962.]

---. *GOD IN MODERN PHILOSOPHY.* Chicago: Henry Regnery
and Co., 1959. [Dewey, passim.]

---. "The Genesis of Dewey's Naturalism." In *JOHN DEWEY: HIS THOUGHT AND INFLUENCE*, edited by John Blewett, pp. 1-32.

Columbia Alumni News. "Prof. John Dewey Will Retire from Columbia Faculty in June." *Columbia Alumni News*, 28 March 1930, p. 5.

Commager, Henry Steele. *THE AMERICAN MIND: AN INTERPRETATION OF AMERICAN THOUGHT AND CHARACTER SINCE THE 1880s.* New Haven: Yale University Press, 1950. [Dewey, pp. 98-107.]

Comstock, W. Richard. "Dewey and Santayana in Conflict: Religious Dimensions of Naturalism." *Journal of Religion* 45 (1965): 119-36.

Condon, Edward Uhler. "Contemporary Science." *New Republic*, 13 February 1950, pp. 11-15.

Conger, George Perrigo. "Pragmatism and the Physical World." In *PHILOSOPHY FOR THE FUTURE: THE QUEST OF MODERN MATERIALISM*, edited by Roy Wood Sellars, V. J. McGill, and Marvin Farber, pp. 522-43.

Conkin, Paul K. "John Dewey." In his *PURITANS AND PRAGMATISTS*, pp. 345-402. New York: Dodd, Mead and Co., 1968.

Cooley, Edwin G. "Professor Dewey's Criticism of the Chicago Commercial Club and Its Vocational Education Bill." *Vocational Education* 3 (1913): 24-29. [Reply to Dewey's "Some Dangers in the Present Movement for Industrial Education." *Child Labor Bulletin* 1 (1913): 69-74.]

---. "In Reply to Dr. John Dewey's 'Some Dangers in the Present Movement for Industrial Education'." Mimeographed. Chicago, 1913?

Coon, Horace. *COLUMBIA, COLOSSUS ON THE HUDSON.* New York: E. P. Dutton and Co., 1947. [Dewey, pp. 177-80, and passim.]

Coons, John Warren. *THE IDEA OF CONTROL IN JOHN DEWEY'S PHILOSOPHY.* Rochester, N.H.: Record Press, 1936. [Doctoral dissertation, University of Iowa, 1933.]

Copleston, Frederick. "The Experimentalism of John Dewey." In his *A HISTORY OF PHILOSOPHY*, vol. 8, pp. 352-79. Westminster, Md.: Newman Press, 1966. [Also passim.]

Corcoran, Timothy. "Child Labor within School Years from Dewey back to Pestalozzi." *Thought* [Fordham University Quarterly.] 6 (1931): 88-107.

Cork, Jim. "John Dewey, Karl Marx, and Democratic Socialism." *Antioch Review* 9 (1949): 435-52. [Reprinted in *JOHN DEWEY: PHILOSOPHER OF SCIENCE AND FREEDOM*, edited by Sidney Hook, pp. 331-50; and in *ANTIOCH REVIEW ANTHOLOGY*, 1953, pp. 137-52.]

Corya, Florence. "Bust of Professor Dewey." *School and Society* 28 (1928): 684-85.

Costello, Harry Todd. "Professor Dewey's 'Judgments of Practise'." *Journal of Philosophy* 17 (1920): 449-55. [On ch. 14 of Dewey's *ESSAYS IN EXPERIMENTAL LOGIC*.]

---. "Logic in 1914 and Now." *Journal of Philosophy* 54 (1957): 245-64.

Counts, George S. *THE CHALLENGE OF SOVIET EDUCATION*. New York: McGraw-Hill Book Co., 1957. [Dewey, pp. 60-61, 114, 188.]

---, and Chapman, J. Crosby. *PRINCIPLES OF EDUCATION*. Boston: Houghton Mifflin Co., 1924. [Dewey, passim.]

---, and Lodge, Nucia. *THE COUNTRY OF THE BLIND: THE SOVIET SYSTEM OF MIND CONTROL*. Boston: Houghton Mifflin Co., 1949. [Dewey, pp. 271, 277-78.]

Cowan, Thomas Anthony, ed. *THE AMERICAN JURISPRUDENCE READER*. New York: Oceana Publications, 1956. [Dewey, passim.]

---, and Churchman, Charles West. "A Discussion of Dewey's and Bentley's 'Postulations'." *Journal of Philosophy* 43 (1946): 217-19. [On Dewey and A. F. Bentley, "Postulations." Ibid. 42 (1945): 645-62.]

Cowart, Billy F. "John Dewey's Concept of God." *Educational Theory* 17 (1967): 83-90.

Cowley, Malcolm. "Dewey in an Age of Unreason." *New Republic*, 16 June 1952, p. 8.

Crabtree, Walden B. "An Age of Irrelevancy." *Educational Theory* 21 (1971): 33-41. [Dewey, pp. 34, 36, 40.]

Crafter, A. G. "Dewey's Russian Analysis." *New Republic*, 16 January 1929, p. 248.

Craig, Robert C., and Dupuis, Adrian M. *AMERICAN EDUCATION: ITS ORIGINS AND ISSUES*. Milwaukee: Bruce Publishing Co., 1963. [Dewey, pp. 253-63.]

Crary, Ryland W. "John Dewey and American Social Thought." *Teachers College Record* 51 (1949): 133-35.

Crawford, Claude C. "Functional Education in the Light of Dewey's Philosophy." *School and Society* 48 (1938): 381-85.

Cremin, Lawrence A. "The Progressive Movement in American Education: A Perspective." *Harvard Educational Review* 27 (1957): 251-70.

---. "What Happened to Progressive Education?" *Teachers College Record* 61 (1959): 23-29. [Condensed in *Education Digest* 25 (January 1960): 4-7.]

---. "John Dewey and the Progressive Education Movement, 1915-1952." *School Review* 67 (1959): 160-73. [Reprinted in *DEWEY ON EDUCATION: APPRAISALS*, edited by Reginald D. Archambault, pp. 9-25.]

---. "The Origins of Progressive Education." *Educational Forum* 24 (1960): 133-40.

---. *THE TRANSFORMATION OF THE SCHOOL: PROGRESSIVISM IN AMERICAN EDUCATION 1876-1957*. New York: Alfred A. Knopf, 1961. [Dewey, passim.]

Crissman, Paul. "Dewey's Theory of the Moral Good." *Monist* 38 (1928): 592-619.

---. "The Psychology of John Dewey." *Psychological Review* 49 (1942): 441-62. [Abstract by A. G. Bills in *Psychological Abstracts* 17 (1943): 46.]

---. "A Comparison and Critique of Dewey's and Perry's Theories of Value." *University of Wyoming Publications*, 15 July 1951, pp. 55-73.

Croce, Benedetto. "Dewey's Aesthetics and Theory of Knowledge." *Journal of Aesthetics and Art Criticism* 11 (1952): 1-6. [Translated by Frederic S. Simoni. Originally published as "Intorno all'estetica e alla teoria del conoscere del Dewey." *Quaderni della critica* 16 (1950): 60-68.]

Cross, Elizabeth. "The Educational Philosophy of John Dewey." *Aryan Path* 29 (1958): 345-50.

Crosser, Paul K. *THE NIHILISM OF JOHN DEWEY.* New York: Philosophical Library, 1955.

Cua, Antonio S. "Foundations of Dewey's Ethics and Value Theory." *Thought and World Magazine* [Taiwan.] 5 (1967): 1-10.

Cubberly, Ellwood Patterson. *PUBLIC EDUCATION IN THE UNITED STATES.* Boston: Houghton Mifflin Co., 1919. [Dewey, passim.]

Cullum, Leo A. "Trend toward Sanity." *Philippine Studies* 1 (1953): 274-76.

Cully, Kendig Brubaker, ed. *BASIC WRITINGS IN CHRISTIAN EDUCATION.* Philadelphia: Westminster Press, 1960. [Introduction to excerpt from "My Pedagogic Creed," pp. 310-11.]

Cunningham, Gustavus Watts. "On Reason's Reach: Historical Observations." *American Philosophical Quarterly* 6 (1969): 1-16.

Current Opinion. "Professor Dewey Pleads for Faith in Constructive Social Progress." *Current Opinion* 60 (1916): 419-20.

Curti, Merle. "John Dewey." In his *SOCIAL IDEAS OF AMERICAN EDUCATORS*, pp. 499-541. Report of the Commission on Social Studies, American Historical Association, part 10. New York: Charles Scribner's Sons, 1935. [Reprinted "With New Chapter on the Last Twenty-five Years," by Littlefield, Adams, and Co., New Jersey, 1959.]

---. *THE GROWTH OF AMERICAN THOUGHT.* New York: Harper and Brothers, 1943. [Dewey, pp. 560-66, and passim.]

---. "John Dewey and Nationalism." *Orbis* 10 (1967): 1103-19.

Curtin, Andrew. "John Dewey." In his *GALLERY OF GREAT AMERICANS*, p. 25. New York: Franklin Watts, 1965.

Curtis, Tom. "Bourne, Macdonald, Chomsky, and the Rhetoric of Resistance." *Antioch Review* 29 (1969): 245-52.

Cywar, Alan. "John Dewey: Toward Domestic Reconstruction, 1915-1920." *Journal of the History of Ideas* 30 (1969): 385-400.

---. "John Dewey in World War I: Patriotism and International Progressivism." *American Quarterly* 21 (1969): 578-94.

Daily Illini. [University of Illinois.] Report of Dewey's Lectures on "Types of Philosophy and Types of Educational Theory." *Daily Illini*, 8 December 1907; 10 December 1907; 11 December 1907; 12 December 1907.

Dale, Edgar. *AUDIOVISUAL METHODS IN TEACHING*. 3d ed. New York: Holt, Rinehart and Winston, 1969. [Dewey, passim.]

Daum, N. F. "Culture-Epoch Theory." *Public School Journal* 15 (1896): 509-10. [Discussion of Dewey's "Interpretation of the Culture-Epoch Theory." Ibid.: 233-37 (*Early Works of John Dewey* 5: 247-53.)]

Davidson, Robert Franklin. "Naturalistic Humanism: John Dewey." In his *PHILOSOPHIES MEN LIVE BY*, pp. 251-93. New York: Dial Press, 1952.

---. "From Naturalism to Humanism: John Dewey." In his *THE SEARCH FOR MEANING IN LIFE*, pp. 218-20. New York: Holt, Rinehart and Winston, 1962.

---. "The Pragmatist as Instrumentalist: John Dewey." In his *THE SEARCH FOR MEANING IN LIFE*, pp. 265-66.

Dearborn, Ned H. "Democracy and Education." In *The Educational Frontier*, Progressive Education Booklet, no. 13, pp. 58-63. Columbus, Ohio: Progressive Education Association, 1939.

De Boer, Cecil. "John Dewey." In his *RESPONSIBLE*

PROTESTANTISM: ESSAYS ON THE CHRISTIAN'S ROLE IN A SECULAR SOCIETY, pp. 77-84. Grand Rapids, Mich.: William B. Eerdmans, 1957. [Abridged in *Christianity Today* 1 (1957): 8-10.]

De Boer, John J. "The Influence of John Dewey on Education." *Educational Trends* 7 (November-December 1939): 15-19.

De Casterline, Grace. "The Religious." In *Some Interpretations of John Dewey's Educational Philosophy*. Bulletin of Florida Southern College, vol. 67, pp. 19-24. Lakeland: Florida Southern College, 1951.

Deely, John N. "The Philosophical Dimensions of the Origin of Species. Part One." *Thomist* 33 (1969): 75-149.

De Grood, David H. "Intelligence and 'Radicalism' in John Dewey's Philosophy." *Telos* 2 (1969): 72-81.

---. "Dewey's Experimental Theory of Essence." In his *PHILOSOPHIES OF ESSENCE*, pp. 127-40. Groningen, Holland: Wolters-Noordhoff, 1970.

De Hovre, Franz. "Some Radical-Social Educators: John Dewey." In his *PHILOSOPHY AND EDUCATION*, pp. 101-16. Translated by Edward Benedict Jordan. New York: Benziger Brothers, 1931. [Also passim.]

De Laguna, Grace Andrus. "The Practical Character of Reality." *Philosophical Review* 18 (1909): 396-415.

De Laguna, Theodore. "Evolutionary Method in Ethical Research." *Philosophical Review* 13 (1904): 328-37. [Reply to Dewey's "The Evolutionary Method as Applied to Morality." Ibid. 11 (1902): 107-24, 353-71.]

de Lone, Richard H., and Susan T. "John Dewey Is Alive and Well in New England." *Saturday Review*, 21 November 1970, pp. 69-71, 83-85.

de Lone, Susan T., and Richard H. "John Dewey Is Alive. . . ." *Saturday Review*, 21 November 1970, pp. 69-71, 83-85.

Dennes, William Ray. *SOME DILEMMAS OF NATURALISM*. New

York: Columbia University Press, 1960. [Dewey, passim.]

Dennett, Tyler. "Education Cannot Lead." *Forum* 93 (1935): 335-37. [Second part of a debate with Dewey, "Education and Our Society, A Debate." First part by Dewey, "The Need for Orientation." Ibid.: 333-35.]

Dennis, Lawrence J. "Dewey's Contribution to Aesthetic Education." *Journal of Aesthetic Education* 2 (1968): 23-35.

———. "Play in Dewey's Theory of Education." *Young Children* 25 (1970): 230-35.

———. "Dewey's Brief For the Fine Arts." *NAEA* [National Art Education Association, Studies in Art Education] 11 (1970): 3-8.

———. "Dewey's Debt to Albert Coombs Barnes." *Educational Theory* 22 (1972): 325-33. [In response to C. M. Smith, "The Aesthetics of John Dewey and Aesthetic Education." Ibid. 21 (1971): 131-45.]

Dennison, George. "The First Street School." *New American Review* 3 (1968): 159.

———. *THE LIVES OF CHILDREN: THE STORY OF THE FIRST STREET SCHOOL.* New York: Random House, 1969. [Dewey, passim.]

Densford, John P. "Value Theory as Basic to a Philosophy of Education." *History of Education Quarterly* 3 (1963): 102-6.

———. "A Dialogue with John Dewey." *Clearing House* 42 (1968): 553-55.

Denton, William H. "Problem-Solving as a Theory of Learning and Teaching." *High School Journal* 49 (1966): 382-90.

De Pencier, Ida B. *THE HISTORY OF THE LABORATORY SCHOOLS. THE UNIVERSITY OF CHICAGO, 1896-1965.* Chicago: Quadrangle Books, 1967. [Dewey, passim.]

Derrick (Oil City, Pa.). "Its Famous Ex-Resident," and

"John Dewey Taught for Two Years at Central Avenue High School." *Derrick*, 28 January 1965.

De Ruggiero, Guido. *MODERN PHILOSOPHY*. Translated by A. Howard Hannay and R. G. Collingwood. London: George Allen and Unwin, 1921. [Dewey, p. 257.]

Destler, Chester McArthur. "Some Observations on Contemporary Historical Theory." *American Historical Review* 55 (1950): 503-29. [Communication in ibid. 56 (1951): 450-52, from Merle Curti, Bert James Loewenberg, John Herman Randall, Jr., and Harold Taylor.]

Detroit Tribune. "'Thought News'--a Journal of Inquiry and a Record of Fact." *Detroit Tribune*, 10 April 1892.

---. "News for Thought." *Detroit Tribune*, 11 April 1892.

---. "He's Planned No Revolution." *Detroit Tribune*, 13 April 1892.

---. "Ethics in Schools." *Detroit Tribune*, 5 November 1893.

Dettering, R. W. "Philosophical Semantics and Education." *Educational Theory* 8 (1958): 143-49, 168. [Dewey, p. 168.]

Devadutt, V. E. "The Church's Mission and Syncretism. Crisis in the Christian West." *Encounter* 19 (1958): 280-91.

Dewey, Adelbert M., and Louis M. *LIFE OF GEORGE DEWEY, REAR ADMIRAL, U.S.N., AND DEWEY FAMILY HISTORY*. Westfield, Mass.: Dewey Publishing Co., 1898. [Genealogy of John Dewey, pp. 910, 961, and passim.]

Dewey, Louis Marinus, and Adelbert M. *LIFE OF GEORGE DEWEY,* . . . Westfield, Mass.: Dewey Publishing Co., 1898. [Genealogy of John Dewey, pp. 910, 961, and passim.]

Dewey, Jane Mary, ed. "Biography of John Dewey." In *THE PHILOSOPHY OF JOHN DEWEY*, edited by Paul Schilpp, pp. 3-45.

De Witt, Dale, and Kilpatrick, William Heard. "John Dewey: Humanist and Educator." *Humanist* 12 (1952): 161-65. [Reprinted in *Michigan Education Journal* 30 (1953): 522-23.]

Dicker, Georges. "John Dewey: Instrumentalism in Social Action." *Transactions of the Charles S. Peirce Society* 7 (1971): 221-32.

---. "John Dewey on the Object of Knowledge." *Transactions of the Charles S. Peirce Society* 8 (1972): 152-66.

---. "Warranted Assertibility and the Uniformity of Nature." *Transactions of the Charles S. Peirce Society* 9 (1973): 110-15.

Diggins, John P. "Flirtation with Fascism: American Pragmatic Liberals and Mussolini's Italy." *American Historical Review* 71 (1966): 487-506.

Dodd, Stuart C. "Can We Be Scientific about Humanism?" *Humanist* 18 (1958): 259-65.

Doescher, Waldemar Oswald. "Dewey's Educational Philosophy and Its Implications for Christian Education." *Christian Education* 22 (1939): 377-89.

Doll, William E., Jr. "Methodology of Experience: An Alternative to Behavioral Objectives." *Educational Theory* 22 (1972): 309-24. [Dewey, pp. 312, 313, 317-23.]

Donahue, Charles. "God, Caesar and Social Integration." *Social Order* 4 (1954): 173-78.

Donohue, John W. "John Dewey: Centennial of An Educator." *Catholic Educational Review* 58 (1960): 16-27.

---. "Dewey and the Problem of Technology." In *JOHN DEWEY: HIS THOUGHT AND INFLUENCE*, edited by John Blewett, pp. 117-44.

---. "Dewey's Theory of Work in Education." In his *WORK AND EDUCATION: THE ROLE OF TECHNICAL CULTURE IN SOME DISTINCTIVE THEORIES OF HUMANISM*, pp. 57-94. Chicago: Loyola University Press, 1959.

Donoso, Anton. "John Dewey's Philosophy of Law." *University of Detroit Law Journal* 36 (1959): 579-606.

Donovan, Charles F. "Dilution in American Education."

America 86 (1951): 121-22.

Dorfman, Joseph. "Philosophers and Social Reforms: John Dewey." In his *THE ECONOMIC MIND IN AMERICAN CIVILIZATION*, vol. 4, pp. 125-26. New York: Viking Press, 1959.

Dougherty, Jude P. "Recent Development in Naturalistic Ethics." In *PROCEEDINGS OF THE AMERICAN CATHOLIC PHILOSOPHICAL ASSOCIATION*, vol. 33, pp. 97-108. Washington, D.C.: Catholic University of America, 1959.

Douglas, George H. "A Reconsideration of the Dewey-Croce Exchange." *Journal of Aesthetics and Art Criticism* 28 (1970): 497-504.

Downes, Chauncey B. "Some Problems concerning Dewey's View of Reason." *Journal of Philosophy* 58 (1961): 121-37.

Drake, Durant. "What Kind of Realism?" *Journal of Philosophy* 9 (1912): 149-54. [In reply to Dewey's "Brief Studies in Realism." Ibid. 8 (1911): 393-400, 546-54.]

---. "Dr. Dewey's Duality and Dualism." *Journal of Philosophy* 14 (1917): 660-63. [In reply to Dewey's "Duality and Dualism." Ibid.: 491-93.]

Drake, William E. "Philosophy of Education and the American Culture." *Educational Theory* 18 (1968): 365-75.

Dubinsky, David. "Dewey and the World of Labor." In *JOHN DEWEY AT NINETY*, edited by Harry W. Laidler, p. 15.

Ducasse, Curt John. *THE PHILOSOPHY OF ART*. Rev. and enl. ed. New York: Dover Publications, 1966. [Dewey, pp. 25-32, 84-94.]

Duncan, Hugh Dalziel. "Society as Determined by Communication: Dewey's Theory of Art as Communication." In his *COMMUNICATION AND SOCIAL ORDER*, pp. 49-72. New York: Bedminster Press, 1962.

Dunkel, Harold Baker. "Dewey and the Fine Arts." *School Review* 67 (1959): 229-45.

---. "The Sniper's Nest: Dewey in 2059?" *School Review* 67 (1959): 368-69.

---, and McCaul, Robert L. "Dewey: 1859-1959." *School Review* 67 (1959): 123-24.

Dupuis, Adrian M., and Craig, Robert C. *AMERICAN EDU-CATION: ITS ORIGINS AND ISSUES*. Milwaukee: Bruce Publishing Co., 1963. [Dewey, pp. 253-63.]

Dupuis, Adrian M., and Nordberg, Robert B. "Progres-sivism and John Dewey's Instrumentalism." In their *PHILOSOPHY AND EDUCATION: A TOTAL VIEW*, pp. 108-68. Rev. ed. Milwaukee: Bruce Publishing Co., 1968.

Durant, William James. *Contemporary American Philoso-phers: Santayana, James and Dewey*. Little Blue Book no. 813. Girard, Kans.: Haldeman-Julius Co., 1925.

---. *THE STORY OF PHILOSOPHY: THE LIVES AND OPINIONS OF THE GREATER PHILOSOPHERS*. New York: Simon and Schuster, 1926. [Dewey, pp. 565-75.]

---. *TRANSITION: A SENTIMENTAL STORY OF ONE MIND AND ONE ERA*. Garden City, N.Y.: Garden City Publishing Co., 1927. [Dewey, pp. 262-63.]

Dworkin, Martin S. "John Dewey." *Canadian Commentator* 3 (November 1959): 5-7, 14-15.

---. "John Dewey: A Centennial Review." In *DEWEY ON EDUCATION, SELECTIONS*. . .Classics in Education, no. 3, edited by Martin S. Dworkin, pp. 1-18. New York: Bureau of Publications, Teachers College, 1959. [Abridged version in *School Executive* 79 (1959): 52-55.]

Dykhuizen, George. "Dewey's Philosophy and Theory of Education." *Vermont Alumni Weekly*, 20 March 1935, pp. 247-48, 254-55.

---. "John Dewey Vermonter." *Vermont Life* 5 (Winter 1950-51): 11-15.

---. "An Early Chapter in the Life of John Dewey." *Journal of the History of Ideas* 13 (1952): 563-72.

---. "John Dewey: American Philosopher and Educator." *Educational Theory* 7 (1957): 263-68.

---. "John Dewey: The Vermont Years." *Journal of the*

History of Ideas 20 (1959): 515-44. [Abstract in *Journal of Philosophy* 55 (1958): 881-82.]

---. "John Dewey at Johns Hopkins (1882-1884)." *Journal of the History of Ideas* 22 (1961): 103-16.

---. "John Dewey's Liberalism." *Educational Theory* 12 (1962): 45-52.

---. "John Dewey and the University of Michigan." *Journal of the History of Ideas* 23 (1962): 513-44.

---. "John Dewey: The Chicago Years." *Journal of the History of Philosophy* 2 (1964): 227-53.

---. "John Dewey in Chicago: Some Biographical Notes." *Journal of the History of Philosophy* 3 (1965): 217-33.

---. *THE LIFE AND MIND OF JOHN DEWEY*. Edited by Jo Ann Boydston. Carbondale: Southern Illinois University Press, 1973.

Dynnik, M. "Contemporary Bourgeois Philosophy in the U.S." *Modern Review* 1 (1947): 653-60. [Abridged translation by Mirra Ginsburg. Original in Russian appeared in *Bolshevik*, March 1947.] [Foreword by Sidney Hook, "The U.S.S.R. Views American Philosophy." *Modern Review* 1 (1947): 649-52. Comments by Ralph Barton Perry, George Boas, Frederick Burkhardt, Curt John Ducasse, Edgar Sheffield Brightman, Filmer Stuart Cuckow Northrup, Horace Meyer Kallen, and Glen Raymond Morrow in ibid. 2 (1948): 157-60.]

Eames, Elizabeth R. "Quality and Relation as Metaphysical Assumptions in the Philosophy of John Dewey." *Journal of Philosophy* 55 (1958): 166-69. [Reply to Paul Welsh, "Some Metaphysical Assumptions in Dewey's Philosophy." Ibid. 51 (1954): 861-67.]

---. "The Relation of Philosophy to Education." In *PHILOSOPHY OF EDUCATION 1966: Proceedings of the Twenty-Second Annual Meeting of the Philosophy of Education Society*, pp. 32-41. Edwardsville, Ill.: Studies in Philosophy and Education, 1966. [Dewey, passim.]

---. "Is There a Philosophical Problem of Perception?"

Modern Schoolman 48 (1970): 53-58. [Dewey, pp. 57-58.]

---, and S. Morris. "The Leading Principles of Pragmatic Naturalism." *Personalist* 43 (1962): 322-37.

Eames, S. Morris. "Experience, Language, and Knowledge." *Philosophy and Phenomenological Research* 22 (1961): 102-5.

---. "Dewey's Views of Truth, Beauty, and Goodness." *Educational Theory* 11 (1961): 174-85.

---. "The Cognitive and Non-Cognitive in Dewey's Theory of Valuation." *Journal of Philosophy* 58 (1961): 179-95.

---. "The First Course in Logic: A Deweyan Approach." *Journal of General Education* 15 (1963): 46-54.

---. "Determinism and Deliberate Action in Karl Marx and John Dewey." In *Memorias del xiii Congreso Internacional de Filosofia*, vol. 6, pp. 241-47. Mexico City: National University, 1964.

---. "Valuing, Obligation, and Evaluation." *Philosophy and Phenomenological Research* 24 (1964): 318-28.

---. "Primary Experience in the Philosophy of John Dewey." *Monist* 48 (1964): 407-18.

---. "The Lost Individual and Religious Unity." *Personalist* 46 (1965): 485-500. [Dewey, passim.]

---. Introduction to *The Early Works of John Dewey, 1882-1898*, edited by Jo Ann Boydston, vol. 3, pp. xxi-xxxviii.

---. "Dewey's Theory of Valuation." In *GUIDE TO THE WORKS OF JOHN DEWEY*, edited by Jo Ann Boydston, pp. 183-99.

---. "Liberalism and the Problem of Alienation." *Religious Humanism* 4 (1970): 56-60. [Dewey, p. 59.]

---, and Elizabeth R. "The Leading Principles of Pragmatic Naturalism." *Personalist* 43 (1962): 322-37.

Eastman, George Herbert. "John Dewey's Literary Style:

Theory and Practice." *Educational Theory* 16 (1966): 110-27.

---. "The Ideologizing of Theories: John Dewey's Educational Theory, A Case in Point." *Educational Theory* 17 (1967): 103-19.

Eastman, Max. "John Dewey." *Atlantic Monthly*, December 1941, pp. 671-85. [Reprinted with revisions and additions as "The Hero as Teacher: The Life Story of John Dewey." In his *HEROES I HAVE KNOWN*, edited by Arno L. Bader and C. F. Wells, pp. 275-321. New York: Simon and Schuster, 1942. Also reprinted as "John Dewey: My Teacher and Friend." In his *GREAT COMPANIONS*, pp. 249-98. New York: Farrar, Straus and Cudahy, 1959.]

---. "America's Philosopher." *Saturday Review of Literature*, 17 January 1953, pp. 23-24, 38. [Condensed in *Reader's Digest*, February 1953, pp. 104-8, with the title "Our Children's Debt to John Dewey."]

---. "John Dewey." In *JUBILEE: ONE HUNDRED YEARS OF THE ATLANTIC*, edited by Edward Weeks and Emily Flint, pp. 315-26. Boston: Little, Brown and Co., 1957.

Easton, Lloyd David. "Empiricism and Ethics in Dietzgen." *Journal of the History of Ideas* 19 (1958): 77-90.

Eby, Frederick, and Arrowood, Charles Flinn. *THE DEVELOPMENT OF MODERN EDUCATION*. New York: Prentice-Hall, 1947. [Dewey, pp. 855-79.]

Ecker, David W. "The Artistic Process as Qualitative Problem Solving." *Journal of Aesthetics and Art Criticism* 21 (1963): 283-90. [Dewey, pp. 286-90.]

Eddy, Philip. "On the Statability of Dewey's Theory of Inquiry." *Educational Theory* 15 (1965): 321-26. [Reply to Robert R. Wellman, "Dewey's Theory of Inquiry: The Impossibility of Its Statement." Ibid. 14 (1964): 103-10. Response by Wellman, "Further Notes on Dewey's Logic: A Response." Ibid. 15 (1965): 327-29.]

Edel, Abraham. "Some Trends in American Naturalistic Ethics." In *PHILOSOPHIC THOUGHT IN FRANCE AND THE UNITED STATES*, edited by Marvin Farber, pp. 589-611.

---. *ETHICAL JUDGMENT: THE USE OF SCIENCE IN ETHICS*.
Glencoe, Ill.: Free Press, 1955. [Dewey, passim.]

---. *SCIENCE AND THE STRUCTURE OF ETHICS*. Foundations
of the Unity of Science, vol. 2. Chicago: University
of Chicago Press, 1961. [Dewey, passim.]

Edman, Irwin. "The New Puritanism." *Columbia University Quarterly* 21 (1919): 38-50.

---. "Our Foremost Philosopher at Seventy." *New York
Times Magazine*, 13 October 1929, pp. 3, 23. [Re-
sponse by J. J. Scott, "Parker Called Originator of
the School of Education." *New York Times*, 24 November 1929, p. 5.] [Edman's article reprinted in part
in "Some Popular Appraisals of John Dewey," edited
by Clyde R. Miller, pp. 214-15.]

---. "John Dewey, American." In his *ADAM, THE BABY,
AND THE MAN FROM MARS*, pp. 68-79. Cambridge, Mass.:
Houghton Mifflin Co., 1929.

---. *FOUR WAYS OF PHILOSOPHY*. New York: Henry Holt
and Co., 1937. [Dewey, passim.]

---. "The Resources of Art in American Life." In
Resources for Building America, Progressive Educa-
tion Booklet, no. 15, pp. 33-40. Columbus, Ohio:
Progressive Education Association, 1939.

---. "Former Teachers: John Dewey." In his *PHILOSO-
PHER'S HOLIDAY*, pp. 138-43. New York: Viking Press,
1938. [Reprinted in *MODERN AMERICAN VISTAS*, edited
by Howard W. Hintz and Bernard D. N. Grebanier, pp.
357-71. New York: Dryden Press, 1940. Also reprinted as "Columbia Galaxy: John Dewey and Others."
In *GREAT TEACHERS PORTRAYED BY THOSE WHO STUDIED
UNDER THEM*, edited by Houston Peterson, pp. 195-99.
New Brunswick, N.J.: Rutgers University Press, 1946.]

---. "America's Philosopher Attains an Alert 90." *New
York Times Magazine*, 16 October 1949, pp. 17, 74-75.

---. "The Victories of the Imagination." *New Republic*,
17 October 1949, pp. 36-39.

---. "Dewey's Contribution to Art." In *JOHN DEWEY AT
NINETY*, edited by Harry W. Laidler, pp. 19-21.

---. "Dewey and Art." In *JOHN DEWEY: PHILOSOPHER OF SCIENCE AND FREEDOM*, edited by Sidney Hook, pp. 47-65.

---. Introduction to *JOHN DEWEY: HIS CONTRIBUTION TO THE AMERICAN TRADITION*, edited by Irwin Edman. Indianapolis: Bobbs Merrill Co., 1955.

Educational Trends. [Special John Dewey Issue.] *Educational Trends* 7 (November-December 1939): 5-29.

Edwards, Anna Camp, and Mayhew, Katherine Camp. *THE DEWEY SCHOOL: THE LABORATORY SCHOOL OF THE UNIVERSITY OF CHICAGO 1896-1903.* New York: D. Appleton-Century Co., 1936. [Reprinted, New York: Atherton Press, 1965.]

Egbert, Donald Drew, and Persons, Stow Spaulding, eds. *SOCIALISM IN AMERICAN LIFE.* 2 vols. Princeton: Princeton University Press, 1952. [Dewey, passim.]

Eiseley, Loren. *THE MIND AS NATURE.* John Dewey Society Lectureship Series, no. 5. New York: Harper and Row, 1962. [Dewey, passim.]

Elliott, John Lovejoy. "Personality in Education." In *Freedom and Education*, Progressive Education Booklet, no. 12, pp. 24-32. Columbus, Ohio: Progressive Education Association, 1939.

Elliott, William Yandell. *THE PRAGMATIC REVOLT IN POLITICS: SYNDICALISM, FASCISM, AND THE CONSTITUTIONAL STATE.* New York: Macmillan Co., 1928. [Dewey, passim.]

Ellis, Frederick Eugene. "Dewey's Conception of Education for Growth." *Educational Theory* 5 (1955): 12-15.

Endres, Raymond J. "Elementary School Functions in the United States: An Historical Analysis." *Paedagogica historica* [Belgium.] 7 (1967): 378-416. [Dewey, pp. 388, 392-98, 402-4, 414-15.]

Engle, William. "Setting New Goals at Seventy." *New York World-Telegram*, 4 November 1931. [Interview.]

Ernst, Frederic. "How Dangerous is John Dewey?"

Atlantic Monthly, May 1953, pp. 59-62. [In reply to
Albert Lynd, "Who Wants Progressive Education? The
Influence of John Dewey on the Public Schools."
Ibid., April 1953, pp. 29-34.]

Esbensen, Thorwald. "John Dewey: Whipping Boy for
Critics." *Wisconsin Journal of Education* 91 (April
1959): 7-10.

Eschenbacher, Herman F. "John Dewey and the Reconstruction in History: The Historian as Social Engineer."
New England Social Studies Bulletin 17 (Spring 1960):
8-15.

Esper, Erwin A. *A HISTORY OF PSYCHOLOGY*. Philadelphia:
W. B. Saunders Co., 1964. [Dewey, passim.]

Evans, Luther H. Statement about Dewey in "Psychology
and the Fourth R," by Gordon Allport. *New Republic*,
17 October 1949, p. 24.

Ezorsky, Gertrude. "Inquiry as Appraisal: The Singu-
larity of John Dewey's Theory of Valuation." *Journal
of Philosophy* 55 (1958): 118-24.

---. "Truth in Context." *Journal of Philosophy* 60
(1963): 113-35. [Reprinted in *PRAGMATIC PHILOSOPHY*,
edited by Amelie Rorty, pp. 495-520.]

Fackenthal, Frank D. "Columbia Greets Dewey." In *JOHN
DEWEY AT NINETY*, edited by Harry W. Laidler, pp. 7-9.

Fagothey, Austin. "The Problem of Being and Value in
Contemporary American Axiology." In *PROCEEDINGS OF
THE AMERICAN CATHOLIC PHILOSOPHICAL ASSOCIATION*, vol.
33, pp. 73-83. Washington, D.C.: Catholic University
of America, 1959.

Farber, Marvin. "Dewey on Immediate Knowledge and the
Nature of the 'Given'." In *PHILOSOPHY FOR THE
FUTURE: THE QUEST OF MODERN MATERIALISM*, edited by
Roy Wood Sellars, V. J. McGill, and Marvin Farber,
pp. 604-10.

---. "The Idea of a Naturalistic Logic." *Philosophy
and Phenomenological Research* 29 (1969): 598-601.

---, ed. *PHILOSOPHIC THOUGHT IN FRANCE AND THE UNITED*

*STATES: ESSAYS REPRESENTING MAJOR TRENDS IN CONTEM-
PORARY FRENCH AND AMERICAN PHILOSOPHY.* University
of Buffalo Publications in Philosophy. Buffalo:
University of Buffalo, 1950. ["The Place of John
Dewey in Modern Thought," by Sidney Hook, pp. 483-
503; "Some Trends in American Naturalistic Ethics,"
by Abraham Edel, pp. 589-611. Also passim.]

Farforth, F. W., ed. *JOHN DEWEY. SELECTED EDUCATIONAL
WRITINGS, WITH AN INTRODUCTION AND COMMENTARY.* London: Heinemann, 1966.

Farrand, Harriet A. "Dr. Dewey's University Elementary
School: An Experiment in Education." *Journal of
Education* 48 (1898): 172.

Farrell, James T. "John Dewey's Philosophy." *Saturday
Review of Literature*, 12 July 1930, p. 1194. [In
reply to Lewis Mumford, "A Modern Synthesis." Ibid.,
12 April 1930, pp. 920-21.]

---. "Dewey in Mexico." In *JOHN DEWEY: PHILOSOPHER OF
SCIENCE AND FREEDOM*, edited by Sidney Hook, pp. 351-
77. [Reprinted in Farrell's *REFLECTIONS AT FIFTY
AND OTHER ESSAYS*, pp. 97-123. New York: Vanguard
Press, 1954.]

---. "Topics: The Democratic Faith of John Dewey."
New York Times, 22 October 1966, p. 30.

---. "Reflections on John Dewey." *Thought* [Delhi.] 19
(1967): 14-16.

---. "The New Relevancy of John Dewey." *Scholastic
Teacher*, 13 September 1968, p. 28, secondary edition; p. 17, elementary edition.

Farrell, Sally Ganong. *DEWEY'S PHILOSOPHY OF HISTORY:
ITS IMPLICATIONS FOR TEACHING.* Inter-University
Project One Publications Series. Ithaca: Cornell
University, 1965. [Master's thesis.]

Faulkner, Harold U. *POLITICS, REFORM AND EXPANSION,
1890-1900.* New York: Harper and Brothers, 1959.
[Dewey, passim.]

Fay, Jay Wharton. *AMERICAN PSYCHOLOGY BEFORE WILLIAM
JAMES.* New Brunswick, N.J.: Rutgers University

Press, 1939. [Dewey, passim.]

Fearon, John D., and Barry, Robert M. "John Dewey and
American Thomism." *American Benedictine Review* 10
(1959): 219-28; 11 (1960): 262-70.

Featherstone, Joseph. "Reconsideration: John Dewey."
New Republic, 8 July 1972, pp. 27-32.

Feibleman, James Kern. "The Influence of Peirce on
Dewey's Logic." *Education* 66 (1945): 18-24. [Ab-
stracted in *Journal of Philosophy* 36 (1939): 682.]

---. "An Estimate of Dewey." In his *REVIVAL OF REAL-
ISM: CRITICAL STUDIES IN CONTEMPORARY PHILOSOPHY*,
pp. 84-98. Chapel Hill: University of North Carolina Press, 1946.

---. "On Dewey's Logic of Inquiry." In his *AN INTRO-
DUCTION TO PEIRCE'S PHILOSOPHY*, pp. 474-86. New
York: Harper and Brothers, 1946.

---. *MORAL STRATEGY*. Hague: Martinus Nijhoff, 1967.
[Dewey, passim.]

Feinberg, Walter. "The Conflict between Intelligence
and Community in Dewey's Educational Philosophy."
Educational Theory 19 (1969): 236-48. [Response by
Frederick M. Schultz, "Intelligence and Community
as Concepts in the Philosophy of John Dewey." Ibid.
21 (1971): 81-89. Reply by Feinberg, "Reply to Professor Schultz." Ibid.: 90-92.]

---. "Progressive Education and Social Planning."
Teachers College Record 73 (1972): 485-505.

Feldman, William Taft. *THE PHILOSOPHY OF JOHN DEWEY:
A CRITICAL ANALYSIS*. Baltimore: Johns Hopkins
Press, 1934. [Doctoral dissertation.] [Reprinted,
New York: Greenwood Press, 1968.]

Fen, Sing-Nan. "Dewey's Philosophy as a Program of
Action." *Progressive Education* 27 (1949): 27-30.
[Reprinted in *Essays for John Dewey's Ninetieth
Birthday*, edited by Kenneth D. Benne and William O.
Stanley, pp. 82-87.]

---. "On Learning as Disposition." *Educational Theory*
13 (1963): 39-43.

---. "A Critical View of 'The Educational Theory of

John Dewey' by Charles D. Hardie." *Educational Theory* 14 (1964): 294-99, 304. [Response by Hardie, "Language, Pragmatism and Dewey." Ibid.: 305-7.]

---. "Social Relations as the Content of Intellectual Learning--Dewey's Point of View." *Social Studies* 55 (1964): 138-43.

---. "How is Philosophy a General Theory of Education?" *Educational Theory* 18 (1968): 178-83.

Fenner, Mildred Sandison. "Tribute to John Dewey, Honorary President of the N.E.A." *Journal of the National Education Association* 38 (1949): 528-29.

Ferm, Vergilius. *BASIC PHILOSOPHY FOR BEGINNERS.* North Quincy, Mass.: Christopher Publishing House, 1969. [Dewey, passim.]

Ferree, George. "The Development and Substance of John Dewey's Religious Thought." *Educational Theory* 10 (1960): 50-56.

Feuer, Lewis Samuel. "Ethical Theories and Historical Materialism." *Science and Society* 6 (1942): 242-72. [Dewey, pp. 264-68.]

---. "H. A. P. Torrey and John Dewey: Teacher and Pupil." *American Quarterly* 10 (1958): 34-54.

---. "John Dewey's Reading at College." *Journal of the History of Ideas* 19 (1958): 415-21.

---. "John Dewey and the Back-to-the-People Movement in American Thought." *Journal of the History of Ideas* 20 (1959): 545-68. [Abstract entitled "The Social Sources of Dewey's Thought," in *Journal of Philosophy* 55 (1958): 882-84.]

---. "The Standpoints of Dewey and Freud: A Contrast and Analysis." *Journal of Individual Psychology* 16 (1960): 119-36.

---. "John Dewey's Sojourn in Japan." *Teachers College Record* 71 (1969): 123-45.

Fiess, Edward. "Dewey's View of Art." *Humanist* 4 (1944): 161-65.

Filler, Louis. *RANDOLPH BOURNE*. Washington, D.C.: American Council on Public Affairs, 1950. [Dewey, passim.]

---. "Main Currents in Progressivist American Education." *History of Education Journal* 8 (1957): 33-57.

Fine, Benjamin. "John Dewey at 88 Holds that Attracting the Best Minds to Teaching is a Major Problem." *New York Times*, 19 October 1947, p. 11.

---. "John Dewey, at 90, Reiterates His Belief that Good Schools are Essential in a Democracy." *New York Times*, 16 October 1949, p. 9.

---. "John Dewey at 90 to Get $90,000 Gift." *New York Times*, 19 October 1949, p. 31.

---. "Burlington, Vt., Fetes John Dewey; at 90, He Visits Childhood Scenes." *New York Times*, 27 October 1949, pp. 29, 40.

---. "Task of Educators Cited by Dr. Dewey." *New York Times*, 12 June 1951, p. 24.

Fingarette, Herbert. "How Normativeness Can Be Cognitive but not Descriptive in Dewey's Theory of Valuation." *Journal of Philosophy* 48 (1951): 625-35. [See Lester Meckler, "Normative and Descriptive Expressions." Ibid. 50 (1953): 577-83.]

Finnegan, J. F. "Remarks concerning Certain Phases of the Moral Philosophy of John Dewey." *PROCEEDINGS OF THE AMERICAN CATHOLIC PHILOSOPHICAL ASSOCIATION*, vol. 6, pp. 125-34. Washington, D.C.: Catholic University of America, 1931.

Finney, Ross. *A SOCIOLOGICAL PHILOSOPHY OF EDUCATION*. New York: Macmillan Co., 1928. [Dewey, passim.]

Fisch, Max Harold. "Justice Holmes, the Prediction Theory of Law, and Pragmatism." *Journal of Philosophy* 39 (1942): 85-97.

---. "Dewey's Place in the Classic Period of American Philosophy." In *Essays for John Dewey's Ninetieth Birthday*, edited by Kenneth D. Benne and William O.

Stanley, pp. 9-36.

---. "Dewey's Critical and Historical Studies." In *GUIDE TO THE WORKS OF JOHN DEWEY*, edited by Jo Ann Boydston, pp. 306-38.

---. "General Introduction: The Classic Period in American Philosophy." In *CLASSIC AMERICAN PHILOSO- PHERS: PEIRCE, JAMES, ROYCE, SANTAYANA, DEWEY, WHITEHEAD*, edited by Max H. Fisch and Gail Kennedy, pp. 1-39. New York: Appleton-Century-Crofts, 1951.

---, and Anderson, Paul Russell, eds. *PHILOSOPHY IN AMERICA: FROM THE PURITANS TO JAMES*. New York: D. Appleton-Century Co., 1939. [Dewey, passim.]

Fischer, Wolfgang K. H. "John Dewey's Life, Philoso- phy, Critics." In *JOHN DEWEY: ESSAYS*, edited and annotated by Wolfgang K. H. Fischer, pp. 5-10. Göttingen: Vandenhoeck and Ruprecht, 1966.

Fisher, Dorothy Canfield. "John Dewey." In her *AMER- ICAN PORTRAITS*, pp. 37-39. New York: Henry Holt and Co., 1946. [Pictures by Enid Kaufman, text by Dorothy Canfield Fisher.]

---. "John Dewey." In her *VERMONT TRADITION: THE BIOGRAPHY OF AN OUTLOOK ON LIFE*, pp. 366-83. Boston: Little, Brown and Co., 1953.

Fisher, William H. "Is Progressivism Passé?" *Education* 81 (1961): 563-65.

Fitch, Robert Elliot. "John Dewey and Jahweh." *Journal of Religion* 23 (1943): 12-22.

---. "John Dewey--the 'Last Protestant'." *Pacific Spectator* 7 (1953): 224-30.

---. "Character Education à la Mode." *Religion in Life* 23 (1954): 528-36.

Fite, Warner. "The Pragmatic Attitude." In his *MORAL PHILOSOPHY: THE CRITICAL VIEW OF LIFE*, pp. 103-18. New York: Lincoln MacVeagh, Dial Press, 1926.

---. "The Impersonal Point of View and the Personal." In *A REFLECTIVE READER: ESSAYS FOR WRITING*, edited

by H. James Rockel, pp. 434-57. New York: Henry
Holt and Co., 1956.

Fitzgerald, James, and Patricia. *METHODS AND CURRICULA
IN ELEMENTARY EDUCATION*. Milwaukee: Bruce Publishing
Co., 1955. [Dewey, passim.]

Fitzgerald, Patricia, and James. *METHODS AND CURRICULA
. . . .* Milwaukee: Bruce Publishing Co., 1955.
[Dewey, passim.]

Flay, Joseph Charles. "Alienation and the Status Quo."
Man and World 2 (1969): 248-62.

Fleckenstein, Norbert J. *A CRITIQUE OF JOHN DEWEY'S
THEORY OF THE NATURE AND KNOWLEDGE OF REALITY IN THE
LIGHT OF THE PRINCIPLES OF THOMISM*. Washington,
D.C.: Catholic University of America, 1954. [Doc-
toral dissertation.]

Fletcher, Ralph V. "Reply to Criticism of Dewey." *Art
Journal* 20 (1961): 173-74. [In response to David B.
Manzella, "John Dewey and the Materialism of Art
Education." Ibid.: 19-21.]

Flugel, J. C. *A HUNDRED YEARS OF PSYCHOLOGY, 1833-1933*.
[With an additional Part(s) 1933-1963 by Donald J.
West.] New York: Basic Books, 1964. [Dewey, passim.]

Foerster, Norman. "Education Leads the Way." *American
Review* 1 (1933): 385-408.

Follin, Maynard D. "A Citizen Looks at Politics."
Outlook and Independent 155 (1930): 542-43, 556.

Forcey, Charles. *THE CROSSROADS OF LIBERALISM: CROLY,
WEYL, LIPPMANN, AND THE PROGRESSIVE ERA, 1900-1925*.
New York: Oxford University Press, 1961. [Dewey,
passim.]

Forest, Ilse. "The Meaning of Faith." *Thomist* 6
(1943): 231-38. [The Scholastics vs. the Non-
Scholastics.]

Fox, June T. "Epistemology, Psychology and Their Relevance for Education in Bruner and Dewey." *Educational Theory* 19 (1969): 58-75.

Fox, Marvin. "On the Diversity of Methods in Dewey's

Ethical Theory." *Philosophy and Phenomenological Research* 12 (1951): 123-29.

Frank, Jerome. "Modern and Ancient Legal Pragmatism--John Dewey and Co. vs. Aristotle." *Notre Dame Lawyer* 25 (1950): 207-57, 460-504.

---. "Some Tame Reflections on Some Wild Facts." In *VISION AND ACTION: ESSAYS IN HONOR OF HORACE M. KALLEN ON HIS 70TH BIRTHDAY*, edited by Sidney Ratner, pp. 56-82. New Brunswick, N.J.: Rutgers University Press, 1953.

Frank, Lawrence K. "Culture and Personality." In *JOHN DEWEY: PHILOSOPHER OF SCIENCE AND FREEDOM*, edited by Sidney Hook, pp. 88-105.

Frank, Waldo David [Search-Light]. "The Man Who Made Us What We Are." *New Yorker*, 22 May 1926, pp. 15-16. [Reprinted in *TIME EXPOSURES* (by Search-Light), pp. 121-27. New York: Boni and Liveright, 1926.]

---. "Our Leaders. The Re-discovery of America: XIV b." *New Republic*, 20 June 1928, pp. 114-17. [Reply by Philip M. Glick, with Frank's rejoinder, in ibid., 1 August 1928, pp. 281-82.] [Frank's article reprinted in his *THE RE-DISCOVERY OF AMERICA*, pp. 168-77. New York: Charles Scribner's Sons, 1929.] [Also passim.]

Frankel, Charles. "John Dewey's Legacy." *American Scholar* 29 (1960): 313-31. [Abridged version, with title, "John Dewey: Where He Stands," in *Johns Hopkins Magazine* 11 (December 1959): 7, 19-23.] [Reprinted in full, with the title, "John Dewey's Legacy," in his *THE LOVE OF ANXIETY AND OTHER ESSAYS*, pp. 148-71. New York: Harper and Row, 1965.]

---. Introduction to *THE GOLDEN AGE OF AMERICAN PHILOSOPHY*, edited by Charles Frankel. New York: George Braziller, 1960.

---. "John Dewey (1859-1952)." In *THE GOLDEN AGE OF AMERICAN PHILOSOPHY*, edited by Charles Frankel, pp. 381-84. [Preface to Dewey reprints.]

Frankena, William K. *THREE HISTORICAL PHILOSOPHIES OF EDUCATION: ARISTOTLE, KANT, DEWEY*. Chicago: Scott, Foresman and Co., 1965.

Frankfurter, Felix. "The Meaning of Dewey to Us All."
In *JOHN DEWEY AT NINETY*, edited by Harry W. Laidler,
pp. 9-13. [Reprinted in *OF LAW AND MEN: PAPERS AND
ADDRESSES OF FELIX FRANKFURTER, 1939-1956*, edited by
Philip Elman, pp. 284-87. New York: Harcourt, Brace
and Co., 1956.]

Friedman, Maurice. "The Pragmatist's Image of Man."
Philosophy Today 9 (1965): 238-49.

---. *TO DENY OUR NOTHINGNESS: CONTEMPORARY IMAGES OF
MAN*. New York: Dell Publishing Co., Delta Book,
1967. [Dewey, pp. 209-26.]

Friedman, Rose. *FREEDOM BUILDERS: GREAT TEACHERS FROM
SOCRATES TO JOHN DEWEY*. Boston: Little, Brown, and
Co., 1968. [Dewey, pp. 248-50.]

Fries, Horace Snyder. "The Method of Proving Ethical
Realism." *Philosophical Review* 46 (1937): 485-502.

---. "Dewey's Theory of Method." *New Leader*, 22 October 1949, S-7.

---. "Educational Foundations of Social Planning."
In *Essays for John Dewey's Ninetieth Birthday*, edited
by Kenneth D. Benne and William O. Stanley, pp.
59-73.

---. "John Dewey's Philosophy." In *IN HONOR OF JOHN
DEWEY ON HIS NINETIETH BIRTHDAY*, pp. 38-40. Madison: University of Wisconsin, 1951.

---. "Social Planning." In *THE CLEAVAGE IN OUR CUL-
TURE: STUDIES IN SCIENTIFIC HUMANISM IN HONOR OF
MAX OTTO*, edited by Frederick Burkhardt, pp. 81-104.
Boston: Beacon Press, 1952. [Also passim.]

Friess, Horace Leland. "The Sixth International Congress of Philosophy." *Journal of Philosophy* 23
(1926): 617-38. [On Dewey's "The Role of Philosophy
in the History of Civilization." In *Proceedings of
the Sixth International Congress of Philosophy*,
edited by Edgar Sheffield Brightman, pp. 536-42.
New York: Longmans, Green and Co., 1927.]

---. "Social Inquiry and Social Doctrine." In *JOHN
DEWEY: PHILOSOPHER OF SCIENCE AND FREEDOM*, edited by

Sidney Hook, pp. 106-17.

---. "Dewey's Philosophy of Religion." In *GUIDE TO THE WORKS OF JOHN DEWEY*, edited by Jo Ann Boydston, pp. 200-217.

Froese, Leonhard. "Reflections on the Defeat of 'Deweyism' in the USA." *International Review of Education* 12 (1966): 35-36.

Gale, Richard Milton. "Russell's Drill Sergeant and Bricklayer and Dewey's Logic." *Journal of Philosophy* 56 (1959): 401-6.

---. "Dewey and the Problem of the Alleged Futurity of Yesterday." *Philosophy and Phenomenological Research* 22 (1962): 501-11.

---. "A Reply on the Alleged Futurity of Yesterday." *Philosophy and Phenomenological Research* 24 (1964): 421-22. [Response to Leon J. Goldstein, "The 'Alleged' Futurity of Yesterday." Ibid.: 417-20.]

Gallagher, Buell Gordon. "Mr. Hutchins and Mr. Dewey." *Christian Century* 62 (1945): 106-7.

Gallant, Thomas F. "Dewey Then--Experiential Education Now." *School and Society* 100 (1972): 303-308.

---. "Dewey, Social Reconstruction, and Institutional Neutrality." *Educational Theory* 22 (1972): 427-33.

Gallie, W. B. *PEIRCE AND PRAGMATISM*. Rev. ed. New York: Dover Publications, 1966. [Dewey, pp. 31, 42, 221.]

Gangel, Kenneth O. "John Dewey: An Evangelical Evaluation," Part One, *Bibliotheca Sacra* 123 (1966): 325-33; Part Two, ibid. 124 (1967): 22-29.

Gans, Roma. "John Dewey and the Understanding of Children." *Teachers College Record* 51 (1949): 136-38.

García, Joaquín. "Deweyism and Democracy." *Tablet* [Brooklyn, N.Y.], 25 August 1945. [Condensed in *Catholic Digest* 9 (October 1945): 78-80.] [See Dewey's comment in *Humanist* 20 (1960): 6.]

Garforth, F. W., ed. *JOHN DEWEY. SELECTED EDUCATIONAL WRITINGS, WITH AN INTRODUCTION AND COMMENTARY.* London: Heinemann, 1966.

Garland, H. B. "John Dewey: Father of the New Education." *National Education* [New Zealand.] 41 (1959): 488-89.

Garner, Richard T., and Rosen, Bernard. *MORAL PHILOSOPHY: A SYSTEMATIC INTRODUCTION TO NORMATIVE ETHICS AND METAETHICS.* New York: Macmillan Co., 1967. [Dewey, pp. 129-32, 134.]

Garnett, Arthur Campbell. "Intrinsic Good: Its Definition and Referent." In *VALUE: A COOPERATIVE INQUIRY*, edited by Ray Lepley, pp. 78-92.

---. *RELIGION AND THE MORAL LIFE.* New York: Ronald Press Co., 1955. [Dewey, pp. 43-59.]

---, and Geiger, George. "Criticisms by Garnett; Rejoinder by Geiger." In *VALUE: A COOPERATIVE INQUIRY*, edited by Ray Lepley, pp. 312-20.

Garrett, Roland W. "Changing Events in Dewey's *EXPERIENCE AND NATURE*." *Journal of the History of Philosophy* 10 (1972): 439-55.

---. "Dewey's Struggle with the Ineffable." *Transactions of the Charles S. Peirce Society* 9 (1973): 95-109.

Garvin, Lucius. "Normative Utilitarianism and Naturalism." *Ethics* 60 (1949): 49-54.

Gauss, Charles Edward. "Some Reflections on John Dewey's Aesthetics." *Journal of Aesthetics and Art Criticism* 19 (1960): 127-32.

Gehring, Ralph B. "Origins of Religion, According to John Dewey." *Philippine Studies* 3 (1955): 275-87.

---. "John Dewey's Substitute for Religion." *Philippine Studies* 4 (1956): 41-56.

Geiger, George Raymond. "Dewey's Social and Political Philosophy." In *THE PHILOSOPHY OF JOHN DEWEY*, edited by Paul Schilpp, pp. 335-68.

---. "Can We Choose between Values?" *Journal of Philosophy* 41 (1944): 292-98. [Dewey's response, "Some Questions about Value." Ibid.: 449-55.]

———. *PHILOSOPHY AND THE SOCIAL ORDER: AN INTRODUCTORY APPROACH*. Boston: Houghton Mifflin Co., 1947. [Dewey, passim.]

———. "Values and Inquiry." In *VALUE: A COOPERATIVE INQUIRY*, edited by Ray Lepley, pp. 93-111.

———. "Dewey and the Experimental Attitude in American Culture: An Essay in Memory of John Dewey, 1859-1952." *American Journal of Economics and Sociology* 12 (1953): 111-21.

———. *JOHN DEWEY IN PERSPECTIVE*. New York: Oxford University Press, 1958.

———. "Preface to a Consistent Philosophy of Education." *Saturday Review*, 21 November 1959, pp. 17-18.

———. "The Scientific Quest for Values." *Humanist* 19 (1959): 259-61. [The Centennial of John Dewey.]

———. "John Dewey in Perspective." *Antioch Review* 19 (1959): 293-98. [Introduction to special issue devoted to Dewey.]

———. "Dewey's Challenge to Irrational Man: Human Possibilities." *Unitarian Register* 138 (Mid-Summer 1959): 3-5.

———. "John Dewey's Social Philosophy." In *EDUCATION IN TRANSITION*, edited by Frederick Charles Gruber, pp. 243-55. Philadelphia: University of Pennsylvania Press, 1960. [Followed by "Comments on Professor Geiger's Paper," by Israel Scheffler, pp. 256-59.]

———, and Garnett, Arthur Campbell. "Criticisms by Garnett; Rejoinder by Geiger." In *VALUE: A COOPERATIVE INQUIRY*, edited by Ray Lepley, pp. 312-20.

Geiger, George, and Ayres, C. E. "Criticisms by Geiger; Rejoinder by Ayres." In *VALUE: A COOPERATIVE INQUIRY*, edited by Ray Lepley, pp. 321-33.

Gerber, D. "A Note on Woody on Dewey on Austin." *Ethics* 79 (1969): 303-8.

Getman, Arthur K. "The Influence of John Dewey in

Education." *Agricultural Education* 5 (December 1932): 83-84, 96.

Geyer, Denton Loring. "The Wavering Aim of Education in Dewey's Educational Philosophy." *Education* 37 (1917): 484-91.

---. "Three Types of Education for Freedom." *School and Society* 66 (1947): 406-9. [Hegelian, Classical, Deweyan.]

Gillis, Adolph, and Ketchum, Roland. "John Dewey: Educator of Democracy." In their *OUR AMERICA*, pp. 67-82. Boston: Little, Brown, and Co., 1936.

Ginger, Ray. "The Idea of Process in American Social Thought." *American Quarterly* 4 (1952): 253-65.

---. *ALTGELD'S AMERICA. THE LINCOLN IDEAL VS. CHANGING REALITIES*. New York: Funk and Wagnalls Co., 1958. [Dewey, passim.]

Girdler, John. "What's Wrong with Our Teachers: Reply to John Dewey." *Rotarian* 46 (January 1935): 36-37. [In reply to Dewey's "Character Training for Youth." Ibid. 45 (September 1934): 6-8, 58-59.]

Givens, Willard Earl, and Santee, Joseph Frederick. "John Dewey, Educational Philosopher." *Phi Delta Kappan* 34 (1952): 9-10.

Giventer, Edwin B., and Kenworthy, Leonard S., eds. "John Dewey Speaks." World Affairs Materials, Brooklyn, N.Y.: Brooklyn College, 1972. [One page of biography and seven pages of quotations from Dewey.]

Glick, Philip M. "The Philosophy of John Dewey." *New Republic*, 1 August 1928, pp. 281-82. [Reply to Waldo Frank, "Our Leaders. The Re-discovery of America: XIV b." Ibid., 20 June 1928, pp. 114-17. Rejoinder by Frank, ibid., 1 August 1928, p. 282.]

Glicksberg, Charles Irving. "John Dewey, 1859-1952." In his *AMERICAN LITERARY CRITICISM 1900-1950*, pp. 349-52. New York: Hendricks House, 1951.

Glover, Katherine. "Tomorrow May Be Too Late: Save

the Schools Now." *Good Housekeeping*, March 1934, pp. 20-21, 222, 225-27. [Interview with Dewey.]

Goldman, Eric Frederick. *RENDEZVOUS WITH DESTINY: A HISTORY OF MODERN AMERICAN REFORM*. New York: Alfred A. Knopf, 1952. [Dewey, pp. 155-59, and passim.]

Goldstein, Leon J. "The 'Alleged' Futurity of Yesterday." *Philosophy and Phenomenological Research* 24 (1964): 417-20. [In response to Richard M. Gale, "Dewey and the Problem of the Alleged Futurity of Yesterday." Ibid. 22 (1962): 501-11.]

Gotshalk, D. W. "On Dewey's Esthetics." *Journal of Aesthetics and Art Criticism* 23 (1964): 131-38.

Gotshalk, Richard. "Dewey's Conception of Being and Philosophical Reflection." *Dialogue* 3 (1964-65): 142-52.

Goudge, Thomas A. "Further Reflections on Peirce's Doctrine of the Given." *Journal of Philosophy* 33 (1936): 289-95. [In response to Dewey's "Peirce's Theory of Quality." Ibid. 32 (1935): 701-8.]

Gouinlock, James. *JOHN DEWEY'S PHILOSOPHY OF VALUE*. New York: Humanities Press, 1972.

Gowin, D. Bob. "Is Dewey's Experimentalism Compatible with Gestalt Theory?" *School Review* 67 (1959): 195-212.

---. "Bode, Dewey, and Gestalt Psychology." *Educational Theory* 15 (1965): 169-87.

Graña, César. "John Dewey's Social Art and the Sociology of Art." *Journal of Aesthetics and Art Criticism* 20 (1962): 405-12. [Reprinted in his *FACT AND SYMBOL: ESSAYS IN THE SOCIOLOGY OF ART AND LITERATURE*, pp. 135-50. New York: Oxford University Press, 1971.]

Grant, Lester. "John Dewey, at 90, Finds Tension of World May Result in Good." *New York Herald Tribune*, 15 October 1949.

Gray, Jesse Glenn. "Is Progressive Education a Failure? Some of the Current Criticisms Examined." *Commentary* 14 (1952): 107-16.

Green, Maurice R. "Prelogical Processes and Partici-

pant Communication." *Psychiatric Quarterly* 35
(1961): 726-40.

Greene, M. "The New Revolt Is of the Mind. . . ."
Teachers College Record 70 (1968): 159-64.

Greene, Maxine. "Dewey and American Education, 1894-
1920." *School and Society* 87 (1959): 381-86. [Re-
printed in *JOHN DEWEY: MASTER EDUCATOR*, edited by
William W. Brickman and Stanley Lehrer, 2d ed., pp.
75-92.]

Gretzinger, Marguerite. "Commonsense in the Classroom."
Michigan Education Journal 27 (1950): 425-27.

Grey, Loren. "A Comparison of the Educational Philosophy of John Dewey and Alfred Adler." *American
Journal of Individual Psychology* 2 (1954): 71-80.

Griffith, Francis. "John Dewey: Theory and Practice."
Commonweal, 24 September 1954, pp. 603-6. [Reply
by Adelbert James. Ibid., 15 October 1954, pp. 38-
39.]

Gross, Mason W. Announcement of the Dewey Archive at
Rutgers University. *Saturday Review*, 21 November
1959, p. 26.

Gruender, C. David. "Language, Society, and Knowledge."
Antioch Review 28 (1968): 187-212.

Grunewald, Robert N. "Dewey's 'Situation' and the Ames
Demonstrations." *Educational Theory* 15 (1965): 293-
304.

---. "Dewey and Discovery Learning." *Proceedings of
the Philosophy of Education Society* 24 (1968): 195-
204.

Gumbert, Edgar B. "John Dewey and the New Liberalism:
Reactions to the USSR." *Educational Theory* 22
(1972): 344-59.

Gustafson, G. J. "John Dewey." *Priest* 8 (1952): 495-
502. [Reprinted in *Catholic Mind* 50 (1952): 513-19.]

Gutek, Gerald L. *THE EDUCATIONAL THEORY OF GEORGE S.
COUNTS*. Studies in Educational Theory of the John

Dewey Society, no. 8. Columbus: Ohio State University Press, 1970. [Dewey, passim.]

Guterman, Norbert. Review of Dewey's *A COMMON FAITH*. *New Republic*, 20 February 1935, p. 53. [Dewey's reply, ibid., 13 March 1935, p. 132. Rejoinder by Guterman and letter of Irvin Kelley, ibid., 20 March 1935, p. 161.]

Gutmann, James. "Toward a Philosophy of Educational Liberation." *Virginia Quarterly Review* 46 (1970): 433-38.

Guttchen, Robert S. "The Logic of Practice." *Studies in Philosophy and Education* 7 (1969): 28-43.

Gutzke, Manford George. *JOHN DEWEY'S THOUGHT AND ITS IMPLICATIONS FOR CHRISTIAN EDUCATION*. New York: King's Crown Press, 1956.

Hagedorn, Hermann. "John Dewey." In his *AMERICANS: A BOOK OF LIVES*, pp. 181-204. New York: John Day Co., 1946.

Hahn, Lewis E. "A Contextualist Looks at Values." In *VALUE: A COOPERATIVE INQUIRY*, edited by Ray Lepley, pp. 112-24.

---. "John Dewey on Teaching Philosophy in High School." *Educational Theory* 17 (1967): 219-21. [Reprinted in *Journal of Critical Analysis* 1 (1969): 115-18.]

---. "From Intuitionalism to Absolutism." Introduction to *The Early Works of John Dewey, 1882-1898*, edited by Jo Ann Boydston, vol. 1, pp. xxiii-xxxviii.

---. "Dewey's Philosophy and Philosophic Method." In *GUIDE TO THE WORKS OF JOHN DEWEY*, edited by Jo Ann Boydston, pp. 15-60.

---; Lepley, Ray; and Mitchell, E. T. "Criticisms by Hahn; Rejoinders by Lepley and Mitchell." In *VALUE: A COOPERATIVE INQUIRY*, edited by Ray Lepley, pp. 334-49.

Haines, Nicolas. "Situational Method: A Proposal for Political Education in a Democracy." *Educational*

Theory 19 (1969): 17-28.

Halbach, Arthur Anthony. *A DEFINITION OF MEANING FOR AMERICAN EDUCATION*. Washington, D.C.: Catholic University of America, 1948. [Doctoral dissertation.]

Hall, Clifton L. "Exegit monumentum aere perennius. . . ." *Peabody Journal of Education* 30 (1952): 2-7.

Hall, David L. "Whitehead's Speculative Method." *Philosophy Today* 16 (1972): 193-209. [Dewey, pp. 205-9.]

Hall, Everett W. "Some Meanings of Meaning in Dewey's *EXPERIENCE AND NATURE*." *Journal of Philosophy* 25 (1928): 169-81. [Dewey's reply, "Meaning and Existence." Ibid.: 345-53.]

Hall, Granville Stanley. *LIFE AND CONFESSIONS OF A PSYCHOLOGIST*. New York: D. Appleton and Co., 1923. [Dewey, pp. 499-500.]

Hall, Royal G. "The Significance of John Dewey for Religious Interpretation." *Open Court* 42 (1928): 331-40.

Hallman, Ralph J. "Concept of Creativity in Dewey's Educational Philosophy." *Educational Theory* 14 (1964): 270-85.

Hallowell, John. *MAIN CURRENTS IN MODERN POLITICAL THOUGHT*. New York: Henry Holt and Co., 1950. [Dewey, pp. 547-49.]

Hamilton, Walter H. "Our Man-Made Natural Resources." In *Resources for Building America,* Progressive Education Booklet, no. 15, pp. 58-63. Columbus, Ohio: Progressive Education Association, 1939.

Hamilton, Walton. "A Deweyesque Mosaic." In *THE PHILOSOPHER OF THE COMMON MAN*, edited by Sidney Ratner, pp. 146-71.

Hammer, Louis Z. "God, Faith, and Religious Thought." In his *VALUE AND MAN*, pp. 79-83. New York: McGraw-Hill Book Co., 1966.

---. "Norms, Value, and Ethical Thought." In his *VALUE AND MAN*, pp. 135-39.

Han Lih Wu. "Professor Dewey's Second Visit to China."

China Weekly Review, 4 April 1931, pp. 176-77.

Handlin, Oscar. "Rejoinder to Critics of John Dewey."
New York Times Magazine, 15 June 1958, pp. 13, 19-
20. [Condensed in *Education Digest* 24 (November
1958): 1-4.]

---. "American Secondary Education at the Dewey Cen-
tennial." In *FRONTIERS OF SECONDARY EDUCATION*,
vol. 4, pp. 1-7. Papers prepared for the Fourth
Annual Conference on Secondary Education, Syracuse
University, 1959. New York: Syracuse University
Press, 1960.

---. *JOHN DEWEY'S CHALLENGE TO EDUCATION: HISTORICAL
PERSPECTIVES ON THE CULTURAL CONTEXT*. John Dewey
Society Lectureship Series, no. 2. New York: Harper
and Brothers, 1959. [Reprinted in *DEWEY ON EDUCA-
TION: APPRAISALS*, edited by Reginald D. Archambault,
pp. 25-36.]

Handschy, Harriet Wild. "The Educational Theories of
Cardinal Newman and John Dewey." *Education* 49
(1928): 129-37.

Handy, Rollo. "Dewey's Theory of Valuation." In his
VALUE THEORY AND THE BEHAVIORAL SCIENCES, pp. 96-
119. Springfield, Ill.: Charles C. Thomas, 1969.
[Also passim.]

Hansen, Harry. "Seventieth Birthday of John Dewey."
In "Some Popular Appraisals of John Dewey," edited
by Clyde R. Miller, pp. 222-23. [Reprinted from his
book review column, "The First Reader," in *New York
World*.]

Harap, Henry. "The Beginnings of the John Dewey Society." *Educational Theory* 20 (1970): 157-63.

Hardie, Charles D. "The Educational Theory of John
Dewey." In his *TRUTH AND FALLACY IN EDUCATIONAL
THEORY*, pp. 48-65. Cambridge, England: University
Press, 1942. [Also passim.] [See comments by Bruce
L. Hood, *Educational Theory* 14 (1964): 300-304.]
[Hardie's essay reprinted in *DEWEY ON EDUCATION:
APPRAISALS*, edited by Reginald D. Archambault, pp.
111-27.]

---. "Language, Pragmatism and Dewey." *Educational
Theory* 14 (1964): 305-7. [In response to Sing-Nan
Fen, "A Critical View of 'The Educational Theory of
John Dewey,' by Charles D. Hardie." Ibid.: 294-99,
304; and B. L. Hood, "Some Comments on C. D. Hardie's
'Refutation' of Dewey." Ibid.: 300-304.]

Hardon, John A. "John Dewey, Prophet of American Naturalism." *Catholic Educational Review* 50 (1952):
433-45.

---. "John Dewey--Radical Social Educator." *Catholic
Educational Review* 50 (1952): 505-17.

---. "The Dewey Legend in American Education." *Catholic Educational Review* 50 (1952): 577-88.

Harnack, R. Victor. "John Dewey and Discussion."
Western Speech 32 (1968): 137-49. [Symposium entitled "The Influence of John Dewey upon Speech,"
with Don M. Burks and Gladys L. Borchers.]

Harris, Pickens E. "John Dewey as Pioneer in the Newer
Discipline of the Child." *Understanding the Child* 3
(June 1933): 23-25, 31.

Harris, Robert T. *SOCIAL ETHICS.* Philadelphia: J. B.
Lippincott Co., 1962. [Dewey, pp. 278-80, 289-90.]

Harris, William Torrey. "A Letter from Dr. Harris."
Public School Journal 11 (1891): 179. [Comment on
Dewey's "How Do Concepts Arise from Percepts?"
Ibid.: 128-30 (*Early Works of John Dewey* 3: 142-
46.)]

---. "Professor John Dewey's Doctrine of Interest as
Related to Will." *Educational Review* 11 (1896):
486-93.

Hart, Hendrik. *COMMUNAL CERTAINTY AND AUTHORIZED
TRUTH: AN EXAMINATION OF JOHN DEWEY'S PHILOSOPHY OF
VERIFICATION.* Amsterdam: Swets and Seitlinger, 1966.

Hart, Henry. *DR. BARNES OF MERION: A BIOGRAPHY.* New
York: Farrar, Straus and Co., 1963. [Dewey, passim.]

Hart, Joseph Kinmont. *INSIDE EXPERIENCE: A NATURALISTIC
PHILOSOPHY OF LIFE AND THE MODERN WORLD.* New York:

Longmans, Green and Co., 1927. [Dewey, pp. 133-41, and passim.]

---. "What Price System?" *Survey* 57 (1927): 522-56.

---. "Principles of Character Development in the Philosophy of John Dewey." *Religious Education* 24 (1929): 113-16.

---. ".Judging Our Progressive Schools." *New Republic*, 11 June 1930, pp. 93-96. [See Boyd H. Bode, "The New Education Ten Years After, I; Apprenticeship or Freedom?" Ibid., 4 June 1930, pp. 61-64, for first article in series.]

---. "Edmund Wilson and the American Mind." *New Republic*, 11 May 1932, pp. 354-55.

Hart, Merwin Kimball. "Dr. Dewey's Stand Disputed." *New York Times*, 9 May 1940, p. 22. [In response to Dewey's "Investigating Education." Ibid., 6 May 1940, p. 16. Dewey's rejoinder, "Censorship Not Wanted." Ibid., 14 May 1940, p. 22.]

Hart, Samuel. "Dewey's Humanistic Legacy." In *THE HUMANITIES IN THE AGE OF SCIENCE*, edited by Charles Angoff, pp. 87-100. Rutherford, N.J.: Fairleigh Dickinson University Press, 1968.

---. "Dewey's Theory of Value." *Akten des XIV. Internationalen Kongresses für Philosophie*, vol. 4, pp. 58-64. Vienna: Herder, 1968.

---. "Axiology--Theory of Values." *Philosophy and Phenomenological Research* 32 (1971): 29-41.

Hartshorne, Charles. "Dewey's Philosophy of Religion." In his *BEYOND HUMANISM*, pp. 39-57. Chicago: Willett, Clark and Co., 1937. [Reprinted, University of Nebraska Press, Bison Book, 1968.]

Haubricht, Vernon F. "Pragmatism and Liberalism." *New Republic*, 12 September 1955, p. 23. [Reply to Arthur E. Bestor, Jr., "John Dewey and American Liberalism." Ibid., 29 August 1955, pp. 18-19.]

Havelock, E. A. "The Philosophy of John Dewey." *Canadian Forum* 19 (1939): 121-23.

Hawaii Educational Review. John Dewey Number. *Hawaii Educational Review* 18 (1929).

Haworth, Lawrence Lindley. "The Experimental Society: Dewey and Jordan." *Ethics* 71 (1960): 27-40.

---. "Dewey's Philosophy of the Corporation." *Ethics* 72 (1962): 120-31. [Reprinted in *Educational Theory* 20 (1970): 345-63.]

Hay, William H. "John Dewey on Freedom and Choice." *Monist* 48 (1964): 346-55.

---; Singer, Marcus; and Murphy, Arthur E., eds. *REASON AND THE COMMON GOOD*. Englewood Cliffs, N.J.: Prentice-Hall, 1963. [Dewey, passim.]

Haydon, Albert Eustace. "Mr. Dewey on Religion and God." *Journal of Religion* 15 (1935): 22-25.

Hechinger, Fred M. "John Dewey's Philosophy of Education and the Issues of the Day." *New York Times*, 18 October 1959, p. 9.

Heidbreder, Edna. "Functionalism and the University of Chicago." In her *SEVEN PSYCHOLOGIES*, pp. 201-33. New York: Century Co., 1933.

Helsel, Paul R. "Ideologies Motivating American Education." *Personalist* 26 (1945): 190-92.

Hendel, Chárles William. "John Dewey and the Philosophical Tradition: A Study of Some Significant Affiliations." *Journal of Philosophy* 55 (1958): 884-86.

---. "The New Empiricism and the Philosophical Tradition." In *JOHN DEWEY AND THE EXPERIMENTAL SPIRIT IN PHILOSOPHY*, edited by Charles W. Hendel, pp. 1-31. New York: Liberal Arts Press, 1959.

Henderson, Stella Van Petten. *INTRODUCTION TO PHILOSOPHY OF EDUCATION*. Chicago: University of Chicago Press, 1947. [Dewey, passim.]

Henle, Paul. "Dewey's Views on Truth and Verification." In *University of Colorado Studies*. Series in Philosophy, no. 2, pp. 11-25. Boulder: University of Colorado Press, 1961.

Henle, Robert J. "Hutchins and Dewey Again." *Modern Schoolman* 15 (January and March 1938): 30-33, 56-59.

Hilgard, Ernest R., and Bower, Gordon H. *THEORIES OF LEARNING.* 3d ed. New York: Appleton-Century-Crofts, 1966. [Dewey, pp. 298-300.]

Hill, Knox Calvin. *INTERPRETING LITERATURE.* Chicago: University of Chicago Press, 1966. [Dewey, pp. 139-50, 175-81.]

Hill, Thomas English. *CONTEMPORARY ETHICAL THEORIES.* New York: Macmillan Co., 1950. [Dewey, pp. 156-75, 177-80.]

---. "Instrumentalism." In his *CONTEMPORARY THEORIES OF KNOWLEDGE*, pp. 321-61. New York: Ronald Press Co., 1961.

Hill, Walker H. "Peirce and Pragmatism." *Journal of Philosophy* 36 (1939): 682-83. [Abstract of his doctoral dissertation, University of Wisconsin, 1938.]

---. "The Founder of Pragmatism." In *IN COMMEMORATION OF WILLIAM JAMES 1842-1942*, pp. 223-34. New York: Columbia University Press, 1942. [Also passim.]

Hillyer, Robert. Statement on Dewey. In "The Victories of the Imagination," by Irwin Edman. *New Republic*, 17 October 1949, p. 38.

Hindle, Wilfrid Hope. "Representative Men: VI--John Dewey." *English Review* 62 (1936): 644-46.

Hines, V. A. "Progressivism in Practice; The Dewey School, 1896-1904." Association for Supervision and Curriculum Development *YEARBOOK*, Washington, D.C., 1972, pp. 119-38.

Hocking, William Ernest. "Political Philosophy in Germany." *New Republic*, 2 October 1915, pp. 234-36. [Dewey's reply, ibid., p. 236.]

---. "Action and Certainty." *Journal of Philosophy* 27 (1930): 225-38. [Dewey's reply, ibid.: 271-77.]

---. "Dewey's Concepts of Experience and Nature." *Philosophical Review* 49 (1940): 228-44. [Dewey's reply, "Nature and Experience." Ibid.: 244-48.]

---. "A Discussion of the Theory of International Relations." *Journal of Philosophy* 42 (1945): 477-97.
[A discussion by several philosophers of two paragraphs of Dewey's Introduction to Jane Addams, *PEACE
AND BREAD IN TIME OF WAR*. New York: King's Crown
Press, 1945.] [Hocking, pp. 484-86. Other philosophers: E. A. Burtt, Joseph P. Chamberlain, Sidney
Hook, Arthur O. Lovejoy, Glen R. Morrow, Jerome Nathanson, and Thomas V. Smith.]

---. *TYPES OF PHILOSOPHY*. 3d ed. New York: Charles
Scribner's Sons, 1959. [Dewey, passim.]

Hodgson, Shadworth Holloway. "Illusory Psychology."
Mind 11 (1886): 478-94 [*Early Works of John Dewey* 1:
xli-lvii.] [In response to Dewey's "The Psychological Standpoint" and "Psychology as Philosophic
Method." *Mind* 11 (1886): 1-19, 153-73 (*Early Works*
1: 122-43, 144-67.)] [Dewey's reply, "'Illusory
Psychology'." *Mind* 12 (1887): 83-88 (*Early Works* 1:
168-75.)] [Hodgson's rejoinder, "'Illusory Psychology'--A Rejoinder." *Mind* 12 (1887): 314-18.]

Hodysh, Henry W. "Historical Theory and Social Change
in Dewey's Philosophy." *Educational Theory* 20
(1970): 245-52.

Hoffman, Alice. "Teachers and Students of America Pay
Tribute." In *JOHN DEWEY AT NINETY*, edited by Harry
W. Laidler, pp. 26-27.

Hofmann, David C. "The Schools and Neutrality: In Re-
sponse to Professor Robert Ennis." *Educational
Theory* 14 (1964): 182-85. [Reply to "Is It Impos-
sible for the Schools to be Neutral?" In *LANGUAGE
AND CONCEPTS IN EDUCATION*, edited by B. Othanel
Smith and Robert H. Ennis, pp. 102-11. Chicago:
Rand McNally, 1961.] [Also passim.]

Hofstadter, Albert. "Concerning a Certain Deweyan Conception of Metaphysics." In *JOHN DEWEY: PHILOSOPHER
OF SCIENCE AND FREEDOM*, edited by Sidney Hook, pp.
249-70.

Hofstadter, Richard. "The Current of Pragmatism." In
his *SOCIAL DARWINISM IN AMERICAN THOUGHT*, rev. ed.,
pp. 123-42. New York: George Braziller, 1959.

---. *ANTI-INTELLECTUALISM IN AMERICAN LIFE*. New York:

Alfred A. Knopf, 1963. [Dewey, pp. 372-83, and passim.]

Holden, David. "John Dewey and His Aims of Education." *Educational Forum* 18 (1953): 72-81. [Reprinted in *PUBLIC SCHOOLS IN CRISIS: SOME CRITICAL ESSAYS*, edited by Mortimer B. Smith, pp. 15-29. Chicago: Henry Regnery Co., 1956.]

Hole, Myra Cadwalader. *EMERSON, JAMES AND DEWEY IN RHYME*. Chicago: Published by the Estate of Myra C. Hole, 1961.

Hollins, T. H. B. "The Problem of Values and John Dewey." In *AIMS IN EDUCATION, THE PHILOSOPHIC APPROACH*, edited by T. H. B. Hollins, pp. 91-108. Manchester, England: Manchester University Press, 1964.

Holmes, Brian. "The Reflective Man: Dewey." In *THE EDUCATED MAN: STUDIES IN THE HISTORY OF EDUCATIONAL THOUGHT*, by Paul Nash, Andreas M. Kazamias, and Henry J. Perkinson, pp. 304-34. New York: John Wiley and Sons, 1965.

Holmes, Henry Wyman. Foreword to *JOHN DEWEY, THE MAN AND HIS PHILOSOPHY*. Addresses Delivered in New York in Celebration of His Seventieth Birthday. Cambridge: Harvard University Press, 1930.

Holmes, John Haynes. "Dewey a Leader in Public Affairs." In *JOHN DEWEY AT NINETY*, edited by Harry W. Laidler, pp. 13-14.

Holmes, Oliver Wendell. *HOLMES-POLLOCK LETTERS: THE CORRESPONDENCE OF MR. JUSTICE HOLMES AND SIR FREDERICK POLLOCK 1874-1932*, edited by Mark DeWolfe Howe. 2 vols. Cambridge: Harvard University Press, 1941. [Dewey, vol. 2, passim.]

---. *HOLMES-LASKI LETTERS: THE CORRESPONDENCE OF MR. JUSTICE HOLMES AND HAROLD J. LASKI 1916-1935*, edited by Mark DeWolfe Howe. 2 vols. Cambridge: Harvard University Press, 1953. [Dewey, passim.]

Holmes, Robert L. "The Development of John Dewey's Ethical Thought." *Monist* 48 (1964): 392-406.

---. "John Dewey's Moral Philosophy in Contemporary

Perspective." *Review of Metaphysics* 20 (1966): 42-70.

Holtzman, Filia. "A Mission That Failed: Gor'kij in America." *Slavic and East European Journal* 6 (1962): 227-35.

Homberger, Conrad Paul. "An Introduction to John Dewey." *Educational Theory* 5 (1955): 98-109.

Honeywell, J. A. "Dewey's Transcendentals." *New Scholasticism* 45 (1971): 517-46.

Hood, Bruce L. "Some Comments on C. D. Hardie's 'Refutation' of Dewey." *Educational Theory* 14 (1964): 300-304. [Review of Chapter 3 of Hardie's *TRUTH AND FALLACY IN EDUCATIONAL THEORY*.]

---, and Bayles, Ernest E. *GROWTH OF AMERICAN EDUCATIONAL THOUGHT AND PRACTICE*. New York: Harper and Row, 1966. [Dewey, pp. 249-95, and passim.]

Hook, Sidney. *THE METAPHYSICS OF PRAGMATISM*. Chicago: Open Court Publishing Co., 1927. [Dewey, passim.]

---. "John Dewey and His Critics." *New Republic*, 3 June 1931, pp. 73-74. [Reprinted in *PRAGMATISM AND AMERICAN CULTURE*, edited by Gail Kennedy, pp. 92-94.]

---. "Dewey on Thought and Action." *New Republic*, 21 March 1934, p. 165.

---. "Our Philosophers." *Current History* 41 (1935): 698-704.

---. "Corliss Lamont: 'Friend of the G.P.U.'" *Modern Monthly* 10 (March 1938): 5-8.

---. "Broun vs. Dewey." *New Republic*, 16 February 1938, p. 48. [Reply to Heywood Broun, "Dr. Dewey Finds Communists in the C.I.O." Ibid., 12 January 1938, p. 280.]

---. *JOHN DEWEY: AN INTELLECTUAL PORTRAIT*. New York: John Day Co., 1939.

---. "The Importance of John Dewey in Modern Thought."

Modern Quarterly 11 (1939): 30-35.

———. *REASON, SOCIAL MYTHS, AND DEMOCRACY.* New York: John Day Co., 1940. [Dewey, passim.]

———. "Is Physical Realism Sufficient?" *Journal of Philosophy* 41 (1944): 544-51.

———. "A Discussion of the Theory of International Relations." *Journal of Philosophy* 42 (1945): 477-97. [A discussion by several philosophers of two paragraphs of Dewey's Introduction to Jane Addams, *PEACE AND BREAD IN TIME OF WAR.* New York: King's Crown Press, 1945.] [Hook, pp. 493-95. Other philosophers: E. A. Burtt, Joseph P. Chamberlain, William Ernest Hocking, Arthur O. Lovejoy, Glenn R. Morrow, Jerome Nathanson, and Thomas V. Smith.]

———. *EDUCATION FOR MODERN MAN.* New York: Dial Press, 1946. [Dewey, passim.]

———. "The USSR Views American Philosophy." *Modern Review* 1 (1947): 649-53. [Foreword to M. Dynnik, "Contemporary Bourgeois Philosophy in the U.S." Ibid.: 653-68.]

———. "Portrait . . . John Dewey." *American Scholar* 17 (1947-48): 105-10.

———. "John Dewey at Ninety: The Man and His Philosophy." *New Leader*, 22 October 1949, S-3, S-8.

———. "The Desirable and Emotive in Dewey's Ethics." In *JOHN DEWEY: PHILOSOPHER OF SCIENCE AND FREEDOM. A SYMPOSIUM*, edited by Sidney Hook, pp. 194-216. New York: Dial Press, 1950.

———. "The Place of John Dewey in Modern Thought." In *PHILOSOPHIC THOUGHT IN FRANCE AND THE UNITED STATES*, edited by Marvin Farber, pp. 483-503.

———. "Some Memories of John Dewey." *Commentary* 14 (1952): 245-53.

———. "John Dewey and Dr. Barnes." *Commentary* 14 (1952): 504.

———. "The Quest for 'Being'." *Journal of Philosophy*

50 (1953): 709-31. [Reprinted in *LIFE, LANGUAGE, LAW: ESSAYS IN HONOR OF ARTHUR F. BENTLEY*, edited by Richard Wirth Taylor, pp. 132-54. Yellow Springs, Ohio: Antioch Press, 1957.]

---. "Exposing Soviet Purges." *New York Times*, 1 April 1956, p. 8.

---. "The Scope of Philosophy of Education." *Harvard Educational Review* 26 (1956): 145-58.

---. *AMERICAN PHILOSOPHERS AT WORK: THE PHILOSOPHIC SCENE IN THE UNITED STATES*. New York: Criterion Books, 1956. [Dewey, passim.]

---. "Marx, Dewey and Lincoln." *New Leader*, 21 October 1957, pp. 16-18.

---. "John Dewey, 1859-1952." In *PHILOSOPHY IN MID-CENTURY*, edited by Raymond Klibansky, vol. 4, pp. 210-14. Florence: La Nuova Italia, 1959.

---. "The Ends and Content of Education." *Daedalus* 88 (1959): 7-24.

---. "John Dewey--Philosopher of Growth." *Journal of Philosophy* 56 (1959): 1010-18.

---. "John Dewey: His Philosophy of Education and Its Critics." *New Leader*, 2 November 1959, S-2, pp. 3-23. [Correction in ibid., 9 November 1959, p. 30.] [Elaboration of an address at the League for Industrial Democracy Conference, April 1959.] [Also issued as a Tamiment Institute Public Service Pamphlet. New York: Tamiment Institute, 1959.] [Reprinted in *DEWEY ON EDUCATION: APPRAISALS*, edited by Reginald D. Archambault, pp. 127-60.]

---. "The Ethical Theory of John Dewey." In his *THE QUEST FOR BEING*, pp. 49-70. New York: St. Martin's Press, 1961.

---. "Experimental Naturalism." In *AMERICAN PHILOSOPHY TODAY AND TOMORROW*, edited by Horace Meyer Kallen and Sidney Hook, pp. 205-25. New York: Lee Furman, 1935. [Reprinted, Freeport, N.Y.: Books for Libraries Press, 1968.]

---. "Reason and Violence--Some Truths and Myths about

John Dewey." *Humanist* 29 (1969): n.p. [Address delivered at First Day of Issue Ceremonies Celebrating
the Dewey Stamp, Burlington, Vt., 21 October 1968.]

---. "John Dewey and the Crisis of American Liberalism." *Antioch Review* 29 (1969): 218-32.

---. "Philosophy and Public Policy." *Journal of Philosophy* 67 (1970): 461-70.

---. "John Dewey and His Betrayers." In *PAPERS ON ED-
UCATIONAL REFORM*, vol. 2, pp. 111-33. La Salle, Ill.:
Open Court Publishing Co., 1971. [Shortened version
in *Change* 3 (1971): 22-26.]

---; Nagel, Ernest; and Dewey, John. "Are Naturalists
Materialists?" *Journal of Philosophy* 42 (1945):
515-30. [In reply to Wilmon Henry Sheldon, "A Critique of Naturalism." Ibid.: 253-70.]

Horne, Herman Harrell. *THE PHILOSOPHY OF EDUCATION:
BEING THE FOUNDATIONS OF EDUCATION IN THE RELATED
NATURAL AND MENTAL SCIENCES*. Rev. ed., with special
reference to the educational philosophy of John
Dewey. New York: Macmillan Co., 1927. [Dewey,
passim.]

---. "John Dewey's Philosophy, Especially *THE QUEST
FOR CERTAINTY*." Boston: Boston University School of
Religious Education and Social Service, 1931. [Con-
vocation addresses, essays and occasional papers.]

---. *THE DEMOCRATIC PHILOSOPHY OF EDUCATION: COMPANION
TO DEWEY'S DEMOCRACY AND EDUCATION: Exposition and
Comment*. New York: Macmillan Co., 1932.

Howard, Delton Thomas. *JOHN DEWEY'S LOGICAL THEORY*.
Cornell Studies in Philosophy, no. 11. New York:
Longmans, Green and Co., 1918. [Doctoral disserta-
tion, Cornell University, 1916.]

---. "John Dewey as a Philosopher." *Educational
Trends* 7 (November-December 1939): 20-22.

Hu Shih. "The Political Philosophy of Instrumentalism."
In *THE PHILOSOPHER OF THE COMMON MAN*, edited by
Sidney Ratner, pp. 205-19.

---. "Salute from the Orient." In *JOHN DEWEY AT*

NINETY, edited by Harry W. Laidler, pp. 28-29.

---. "John Dewey in China." In *PHILOSOPHY AND CUL-
TURE--EAST AND WEST*, edited by Charles A. Moore, pp.
762-69.

Hudson, Manley Ottmer. "Shall the United States Join
the World Court?" *Christian Century* 40 (1923):
1292-97. [Part 1 in a debate with Dewey.] [Dewey,
Part 2. Ibid.: 1329-34. Part 3, with statements
by both Hudson and Dewey. Ibid.: 1367-70.]

Hughes, Ernest Richard. *THE INVASION OF CHINA BY THE
WESTERN WORLD*. New York: Macmillan Co., 1938.
[Dewey's visit to China, pp. 183-85, and passim.]

Hullfish, Henry Gordon. "Educational Confusion." *Educational Research Bulletin* 11 (1932): 85-90, 113-19.

---. "On the Agenda of Pragmatism." *Educational
Theory* 1 (1951): 241-47.

---. "John Dewey: A Mind Ever Young." *Progressive Education* 30 (1952): 16-18.

---. "John Dewey." In his *TOWARD A DEMOCRATIC EDUCA-
TION*, pp. 76-90. Columbus: College of Education,
Ohio State University, 1960.

---, and Smith, Philip G. *REFLECTIVE THINKING*. New
York: Dodd, Mead and Co., 1961. [Dewey, passim.]

Hullfish, Henry Gordon, ed. *EDUCATIONAL FREEDOM IN AN
AGE OF ANXIETY*. Twelfth Yearbook of the John Dewey
Society. New York: Harper and Brothers, 1953.
[Dewey, passim.]

Humphries, B. M. "Dewey's *STUDIES IN LOGICAL THEORY*."
Journal of the History of Philosophy 9 (1971):
485-90.

Huskins, C. Leonard. "John Dewey and Science." In *IN
HONOR OF JOHN DEWEY ON HIS NINETIETH BIRTHDAY*, pp.
34-37. Madison: University of Wisconsin, 1951.

Hutchins, Robert Maynard. "Grammar, Rhetoric, and Mr.
Dewey." *Social Frontier* 3 (1937): 137-39. [In re-
sponse to Dewey's "Rationality in Education."
Ibid.: 71-73; and "President Hutchins' Proposals to

Remake Higher Education." Ibid.: 103-4.]

---. "Education for Freedom." *Christian Century* 61 (1944): 1314-16.

---. *THE CONFLICT IN EDUCATION IN A DEMOCRATIC SOCI-ETY*. New York: Harper and Brothers, 1953. [Dewey, pp. 15, 49-55, 86.]

Hyman, Stanley Edgar. *THE ARMED VISION: A STUDY IN THE METHODS OF MODERN LITERARY CRITICISM*. Rev. ed. New York: Alfred A. Knopf, Vintage Book, 1961. [Dewey, passim.]

Hyslop, James Hervey. "The Ego, Causality, and Free-dom." *Philosophical Review* 3 (1894): 717-22. [Reply to Dewey's "The Ego as Cause." Ibid.: 337-41 *(Early Works of John Dewey* 4: 91-95.)]

Illson, Murray. "School Program Sharply Debated." *New York Times*, 6 May 1948, p. 27.

Inatomi, Eiijiro. "Present Situation of the Study of Educational Philosophy." *Education in Japan* 1 (1966): 75-82.

Ireland, Alleyne. "John Dewey on Making People Citi-zens." *New York World*, 21 April 1915.

Irving, John Allan. *SCIENCE AND VALUES: EXPLORATIONS IN PHILOSOPHY AND THE SOCIAL SCIENCES*. Toronto: Ryerson Press, 1952. [Dewey, passim.]

---. "Comments." *Journal of Philosophy* 57 (1960): 442-50. [On Edwin A. Burtt, "The Core of Dewey's Way of Thinking"; and Arthur E. Murphy, "John Dewey and American Liberalism." Ibid.: 401-19, 420-36.]

Isenberg, Arnold. Introduction to *THEORY OF THE MORAL LIFE*. New York: Holt, Rinehart and Winston, 1960. [Reissuance, with new introd. by Isenberg, of pt. 2 of the 1932 ed. of the Dewey and Tufts *ETHICS*.]

Ivie, Stanley D. "Comparison in Educational Philoso-phy: José Vasconcelos and John Dewey." *Comparative Education Review* 10 (1966): 404-17.

Jablonower, Joseph. "John Dewey Memorial Address." *American Teacher* 37 (1952): 12-16. [Delivered at the 35th

Annual American Federation of Teachers Convention.]

Jackson, Philip W., and Belford, Elizabeth. "Educational Objectives and the Joys of Teaching." *School Review* 73 (1965): 267-91.

Jacobson, Leon. *"ART AS EXPERIENCE* and American Visual Art Today." *Journal of Aesthetics and Art Criticism* 19 (1960): 117-26.

Jacobson, Nolan Pliny. "The Faith of John Dewey." *Journal of Religion* 40 (1960): 191-97.

Jaffe, Raymond. *THE PRAGMATIC CONCEPTION OF JUSTICE.* Publications in Philosophy, vol. 34. Berkeley: University of California Press, 1960. [Dewey, passim.]

Jamali, Mohammed Fadhel. "John Dewey, the Philosopher Educator." *Middle East Forum* 45 (1969): 75-89.

James, Adelbert. "Reply to 'John Dewey, Theory and Practice'." *Commonweal,* 15 October 1954, pp. 38-39. [Response to Francis Griffith, "John Dewey: Theory and Practice." Ibid., 24 September 1954, pp. 603-6.]

James, William. Discussion of Dewey's *STUDIES IN LOGICAL THEORY.* In his *LETTERS,* vol. 2, pp. 201-2.

---. *PRAGMATISM, A NEW NAME FOR SOME OLD WAYS OF THINKING.* New York: Longmans, Green and Co., 1907. [Dewey, passim.]

---. "The Chicago School." In his *COLLECTED ESSAYS AND REVIEWS,* pp. 445-47. New York: Russell and Russell, 1969.

Jarrett, James L. "Art as Cognitive Experience." *Journal of Philosophy* 50 (1953): 681-88.

Jeffrey, Richard C. "Symposium: Ethics and Decision Theory: Ethics and the Logic of Decision." *Journal of Philosophy* 62 (1965): 528-39.

Jessup, Bertram. "On Value." In *VALUE: A COOPERATIVE INQUIRY,* edited by Ray Lepley, pp. 125-46.

---; Aiken, Henry; and Mitchell, E. T. "Criticisms by Jessup; Rejoinders by Aiken and Mitchell." In *VALUE: A COOPERATIVE INQUIRY,* edited by Ray Lepley, pp. 350-65.

Johann, Robert O. *THE PRAGMATIC MEANING OF GOD.* Milwaukee: Marquette University Press, 1966.

[Dewey, passim.]

---. "Lonergan and Dewey on Judgment." *International Philosophical Quarterly* 11 (1971): 461-74.

JOHN DEWEY: THE MAN AND HIS PHILOSOPHY. Addresses Delivered in New York in Celebration of His Seventieth Birthday. Cambridge: Harvard University Press, 1930.

Johns Hopkins Magazine. "Profile of a Visionary: John Dewey, 1859-1952." *Johns Hopkins Magazine* 11 (1959): 3-6.

Johnson, Allison Heartz. Introduction to *THE WIT AND WISDOM OF JOHN DEWEY*, edited by Allison Heartz Johnson. Boston: Beacon Press, 1949.

---. "Religion has Lost Itself." *Christian Register* 128 (November 1949): 16-18, 39.

---. "John Dewey. 1859-1952." *Nation*, 25 October 1952, pp. 381-82.

Johnson, Alvin S. "Dewey, the Greek." *New Republic*, 31 October 1949, p. 9.

---. *PIONEER'S PROGRESS*. New York: Viking Press, 1952. [Dewey, passim.]

Johnson, F. E. "Is Saul Also among the Prophets?" *Christianity and Crisis*, 12 December 1949, pp. 161-62.

Johnson, Glen. *SOME ETHICAL IMPLICATIONS OF A NATURALISTIC PHILOSOPHY OF EDUCATION*. New York: Bureau of Publications, Teachers College, Columbia University, 1947. [Dewey, passim.]

Johnson, Henry C., Jr. "Progressive Education. A Case of Arrested Development?" *Educational Theory* 15 (1965): 188-97.

Joly, Ralph Philip. *THE HUMAN PERSON IN A PHILOSOPHY OF EDUCATION*. Hague: Mouton, 1965.

Jones, Frank P. "The Work of F. M. Alexander as an Introduction to Dewey's Philosophy of Education." *School and Society* 57 (1943): 1-4.

---. "Letters from John Dewey in the Wessell Library,

Tufts University." *Educational Theory* 17 (1967): 92-93.

Jones, Marc Edmund. *GEORGE SYLVESTER MORRIS: HIS PHILOSOPHICAL CAREER AND THEISTIC IDEALISM.* Philadelphia: David McKay Co., 1948. [Dewey, passim.] [Doctoral dissertation, Columbia University.]

Jones, William Thomas. "Dewey." In his *KANT TO WITTGENSTEIN AND SARTRE: A HISTORY OF WESTERN PHILOSOPHY*, vol. 4, pp. 281-317. 2d ed. New York: Harcourt, Brace and World, 1969. [Also passim.]

Joost, Nicholas. "Culture vs. Power: Randolph Bourne, John Dewey, and the *Dial*." *Midwest Quarterly* [Kansas State College of Pittsburgh] 9 (1968): 245-59.

Jordan, David Starr. "An Appraisal of War Purposes." *New Republic*, 25 August 1917, pp. 104-5. [Reply to Dewey's "The Future of Pacifism." Ibid., 28 July 1917, pp. 358-60.]

Jordan, Elijah. *FORMS OF INDIVIDUALITY: AN INQUIRY INTO THE GROUNDS OF ORDER IN HUMAN RELATIONS.* Indianapolis: Progress Publishing Co., 1927. [Dewey, pp. 62-79.]

Jordan, James A., Jr. "Interest, Choice, and Desirability." *School Review* 67 (1959): 174-85.

Journal of the National Education Association. "The Seventieth Birthday of John Dewey." *Journal of the National Education Association* 18 (1929): 281. [Editorial.]

---. "The Influence of John Dewey." *Journal of the National Education Association* 18 (1929): 282.

---. "John Dewey's Contribution to Education." *Journal of the National Education Association* 18 (1929): 285.

---. "John Dewey, the Humanist." *Journal of the National Education Association* 18 (1929): 286.

---. "The Books of John Dewey." *Journal of the National Education Association* 18 (1929): 296.

Judd, Charles Hubbard. "Motor Processes and Consciousness." *Journal of Philosophy* 6 (1909): 85-91. [Dewey, pp. 85-86.]

---, and Russell, John Dale. *THE AMERICAN EDUCATIONAL SYSTEM*. Boston: Houghton Mifflin Co., 1940. [Dewey, passim.]

Kahn, Sholom J. "Transaction vs. Interaction." *Journal of Philosophy* 44 (1947): 660-63. [Reply by Benjamin Wolstein, "A Transaction with Mr. Kahn." Ibid.: 663-66.]

---. "Experience and Existence in Dewey's Naturalistic Metaphysics." *Philosophy and Phenomenological Research* 9 (1948): 316-21. [Response by Dewey, "Experience and Existence: A Comment." Ibid.: 709-13. Kahn's reply, "The Status of the Potential." Ibid.: 714-16.]

Kallen, Horace Meyer. "Pragmatism and Its 'Principles'." *Journal of Philosophy* 8 (1911): 617-36.

---. "John Dewey, America's Foremost Thinker." *Forward* [English section.], 20 October 1929, pp. 1, 2.

---. *INDIVIDUALISM: AN AMERICAN WAY OF LIFE*. New York: Liveright, 1933. [Dewey, pp. 3-5.]

---. "Freedom and Education." In *Freedom and Education*, Progressive Education Booklet no. 12, pp. 5-15. Columbus, Ohio: Progressive Education Association, 1939. [Reprinted in *THE PHILOSOPHER OF THE COMMON MAN*, edited by Sidney Ratner, pp. 15-32.]

---. "John Dewey on the Power and Function of Art in Free Society." In his *ART AND FREEDOM*, vol. 2, pp. 906-16. New York: Duell, Sloan and Pearce, 1942. [Also passim.]

---. "John Dewey and the Spirit of Pragmatism." In *JOHN DEWEY: PHILOSOPHER OF SCIENCE AND FREEDOM*, edited by Sidney Hook, pp. 3-46.

---. "Human Rights and the Religion of John Dewey." *Ethics* 60 (1950): 169-77.

---. "Of Truth." In *THE CLEAVAGE IN OUR CULTURE:*

STUDIES IN SCIENTIFIC HUMANISM IN HONOR OF MAX OTTO, edited by Frederick Burkhardt, pp. 30-50.

---. "Individuality, Individualism, and John Dewey." *Antioch Review* 19 (1959): 299-314.

---. "Creative Intelligence." *Humanist* 19 (1959): 262-65. [The Centennial of John Dewey.]

---, and Hook, Sidney, eds. *AMERICAN PHILOSOPHY TODAY AND TOMORROW*. New York: Lee Furman, 1935. [See Sidney Hook, "Experimental Naturalism," pp. 205-35. Also passim.] [Reprinted, Freeport, N.Y.: Books for Libraries Press, 1968.]

Kaminsky, Jack. "Dewey's Defense of the Humanities." *Journal of General Education* 9 (1956): 66-72.

---. "Dewey's Concept of *An* Experience." *Philosophy and Phenomenological Research* 17 (1957): 316-30.

---. "The Challenge of Dewey." *Indian Journal of Philosophy* 4 (1962): 243-55.

---. *LANGUAGE AND ONTOLOGY*. Carbondale: Southern Illinois University Press, 1969. [Dewey, passim.]

Kandel, Isaac Leon. *TWENTY-FIVE YEARS OF AMERICAN EDUCATION: COLLECTED ESSAYS*. New York: Macmillan Co., 1924. [Dewey, passim.]

---. "The Influence of Dewey Abroad." *School and Society* 30 (1929): 700-704. [Also printed in *Teachers College Record* 31 (1929): 239-44.]

---. "John Dewey's Influence on Education in Foreign Lands." In *JOHN DEWEY: THE MAN AND HIS PHILOSOPHY*. Addresses Delivered in New York in Celebration of His Seventieth Birthday, pp. 65-74. Cambridge: Harvard University Press, 1930.

---. "John Dewey." *School and Society* 70 (1949): 250.

---. "The Influence of Educational Theorists." *School and Society* 70 (1949): 379.

---. "John Dewey, 1859-1952." *School and Society* 75 (1952): 363.

---. "A Controversy Ended." *Educational Forum* 22 (1958): 175-81. [Condensed in *Education Digest* 23 (April 1958): 16-19.]

Kantorovich, Haim. "A Revolutionary Interpretation of Philosophy." *Modern Quarterly* 2 (1924): 22-31.

Kao Chien. "Progressive Education Underminded China." *Freeman* 5 (1954): 216-18.

Kaplan, Abraham. THE NEW WORLD OF PHILOSOPHY. New York: Random House, 1961. [Dewey, passim.]

---. THE CONDUCT OF INQUIRY: METHODOLOGY FOR BEHAV- IORAL SCIENCE. Scranton, Pa.: Chandler Publishing Co., 1964. [Dewey, passim.]

Kaplan, Sidney. "Social Engineers as Saviors: Effects of World War I on Some American Liberals." *Journal of the History of Ideas* 17 (1956): 247-69.

Kariel, Henry S. "Faith in Process: John Dewey." In his IN SEARCH OF AUTHORITY, pp. 204-20. Glencoe, Ill.: Free Press, 1964.

Karier, Clarence J. "The Rebel and the Revolutionary: Sigmund Freud and John Dewey." *Teachers College Record* 64 (1963): 605-13.

---. "Humanitas and the Triumph of the Machine." *Journal of Aesthetic Education* 3 (1969): 11-28.

---. "Liberalism and the Quest for Orderly Change." *History of Education Quarterly* 12 (1972): 57-80.

Kaufmann, Felix. "John Dewey's Theory of Inquiry." In JOHN DEWEY: PHILOSOPHER OF SCIENCE AND FREEDOM, edited by Sidney Hook, pp. 217-30. [Reprinted in *Journal of Philosophy* 56 (1959): 826-36, from manuscript.]

Kazin, Alfred. "Progressivism: Some Insurgent Scholars." In his ON NATIVE GROUNDS, pp. 127-64. New York: Reynal and Hitchcock, 1942.

Keating, James W. THE FUNCTION OF THE PHILOSOPHER IN AMERICAN PRAGMATISM. Washington, D.C.: Catholic University of America, 1953. [Doctoral dissertation.]

Keel, John S. "John Dewey and Education through Art."
School Arts 66 (February 1967): 33-37.

Kelley, Truman Lee. "The Passing of the Progressive
Education Association." *School and Society* 60
(1944): 401-2.

Kellison, Chery L. "John Dewey's Theory of Truth."
Dialogue 11 (1969): 36-40.

Kennedy, Gail. "Science and the Transformation of
Common Sense: The Basic Problem of Dewey's Philosophy." *Journal of Philosophy* 51 (1954): 313-25.

---. "The Hidden Link in Dewey's Theory of Evaluation."
Journal of Philosophy 52 (1955): 85-94. [Also printed
in *Teachers College Record* 56 (1955): 421-28.]

---. "Pragmatism, Pragmaticism, and the Will to Be-
lieve--A Reconsideration." *Journal of Philosophy* 55
(1958): 578-88.

---. "The Process of Evaluation in a Democratic Community." *Journal of Philosophy* 56 (1959): 253-63.

---. "Dewey's Concept of Experience: Determinate, Indeterminate, and Problematic." *Journal of Philosophy*
56 (1959): 801-14.

---. "Comments." *Journal of Philosophy* 57 (1960):
436-42. [On Edwin Arthur Burtt, "The Core of Dewey's
Way of Thinking"; and Arthur Edward Murphy, "John
Dewey and American Liberalism."]

---. "Comment on Professor Bernstein's Paper, 'John
Dewey's Metaphysics of Experience'." *Journal of
Philosophy* 58 (1961): 14-21.

---. "Education and the Three Cultures." In *VALUES IN
AMERICAN EDUCATION*, edited by Theodore Brameld and
Stanley Elam, pp. 1-17. Bloomington, Ind.: Phi
Delta Kappa, 1964.

---. "Science and Social Control in Dewey's Philosophy." In *INNOVATION AND ACHIEVEMENT IN THE PUBLIC
INTEREST*, Essays in Honor of Edward W. Morehouse,
edited by Ward Morehouse and Nancy Morehouse Gordon,
pp. 129-63. Croton-on-Hudson, N.Y.: Wayward Press,
1966.

---. "A Naturalistic Rejoinder: Dewey's Answer to Some Questions about Value." In *SIDNEY HOOK AND THE CON TEMPORARY WORLD*, edited by Paul Kurtz, pp. 218-35. New York: John Day Co., 1968.

---. "Dewey's Logic and Theory of Knowledge." In *GUIDE TO THE WORKS OF JOHN DEWEY*, edited by Jo Ann Boydston, pp. 61-98.

---. Introduction to *PRAGMATISM AND AMERICAN CULTURE*, edited by Gail Kennedy. Boston: D. C. Heath and Co., 1950.

---, and Fisch, Max, eds. *CLASSIC AMERICAN PHILOSO-PHERS: PEIRCE, JAMES, ROYCE, SANTAYANA, DEWEY, WHITE-HEAD.* New York: Appleton-Century-Crofts, 1959. [Dewey, pp. 327-35.]

Kennedy, Gail, and Konvitz, Milton Ridvas, eds. *THE AMERICAN PRAGMATISTS*. New York: World Publishing Co., Meridian Books, 1960. [Dewey, pp. 173-75.]

Kennedy, William F. "John Dewey and the Platoon School." *Platoon School* 3 (1929-30): 150.

Kent, William Phelps. "John Dewey's Philosophical Principles and Their Political Significance." *Western Political Quarterly* 6 (1953): 446-57.

Kenworthy, Leonard S., and Giventer, Edwin B., eds. "John Dewey Speaks." World Affairs Materials, Brooklyn, N.Y.: Brooklyn College, 1972. [One page of biography and seven pages of quotations from Dewey.]

Keohane, Mary. "A. S. Neill: Latter-day Dewey?" *Elementary School Journal* 70 (1970): 401-10.

Kerlinger, Fred N. "The Origin of the Doctrine of Permissiveness in American Education." *Progressive Education* 33 (1956): 161-65.

---. *FOUNDATIONS OF BEHAVIORAL RESEARCH: EDUCATIONAL AND PSYCHOLOGICAL INQUIRY.* New York: Holt, Rinehart and Winston, 1964. [Dewey, pp. 13-17.]

Kersey, Shirley J., and Beck, Carlton E. "Dewey's Aesthetics: Implications for Teachers." *Journal of Thought* 5 (1970): 92-100.

Kestenbaum, Victor. "Phenomenology and Dewey's Empiricism: A Response to Leroy Troutner." *Educational Theory* 22 (1972): 99-108. [Response to Leroy F. Troutner, "What Can the Educator Learn from the Existential Philosopher?" In *PHILOSOPHY AND EDUCATION 1966: Proceedings of the Twenty-Second Annual Meeting of the Philosophy of Education Society*, pp. 98-105. Edwardsville, Ill.: Studies in Philosophy of Education, 1966.]

Killeen, Mary Vincent. *MAN IN THE NEW HUMANISM*. Washington, D.C.: Catholic University of America, 1934. [Doctoral dissertation.]

Kilpatrick, Franklin Pierce, ed. *EXPLORATIONS IN TRANSACTIONAL PSYCHOLOGY*. New York: New York University Press, 1961. [Dewey, passim.]

Kilpatrick, William Heard. "Remarks at the Unveiling of Dr. Dewey's Bust." *School and Society* 28 (1928): 778-80.

---. Introduction to *JOHN DEWEY, THE MAN AND HIS PHILOSOPHY*. Addresses Delivered in New York in Celebration of His Seventieth Birthday. Cambridge: Harvard University Press, 1930.

---. "Dewey's Influence on Education." In *THE PHILOSOPHY OF JOHN DEWEY*, edited by Paul Schilpp, pp. 445-74. [Reprinted in *JOHN DEWEY AS EDUCATOR*, edited by William H. Kilpatrick and John L. Childs, pp. 445-74.]

---. "The Child and the Curriculum." In *Freedom and Education*, Progressive Education Booklet no. 12, pp. 33-36. Columbus, Ohio: Progressive Education Association, 1939.

---. "John Dewey in American Life." In *John Dewey and the Promise of America*, Progressive Education Booklet no. 14, pp. 5-11. Columbus, Ohio: Progressive Education Association, 1939.

---. "John Dewey's Ninetieth Birthday." *Education* 70 (1949): 95. [Also appears in *Journal of the National Education Association* 38 (1949): 529.]

---. *JOHN DEWEY AND HIS CONTRIBUTIONS TO AMERICAN EDU-*

CATION, Henry Barnard Lecture no. 1. New Britain: Connecticut Teachers College, 1949.

———. Statement on Dewey. In "The Literature of Diversity," by George Boas. *New Republic*, 17 October 1949, p. 27.

———. "Apprentice Citizens." *Saturday Review of Literature*, 22 October 1949, p. 12.

———. "What Has John Dewey Meant to Childhood Education?" *Childhood Education* 26 (1950): 380-81.

———. "Dewey and Education for Democracy." In *JOHN DEWEY AT NINETY*, edited by Harry W. Laidler, pp. 21-24.

———. *PHILOSOPHY OF EDUCATION*. New York: Macmillan Co., 1951. [Dewey, passim.]

———. "John Dewey and His Educational Theory." *Educational Theory* 2 (1952): 217-21. [Also printed in *Progressive Education* 30 (1952): 5-8.]

———. "Dewey's Philosophy of Education." *Educational Forum* 17 (1953): 143-54.

———. "Education by Interest and Effort." *Humanist* 19 (1959): 265-66. [The Centennial of John Dewey.]

———. "Personal Reminiscences of Dewey and My Judgment of His Present Influence." *School and Society* 87 (1959): 374-75. [Reprinted in *JOHN DEWEY: MASTER EDUCATOR*, edited by William W. Brickman and Stanley Lehrer, 2d ed., pp. 13-16.] [Also reprinted in *DEWEY ON EDUCATION: APPRAISALS*, edited by Reginald D. Archambault, pp. 3-6.]

———, and Childs, John L. *JOHN DEWEY AS EDUCATOR*. New York: Progressive Education Association, 1940. [Reprint of "The Educational Philosophy of John Dewey," by John L. Childs and "Dewey's Influence on Education," by William H. Kilpatrick, with a separate preface by Childs and Kilpatrick, and the complete table of contents of *THE PHILOSOPHY OF JOHN DEWEY*, edited by Paul Schilpp.]

Kilpatrick, William Heard, and De Witt, Dale. "John

Dewey: Humanist and Educator." *Humanist* 12 (1952): 161-65. [Reprinted in *Michigan Education Journal* 30 (1953): 522-23.]

Kimpton, Lawrence Alpheus. "The University and the High School." *School and Society* 86 (1958): 100-102. [Reprinted in *THE HIGH SCHOOL IN A NEW ERA*, edited by Francis S. Chase and Harold A. Anderson, pp 31-37. Chicago: University of Chicago Press, 1958; and in part in *School Review* 67 (1959): 125-27, with the title, "Dewey and Progressive Education."]

Klein, Julius. "Secretary Klein's Reply to Prof. Dewey--And Rejoinder." *People's Lobby Bulletin*, August 1931, pp. 3-4. [Reply to Dewey's "Secretary Klein Asked Basis of Optimism." Ibid., June 1931, pp. 3-4. Rejoinder by Dewey. Ibid., August 1931, pp. 4-5.]

Kling, Carlos. "On the Instrumental Analysis of Thought." *Journal of Philosophy* 29 (1932): 259-65. [Apropos of Laurence Buermeyer, "Professor Dewey's Analysis of Thought." Ibid. 17 (1920): 673-81; and Dewey, "An Analysis of Reflective Thought." Ibid. 19 (1922): 29-38.]

Klubertanz, George Peter. "The Man Whom Dewey Would Educate." *Modern Schoolman* 16 (1939): 60-64.

Klyce, Scudder. "Dewey's Suppressed Psychology . . . Being Correspondence between John Dewey and Scudder Klyce." Mimeographed. Winchester, Mass.: S. Klyce, 1928.

Knight, Frank H. "Pragmatism and Social Action." *International Journal of Ethics* 46 (1936): 229-36.

Knode, Jay C. "The Influence of John Dewey on Higher Education." *New Mexico Quarterly Review* 10 (1940): 17-29.

Kobayashi, Victor N. "The Quest for Experience: Zen, Dewey, and Education." *Comparative Education Review* 5 (1962): 217-22.

---. *JOHN DEWEY IN JAPANESE EDUCATIONAL THOUGHT*. Ann Arbor: University of Michigan Press, 1964.

---. "Japan's Hoashi Riichirō and John Dewey." *Educational Theory* 14 (1964): 50-53.

Koch, Adrienne. "John Dewey's Influence Pervades Most of Society." *Washington Post*, 8 June 1952.

Koehler, Conrad J. "A Study in Wittgenstein's Theory of Meaning." *Kinesis* 1 (1968): 36-42.

Kohl, Herbert. "Dewey-James-Peirce." In his *THE AGE OF COMPLEXITY*, pp. 29-34. New York: New American Library, Mentor Books, 1965.

Kohlberg, Lawrence, and Mayer, Rochelle. "Development as the Aim of Education." *Harvard Educational Review* 42 (1972): 449-96.

Kolko, Gabriel. "Morris R. Cohen: The Scholar and/or Society." *American Quarterly* 9 (1957): 325-36.

Konvitz, Milton Ridvas. "Dewey, Society, and Religion." *New Leader*, 22 October 1949, S-6.

---. "Dewey's Revision of Jefferson." In *JOHN DEWEY: PHILOSOPHER OF SCIENCE AND FREEDOM*, edited by Sidney Hook, pp. 164-76.

---, and Kennedy, Gail, eds. *THE AMERICAN PRAGMATISTS*. New York: World Publishing Co., Meridian Books, 1960. [Dewey, pp. 173-75.]

Kraft, Ivor. "What John Dewey Taught." *Nation*, 9 June 1962, pp. 521-22. [Review of *THE TRANSFORMATION OF THE SCHOOL* by Lawrence A. Cremin.]

Krikorian, Yervant Hovhannes. "The Ethics of Naturalism." *New Republic*, 17 October 1949, pp. 32-36.

---, ed. *NATURALISM AND THE HUMAN SPIRIT*. Columbia Studies in Philosophy, no. 8. New York: Columbia University Press, 1944. [One essay by Dewey. Other essays, Dewey, passim.]

Krutch, Joseph Wood. Statement on Dewey in "Psychology and the Fourth R," by Gordon Allport. *New Republic*, 17 October 1949, p. 25.

Kuhn, Manford H. "Self-Attitudes by Age, Sex, and Professional Training." *Sociological Quarterly* 1 (1960): 39-55.

Kuhn, Philip A. "T'ao Hsing-Chih, 1891-1946, An Educational Reformer." In *PAPERS ON CHINA*, vol. 13, pp. 163-92. Cambridge: Center for East Asian

Studies, Harvard University, 1959.

Kunitz, Stanley J. "John Dewey." In *AUTHORS TODAY AND YESTERDAY*, edited by Stanley J. Kunitz, pp. 195-97. New York: J. W. Wilson Co., 1933.

---, and Haycraft, Howard, ed. *TWENTIETH CENTURY AUTHORS*. New York: J. W. Wilson Co., 1942. [Dewey, pp. 378-79.] [Dewey, p. 279 of *FIRST SUPPLEMENT*, edited by Stanley J. Kunitz. New York: J. W. Wilson Co., 1955.]

Kurita, Osamu. "John Dewey's Philosophic Frame of Reference in His First Three Articles." *Educational Theory* 21 (1971): 338-46.

Kurtz, Paul. "Has Ethical Naturalism Been Refuted?" *Journal of Value Inquiry* 4 (1970): 161-71.

---, ed. *AMERICAN PHILOSOPHY IN THE TWENTIETH CENTURY: A SOURCEBOOK FROM PRAGMATISM TO PHILOSOPHICAL ANALYSIS*. Classics in the History of Thought, edited by Crane Brinton and Paul Edwards. New York: Macmillan Co., 1966. [Dewey, pp. 161-63.]

Kuspit, Donald P. "Dewey's Critique of Art for Art's Sake." *Journal of Aesthetics and Art Criticism* 27 (1968): 93-98. [Response by Lincoln Rothschild and rejoinder by Kuspit. Ibid. 27 (1969): 461.]

La Brecque, Richard. "Social Planning and the Imperium Humanum: John Dewey, circa 1960's." *Educational Theory* 19 (1969): 363-71.

Ladd, John. "'Desirability' and 'Normativeness' in White's Article on Dewey." *Philosophical Review* 60 (1951): 91-98. [Reply to Morton G. White, "Value and Obligation in Dewey and Lewis." Ibid. 58 (1949): 321-29.]

Lafferty, Theodore Thomas. "Inter-Communication in Philosophy." *Journal of Philosophy* 43 (1946): 449-66.

---. "Empiricism and Objective Relativism in Value Theory." *Journal of Philosophy* 46 (1949): 141-55.

Laidler, Harry Wellington, ed. "Introductory Remarks."

In *JOHN DEWEY AT NINETY*. Addresses and Greetings on the Occasion of Dr. Dewey's Ninetieth Birthday Dinner, pp. 5-7. New York: League for Industrial Democracy, 1950.

Lamont, Corliss. "John Dewey Capitulates to 'God'." *New Masses*, 31 July 1934, pp. 23-24.

---. "John Dewey, Marxism and the United Front." *New Masses*, 3 March 1936, pp. 22-23.

---. "The Pragmatism of John Dewey." *Marxist Quarterly* 1 (1937): 298-300.

---. "John Dewey in Theory and Practice." *Science and Society* 5 (1941): 61-64. [Comment on Vivian J. McGill, "Pragmatism Reconsidered: An Aspect of John Dewey's Philosophy." Ibid. 3 (1939): 289-322. Reply by McGill, "Further Considerations." Ibid. 5 (1941): 65-71.]

---. *HUMANISM AS A PHILOSOPHY*. New York: Philosophical Library, 1949. [Dewey, passim.]

---. "John Dewey: Philosopher and Educator." *Humanist* 19 (1959): 133-34.

---. "John Dewey and the American Humanist Association." *Humanist* 20 (1960): 3-10.

---. "New Light on Dewey's *COMMON FAITH*." *Journal of Philosophy* 58 (1961): 21-28. [Sections of this article reprinted in *Religious Humanism* 2 (1968): 27-29, with the title, "A Critical Response to Law, Angeles, and Others."]

---. *THE PHILOSOPHY OF HUMANISM*. 5th ed., rev. and enl. New York: Frederick Ungar Publishing Co., 1965. [Dewey, passim.]

---. *FREEDOM OF CHOICE AFFIRMED*. New York: Horizon Press, 1967. [Dewey, passim.]

---, and Selsam, Howard. "Materialism and John Dewey-- A Discussion." *New Masses*, 25 February 1947, pp. 17-23.

---. "'Philosophy in Revolution': A Discussion."

Science and Society 22 (1958): 56-68. [Discussion of Selsam's *PHILOSOPHY IN REVOLUTION* (1957), especially his treatment of Dewey. Lamont's review, pp. 56-62. Reply by Selsam, pp. 62-68.]

Lamont, Corliss, ed. *DIALOGUE ON JOHN DEWEY*. New York, Horizon Press, 1959.

Lamprecht, Sterling Power. "A Note on Professor Dewey's Theory of Knowledge." *Journal of Philosophy* 20 (1923): 488-94. [In response to Dewey's "Realism without Monism or Dualism." Ibid. 19 (1922): 309-17, 351-61. Reply by Dewey, "Some Comments on Philosophical Discussion." Ibid. 21 (1924): 197-209.]

---. "An Idealistic Source of Instrumentalist Logic." *Mind* n.s. 33 (1924): 415-27.

---. "The Philosophy of John Dewey." *New World Monthly* 1 (1930): 1-16.

---. *Empiricism and Natural Knowledge*. University of California Publications in Philosophy, vol. 16, no. 4, pp. 71-94. Berkeley and Los Angeles: University of California Press, 1940.

---. "Philosophy in the United States: Dewey." In his *OUR PHILOSOPHICAL TRADITIONS: A BRIEF HISTORY OF PHILOSOPHY IN WESTERN CIVILIZATION*, pp. 497-512. New York: Appleton-Century-Crofts, 1955.

Lancaster, Lane W. "John Dewey." In his *MASTERS OF POLITICAL THOUGHT, HEGEL TO DEWEY*, vol. 3, pp. 332-68. Boston: Houghton Mifflin Co., 1960.

Lane, Alfred Church. "Authority and Freedom." *School and Society* 44 (1936): 376-77. [Comment on Dewey's "Authority and Resistance to Social Change." Ibid.: 457-66.]

Larrabee, Harold Atkins. "The Twenty-Ninth Meeting of the American Philosophical Association [at Columbia University, 30-31 December 1929]." *Journal of Philosophy* 27 (1930): 70-79.

---. *RELIABLE KNOWLEDGE*. Rev. ed. Boston: Houghton Mifflin Co., 1964. [Dewey, passim.]

---. "John Dewey as Teacher." *School and Society* 86 (1959): 378-81. [Condensed in *Education Digest* 25 (January 1960): 20-23.] [Reprinted in *JOHN DEWEY: MASTER EDUCATOR*, edited by William W. Brickman and

Stanley Lehrer, 2d ed., pp. 93-100.]

Lasch, Christopher. *THE NEW RADICALISM IN AMERICA,
1889-1963.* New York: Alfred A. Knopf, 1965.
[Dewey, pp. 202-17, and passim.]

Lavine, Thelma Z. "Note to Naturalists on the Human
Spirit." *Journal of Philosophy* 50 (1953): 145-54.

---. "What is the Method of Naturalism?" *Journal of
Philosophy* 50 (1953): 157-61.

Law, David A., and Angeles, Peter A. "Dewey's Idea of
the Religious and Unreligious." *Religious Humanism*
2 (1968): 25-26.

Lawrence, Nathaniel Morris. "Education as Social Process." In *JOHN DEWEY AND THE EXPERIMENTAL SPIRIT IN
PHILOSOPHY*, edited by Charles W. Hendel, pp. 33-61.

Lawson, Douglas E., and Lean, Arthur E., eds. *JOHN
DEWEY AND THE WORLD VIEW.* Carbondale: Southern Illinois University Press, 1964; Arcturus Books, 1966.

Lawson, R. Alan. *THE FAILURE OF INDEPENDENT LIBER-
ALISM, 1930-1941.* New York: G. P. Putnam's Sons,
1971. [Dewey, pp. 99-130, and passim.]

Lean, Arthur E. "John Dewey on Psychology in High
Schools." In *JOHN DEWEY AND THE WORLD VIEW*, edited
by Douglas Lawson and Arthur Lean, pp. 26-34.

Leander, Folke. "John Dewey and the Classical Tradition." *American Review* 9 (1937): 504-27.

---. *THE PHILOSOPHY OF JOHN DEWEY, A CRITICAL STUDY.*
Göteborg: Wettergren and Kerber, 1939.

Learning How To Learn. An Introduction to the Educational Methods and Theories Taught by John Dewey.
Detroit: Solidarity House, 1952. [A worker education pamphlet of the UAW-CIO education department.]

LeBoutillier, Cornelia Throop. "The Religious Phi-
losophy of John Dewey." In her *RELIGIOUS VALUES IN
THE PHILOSOPHY OF EMERGENT EVOLUTION*, pp. 71-89.
New York, 1936. [Doctoral dissertation, Columbia
University.]

---. "The Doctrine of the Trinity: An Indispensable
Norm." *Journal of Religion* 23 (1943): 33-42.

[Dewey, passim.]

Lee, Grace Chin. *GEORGE HERBERT MEAD: PHILOSOPHER OF THE SOCIAL INDIVIDUAL*. New York: King's Crown Press, 1945. [Dewey, passim.] [Doctoral dissertation, Bryn Mawr College.]

Lee, Harold Newton. "Methodology of Value Theory." In *VALUE: A COOPERATIVE INQUIRY*, edited by Ray Lepley, pp. 147-66.

---; Aiken, Henry; and Pepper, Stephen. "Criticisms by Lee; Rejoinders by Aiken and Pepper." In *VALUE: A COOPERATIVE INQUIRY*, edited by Ray Lepley, pp. 366-80.

Lee, Leon. "Institutions and Ideas in Social Change." *American Journal of Economics and Sociology* 18 (1959): 127-38.

Lee, Otis. "Instrumentalism and Action." *Journal of Philosophy* 37 (1940): 57-75.

Lehrer, Stanley, and Brickman, William W., eds. *JOHN DEWEY: MASTER EDUCATOR*. New York: Society for the Advancement of Education, 1959. [2d ed., 1961.]

Leighton, Joseph Alexander. "Pragmatism." *Journal of Philosophy* 1 (1904): 148-56.

---. "Cognitive Thought and 'Immediate' Experience." *Journal of Philosophy* 3 (1906): 174-80. [On Dewey's "The Postulate of Immediate Empiricism." Ibid. 2 (1905): 393-99.]

Leonard, Henry S. "Authorship of Signs." *Papers of the Michigan Academy of Science, Arts, and Letters* 45 (1960): 329-40.

Lepley, Ray. *VERIFIABILITY OF VALUE*. Columbia Studies in Philosophy, no. 7. New York: Columbia University Press, 1944. [Dewey, passim.]

---. "Sequel on Value." In *VALUE: A COOPERATIVE INQUIRY*, edited by Ray Lepley, pp. 167-89. New York: Columbia University Press, 1949.

---; Morris, Charles; and Parker, DeWitt. "Criticisms

by Lepley; Rejoinders by Morris and Parker." In *VALUE: A COOPERATIVE INQUIRY*, edited by Ray Lepley, pp. 381-99.

---, ed. *THE LANGUAGE OF VALUE*. New York: Columbia University Press, 1957. [Dewey, passim.]

Lerner, Max. "Randolph Bourne and Two Generations." *Twice a Year* 5-6 (1940-41): 54-78.

Leslie, Elmer A. "John Dewey." In *VOCATIONS AND PRO-FESSIONS*, edited by Philip Lotz, pp. 63-72. New York: Association Press, 1940.

Levi, Albert William. "Reason in Society: John Dewey." In his *PHILOSOPHY AND THE MODERN WORLD*, pp. 283-330. Bloomington: Indiana University Press, 1959.

---. "The Value of Freedom: Mill's Liberty (1859-1959)." *Ethics* 70 (1959): 37-46. [Dewey, pp. 44-46.]

Levin, Samuel M. "John Dewey's Evaluation of Technology." *American Journal of Economics and Sociology* 15 (1955): 123-36.

Levine, Daniel. "Randolph Bourne, John Dewey and the Legacy of Liberalism." *Antioch Review* 29 (1969): 234-44.

Levit, Martin. "Soviet Version of John Dewey and Pragmatism." *History of Education Journal* 4 (1953): 135-41.

---. "The Context of a Contextualist Philosophy." *School Review* 67 (1959): 246-57.

Levitt, Morton. *FREUD AND DEWEY ON THE NATURE OF MAN*. New York: Philosophical Library, 1960. [From his doctoral dissertation, "Freud and Dewey: A Comparative Study of Their Psychological Systems." University of Michigan, 1956.]

Lewis, Clarence Irving. "Pragmatism and Current Thought." *Journal of Philosophy* 27 (1930): 238-46. [Response by Dewey, "In Reply to Some Criticisms." Ibid.: 271-77.]

Leys, Wayne A. R. "Dewey's Instrumental Thinking."

In his *ETHICS FOR POLICY DECISIONS*, pp. 150-75. New York: Prentice-Hall, 1952. [Also passim.]

---. "Dewey's Social, Political, and Legal Philosophy." In *GUIDE TO THE WORKS OF JOHN DEWEY*, edited by Jo Ann Boydston, pp. 131-55.

---. Introduction to *The Early Works of John Dewey, 1882-1898*, edited by Jo Ann Boydston, vol. 4, pp. xiii-xxiv.

Libraries. "Celebration of John Dewey's Seventieth Birthday." *Libraries* 35 (1930): 310.

Librome, Jack, and Salter, Paul. "Dewey, Russell and Cohen: Why They Are Anti-Communist." *New Masses*, 17 July 1934, pp. 24-27; 24 July 1934, pp. 22-23.

Lidman, David. "John Dewey Honored." *New York Times*, 18 August 1968, p. 27.

Life. "*Life* Congratulates John Dewey." *Life*, 31 October 1949, p. 43.

Lilge, Frederic. "Meanings of Nature in Education." *Educational Theory* 1 (1951): 116-30.

---. "The Vain Quest for Unity: John Dewey's Social and Educational Thought." In "Proceedings of the 15th Annual Meeting of the Philosophy of Education Society, 1959," pp. 132-42. Mimeographed. [Reprinted in *DEWEY ON EDUCATION: APPRAISALS*, edited by Reginald D. Archambault, pp. 52-71.]

---. "John Dewey in Retrospect: An American Reconsideration." *British Journal of Educational Studies* 8 (1960): 99-111.

---. "John Dewey, 1859-1959: Reflections on His Educational and Social Thought." *Educational Forum* 24 (1960): 351-56.

Lind, Levi Robert. "Dewey Pictured as Prophet and Reconstructionist." *Daily Illini* [University of Illinois.], 26 February 1928.

Lindeman, Eduard C. "John Dewey and Social Action." In *The Educational Frontier*, Progressive Education

Booklet no. 13, pp. 42-57. Columbus, Ohio: Progressive Education Association, 1939. [Reprinted in *School and Society* 51 (1940): 33-37, with the title "John Dewey as Educator."]

---. "John Dewey on the Doctrine of the Golden Mean." *Progressive Education* 30 (1952): 8-19.

Link, Eugene P. "John Dewey and Mohandas K. Gandhi as Educational Thinkers." *Comparative Education Review* 5 (1962): 212-16.

Linville, Henry Richardson. "The Dewey Anniversary." *Nation*, 16 October 1929, p. 408.

---. "John Dewey at Seventy." *New Republic*, 16 October 1929, p. 245.

---. "Inaugurating the Plan." In *JOHN DEWEY: THE MAN AND HIS PHILOSOPHY*. Addresses Delivered in New York in Celebration of His Seventieth Birthday, pp. 1-2. Cambridge: Harvard University Press, 1930.

Lippmann, Walter. "The Footnote." *New Republic*, 17 July 1915, p. 285. [Following an extract from Dewey's *GERMAN PHILOSOPHY AND POLITICS* and a review by Francis Hackett. Ibid., pp. 281-84.]

Literary Digest. "Young Men's Report Stirs Interest." *Literary Digest*, 16 February 1935, pp. 16, 27.

Locigno, Joseph P. "Religion in the Thought of Dewey and Bonhoeffer." *Religious Education* 65 (1970): 5-8.

Lodge, Nucia, and Counts, George S. *THE COUNTRY OF THE BLIND: THE SOVIET SYSTEM OF MIND CONTROL*. Boston: Houghton Mifflin Co., 1949. [Dewey, pp. 261, 271, 277-78.]

Lodge, Rupert Clendon. *PLATO'S THEORY OF ART*. New York: Humanities Press, 1953. [Dewey, passim.]

Logan, Frederick Manning. "John Dewey's Influence on the Arts and on Art Education." In *IN HONOR OF JOHN DEWEY ON HIS NINETIETH BIRTHDAY*, pp. 28-31. Madison: University of Wisconsin, 1951.

Long, Wilbur. "Mr. Dewey's Faith without Religion."

Personalist 18 (1937): 239-53, 369-88.

Lovejoy, Arthur Oncken. "Pragmatism as Interactionism, I and II." *Journal of Philosophy* 17 (1920): 589-96, 622-32.

---. "Pragmatism *versus* the Pragmatist." In *ESSAYS IN CRITICAL REALISM*, by Arthur Oncken Lovejoy, Durant Drake, James Bissett Pratt, Arthur K. Rogers, George Santayana, Roy Wood Sellars, and C. A. Strong, pp. 35-81. London: Macmillan and Co., 1920. [Reprinted. New York: Gordian Press, 1968.] [Dewey's reply, "Realism without Monism or Dualism." *Journal of Philosophy* 19 (1922): 309-17, 351-61.]

---. "Pragmatism and the New Materialism." *Journal of Philosophy* 19 (1922): 5-15.

---. "Time, Meaning and Transcendence, Part I. The Alleged Futurity of Yesterday." *Journal of Philosophy* 19 (1922): 505-15. "Part II. Professor Dewey's *Tertium Quid*." Ibid.: 533-41. [In response to Dewey's "Realism without Monism or Dualism." Ibid.: 309-17, 351-61. Reply by Dewey, "Some Comments on Philosophical Discussion." Ibid. 21 (1924): 197-209. Rejoinder by Lovejoy, "Pastness and Transcendence." Ibid.: 601-11.]

---. "Shall We Join the League of Nations?" *New Republic*, 28 March 1923, pp. 138-39. [Letter in response to Dewey's "Shall We Join the League?" Ibid., 7 March 1923, pp. 36-37. Reply by Dewey, ibid., 28 March 1923, pp. 139-40.]

---. *THE REVOLT AGAINST DUALISM*. Chicago: Open Court Publishing Co., 1930. [Dewey, passim.]

---. "A Discussion of the Theory of International Relations." *Journal of Philosophy* 42 (1945): 477-97. [A discussion by several philosophers of two paragraphs of Dewey's Introduction to Jane Addams, *PEACE AND BREAD IN TIME OF WAR*. New York: King's Crown Press, 1945.] [Lovejoy, pp. 480-82. Other philosophers: E. A. Burtt, Joseph P. Chamberlain, William Ernest Hocking, Sidney Hook, Glenn R. Morrow, Jerome Nathanson, and Thomas V. Smith.]

---. *THE THIRTEEN PRAGMATISTS AND OTHER ESSAYS*. Baltimore: Johns Hopkins Press, 1963. [Dewey, passim.]

Lovett, Robert Morss. "A Task for Pacifists." *New Republic*, 25 August 1917, pp. 106-7. [Reply to Dewey's "The Future of Pacifism." Ibid., 28 July 1917, pp. 358-60.]

---. "John Dewey at Seventy." *New Republic*, 23 October 1929, pp. 262-64. [Reprinted in "Some Popular Appraisals of John Dewey," edited by Clyde R. Miller, pp. 218-20.]

Lu, Henry Chung-Ming. "The Problem of Verification in Moral Judgments." *Educational Theory* 17 (1967): 67-72.

---. "Dewey's Logical Theory and His Conception of Education." *Educational Theory* 18 (1968): 388-95.

---. "The Goal of Inquiry in Dewey's Philosophy." *Educational Theory* 20 (1970): 65-72.

Lugton, Robert C. "John Dewey's Theory of Language." *Journal of English as a Second Language* 2 (1967): 75-82.

Lyman, Eugene William. "The Influence of Pragmatism upon the Status of Theology." In *STUDIES IN PHILOSOPHY AND PSYCHOLOGY BY FORMER STUDENTS OF CHARLES E. GARMAN*, edited by James H. Tufts, Edmund Burke Delabarre, Frank Chapman Sharp, Arthur Henry Pierce, and Frederick J. E. Woodbridge, pp. 219-36. Cambridge, Mass.: Riverside Press, 1906.

Lynch, Jarmon Alvis. "Two Ways of Misconstruing the Doctrine of Interest." *Texas Outlook* 15 (August 1931): 18-19.

---. "Concerning the Emphasis on Methods." *Journal of Philosophy* 37 (1940): 269-73.

---. "A Criticism of Dewey's Theory of the Stimulus." *Philosophical Review* 49 (1940): 356-60.

Lynd, Albert. "Who Wants Progressive Education? The Influence of John Dewey on the Public Schools." *Atlantic Monthly*, April 1953, pp. 29-34. [Reply by Frederic Ernst, "How Dangerous is John Dewey?"

Ibid., May 1953, pp. 59-62.] [Reprinted in Lynd's
QUACKERY IN THE PUBLIC SCHOOLS, pp. 183-211. Bos-
ton: Little, Brown and Co., 1953. Also reprinted in
DEWEY ON EDUCATION: APPRAISALS, edited by Reginald
D. Archambault, pp. 191-208.]

Maccia, George S. "A Comparison of the Educational
Aims of Charles Peirce and John Dewey." *Educational
Theory* 4 (1954): 289-96.

McCadden, Helen M. "John Dewey and Education." *Commonweal*, 27 November 1929, p. 113.

McCarthy, Harold E. "Dewey, Suzuki, and the Elimina-
tion of Dichotomies." *Philosophy East and West* 6
(1956): 35-48.

McCaul, Robert L. "Educational Biography: Dewey and
[Samuel Gridley] Howe." *Elementary School Journal*
58 (1957): 1-7.

---. "A Preliminary Listing of Dewey Letters, 1894-
1904." *School and Society* 87 (1959): 395-99. [Re-
printed in *JOHN DEWEY: MASTER EDUCATOR*, edited by
William W. Brickman and Stanley Lehrer, 2d ed.,
pp. 154-68.]

---. "Dewey's Chicago." *School Review* 67 (1959):
258-80.

---. "Dewey and the University of Chicago. I. July,
1894-March, 1902." *School and Society* 89 (1961):
152-57; "II. April, 1902-May, 1903." Ibid.: 179-83;
"III. September, 1903-June, 1904." Ibid.: 202-6.
[Reprinted in *JOHN DEWEY: MASTER EDUCATOR*, edited
by William W. Brickman and Stanley Lehrer, 2d ed.,
pp. 31-74.]

---. "Dewey's School Days, 1867-1875." *Elementary
School Journal* 63 (1962): 15-21.

---. "Dewey in College, 1875-1879." *School Review* 70
(1962): 437-56.

---, and Dunkel, Harold B. "Dewey: 1859-1952." *School
Review* 67 (1959): 123-24.

McClellan, James E. "Dewey and the Concept of Method:
Quest for the Philosopher's Stone in Education."

School Review 67 (1959): 213-28. [Reprinted in *PHI-LOSOPHICAL ESSAYS ON TEACHING*, edited by Bertram Bandman and Robert S. Guttchen, pp. 135-228. New York: J. B. Lippincott, 1969.]

McCluskey, Neil Gerard. *PUBLIC SCHOOLS AND MORAL EDU-CATION: THE INFLUENCE OF HORACE MANN, WILLIAM TORREY HARRIS, AND JOHN DEWEY*. New York: Columbia University Press, 1958. [Doctoral dissertation.]

McCool, Gerald A. "Philosophy and Christian Wisdom." *Thought* 44 (1969): 485-512. [Dewey, pp. 502-509.]

McCreary, John Kenneth. "The Matrix of Dewey's Theory of Education." *Education* [Boston] 68 (1948): 439-48.

McDermott, John J. "Dewey's Logic." *Transactions of the Charles S. Peirce Society* 6 (1970): 34-45.

MacDonald, A. A. "Teachers Uphold Ouster of 'Reds'." *New York Times*, 24 August 1941, p. 18.

McDonald, Gerald Edmund. "Cooperation in Education between the Thomist and the Experimentalist." *Educational Administration and Supervision* 45 (1959): 13-25.

McDougall, William. "Can Sociology and Social Psychology Dispense with Instincts?" *American Journal of Sociology* 29 (1924): 657-70.

McElroy, Howard Clifford. "John Dewey." In his *MODERN PHILOSOPHERS: WESTERN THOUGHT SINCE KANT*, pp. 101-22. New York: Russell F. Moore Co., 1950.

McGann, Thomas F. "John Dewey and Vatican Council II." *America*, 5 April 1969, pp. 411-15.

McGilvary, Evander Bradley. "Pure Experience and Reality." *Philosophical Review* 16 (1907): 266-84.

---. "Pure Experience and Reality: A Reassertion." *Philosophical Review* 16 (1907): 422-24. [Reply to Dewey's "Pure Experience and Reality: A Disclaimer." Ibid.: 419-22.]

---. "The Chicago 'Idea' and Idealism." *Journal of*

Philosophy 5 (1908): 589-97. [Reply by Dewey, "Objects, Data and Existence." Ibid. 6 (1909): 13-21.]

---. "Professor Dewey's 'Action of Consciousness'." *Journal of Philosophy* 8 (1911): 458-60. [In response to Dewey's "Does Reality Possess Practical Character?" In *ESSAYS, PHILOSOPHICAL AND PSYCHOLOGICAL, IN HONOR OF WILLIAM JAMES*, pp. 53-80. New York: Longmans, Green and Co., 1908.]

---. "Professor Dewey's 'Brief Studies in Realism'." *Journal of Philosophy* 9 (1912): 344-49. [In response to Dewey's "Brief Studies in Realism." Ibid. 8 (1911): 393-400, 546-54.]

---. "Professor Dewey's 'Awareness'." *Journal of Philosophy* 9 (1912): 301-2. [In response to Dewey's "Brief Studies in Realism." Ibid. 8 (1911): 393-400, 546-54.]

---. "Realism and the Ego-centric Predicament." *Philosophical Review* 21 (1912): 351-56. [In response to Dewey's "Brief Studies in Realism." *Journal of Philosophy* 8 (1911): 393-400, 546-54.]

MacGowan, Robert. "John Dewey as a Moral Philosopher." In *Some Interpretations of John Dewey's Educational Philosophy*. Bulletin of Florida Southern College, vol. 67, pp. 25-27. Lakeland: Florida Southern College, 1951.

Macintosh, Douglas Clyde, and Wieman, Henry Nelson. "Mr. Wieman and Mr. Macintosh 'Converse' with Mr. Dewey." *Christian Century* 50 (1933): 299-302. [In response to Dewey's "A God or The God?" Ibid.: 193-96. Rejoinder by Dewey, "Dr. Dewey Replies." Ibid.: 394-95.]

MacIver, D. A. "Philosophy, Education, Archetypes, and Dewey." *Educational Philosophy and Theory* 4 (March 1972): 1-9.

Mack, Robert Donald. *THE APPEAL TO IMMEDIATE EXPERIENCE: PHILOSOPHIC METHOD IN BRADLEY, WHITEHEAD, AND DEWEY*. New York: King's Crown Press, 1945. [Reprinted. Freeport, N.Y.: Books for Libraries Press, 1968.]

Mackay, Donald Sage. "What Does Mr. Dewey Mean by an 'Indeterminate Situation'?" *Journal of Philosophy* 39 (1942): 141-48. [Replies by Dewey, "Inquiry and Indeterminateness of Situations." Ibid.: 290-96, and Arthur Fisher Bentley, "As through a Glass Darkly." Ibid.: 432-39. Comment by Mackay, "Outcome of Inquiry, as 'End-Result' or as 'End-In-View'?" Ibid.: 547-50.]

McKenney, John L. "Dewey and Russell: Fraternal Twins in Philosophy." *Educational Theory* 9 (1959): 24-30.

McKenzie, William Robert. "Toward Unity of Thought and Action." Introduction to *The Early Works of John Dewey, 1892-1898*, edited by Jo Ann Boydston, vol. 5, pp. xiii-xx.

McKeon, Richard. "The Problematic Analysis of Freedom and History." In his *FREEDOM AND HISTORY*, pp. 69-82. New York: Noonday Press, 1952.

---. *THOUGHT, ACTION AND PASSION*. Chicago: University of Chicago Press, 1954. [Dewey, passim.]

---. "The Ethics of International Influence." *Ethics* 70 (1960): 187-203.

Mackintosh, William Davis. Letter on Dewey's *PSYCHOLOGY OF NUMBER*. *Nation*, 9 January 1896, pp. 32-33.

McManis, John T. *ELLA FLAGG YOUNG AND A HALF CENTURY OF THE CHICAGO PUBLIC SCHOOLS*. Chicago: A. C. McClurg and Co., 1916. [Dewey, pp. 101-22.]

McMurray, Foster. "The Problem of Verification in Formal School Learning." In *Essays for John Dewey's Ninetieth Birthday*, edited by Kenneth D. Benne and William O. Stanley, pp. 47-58.

---. "Pragmatism in Music Education." In *BASIC CONCEPTS IN MUSIC EDUCATION*, edited by Nelson B. Henry, pp. 30-61. Chicago: National Society for the Study of Education, 1958.

---. "The Present Status of Pragmatism in Education." *School and Society* 87 (1959): 14-17. [Reprinted in *EDUCATIONAL THEORY TODAY*, edited by William W. Brickman and Stanley Lehrer, pp. 12-15. New York:

Society for the Advancement of Education, 1959.]

---. "Dewey's Lectures. An Essay Review." *Educational Forum* 32 (1968): 227-32.

McMurry, Charles Alexander. "The Culture Epochs." *Public School Journal* 15 (1896): 279-99. [Discussion of Dewey's "Interpretation of the Culture-Epoch Theory." Ibid.: 233-36 (*Early Works of John Dewey* 5: 247-53.)]

McNutt, Walter Scott. "Instrumentalism at Its Best." *Education* 46 (1925): 149-53.

MacPartland, John. "Aristotle and the Spectator Theory of Knowledge." *Journal of Philosophy* 42 (1945): 291-93.

MacPherson, Jessie. "Ends of Education." *Food for Thought* 14 (1954): 3-7.

McWilliams, James Aloysius. "Dewey's Esthetic Experience as a Substitute for Religion." *Modern Schoolman* 15 (1937): 9-13.

---. "Education for Progress." *Modern Schoolman* 19 (1942): 27-29.

---. "John Dewey's Educational Philosophy." *Modern Schoolman* 22 (1945): 144-54.

---. "John Dewey, Nonagenarian." *America* 82 (1949): 39-40.

Maddaloni, Arnold. "Two Liberalisms: A Study in Contrasts." *Educational Theory* 2 (1952): 177-85.

Mal'Kova, Z. "Pragmatism and Pedagogy." *Soviet Education* 5 (1963): 42-45.

Manasse, Ernst Moritz. "Moral Principles and Alternatives in Max Weber and John Dewey." *Journal of Philosophy* 41 (1944): 29-48, 57-68.

Mann, Jesse A. "The Role of the Tentative in the Philosophy of John Dewey." In *PROCEEDINGS OF THE AMERICAN CATHOLIC PHILOSOPHICAL ASSOCIATION*, vol. 42, pp. 202-8. Washington, D.C.: Catholic University of America, 1968.

---, and Kreyche, Gerald F., eds. *REFLECTIONS ON MAN: READINGS IN PHILOSOPHICAL PSYCHOLOGY FROM CLASSICAL PHILOSOPHY TO EXISTENTIALISM*. New York: Harcourt, Brace and World, 1966. [Dewey, passim.]

Manny, Frank Addison. "John Dewey." *Seven Arts Magazine* 2 (1917): 214-28.

Manzella, David B. "John Dewey and the Materialism of Art Education." *Art Journal* 20 (1960): 19-21.

March, John Lewis. "The Ichabod Spencer Lectures, 1914." *Union Alumni Monthly* 3 (1914): 309-26.

Marie Theresa. "Two Moderns and Aquinas." *Catholic Education Review* 43 (1945): 159-69.

Maritain, Jacques. *MORAL PHILOSOPHY*. New York: Charles Scribner's Sons, 1964. [Dewey, pp. 396-419, and passim.]

Marsden, Malcolm M. "General Education: Compromise between Transcendentalism and Pragmatism." *Journal of General Education* 8 (1953): 228-39.

Martin, Clyde V. "The Metaphysical Development of John Dewey." *Educational Theory* 8 (1958): 55-58. [Replies by Dorothy June Newbury, "A Note on 'The Metaphysical Development of John Dewey'." Ibid.: 186-87, and Marcus Brown, "Another Note on 'The Metaphysical Development of John Dewey'." Ibid.: 284-85.]

Martland, Thomas Rodolphe. *THE METAPHYSICS OF WILLIAM JAMES AND JOHN DEWEY: PROCESS AND STRUCTURE IN PHILOSOPHY AND RELIGION*. New York: Philosophical Library, 1963.

---. "Dewey's Rejection and Acceptance of a Metaphysic." *Monist* 48 (1964): 382-91.

Martorella, Peter H. "Reflective Thinking and the American Culture." *Peabody Journal of Education* 45 (1967): 87-90.

Marvin, Francis Sydney. "Science and Society." *Nature* [London], 5 March 1932, pp. 329-31.

Mason, Robert Emmett. "Implications of Dewey's Culture Theory for Pedagogy." *School and Society* 87 (1959): 391-95. [Reprinted in *JOHN DEWEY: MASTER EDUCATOR*, edited by William W. Brickman and Stanley Lehrer, 2d ed., pp. 115-25.

Mathur, Dinesh Chandra. "Religious Dimension of Dewey's Philosophy (An Analysis of His Philosophy of Art)." *Philosophical Quarterly* [India] 35 (1962-63): 107-11.

---. "A Note on the Concept of 'Consummatory Experience' in Dewey's Aesthetics." *Journal of Philosophy* 63 (1966): 225-31.

---. *NATURALISTIC PHILOSOPHIES OF EXPERIENCE, Studies in James, Dewey and Farber against the Background of Husserl's Phenomenology*. St. Louis: Warren H. Green, 1971.

Maurer, Armand A. "Pragmatism." In *RECENT PHILOSOPHY: HEGEL TO THE PRESENT*, by Etienne Gilson, Thomas Langan, and Armand Maurer, pp. 649-63. New York: Random House, 1966.

Mayer, Frederick. *A HISTORY OF MODERN PHILOSOPHY*. New York: American Book Co., 1951. [Dewey, pp. 535-50.]

---. *A HISTORY OF AMERICAN THOUGHT: AN INTRODUCTION*. Dubuque, Iowa: William C. Brown Co., 1951. [Dewey, pp. 303-9, and passim.]

---. *A HISTORY OF EDUCATIONAL THOUGHT*. Columbus, Ohio: Charles E. Merrill, 1966. [Dewey, pp. 382-94.]

---. *THE GREAT TEACHERS*. New York: Citadel Press, 1967. [Dewey, pp. 309-26.]

Mayer, Martin. *THE SCHOOLS*. New York: Harper and Brothers, 1961. [Dewey, pp. 68-70, and passim.]

Mayer, Milton, and Adler, Mortimer. *THE REVOLUTION IN EDUCATION*. Chicago: University of Chicago Press, 1958. [Dewey, passim.]

Mayer, Rochelle, and Kohlberg, Lawrence. "Development as the Aim of Education." *Harvard Educational Review* 42 (1972): 449-96.

Mayeroff, Milton. "The Nature of Propositions in John Dewey's 'Logic'." *Journal of Philosophy* 47 (1950): 353-59. [Reply to May Brodbeck, "The New Rationalism: Dewey's Theory of Induction." Ibid. 46 (1949): 780-91.]

---. "A Neglected Aspect of Experience in Dewey's Philosophy." *Journal of Philosophy* 60 (1963): 146-53.

---. "Some Developments in Dewey's Concept of the Unification of the Self." *Personalist* 45 (1964): 15-26.

Mayhew, Katherine Camp, and Edwards, Anna Camp. *THE DEWEY SCHOOL: THE LABORATORY SCHOOL OF THE UNIVERSITY OF CHICAGO 1896-1903*. New York: D. Appleton-Century Co., 1936. [Reprinted, New York: Atherton Press, 1965.]

MD. "Democracy's Schoolmaster." *MD* 3 (1959): 170-74.

Mead, George Herbert. "Suggestions toward a Theory of the Philosophical Disciplines." *Philosophical Review* 9 (1900): 1-17. [Reply to Dewey's "The Reflex Arc Concept in Psychology." *Psychological Review* 3 (1896): 357-70 (*Early Works of John Dewey* 5: 96-109.)]

---. "The Philosophies of Royce, James and Dewey in Their American Setting." *International Journal of Ethics* 40 (1930): 211-31. [Reprinted in *JOHN DEWEY: THE MAN AND HIS PHILOSOPHY*. Addresses Delivered in New York in Celebration of His Seventieth Birthday, pp. 75-105. Cambridge: Harvard University Press, 1930.]

---. "The Philosophy of John Dewey." *International Journal of Ethics* 46 (1935): 64-81.

---. *MOVEMENTS OF THOUGHT IN THE NINETEENTH CENTURY*. Edited by Merritt Hadden Moore. Chicago: University of Chicago Press, 1936. [Dewey, passim.]

---. *THE PHILOSOPHY OF THE ACT*. Edited by Charles W. Morris. Chicago: University of Chicago Press, 1938. [Dewey, passim.]

---. *THE SOCIAL PSYCHOLOGY OF GEORGE HERBERT MEAD*. Edited with an introd. by Anselm Strauss. Chicago: University of Chicago Press, Phoenix Books, 1956. [See introd. for Dewey. Also passim.]

---. *SELECTED WRITINGS*. Edited by Andrew J. Reck. New York: Bobbs-Merrill Co., 1964. [Dewey, pp. 36-42, 386-91, and passim.]

Meckler, Lester. "Normative and Descriptive Expressions." *Journal of Philosophy* 50 (1953): 577-83. [See Herbert Fingarette, "How Normativeness Can Be Cognitive but not Descriptive in Dewey's Theory of Valuation." Ibid. 48 (1951): 625-35.]

Meehan, Francis X. "Absolute and Relative in the Moral Order." In *PROCEEDINGS OF THE AMERICAN CATHOLIC PHILOSOPHICAL ASSOCIATION*, vol. 22, pp. 53-80. Washington, D.C.: Catholic University of America, 1947.

Meenan, Daniel F. X. "John Dewey's Theory of Valuation." *Modern Schoolman* 30 (1953): 187-201.

Megel, Carl J. "The President's Page." *American Teacher Magazine* 47 (1963): 3. [Dewey and teacher unionism.]

Mehl, Bernard. "History of Education." *Review of Educational Research* 31 (1961): 7-19. [Dewey, passim.]

Meiklejohn, Alexander. "The Pragmatic Episode--A Study of John Dewey." In his *EDUCATION BETWEEN TWO WORLDS*, pp. 123-95. New York: Harper and Brothers, 1942. [Reprinted as "Knowledge and Intelligence," in *DEWEY ON EDUCATION: APPRAISALS*, edited by Reginald D. Archambault, pp. 75-95.]

---. "A Reply to John Dewey." *Fortune*, January 1945, pp. 207-8, 210, 212, 214, 217, 219. [In reply to Dewey's "Challenge to Liberal Thought." Ibid., August 1944, pp. 155-57, 180, 184, 186, 188, 190. Rejoinder by Dewey, ibid., March 1945, pp. 10, 14. Further reply by Meiklejohn, ibid., p. 14, and letter from Dewey, ibid., p. 14.]

---. Statement about Dewey. In "Pure Science and Gross Experience," by Ernest Nagel. *New Republic*, 17 October 1949, p. 22.

Melvin, A. Gordon. *THE TECHNIQUE OF PROGRESSIVE TEACHING*. New York: John Day Co., 1932. [Dewey, passim.]

Melvin, Georgiana. "The Social Philosophy underlying Dewey's Theory of Art." In *MILLS COLLEGE FACULTY STUDIES*, no. 1, pp. 124-36. Oakland, Cal.: Eucalyptus Press, 1937.

Mercieca, Charles. "Philosophic Approaches in an Educational Method." *Indian Sociological Bulletin* 5 (1968): 133-45.

Meriam, Junius Lathrop. "John Dewey in History." *School and Society* 87 (1959): 376-78. [Reprinted in *JOHN DEWEY: MASTER EDUCATOR*, edited by William W. Brickman and Stanley Lehrer, 2d ed., pp. 17-24.]

Mesthene, Emmanuel G. "The Role of Language in the Philosophy of John Dewey." *Philosophy and Phenomenological Research* 19 (1959): 511-17.

---. "Dewey." In his *HOW LANGUAGE MAKES US KNOW: SOME VIEWS ABOUT THE NATURE OF INTELLIGIBILITY*, pp. 47-81. Hague: Martinus Nijhoff, 1964. [Doctoral dissertation, Columbia University, 1964, with title, "Some Views about the Nature of Intelligibility."]

Metz, Joseph G. "Democracy and the Scientific Method in the Philosophy of John Dewey." *Review of Politics* [University of Notre Dame] 31 (1969): 242-62.

Meyer, Adolphe E. *JOHN DEWEY AND MODERN EDUCATION, AND OTHER ESSAYS*. New York: Avon Press, 1931. [Dewey, pp. 3-17.]

---. "John Dewey at Ninety." *Tomorrow* 9 (1949): 43-47.

---. *AN EDUCATIONAL HISTORY OF THE AMERICAN PEOPLE*. 2d ed. New York: McGraw-Hill Book Co., 1967. [Dewey, pp. 258-71, 314-20, 359-60.]

Meyer, Agnes. "John Dewey, Great American Liberal, Denounces Russian Dictatorship." *Washington Post*, 19 December 1937. [Interview.] [Reprinted in *International Conciliation*, no. 337 (1938): 53-60.]

---. *The Quest of the Good*. John Dewey Memorial Lecture, no. 2. Bennington, Vt.: Bennington College, 1954.

Michael, Franz Henry, and Taylor, George Edward. *THE FAR EAST IN THE MODERN WORLD*. Rev. ed. New York: Henry Holt and Co., 1964. [Dewey's visit to China, pp. 229, 232, 234-35, 715.]

Michel, Virgil. "Some Thoughts on Professor Dewey."
New Scholasticism 2 (1928): 327-41.

Miller, Clarence. "Moore, Dewey, and the Problem of
the Given." *Modern Schoolman* 39 (1962): 379-82.

Miller, Clyde R., ed. "Some Popular Appraisals of John
Dewey." *Teachers College Record* 31 (1929): 207-38.

Miller, Henry. "Transaction: Dewey's Last Contribution
to the Theory of Learning." *Educational Theory* 13
(1963): 13-28.

---. "John Dewey on Urban Education: An Extrapola-
tion." *Teachers College Record* 69 (1968): 771-83.

Mills, C. Wright. *SOCIOLOGY AND PRAGMATISM: THE HIGHER
LEARNING IN AMERICA*. New York: Paine-Whitman, 1964.
[Dewey, pp. 279-463, and passim.]

Milmed, Bella Kussy. "Dewey's Treatment of Causality."
Journal of Philosophy 54 (1957): 5-19.

Minogue, William John Desmond. "John Dewey--An Appreciation." *National Education* [New Zealand] 34
(1952): 198-99.

Misner, Paul James. "What Did Dewey Do for Education?"
National Parent-Teacher 54 (December 1959): 9.

Mitchell, Edwin Thomas. "Dewey's Theory of Valuation."
Ethics 55 (1945): 287-97.

---. "Values, Valuing, and Evaluation." In *VALUE: A
COOPERATIVE INQUIRY*, edited by Ray Lepley, pp. 190-
210.

---; Lee, Harold; and Rice, Philip. "Criticisms by
Mitchell; Rejoinders by Lee and Rice." In *VALUE: A
COOPERATIVE INQUIRY*, edited by Ray Lepley, pp. 400-
414.

Mitchell, Frank W. "Submission to the Commission on
Education, June 1961." New Zealand Commission on
Education, 1960-62. [Dewey, passim.]

Mitchell, Lucy Sprague. Statement on Dewey. In "The
Conquest of Dualism," by Wilmon H. Sheldon. *New*

Republic, 17 October 1949, p. 30.

---. *TWO LIVES: THE STORY OF WESLEY CLAIR MITCHELL AND MYSELF*. New York: Simon and Schuster, 1953. [John and Alice Dewey, passim.]

Moehlman, Arthur B. "John Dewey: Master Teacher." *Nation's Schools* 38 (November 1946): 19.

Molinaro, Leo. "Closing Remarks." In *Essays for John Dewey's Ninetieth Birthday*, edited by Kenneth D. Benne and William O. Stanley, pp. 88-92.

Monlin, Chiang. *TIDES FROM THE WEST*. New Haven: Yale University Press, 1947. [Dewey, passim.]

Montague, William Pepperell. *THE WAYS OF KNOWING, OR THE METHODS OF PHILOSOPHY*. London: George Allen and Unwin, 1925. [Dewey, passim.]

---. "Citation from the Committee." In *JOHN DEWEY AT NINETY*, edited by Harry W. Laidler, pp. 30-31. [Presented by Mr. Montague for the Committee: William Heard Kilpatrick, Jerome Nathanson, Frederick Redefer, Irwin Edman, Harry W. Laidler, and Harold Taylor.]

Montenegro, Ernesto. "John Dewey's Ideas." *Américas* 4 (1952): 32-33.

Montgomery, Ray. "John Dewey and the Egg-in-the-Bottle." *Phi Delta Kappan* 34 (1952): 95-97, 100.

---. "John Dewey and the Double-Edged Danger." *Phi Delta Kappan* 34 (1953): 114-18.

---. "John Dewey and the Broken Circuit." *Phi Delta Kappan* 34 (1953): 201-3.

---. "John Dewey and the Continuity of Growth." *Phi Delta Kappan* 34 (1953): 215-18.

---. "John Dewey and the Death Valley Daze." *Phi Delta Kappan* 34 (1953): 273-78.

---. "John Dewey and the Oyster's Pain." *Phi Delta Kappan* 34 (1953): 311-15.

---. "John Dewey and the Seven-Eyed Teacher." *Phi*

Delta Kappan 34 (1953): 424-30.

---. "John Dewey and the Blunted Instrument." *Phi Delta Kappan* 36 (1955): 177-80.

Moore, Addison Webster. "'Anti-Pragmatisme'." *Journal of Philosophy* 6 (1909): 291-95.

---. "Pragmatism and Solipsism." *Journal of Philosophy* 6 (1909): 378-83.

---. *PRAGMATISM AND ITS CRITICS*. Chicago: University of Chicago Press, 1910. [Dewey, passim.]

Moore, Charles A., ed. *ESSAYS IN EAST-WEST PHILOSOPHY: AN ATTEMPT AT WORLD PHILOSOPHICAL SYNTHESIS*. Honolulu: University of Hawaii Press, 1951. [Papers presented at the second East-West Philosophers' Conference, University of Hawaii, June-July 1949.] [Dewey, passim.]

---, ed. *PHILOSOPHY AND CULTURE--EAST AND WEST*. Honolulu: University of Hawaii Press, 1962. [Dewey, pp. 342-61, 762-69, and passim.]

Moore, Edward Carter. *AMERICAN PRAGMATISM: PEIRCE, JAMES, AND DEWEY*. New York: Columbia University Press, 1961.

Moore, Ernest Carroll. "John Dewey's Contribution to Educational Theory." *School and Society* 31 (1930): 37-47. [Reprinted in *California Quarterly of Secondary Education* 5 (1930): 113-26, with the title "John Dewey and His Educational Philosophy"; and in *JOHN DEWEY, THE MAN AND HIS PHILOSOPHY*. Addresses Delivered in New York in Celebration of His Seventieth Birthday, pp. 7-36. Cambridge: Harvard University Press, 1930.]

---. "John Dewey." In *FAMOUS AMERICANS*, edited by Warren Huff and Edna Lenore Webb Huff, pp. 153-65. 2d ser. Los Angeles: Charles Webb and Co., 1941.

Moore, Harold. "Dewey and the Philosophy of Science." *Man and World* 5 (1972): 158-68.

Moore, Willis. "Indoctrination as a Normative Conception." *Studies in Philosophy and Education* 4

(1966): 396-403.

More, Paul Elmer. "Religion and Social Discontent."
In *CHRISTIANITY AND PROBLEMS OF TO-DAY*, pp. 75-106.
The William Bross Lectures. New York: Charles
Scribner's Sons, 1922. [Reprinted in his *ON BEING
HUMAN*, pp. 117-43. Princeton: Princeton University
Press, 1936.]

Morgan, Joy Elmer. "Presentation of Life Membership."
Journal of the National Education Association 18
(1929): 281.

---. "John Dewey the Humanist." *Journal of the National Education Association* 18 (1929): 286.

---. "John Dewey's Worldwide Influence." *Journal of
the National Education Association* 38 (1949): 647.

---. "Teachers and Students of America Pay Tribute."
In *JOHN DEWEY AT NINETY*, edited by Harry W. Laidler,
pp. 24-25.

Morison, Elting E., ed. *THE AMERICAN STYLE: ESSAYS IN
VALUE AND PERFORMANCE*. Report on the Dedham Conference of 23-27 May 1957. New York: Harper and Brothers, 1958. [Dewey, passim.]

Morris, Bertram. "'The Public' as Mediator between
Society and Community in Dewey's Political Philosophy." *University of Colorado Studies*, Series in
Philosophy, no. 2, pp. 99-107. Boulder: University
of Colorado Press, 1961.

---. *INSTITUTIONS OF INTELLIGENCE*. Studies in Educa-
tional Theory of the John Dewey Society, no. 6.
Columbus: Ohio State University Press, 1969.
[Dewey, passim.]

---. "Dewey's Theory of Art." In *GUIDE TO THE WORKS
OF JOHN DEWEY*, edited by Jo Ann Boydston, pp. 156-82.

---. "Dewey's Aesthetics: The Tragic Encounter with
Nature." *Journal of Aesthetics and Art Criticism* 30
(1971): 189-96.

Morris, Charles W. "Dewey's Doctrine of Experience as
Adjectival." In his *SIX THEORIES OF MIND*, pp.

290-330. Chicago: University of Chicago Press, 1932. [Also passim.]

---. *Pragmatism and the Crisis of Democracy*. Public Policy Pamphlet no. 12. Chicago: University of Chicago Press, 1934.

---. "Pragmatism and Metaphysics." *Philosophical Review* 43 (1934): 549-64.

---. "Peirce, Mead, and Pragmatism." *Philosophical Review* 47 (1938): 109-27.

---. "General Education and the Unity of Science Movement." In *John Dewey and the Promise of America*, Progressive Education Booklet, no. 14, pp. 26-40. Columbus, Ohio: Progressive Education Association, 1939.

---. Letter in *Journal of Philosophy* 43 (1946): 196. [In reply to Dewey's "Peirce's Theory of Linguistic Signs, Thought and Meaning." Ibid.: 85-95. Dewey's response, ibid.: 280. Rejoinder by Morris, ibid.: 363-64.]

---. *SIGNS, LANGUAGE AND BEHAVIOR*. New York: Prentice-Hall, 1946. [Dewey, passim.]

---. "Axiology as the Science of Preferential Behavior." In *VALUE: A COOPERATIVE INQUIRY*, edited by Ray Lepley, pp. 211-22.

---. *THE PRAGMATIC MOVEMENT IN AMERICAN PHILOSOPHY*. New York: George Braziller, 1970. [Dewey, passim.]

---; Ayres, C. E.; and Hahn, Lewis. "Criticisms by Morris; Rejoinders by Ayres and Hahn." In *VALUE: A COOPERATIVE INQUIRY*, edited by Ray Lepley, pp. 415-23.

Morris, Clarence, ed. *THE GREAT LEGAL PHILOSOPHERS: SELECTED READINGS IN JURISPRUDENCE*. Philadelphia: University of Pennsylvania Press, 1959. [Dewey, pp. 495-510.]

---. "The Political Philosophy of Jacques Maritain." *Daedalus* 88 (1959): 700-711. [Dewey, passim.]

Morris, Lloyd. *POSTSCRIPT TO YESTERDAY. AMERICA:*

THE LAST FIFTY YEARS. New York: Random House, 1947. [Dewey, pp. 368-78.]

Morrison, Charles Clayton. "The New Modernism." *Christian Century* 53 (1936): 351-53.

---. "A Communication." *Christian Century* 69 (1952): 854.

---. "The Past Foreshadows the Future." *Christian Century* 75 (1958): 271-74.

Morrow, Glenn R. "A Discussion of the Theory of International Relations." *Journal of Philosophy* 42 (1945): 477-97. [A discussion by several philosophers of two paragraphs of Dewey's Introduction to Jane Addams, *PEACE AND BREAD IN TIME OF WAR.* New York: King's Crown Press, 1945.] [Morrow, pp. 491-93. Other philosophers: E. A. Burtt, Joseph P. Chamberlain, William Ernest Hocking, Sidney Hook, Arthur O. Lovejoy, Jerome Nathanson, and Thomas V. Smith.]

Mosier, Richard David. "Education as Experience." *Progressive Education* 29 (1952): 200-203.

---. *THE AMERICAN TEMPER: PATTERNS OF OUR INTELLECTUAL HERITAGE.* Berkeley and Los Angeles: University of California Press, 1952. [Dewey, pp. 253, 280-81.]

Mowat, Alex S. "How Progressive are the 'Progressives'?" *University of Toronto Quarterly* 24 (1954): 26-33.

Muelder, Walter George, and Sears, Laurence, eds. *THE DEVELOPMENT OF AMERICAN PHILOSOPHY: A BOOK OF READINGS.* Boston: Houghton Mifflin Co., 1940. [Dewey, pp. 315-16, and passim.] [Rev. ed. 1960. Dewey, pp. 343, 344, 346-47.]

Mueller, Gustav Emil. "John Dewey's Aesthetics." In his *ORIGINS AND DIMENSIONS OF PHILOSOPHY: SOME CORRELATIONS,* pp. 572-85. New York: Pageant Press, 1965.

Mullahy, Patrick. *PSYCHOANALYSIS AND INTERPERSONAL PSYCHIATRY: The Contributions of Henry Stack Sullivan.* New York: Science House, 1970. [Appendix: "Experience and Conduct: The Ethical Philosophy of John Dewey."]

Muller, Herbert Joseph. *SCIENCE AND CRITICISM: THE HUMANISTIC TRADITION IN CONTEMPORARY THOUGHT*. New Haven: Yale University Press, 1943. [Dewey, passim.]

Mullins, James. "The Problem of the Individual in the Philosophies of Dewey and Buber." *Educational Theory* 17 (1967): 76-82.

Mumford, Lewis. "The Pragmatic Acquiescence: A Reply." *New Republic*, 19 January 1927, pp. 250-51. [In response to Dewey's "The Pragmatic Acquiescence." Ibid., 5 January 1927, pp. 186-89. Both articles reprinted, with Mumford's statement on pragmatism from *THE GOLDEN DAY*, in *PRAGMATISM AND AMERICAN CULTURE*, edited by Gail Kennedy, pp. 36-57.]

---. "A Modern Synthesis." *Saturday Review of Literature*, 12 April 1930, pp. 920-21. [See Charles Beard, "Toward Civilization." Ibid., 5 April 1930, pp. 894-95. Response to Mumford, "More on the Same," by Joseph Ratner. Ibid., 12 July 1930, p. 1194.]

Munitz, Milton K., ed. *A MODERN INTRODUCTION TO ETHICS*. Glencoe, Ill.: Free Press, 1958. [Dewey, passim.]

Munk, Arthur W. "John Dewey in Retrospect." *Christian Century* 76 (1959): 1113-14.

Münsterberg, Hugo. "The International Congress of Arts and Science." *Science* n.s. 18 (1903): 559-63. [Reply to Dewey's letter, "The St. Louis Congress of Arts and Sciences." Ibid.: 275-78. Rejoinder by Dewey, ibid.: 665. Reply by Münsterberg, ibid.: 788.]

Murphy, Arthur E. "Objective Relativism in Dewey and Whitehead." *Philosophical Review* 36 (1927): 121-44.

---. "Dewey's Epistemology and Metaphysics." In *THE PHILOSOPHY OF JOHN DEWEY*, edited by Paul Schilpp, pp. 193-226.

---. "John Dewey's Philosophy of Religion." In *The Educational Frontier*, Progressive Education Association Booklet, no. 13, pp. 26-41. Columbus, Ohio: Progressive Education Association, 1939.

---. "Dewey's Theory of the Nature and Function of

Philosophy." In *THE PHILOSOPHER OF THE COMMON MAN*, edited by Sidney Ratner, pp. 33-35.

---. *THE USES OF REASON*. New York: Macmillan Co., 1943. [Dewey, pp. 86-92.]

---. "John Dewey and American Liberalism." *Journal of Philosophy* 57 (1960): 420-36. [Comments by Gail Kennedy and John Allan Irving. Ibid.: 436-50.] [Murphy's article reprinted in *REASON AND THE COMMON GOOD*, edited by William H. Hay, Marcus Singer, and Arthur E. Murphy, pp. 247-61. Englewood Cliffs, N.J.: Prentice-Hall, 1963.]

Murphy, Gardner. "Some Reflections on John Dewey's Psychology." In *University of Colorado Studies*, Series in Philosophy, no. 2, pp. 26-34. Boulder: University of Colorado Press, 1961.

---. *FREEING INTELLIGENCE THROUGH TEACHING*. John Dewey Society Lectureship Series, no. 4. New York: Harper and Brothers, 1961.

Murphy, Jay Wesley. "John Dewey--A Philosophy of Law for Democracy." *Vanderbilt Law Review* 14 (1960): 291-316.

Myers, Caroline E. "Should Teachers' Organizations Affiliate with the American Federation of Labor?" *School and Society* 10 (1919): 594-97.

Myers, Francis M. *THE WARFARE OF DEMOCRATIC IDEALS*. Yellow Springs, Ohio: Antioch Press, 1956. [Dewey, passim.]

---. "Comments on George Axtelle's 'John Dewey's Concept of the Religious'." *Religious Humanism* 1 (1967): 69-70.

Nagano, Yoshio. "John Dewey's Influence in Japan." *Education in Japan: Journal for Overseas* 1 (1966): 66-74.

Nagel, Ernest. "Can Logic Be Divorced from Ontology?" *Journal of Philosophy* 26 (1929): 705-12. [In response to Dewey's "The Sphere of Application of the Excluded Middle." Ibid.: 701-5. Reply by Dewey, "The Applicability of Logic to Existence." Ibid. 27 (1930): 174-79.]

---. "Dewey's Reconstruction of Logical Theory." In
    THE PHILOSOPHER OF THE COMMON MAN, edited by Sidney
    Ratner, pp. 56-86.

---. "Pure Science and Gross Experience." *New Repub-
    lic*, 17 October 1949, pp. 20-23.

---. "Dewey's Theory of Natural Science." In *JOHN
    DEWEY: PHILOSOPHER OF SCIENCE AND FREEDOM*, edited by
    Sidney Hook, pp. 231-48.

---. "On the Method of Verstehen as the Sole Method of
    Philosophy." *Journal of Philosophy* 50 (1953): 154-57.

---. *SOVEREIGN REASON AND OTHER STUDIES IN THE PHILOS-
    OPHY OF SCIENCE*. Glencoe, Ill.: Free Press, 1954.
    [Dewey, pp. 101-17, 118-40, 141-49.]

---. *LOGIC WITHOUT METAPHYSICS*. Glencoe, Ill.: Free
    Press, 1956. [Dewey, passim.]

---. *LIBERALISM AND INTELLIGENCE*. John Dewey Memorial
    Lecture no. 4. Bennington, Vt.: Bennington College,
    1957.

---. "Philosophy of Science and Educational Theory."
    Studies in Philosophy and Education 7 (1969): 5-27.
    [Dewey, pp. 21-23.]

---; Hook, Sidney; and Dewey, John. "Are Naturalists
    Materialists?" *Journal of Philosophy* 42 (1945):
    515-30. [In reply to "A Critique of Naturalism,"
    by Wilmon Henry Sheldon. Ibid.: 253-70.]

Nahem, Joseph. "What Is 'Progressive Education'?"
    Worker, 30 September 1951, p. 8.

Nakosteen, Mehdi. *A THREE-FOLD PHILOSOPHY OF EDUCATION*.
    Denver: Charles Mapes, 1943. [Dewey, pp. 41-53,
    279-88.]

Nash, J. V. "The Ethics of John Dewey." *Open Court* 38
    (1924): 527-38.

Nash, Paul. "The Strange Death of Progressive Educa-
    tion." *Educational Theory* 14 (1964): 65-75, 82.

Naslund, Robert A. "The Impact of the Power Age on the
    Community-School Concept." *National Society For The*

Study of Education Fifty-Second Yearbook, Part 2
(1953): 251-64. [Dewey, pp. 257-59.]

Natanson, Maurice. *THE SOCIAL DYNAMICS OF GEORGE H.
MEAD.* Introduction by Horace M. Kallen. Washington,
D.C.: Public Affairs Press, 1956. [Dewey, passim.]

Nathanson, Jerome. "John Dewey: Democracy as Reconstruction." In his *FORERUNNERS OF FREEDOM: THE RE-
CONSTRUCTION OF THE AMERICAN SPIRIT*, pp. 116-54.
Washington, D.C.: American Council on Public Affairs, 1941.

---. "A Discussion of the Theory of International Relations." *Journal of Philosophy* 42 (1945): 477-97.
[A discussion by several philosophers of two paragraphs of Dewey's Introduction to Jane Addams, *PEACE
AND BREAD IN TIME OF WAR.* New York: King's Crown
Press, 1945.] [Nathanson, pp. 495-97. Other philosophers: E. A. Burtt, Joseph P. Chamberlain, William Ernest Hocking, Sidney Hook, Arthur O. Lovejoy,
Glenn R. Morrow, and Thomas V. Smith.]

---. "John Dewey: American Radical." *Nation*, 22 October 1949, pp. 392-94.

---. *JOHN DEWEY: THE RECONSTRUCTION OF THE DEMOCRATIC
LIFE.* Twentieth Century Library Series, edited by Hiram Hayden. New York: Charles Scribner's Sons, 1951.

---. "John Dewey: Some Reflections." *Progressive Education* 30 (1952): 13-15.

---. "John Dewey." In *GREAT AMERICAN LIBERALS*, edited
by Gabriel R. Mason, pp. 143-53. Boston: Starr King
Press, 1956.

Nation. "Professor Dewey's Advocacy of a Broad Voca-
tionism--Mr. Wirt's Schools at Gary, Indiana."
Nation, 9 September 1915, p. 326.

Naumburg, Margaret. "A Challenge to John Dewey."
Survey, 15 September 1928, pp. 598-600.

---. "The Crux of Progressive Education." *New Republic*, 25 June 1930, pp. 145-46.

---. *THE CHILD AND THE WORLD: DIALOGUES IN MODERN EDU-
CATION.* New York: Harcourt, Brace and Co., 1928.

[Dewey, passim.]

Neff, Frederick C. "Our Debt to John Dewey." *California Journal of Secondary Education* 24 (1949): 466-71.

---. "The Status of John Dewey in American Educational Thought: A Current Appraisal." University of Leeds, Institute of Education, *Researches and Studies* no. 17 (1958): 16-33. [Also printed in *Proceedings of the 14th Annual Meeting of the Philosophy of Education Society*, 1958, pp. 58-68.]

---. "John Dewey and the Luce Ends of Education." *Phi Delta Kappan* 40 (1958): 130-31.

---. *PHILOSOPHY AND AMERICAN EDUCATION.* New York: Center for Applied Research in Education, 1966. [Dewey, passim.]

---. *THE DEWEY TRADITION AND THE AMERICAN SCENE.* Boyd H. Bode Memorial Lecture 1965. Columbus: College of Education, Ohio State University, 1967.

Neill, Thomas P. "Democracy's Intellectual Fifth Column." *Catholic World* 155 (1942): 151-55.

---. "Dewey: Teachers as Social Engineers." In his *MAKERS OF THE MODERN MIND*, 2d enl. ed., pp. 357-84. Milwaukee: Bruce Publishing Co., 1958.

---. "Dewey's Ambivalent Attitude toward History." In *JOHN DEWEY: HIS THOUGHT AND INFLUENCE*, edited by John Blewett, pp. 145-60.

Nelson, Alvin F. "On Life and Mind in Dewey's System." *Darshana International* 7 (July 1967): 1-11.

Neumann, Henry. *EDUCATION FOR MORAL GROWTH.* New York: D. Appleton and Co., 1924. [Dewey, passim.]

---. "Two Letters on Ethical Culture and Pragmatism." *American Review* 3 (1925): 252-53. [Response to Max Otto's review of his *EDUCATION FOR MORAL GROWTH*. Ibid. 2 (1924): 666-75. Reply by Otto, ibid. 3 (1925): 253-54.]

Newbury, Dorothy June. "A Search for the Meaning of

Discipline in John Dewey's Theory of Growth." *Educational Theory* 6 (1956): 236-45.

---. "A Theory of Discipline Derived from Dewey's Theory of Inquiry." *Educational Theory* 7 (1957): 102-11, 159.

---. "A Note on 'The Metaphysical Development of John Dewey'." *Educational Theory* 8 (1958): 186-87. [See Clyde V. Martin, ibid.: 55-58.]

Newhall, David. "U. V. M.'s Favorite Alumni John Dewey Feted by Students, Faculty." [University of] *Vermont Cynic*, 2 November 1949. [Interview with Dewey.]

New Leader. "Salute to John Dewey." [Special Section Commemorating John Dewey's Ninetieth Birthday.] *New Leader*, 22 October 1949. [Greetings from James B. Conant, Oliver Franks, Lady Allen of Hurtwood, C. E. M. Joad, Chih Meng, Prime Minister Nehru, Giuseppe Saraget, Omer Celal Sarc, The Senate of the University of Leiden, Holland, and President Harry S. Truman.]

Newlon, Jesse Homer. "John Dewey's Influence in the Schools." *School and Society* 30 (1929): 691-700. [Reprinted in *Teachers College Record* 31 (1929): 224-38. Adapted, with the title, "Dr. Dewey's Influence in the Schools," and printed in *Journal of the National Education Association* 18 (1929): 283-85. Also reprinted in *JOHN DEWEY, THE MAN AND HIS PHILOSOPHY*. Addresses Delivered in New York in Celebration of His Seventieth Birthday, pp. 37-63. Cambridge: Harvard University Press, 1930.]

---, with Lester Hancil Dix. "John Dewey, Dean of Educational Theorists." *School Executives Magazine* 53 (1933): 99-101, 119.

New Republic. Editorial comment in *New Republic*, 17 June 1922, p. 48. [On Dewey's "Mind in the Making." Ibid., p. 48.]

---. Introduction to special Dewey issue. *New Republic*, 17 October 1949, p. 10

---. "John Dewey: An Appraisal of His Contributions to

Philosophy, Education, and the Affairs of Men." *New
Republic*, 17 October 1949, pp. 10-39. [Papers pre-
sented on the occasion of his ninetieth birthday by
Gordon W. Allport, Clarence E. Ayres, George Boas,
Boyd H. Bode, Irwin Edman, Y. H. Krikorian, Ernest
Nagel, Ralph Barton Perry, and Wilmon H. Sheldon,
qq.v. Statements by Jan C. Smuts, Charles Seymour,
Alexander Meiklejohn, Luther H. Evans, Joseph W.
Krutch, William H. Kilpatrick, Frederick Burkhardt,
Lucy S. Mitchell, Harold Taylor, and Robert Hillyer.]

New Scholasticism. "John Dewey, 1859-1952." *New Scholasticism* 26 (1952): 391-92. [Editorial.]

Newsweek. "Philosopher at 80 Objects to Another 'Can-
onization'." *Newsweek*, 23 October 1939, pp. 33-34.

---. "Married." *Newsweek*, 23 December 1946, p. 52.

---. "John Dewey at 90." *Newsweek*, 24 October 1949,
p. 80.

---. "Death of John Dewey." *Newsweek*, 9 June 1952,
p. 58.

---. "Dewey's Labs." *Newsweek*, 3 June 1963, p. 75.

---. "Does School + Joy = Learning?" *Newsweek*, 3 May
1971, pp. 60-68. [Dewey, p. 66.]

New York Evening Post. Editorial. *New York Evening
Post*, 5 February 1910. [Comment on Dewey's "Science
as Subject-Matter and as Method." *Science* n.s. 31
(1910): 121-27.]

---. "'Motivation' of the War." *New York Evening
Post*, 20 August 1917. [Editorial reply to Dewey's
"What America Will Fight For." *New Republic*, 18
August 1917, pp. 68-69.]

New York Herald Tribune. "John Dewey." *New York
Herald Tribune*, 19 October 1929. [Editorial.] [Re-
printed in "Some Popular Appraisals of John Dewey,"
edited by Clyde R. Miller, pp. 21-22.]

New York Times. "Professor For Suffrage." *New York
Times*, 9 August 1912, p. 3.

---. "Educators and Their Responsibilities." *New

York Times, 13 September 1922, p. 20. [Editorial comment on Dewey's "Education as a Religion." *New Republic*, 13 September 1922, pp. 63-65.]

---. "The American Attitude." *New York Times*, 3 January 1927, p. 18. [Editorial comment on Dewey's "America's Responsibility." *Christian Century* 43 (1926): 1583-84.]

---. "Labor Expunges Tribute to Dewey." *New York Times*, 29 November 1928, p. 12.

---. "The Dewey Tribute." *New York Times*, 21 October 1929, p. 26. [Editorial.]

---. "How Much Freedom?" *New York Times*, 13 July 1930, p. 1. [Editorial.]

---. "Dewey Asks Norris to Lead New Party; Lucas Row Is Cited." *New York Times*, 26 December 1930, p. 1; editorial comment, 27 December 1930, p. 12.

---. "Smoking Them Out." *New York Times*, 1 January 1931, p. 28. [Editorial.]

---. "Dewey Contradicts Borah on Debt Revisions." *New York Times*, 15 July 1931, p. 17.

---. "A Philosopher in Politics." *New York Times*, 24 July 1932, p. 1. [Editorial comment on Dewey's "Prospects for a Third Party." *New Republic*, 27 July 1932, pp. 278-80.]

---. "Socialist Candidates." *New York Times*, 4 November 1932, p. 18. [Editorial.]

---. "Teachers and Textbooks." *New York Times*, 24 April 1933, p. 14. [Editorial.]

---. "Dr. Dewey Regulates Judges but not Children." *New York Times*, 23 February 1937, p. 26. [Editorial.]

---. "John Dewey Cited for Honors." *New York Times*, 28 February 1937, p. 8. [Editorial.]

---. "Philosopher of Americanism." *New York Times*, 20 October 1939, p. 22. [Editorial.]

---. "John Dewey's Aims Held Un-American." *New York*

Times, 27 October 1939, p. 14.

---. "Russell Defended by Four Educators." *New York Times*, 12 March 1940, p. 27. [John Dewey, Alfred North Whitehead, Curt John Ducasse, William Pepperell Montague.]

---. "Past May Be Good." *New York Times*, 15 November 1940, p. 20. [Editorial.]

---. "John Dewey at 85." *New York Times*, 20 October 1944, p. 18. [Editorial.]

---. "John Dewey at 85, Defends Doctrines." *New York Times*, 20 October 1944, p. 32. [Interview.]

---. "John Dewey: American." *New York Times*, 20 October 1949, p. 28. [Editorial.]

---. "Dr. John Dewey Dead at 92: Philosopher a Noted Liberal." *New York Times*, 2 June 1952, p. 1.

---. "John Dewey and His Creed." *New York Times*, 3 June 1952, p. 28. [Editorial.]

---. "Dewey's Missing Years." *New York Times*, 28 July 1963, p. 7.

New York World. "Two Gallant Figures." *New York World*, 3 November 1928. [Editorial on the meeting of Dewey and Governor Smith.]

---. "Dr. Dewey and the Communists." *New York World*, 30 November 1928. [Editorial.]

---. "John Dewey and Our Time." *New York World*, 20 October 1929. [Editorial.] [Reprinted in "Some Popular Appraisals of John Dewey," edited by Clyde R. Miller, pp. 211-12.]

Neilsen, Kai. "Dewey's Conception of Philosophy." *Massachusetts Review* 2 (1960): 111-34.

Nissen, Lowell. "Dewey's Theory of Truth." *Personalist* 46 (1965): 203-10.

---. *JOHN DEWEY'S THEORY OF INQUIRY AND TRUTH*. Hague: Mouton and Co., 1966. [Reprinted. New York:

Humanities Press, 1968.]   [Abstract in *Monist* 54
(1970): 155-56.]

Nordberg, Robert B., and Dupuis, Adrian M. "Progressivism and John Dewey's Instrumentalism." In their
PHILOSOPHY AND EDUCATION: A TOTAL VIEW, rev. ed.,
pp. 108-68. Milwaukee: Bruce Publishing Co., 1968.

Northrop, Filmer Stuart Cuckow. "The Initiation of Inquiry." In his *THE LOGIC OF THE SCIENCES AND THE
HUMANITIES*, pp. 1-18. New York: Macmillan Co.,
1947.

---. "The Mediational Approval Theory of Law in American Legal Realism." *Virginia Law Review* 44 (1958):
347-63. [Dewey, passim.]

---. "The Comparative Philosophy of Comparative Law."
Cornell Law Quarterly 45 (1960): 617-58. [Dewey,
passim.]

O'Connell, Geoffrey. *NATURALISM IN AMERICAN EDUCATION*.
Washington, D.C.: Catholic University of America,
1936. [Doctoral dissertation. Dewey, pp. 104-38.]

O'Connor, John Joseph. "Indeterminate Situation and
Problem in Dewey's Logical Theory." *Journal of Philosophy* 50 (1953): 753-70.

O'Hara, James Henry. *THE LIMITATIONS OF THE EDUCA-
TIONAL THEORY OF JOHN DEWEY*. Washington, D.C.:
Catholic University of America, 1929. [Doctoral
dissertation.]

Okun, Sid. *JOHN DEWEY: A MARXIAN CRITIQUE*. Chicago:
Revolutionary Workers League, 1942.

Olshausen, George. "Dewey, Spengler, and Russia." *New
Republic*, 19 December 1928, p. 142.

O'Meara, William. "John Dewey and Modern Thomism:
Introductory Notes." *Thomist* 5 (1943): 308-18.

---, and Byrns, Ruth K. "Concerning Mr. Hutchins:
Three Philosophies of Education--Dewey, Hutchins,
and a Catholic View." *Commonweal*, 31 May 1940, pp.
114-16.

Omohundro, Arthur T. "'Habit' in Peirce, Dewey, and

Mead." *Philosophy: A Student Journal at the Univer-sity of Chicago* 1 (1961): 55-61.

Oppenheim, James. "What Drives the Machine." *New Re-public*, 23 April 1930, p. 275. [Letter on Dewey's "Toward a New Individualism." Ibid., 19 February 1930, pp. 13-16.]

O'Rourke, Edward W. "John Dewey--Champion of Democracy or Decadence?" *Homiletic and Pastoral Review* 51 (1951): 1080-86.

Otto, Max Carl. "Ethical Culture and Pragmatism." *American Review* 2 (1924): 666-75.

---. "Instrumentalism." In *PHILOSOPHY TODAY*, edited by Edward Leroy Schaub, pp. 37-53. Chicago: Open Court Publishing Co., 1928.

---. "Contemporary Thought around the World: John Dewey." *Christian Register*, 11 January 1934, pp. 19-21.

---. "Mr. Dewey and Religion." *New Humanist* 8 (1935): 41-47.

---. "Philosopher of a New Age." *Social Frontier* 3 (1937): 230-33.

---. "John Dewey's Philosophy." *Social Frontier* 3 (1937): 264-67.

---. "The Social Philosophy of John Dewey." *Journal of Social Philosophy* 5 (1939): 42-60.

---. "Dewey and 'Experience'." *New Leader*, 22 October 1949, S-5.

---. "John Dewey." In *IN HONOR OF JOHN DEWEY ON HIS NINETIETH BIRTHDAY*, pp. 5-23. Madison: University of Wisconsin, 1951.

---. "John Dewey." *Progressive*, July 1952, p. 4. [Reprinted in *Progressive Education* 30 (1952): 1-2.]

---. *TOOLS OF TRUTH*. John Dewey Memorial Lecture no. 1. Bennington, Vt.: Bennington College, 1953.

---, and Neumann, Henry. "Two Letters on Ethical Cul-

ture and Pragmatism." *American Review* 3 (1925):
252-54.

Ou, Tsuin-Chen. "A Re-evaluation of the Educational
Theory and Practice of John Dewey." *Educational
Forum* 25 (1961): 277-300.

———. "Dewey's Lectures and Influence in China." In
GUIDE TO THE WORKS OF JOHN DEWEY, edited by Jo Ann
Boydston, pp. 339-64.

Outlook. "Dr. Dewey's Third Party." *Outlook*, 7 January 1931, pp. 10-11.

Ozmon, Howard. "Progressive Education: Rousseau and
Dewey." *New Era* 47 (1966): 45-48.

Padover, Saul Kussiel. "The American as Pragmatist:
John Dewey." In his *THE GENIUS OF AMERICA*, pp.
271-85. New York: McGraw-Hill Book Co., 1960.

Pap, Arthur. "On the Meaning of Universality."
Journal of Philosophy 40 (1943): 1505-14.

———. "Reply to Dewey's 'Ethical Subject-Matter and
Language'." *Journal of Philosophy* 43 (1946):
412-14. [Dewey's article in ibid. 42 (1945):
701-12.]

Park, Joe. "Experience in Contemporary Education: I.
The Development of the Conception of Experience in
Philosophy and Education." *Educational Theory* 7
(1957): 207-15. "II. Dewey's Concept of Experience." Ibid.: 269-75, 280. "III. The Modification
of Dewey's Viewpoint." Ibid. 8 (1958): 8-16.

———. "John Dewey: Exponent of Intellectual Discipline."
Educational Theory 10 (1960): 32-39, 70.

———. "Three Views of the Problem of Instruction."
Social Studies 52 (1961): 54-58.

———. *BERTRAND RUSSELL ON EDUCATION*. John Dewey Society Studies in Educational Theory, no. 1. Columbus: Ohio State University Press, 1963. [Dewey,
passim.]

Parker, DeWitt Henry. "Discussions of John Dewey:
Some Questions of Value." In *VALUE: A COOPERATIVE*

INQUIRY, edited by Ray Lepley, pp. 223-44.

---; Jessup, Bertram; and Morris, Charles. "Criticisms
by Parker; Rejoinders by Jessup and Morris." In
VALUE: A COOPERATIVE INQUIRY, edited by Ray Lepley,
pp. 424-39.

Parker, Douglas. "On Values and Value Judgments in
Sociology." *American Sociological Review* 32 (1967):
463-66.

Parker, Franklin. "A Golden Age in American Education:
Chicago in the 1890's." *School and Society* 89
(1961): 146-52. [Reprinted in *JOHN DEWEY: MASTER
EDUCATOR*, edited by William W. Brickman and Stanley
Lehrer, 2d ed., pp. 25-30.]

Parkes, Henry Bamford. "John Dewey." *Southern Review*
2 (1936): 260-78. [Reprinted in his *THE PRAGMATIC
TEST: ESSAYS ON THE HISTORY OF IDEAS*, pp. 95-119.
San Francisco: Colt Press, 1941.]

Parodi, Dominique. "Knowledge and Action in Dewey's
Philosophy." In *THE PHILOSOPHY OF JOHN DEWEY*,
edited by Paul Schilpp, pp. 227-42.

Parsons, Howard Lee. "The Meaning and Significance of
Dewey's Religious Thought." *Journal of Religion* 40
(1960): 170-90.

---. "Dewey's Religious Thought: The Challenge of
Evolution." *Journal of Philosophy* 58 (1961): 113-21.

Parsons, J. E., Jr. "John Dewey's Science of Society."
Thought and Word 6 (1968): 121-30, 159-71.

Pasch, Alan. "Dewey and the Analytical Philosophers."
Journal of Philosophy 56 (1959): 814-26.

Pascual, Ricardo R. "The Pragmatism of John Dewey."
Philippine Social Science Review 9 (1937): 142-56.

Passmore, John. *A HUNDRED YEARS OF PHILOSOPHY*. Rev.
ed. New York: Basic Books, 1966. [Dewey, pp.
117-21, 172-74, and passim.]

Patterson, Edwin Wilhite. "Pragmatism as a Philosophy
of Law." In *THE PHILOSOPHER OF THE COMMON MAN*,

edited by Sidney Ratner, pp. 172-204.

---. "John Dewey and the Law: Theories of Legal Reasoning and Valuation." *American Bar Association Journal* 36 (1950): 619-22, 699-701. [Also printed in *JOHN DEWEY, PHILOSOPHER OF SCIENCE AND FREEDOM*, edited by Sidney Hook, pp. 118-33, with the title, "Dewey's Theories of Legal Reasoning and Valuation."]

---. "John Dewey: Instrumental Reasoning," and "John Dewey: Scientific Ethics." In his *JURISPRUDENCE: MEN AND IDEAS OF THE LAW*, pp. 486-94, and pp. 494-500. Brooklyn: Foundation Press, 1953. [Also passim.]

Peake, Cyrus H. *NATIONALISM AND EDUCATION IN MODERN CHINA*. New York: Columbia University Press, 1932. [Dewey, pp. 85-86.]

Peel, James Claudius. "Many of Dewey's Educational Reforms Have Become Accepted Procedure." In *Some Interpretations of John Dewey's Educational Philosophy*. Florida Southern College Bulletin, vol. 67, pp. 7-12. Lakeland: Florida Southern College, 1951.

Pegis, Anton Charles. "Man and the Challenge of Irrationalism." In *RACE: NATION: PERSON: SOCIAL ASPECTS OF THE RACE PROBLEM*, edited by J. M. Corrigan and G. B. O'Toole, pp. 67-93. New York: Barnes and Noble, 1944.

Peirce, Charles Santiago Sanders. "To John Dewey, on the Nature of Logic." In his *COLLECTED PAPERS*, vol. 8, pp. 180-84. Cambridge: Harvard University Press, 1958. [Reprinted in *PRAGMATIC PHILOSOPHY*, edited by Amelie Rorty, pp. 118-20.]

Pennock, J. Roland. *LIBERAL DEMOCRACY: ITS MERITS AND PROSPECTS*. New York: Rinehart and Co., 1950. [Dewey, passim.]

Pepper, Stephen Coburn. "Some Questions on Dewey's Esthetics." In *THE PHILOSOPHY OF JOHN DEWEY*, edited by Paul Schilpp, pp. 369-90.

---. "Observations on Value from an Analysis of Simple Appetition." In *VALUE: A COOPERATIVE INQUIRY*, edited by Ray Lepley, pp. 245-60.

---. "The Concept of Fusion in Dewey's Aesthetic Theory." *Journal of Aesthetics and Art Criticism* 12 (1953): 169-76. [Reprinted in his *THE WORK OF ART*, pp. 151-72. Bloomington: Indiana University Press, 1955.]

---. *THE SOURCES OF VALUE*. Berkeley and Los Angeles: University of California Press, 1958. [Dewey, passim.]

---. "The Development of Contextualistic Aesthetics." *Antioch Review* 28 (1968): 169-85.

---, and Parker, DeWitt. "Criticisms by Pepper; Rejoinder by Parker." In *VALUE: A COOPERATIVE INQUIRY*, edited by Ray Lepley, pp. 440-55.

Perry, Ralph Barton. *PRESENT PHILOSOPHICAL TENDENCIES: A CRITICAL SURVEY OF NATURALISM, IDEALISM, PRAGMATISM, AND REALISM, TOGETHER WITH A SYNOPSIS OF THE PHILOSOPHY OF WILLIAM JAMES*. New York: Longmans, Green and Co., 1912. [Dewey, passim.]

---. "Dewey and Urban on Value Judgments." *Journal of Philosophy* 14 (1917): 169-81. [Reply by Dewey, "The Objects of Valuation." Ibid. 15 (1918): 253-58.]

---. *PHILOSOPHY OF THE RECENT PAST: AN OUTLINE OF EUROPEAN AND AMERICAN PHILOSOPHY SINCE 1860*. New York: Charles Scribner's Sons, 1926. [Dewey, pp. 194-95.]

---. "Salvation by Philosophy." *Saturday Review of Literature*, 26 October 1929, pp. 309-10.

---. "James and Dewey." In his *THE THOUGHT AND CHARACTER OF WILLIAM JAMES*, vol. 2, pp. 514-33. Boston: Little, Brown and Co., 1935.

---. *CHARACTERISTICALLY AMERICAN*. New York: Alfred A. Knopf, 1949. [Dewey, pp. 34, 50-52, 54, 57.]

---. "The Influence of a First-Hand Mind." *New Republic*, 17 October 1949, pp. 11-14.

---. "Dewey as Philosopher." In *JOHN DEWEY AT NINETY*, edited by Harry W. Laidler, pp. 16-19.

Persons, Stow Spaulding. *EVOLUTIONARY THOUGHT IN*

AMERICA. New Haven: Yale University Press, 1950. [Dewey, passim.]

---. "Pragmatism." In his *AMERICAN MINDS: A HISTORY OF IDEAS*, pp. 394-408. New York: Henry Holt and Co., 1958.

---, and Egbert, Donald Drew, eds. *SOCIALISM AND AMERICAN LIFE*. 2 vols. Princeton: Princeton University Press, 1952. ["Commission of Inquiry on Leon Trotsky," vol. 2, pp. 153-60; also Dewey, passim, vols. 1 and 2.]

Petcock, Stuart Jay. "Dewey and Gotshalk on Criticism." *Journal of Aesthetics and Art Criticism* 25 (1967): 387-94.

Peterfreund, Sheldon P. "John Dewey." In his *AN INTRODUCTION TO AMERICAN PHILOSOPHY*, pp. 202-68. New York: Odyssey Press, 1959.

Peterson, Houston. "John Dewey [1859-1952]." In *ESSAYS IN PHILOSOPHY*, edited by Houston Peterson, pp. 381-400. New York: Pocket Books, 1959.

Petras, John W. "John Dewey and the Rise of Interactionism in American Social Theory." *Journal of the History of Behavioral Science* 4 (1968): 18-27.

Pfuetze, Paul E. *SELF, SOCIETY, EXISTENCE*. Rev. ed. New York: Harper and Brothers, Harper Torchbooks, 1961. [Dewey, passim.] [Originally published in 1954 under the title *THE SOCIAL SELF*, by Bookman Associates, New York.]

Phenix, Philip Henry. "John Dewey's War on Dualism: Its Bearing on Today's Educational Problems." *Phi Delta Kappan* 41 (1959): 5-9. [Reprinted in *DEWEY ON EDUCATION: APPRAISALS*, edited by Reginald D. Archambault, pp. 39-51.]

Phillips, D. C. "John Dewey's Philosophy and His Writings on Education." *Educational Philosophy and Theory* 2 (October 1970): 47-56.

---. "James, Dewey, and the Reflex Arc." *Journal of the History of Ideas* 32 (1971): 555-68.

Phillips, Daniel Edward. "Number and Its Application

Psychologically Considered." *Pedagogical Seminary* 5 (1897): 221-81. [*Early Works of John Dewey* 5: xxviii-lxxxv.]

---. "Some Remarks on Number and Its Application." *Pedagogical Seminary* 5 (1898): 590-98. [Rejoinder to Dewey's "Some Remarks on the Psychology of Number." Ibid.: 426-34 (*Early Works of John Dewey* 5: 177-91.)]

Piatt, Donald Ayres. "Immediate Experience." *Journal of Philosophy* 25 (1928): 477-92.

---. "Dewey's Logical Theory." In THE PHILOSOPHY OF JOHN DEWEY, edited by Paul Schilpp, pp. 103-34.

---. "The Import of the Word 'Transaction' in Dewey's Philosophy." *ETC.: A Review of General Semantics* 12 (1955): 299-308.

Pickerell, T. L. "'First' Great Society?" *Chicago Tribune*, 14 April 1968.

Pietrowski, Edward F. "Dewey: Individuality as a Mark of Non-Value." *Studi Internazionali Di Filosofia* 2 (1970): 131-34. [English.]

Pinkevitch, Albert P. THE NEW EDUCATION IN THE SOVIET REPUBLIC. Translated by Nucia Perlmutter. New York: John Day Co., 1929. [Dewey, pp. 163-66, 173-77, and passim.]

Platoon School. "John Dewey and the Public Schools." *Platoon School* 3 (1929-30): 149-51. [Brief statements by Charles L. Spain, Charles A. Rice, William F. Kennedy, and Alice Barrows.]

Plochmann, George Kimball. Foreword to *F. A. TRENDEL-ENBURG, FORERUNNER TO JOHN DEWEY* by Gershon George Rosenstock. Carbondale: Southern Illinois University Press, 1964.

Polakov, Walter N. "Our Productive Potentialities." In *Resources for Building America*, Progressive Education Booklet no. 15, pp. 20-32. Columbus, Ohio: Progressive Education Association, 1939.

Pollock, Robert Channon. "Process and Experience: Dewey and American Philosophy." *Cross Currents* 9

(1959): 341-66. [Reprinted in *JOHN DEWEY: HIS THOUGHT AND INFLUENCE*, edited by John Blewett, pp. 161-98.]

Pope, Arthur Upham. "'Mission to Moscow' Film Viewed as Historical Realism." *New York Times*, 16 May 1943, p. 12. [Letter in reply to John Dewey and Suzanne La Follette, "Several Faults are Found in 'Mission to Moscow' Film." Ibid., 9 May 1943, p. 8. Response by Pope, ibid., 12 June 1943, p. 12. Reply by Dewey and La Follette, ibid., 24 May 1943, p. 14.]

Potter, Robert E. *THE STREAM OF AMERICAN EDUCATION*. New York: American Book Co., 1967. [Dewey, passim.]

Power, Edward J. "John Dewey: Reform for Relevance." In his *EVOLUTION OF EDUCATIONAL DOCTRINE: MAJOR EDUCATIONAL THEORISTS OF THE WESTERN WORLD*, pp. 333-67. New York: Appleton-Century-Crofts, 1969.

Prall, David Wight. "In Defense of a *Worthless* Theory of Value." *Journal of Philosophy* 20 (1923): 128-37. [In response to Dewey's "Valuation and Experimental Knowledge." *Philosophical Review* 31 (1922): 325-51.]

---. "Value and Thought-Process." *Journal of Philosophy* 21 (1924): 117-25. [In response to Dewey's "Values, Liking, and Thought." Ibid. 20 (1923): 617-22. Dewey's reply, "The Meaning of Value." Ibid. 22 (1925): 126-33.]

Pratt, Helen. "A Brief Survey of the Influences Which Have Shaped Education in Hawaii." *Hawaii Educational Review* 18 (1929): 36, 50-52.

Pratt, James Bissett. "Truth and Ideas." *Journal of Philosophy* 5 (1908): 122-31.

---. *WHAT IS PRAGMATISM?* New York: Macmillan Co., 1909. [Dewey, passim.]

Price, Kingsley. "American Thinking: Some Doctrines of John Dewey." In *1957 YEARBOOK OF EDUCATION*, edited by George Z. F. Bereday and Joseph A. Lauwerys, pp. 52-64. New York: Harcourt, Brace and World, 1957. [Reprinted in *Cross Currents* 7 (1958): 335-44. Also reprinted, with additions, with the title, "John Dewey," in *EDUCATION AND PHILOSOPHICAL THOUGHT*, edited by Kingsley Price, pp. 459-78. Boston: Allyn and Bacon, 1962.]

Pringle-Pattison, A. Seth. "Dewey's Studies in Logical Theory." In his *THE PHILOSOPHICAL RADICALS AND OTHER ESSAYS*, pp. 178-94. Edinburgh and London: William Blackwood and Sons, 1907.

Prosch, Harry. "Toward an Ethics of Civil Disobedience." *Ethics* 77 (1967): 176-92.

Punzo, Vincent C. *REFLECTIVE NATURALISM: AN INTRODUCTION TO MORAL PHILOSOPHY*. New York: Macmillan Co., 1969. [Dewey, pp. 315-68.]

Quine, W. V. "Ontological Relativity: The Dewey Lectures 1968." *Journal of Philosophy* 65 (1968): 185-212.

Raby, Joseph Mary. *A CRITICAL STUDY OF THE NEW EDUCATION*. Washington, D.C.: Catholic University of America, 1932. [Doctoral dissertation.]

---. "John Dewey and Progressive Education." In *JOHN DEWEY: HIS THOUGHT AND INFLUENCE*, edited by John Blewett, pp. 85-116.

Rader, Melvin Miller. "The Way of the Pragmatist: John Dewey." In his *THE ENDURING QUESTIONS: MAIN PROBLEMS OF PHILOSOPHY*. New York: Henry Holt and Co., 1956. [Reprint of Dewey's essay, "The Influence of Darwinism on Philosophy," with Rader's introduction and commentary on pp. 134-35, 142-44, and 149-56.]

---. "Morality Based on Experimental Logic." In his *THE ENDURING QUESTIONS: MAIN PROBLEMS OF PHILOSOPHY*. [Reprint of Dewey's chapter, "Reconstruction in Moral Conception," from *RECONSTRUCTION IN PHILOSOPHY*, with Rader's commentary on pp. 430-35.] [Reprinted with the title, "Comment on Dewey's Ethical Views," in *THE STRUCTURE OF SCIENTIFIC THOUGHT: AN INTRODUCTION TO THE PHILOSOPHY OF SCIENCE*, edited by Edward Harry Madden, pp. 358-62. Boston: Houghton Mifflin Co., 1960.]

---. "Community in Time of Stress." In *University of Colorado Studies*, Series in Philosophy, no. 2, pp. 83-98. Boulder: University of Colorado Press, 1961.

Radhakrishnan, Sarvepalli. *HISTORY OF PHILOSOPHY EASTERN AND WESTERN*. London: George Allen and Unwin, 1953. [Dewey, vol. 2, pp. 344-49.]

Ragusa, Thomas Joseph. *THE SUBSTANCE THEORY OF MIND AND CONTEMPORARY FUNCTIONALISM.* Washington, D.C.: Catholic University of America, 1937. [Doctoral dissertation.]

Ramanathan, Gopalakrishna. *EDUCATION FROM DEWEY TO GANDHI: THE THEORY OF BASIC EDUCATION.* Bombay: Asia Publishing House, 1963.

Randall, John Herman, Jr. "Liberalism as Faith in Intelligence." *Journal of Philosophy* 32 (1935): 253-64. [Reply to Dewey's "The Future of Liberalism." Ibid.: 225-30; *School and Society* 41 (1935): 73-77.]

---. "Dewey's Interpretation of the History of Philosophy." In *THE PHILOSOPHY OF JOHN DEWEY*, edited by Paul Schilpp, pp. 75-102.

---. "The Religion of Shared Experience." In *THE PHILOSOPHER OF THE COMMON MAN*, edited by Sidney Ratner, pp. 106-45.

---. "A Note on Mr. Sheldon's Mind." *Journal of Philosophy* 43 (1946): 209-14. [On Wilmon Henry Sheldon's exchange with Dewey. Ibid. 42 (1945): 253-70, 515-30; 43 (1946): 197-209.]

---. "Salute to John Dewey--'Going on 91'." *Survey* 85 (1949): 508-10.

---. "John Dewey 1859-1952." *Journal of Philosophy* 50 (1953): 5-13.

---. "Talking and Looking." *American Philosophical Association Proceedings and Addresses* 30 (1957): 5-24. [Dewey, passim.]

---. "The Department of Philosophy." In *A HISTORY OF THE FACULTY OF PHILOSOPHY, COLUMBIA UNIVERSITY*, edited by Jacques Barzun, pp. 102-45. New York: Columbia University Press, 1957.

---. *NATURE AND HISTORICAL EXPERIENCE: ESSAYS IN NATURALISM AND IN THE THEORY OF HISTORY.* New York: Columbia University Press, 1958. [Dewey, pp. 230-45, 288-95, and passim.]

---. "Dewey's Contribution to Scientific Humanism." *Humanist* 19 (1959): 134-38.

---. "The Future of John Dewey's Philosophy." *Journal of Philosophy* 56 (1959): 1005-10.

---. Foreword to *JOHN DEWEY: DICTIONARY OF EDUCATION*, edited by Ralph B. Winn. New York: Philosophical Library, 1959.

---. *HOW PHILOSOPHY USES ITS PAST*. New York: Columbia University Press, 1963. [Dewey, passim.]

---. "F. H. Bradley and the Working Out of Absolute Idealism." *Journal of the History of Philosophy* 5 (1967): 245-67.

---, and Buchler, Justus. *PHILOSOPHY: AN INTRODUCTION*. New York: Barnes and Noble, 1942. [Dewey, pp. 130-32, 287-90, and passim.]

Randall, Mercedes Irene Moritz, ed. *Pan, the Logos and John Dewey: A Legend of the Green Mountains*, by Herbert Wallace Schneider and *The Realism of Jane Addams* by John Dewey. Philadelphia: Women's International League for Peace and Freedom, 1959. [The two articles reprinted for the John Dewey-Jane Addams Centennial, 1959-1960, with an Introduction, "John Dewey and Jane Addams," by Mrs. Randall.]

Rao, K. Ramakrishna. *GANDHI AND PRAGMATISM*. Calcutta: Oxford and IBH Publishing Co., 1968. ["A systematic account of the philosophies of Peirce, James, Dewey, and Gandhi."]

Rapoport, Anatol. *OPERATIONAL PHILOSOPHY*. New York: Harper and Brothers, 1953. [Dewey, passim.]

Rasmussen, Carl C. "Some Reactions to Dewey's Philosophy." *Personalist* 3 (1922): 171-82.

Ratner, Joseph. Preface to *THE PHILOSOPHY OF JOHN DEWEY*, edited by Joseph Ratner. New York: Henry Holt and Co., 1928.

---. "John Dewey's Theory of Judgment." *Journal of Philosophy* 27 (1930): 253-64.

---. "More on the Same." *Saturday Review of Literature*, 12 July 1930, p. 1194. [In reply to Lewis Mumford, "A Modern Synthesis." Ibid., 12 April 1930, pp. 920-21.]

---. "Dewey's Conception of Philosophy." In *THE PHI-LOSOPHY OF JOHN DEWEY*, edited by Paul Schilpp, pp. 47-74.

---. "Introduction to John Dewey's Philosophy." In *INTELLIGENCE IN THE MODERN WORLD: JOHN DEWEY'S PHI-LOSOPHY*, edited by Joseph Ratner, pp. 3-241. New York: Modern Library, 1939.

---. "Editor!s Note." In *INTELLIGENCE IN THE MODERN WORLD*, pp. 525-66.

---. Foreword to *EDUCATION TODAY* by John Dewey. Edited by Joseph Ratner. New York: G. P. Putnam's Sons, 1940.

---. Foreword to *JOHN DEWEY: PHILOSOPHY, PSYCHOLOGY AND SOCIAL PRACTICE*, edited by Joseph Ratner. New York: G. P. Putnam's Sons, 1963, Capricorn Books, 1965.

---. Reply to George Eastman's review of *PHILOSOPHY, PSYCHOLOGY AND SOCIAL PRACTICE*. *Studies in Philosophy and Education* 4 (1965): 105-7.

Ratner, Sidney. "Evolution and the Rise of the Scientific Spirit in America." *Philosophy of Science* 3 (1936): 104-22.

---. "Dewey's Contribution to Historical Theory." In *JOHN DEWEY: PHILOSOPHER OF SCIENCE AND FREEDOM*, edited by Sidney Hook, pp. 134-52.

---. "The Evolutionary Naturalism of John Dewey." *Social Research* 18 (1951): 435-48.

---. "The Development of Dewey's Evolutionary Naturalism." *Social Research* 20 (1953): 127-54.

---. "Events and the Future, John Dewey." In *ESSAYS IN HONOR OF HORACE M. KALLEN ON HIS 70TH BIRTHDAY*, pp. 184-91. New Brunswick, N.J.: Rutgers University Press, 1953.

---. "The Naturalistic Humanism of John Dewey and Arthur F. Bentley." *Humanist* 14 (1954): 81-87.

---. "Facts and Values in History." *Teachers College Record* 56 (1955): 429-34.

---. "The Ethics of Democracy: Of John Dewey, Liberalism, and Ends and Means." *Humanist* 15 (1955):
15-17.

---. "A. F. Bentley's Inquiries into the Behavioral
Sciences and the Theory of Scientific Inquiry." In
*LIFE, LANGUAGE, LAW: ESSAYS IN HONOR OF ARTHUR F.
BENTLEY*, edited by Richard Wirth Taylor, pp. 26-57.
Yellow Springs, Ohio: Antioch Press, 1957.

---. "History as Experiment." *Antioch Review* 19
(1959): 315-27.

---. "A Salute around the Globe." *Saturday Review*,
21 November 1959, pp. 18, 53.

---. "Pragmatism in America." In *ESSAYS IN AMERICAN
HISTORIOGRAPHY: PAPERS PRESENTED IN HONOR OF ALLAN
NEVINS*, edited by Donald Henry Sheehan and Harold
Coffin Syrett, pp. 193-216. New York: Columbia
University Press, 1960. [Dewey, pp. 204-11.]

---, ed. *THE PHILOSOPHER OF THE COMMON MAN. ESSAYS IN
HONOR OF JOHN DEWEY TO CELEBRATE HIS EIGHTIETH
BIRTHDAY*. New York: G. P. Putnam's Sons, 1940.

---, and Altman, Jules, eds. *JOHN DEWEY AND ARTHUR F.
BENTLEY: A PHILOSOPHICAL CORRESPONDENCE, 1932-1951*.
New Brunswick, N.J.: Rutgers University Press, 1964.

Raup, Robert Bruce. "Dewey's *LOGIC* and Some Problems
of Progressive Education." *Progressive Education* 16
(1939): 264-71.

Ravenhill, Alice. *Special Reports on Educational Sub-
jects*, vol. 15. London: Wyman and Sons, 1905.
[Dewey's views on education, pp. 7-8; Dewey's views
on the training of children, pp. 143-48.]

Raymont, Thomas. "John Dewey, Educationist and Philosopher." *Journal of Education* [London.] 82
(1950): 144.

Reck, Andrew Joseph. "Comments on Dewey, Randall, and
Parker Concerning Experience and Substance."
Journal of Philosophy 58 (1961): 162-66.

---. *RECENT AMERICAN PHILOSOPHY: STUDIES OF TEN*

REPRESENTATIVE THINKERS. New York: Random House, Pantheon Books, 1964. [Dewey, passim.]

---. "Substance and Experience." *Tulane Studies in Philosophy* 15 (1966): 31-45.

---. "Bernard Lonergan's Theory of Inquiry vis-à-vis American Thought." In *PROCEEDINGS OF THE AMERICAN CATHOLIC PHILOSOPHICAL ASSOCIATION*, vol. 41, pp. 239-45. Washington, D.C.: Catholic University of America, 1967. [Dewey, pp. 242-44.]

Reeder, Edwin Hewett. "John Dewey and the Activist Movement." In *THE HISTORICAL APPROACH TO METHODS OF TEACHING THE SOCIAL STUDIES*. National Council for the Social Studies, Fifth Yearbook, pp. 38-49. Philadelphia: McKinley Publishing Co., 1935.

Rehage, Kenneth Joseph. "John Dewey's Ninetieth Birthday." *Elementary School Journal* 50 (1949): 127-28.

Reichenbach, Hans. "Dewey's Theory of Science." In *THE PHILOSOPHY OF JOHN DEWEY*, edited by Paul Schilpp, pp. 157-92.

Reid, John R. "The Apotheosis of Intelligence." *Journal of Philosophy* 32 (1935): 375-85. [Reply by Robert Rothman, "Value and Intelligence." Ibid. 33 (1936): 176-86.]

Reilly, George C. "John Dewey: Philosopher in the Market Place." In *TWENTIETH CENTURY THINKERS*, edited by John K. Ryan, pp. 223-37. Staten Island, N.Y.: Alba House, 1964.

Reinert, Paul C. "Deweyism: The Modern Philosophy of Education and the Catholic Student in a Secular University." *Catholic School Journal* 52 (1952): 13-16.

Renfield, Richard. *IF TEACHERS WERE FREE*. Washington, D.C.: Acropolis Books, 1969. [Dewey, passim.]

Rhine, Robley. Introduction to "Symposium: The Influence of John Dewey upon Speech." *Western Speech* 32 (1968): 114-17. [Symposium by Don M. Burks, Gladys L. Borchers, and R. Victor Harnack.]

Rian, Edwin Harold. *CHRISTIANITY AND AMERICAN EDUCA-*

TION. San Antonio, Tex.: Naylor Co., 1949. [Dewey, passim.]

Rice, Charles A. "Our Debt to John Dewey." *Platoon School* 3 (1929): 149-50.

Rice, Philip Blair. "'Objectivity' in Value Judgments." *Journal of Philosophy* 40 (1943): 5-14. [Reply by Dewey, "Valuation Judgments and Immediate Quality." Ibid.: 309-17.]

---. "Quality and Value." *Journal of Philosophy* 40 (1943): 337-48.

---. "Types of Value Judgment." *Journal of Philosophy* 40 (1943): 533-43. [In response to Dewey's "Valuation Judgments and Immediate Quality." Ibid.: 309-17. Reply by Dewey, "Further as to Valuation as Judgment." Ibid.: 543-52. Response by Rice, "Feelings as Evidence." Ibid.: 552-57.]

---. "Science, Humanism, and the Good." In *VALUE: A COOPERATIVE INQUIRY*, edited by Ray Lepley, pp. 261-90.

---; Garnett, A. C.; and Hahn, Lewis. "Criticisms by Rice; Rejoinders by Garnett and Hahn." In *VALUE: A COOPERATIVE INQUIRY*, edited by Ray Lepley, pp. 456-70.

Rich, John Martin. "Dewey's Concept of Communication and 'Mindful' Behavior." *Educational Theory* 10 (1960): 205-9.

Richards, Robert J. "Materialism and Natural Events in Dewey's Developing Thought." *Journal of the History of Philosophy* 10 (1972): 55-69.

Rickover, Hyman G. *EDUCATION AND FREEDOM*. New York: E. P. Dutton and Co., 1959. [Dewey, passim.]

Riepe, Dale. "The Collapse of American Philosophical Naturalism (1920-1950)." *Telos* 2 (1969): 82-89. [Dewey, passim.]

Riley, Woodbridge. "The Chicago School: John Dewey." In his *AMERICAN THOUGHT, FROM PURITANISM TO PRAGMATISM AND BEYOND*, pp. 289-308. New York: Henry Holt and Co., 1915. [Also passim.] [Reprinted, New York: Peter Smith, 1941.]

Rippa, Sol Alexander. "An Epilogue to the John Dewey Centenary." *Education* 80 (1960): 428-29.

Roback, Abraham Aaron. *WILLIAM JAMES: HIS MARGINALIA, PERSONALITY, AND CONTRIBUTION.* Cambridge, Mass.: Sci-Art Publishers, 1942. [Dewey, passim.]

---. *HISTORY OF AMERICAN PSYCHOLOGY.* New York: Library Publishers, 1952. [Dewey, passim.]

---. *HISTORY OF PSYCHOLOGY AND PSYCHIATRY.* New York: Philosophical Library, 1961. [Dewey, pp. 164-67, and passim.]

Robertson, Robert E. "John Dewey and the Given." *Educational Theory* 8 (1958): 182-85.

Robinson, Daniel Sommer. "An Alleged New Discovery in Logic." *Journal of Philosophy* 14 (1917): 225-37. [On Dewey's *ESSAYS IN EXPERIMENTAL LOGIC.* Dewey's reply, "Concerning Novelties in Logic." *Journal of Philosophy* 14 (1917): 237-45.]

---. "The Chief Types of Motivation to Philosophic Reflection." *Journal of Philosophy* 20 (1923): 29-41. [Dewey's reply, "Tradition, Metaphysics and Morals." Ibid.: 187-92.]

---. "John Dewey's Instrumentalism." In his *AN INTRODUCTION TO LIVING PHILOSOPHY*, pp. 246-49. New York: Thomas Y. Crowell, 1932. [Also, pp. 251-59, 283-97, and passim.]

Robinson, James Harvey. "John Dewey and Liberal Thought." In *JOHN DEWEY, THE MAN AND HIS PHILOSOPHY.* Addresses Delivered in New York in Celebration of His Seventieth Birthday, pp. 153-72. Cambridge: Harvard University Press, 1930.

---. "John Dewey and His World." *Harvard Teachers Record* 2 (1932): 9-16.

Robischon, Thomas Gregory. "What Is Objective Relativism?" *Journal of Philosophy* 55 (1958): 1117-32.

Rodríguez Surillo, Nicolás. "Emmanuel Kant and John

Dewey (Comparison and Contrast)." *Pedagogía* 13 (1965): 89-108.

Rogers, Arthur Kenyon. "The Standpoint of Instrumental Logic." *Journal of Philosophy* 1 (1904): 207-12.

---. "John Dewey." In his *ENGLISH AND AMERICAN PHILOSOPHY SINCE 1800, A CRITICAL SURVEY*, pp. 388-406. New York: Macmillan Co., 1922.

Rogers, Donald. "Pragmatism: The Philosophy of America." *Educational Theory* 9 (1959): 207-16, 222.

Rogers, Robert. "Dewey and the Philosophy of Mathematics." *University of Colorado Studies*, Series in Philosophy, no. 2, pp. 52-66. Boulder: University of Colorado Press, 1961.

Romanelli, Pasquale. "The New Naturalism." *Journal of Philosophy* 38 (1941): 39-48.

Romanell, Patrick. "A Comment on Croce's and Dewey's Aesthetics." *Journal of Aesthetics and Art Criticism* 8 (1949): 125-28. [Reply by Dewey, "Aesthetic Experience as a Primary Phase and as an Artistic Development." Ibid. 9 (1950): 56-58.]

---. "Some Difficulties in John Dewey's Case for a Scientific Ethics." In *PROCEEDINGS OF THE ELEVENTH INTERNATIONAL CONGRESS OF PHILOSOPHY*, vol. 13, pp. 194-99. Amsterdam: North-Holland Publishing Co., 1953.

---. "John Dewey and the Naturalistic Approach to Ethics." In his *TOWARD A CRITICAL NATURALISM: REFLECTIONS ON CONTEMPORARY AMERICAN PHILOSOPHY*, pp. 39-47. New York: Macmillan Co., 1958.

Roodkowsky, Nikita Dmitrievitch. "Marxism's Appeal for American Intellectuals." *Catholic World* 192 (1960): 35-39. [Dewey, pp. 37-39.]

Rorty, Amelie. "John Dewey." In *PRAGMATIC PHILOSOPHY*, edited by Amelie Rorty, pp. 200-202. Garden City, N.Y.: Doubleday and Co., Anchor Books, 1966. [Introduction to reprints of several of Dewey's works.]

Roseman, Norman. "Self-Realization and the Experimentalist Theory of Education." *Educational Theory* 13 (1963): 29-38.

Rosenstock, Gershon George. *F. A. TRENDELENBURG--FORE-RUNNER TO JOHN DEWEY*. Carbondale: Southern Illinois University Press, 1964. [Dewey, pp. 112-24, 129-35, and passim.]

Rosenstock-Huessy, Eugen. "John Dewey." In his *THE CHRISTIAN FUTURE OR THE MODERN MIND OUTRUN*, pp. 43-53. New York: Charles Scribner's Sons, 1946.

Ross, Stephen D. "The Means-End Distinction in Dewey's Philosophy." *Transactions of the Charles S. Peirce Society* 5 (1969): 107-20.

Roth, John K. "William James, John Dewey, and the 'Death-of-God'." *Religious Studies* 7 (1971): 53-61.

Roth, Robert J. "How 'Closed' is John Dewey's Naturalism?" *International Philosophical Quarterly* 3 (1963): 106-20.

---. *JOHN DEWEY AND SELF-REALIZATION*. Englewood Cliffs, N.J.: Prentice-Hall, 1963.

---. "The Challenge of American Naturalism." *Thought* [Fordham University Quarterly] 39 (1964): 559-84. [Reprinted in part, with minor changes, in his *AMERICAN RELIGIOUS PHILOSOPHY*, pp. 14-25. New York: Harcourt, Brace and World, 1967.]

---. "Naturalistic Ethics: Problem of Method." *New Scholasticism* 40 (1966): 285-311.

---. "John Dewey and Religious Experience." In his *AMERICAN RELIGIOUS PHILOSOPHY*, pp. 85-108. [Also passim.]

---. "American Philosophy and the Future of Man." In *PROCEEDINGS OF THE AMERICAN CATHOLIC PHILOSOPHICAL ASSOCIATION*, vol. 42, pp. 209-16. Washington, D.C.: Catholic University of America, 1968.

---. "Humanism and Catholicism." *Humanist* 29 (1969): 28-30.

---. "The Puritan Backgrounds of American Naturalism." *Thought* [Fordham University Quarterly] 45

(1970): 503-20.

---. "Religion and American Experience." *America*, 16 January 1971, pp. 43-44.

Rothman, Robert. "Value and Intelligence." *Journal of Philosophy* 33 (1936): 176-86.

---. "Philosopher Dewey at 91." *American Teacher Magazine* 35 (1951): 5-6.

Rothschild, Lincoln. Letter to the Editor. *Journal of Aesthetics and Art Criticism* 19 (1961): 471. [In reply to Leon Jacobson's "*ART AS EXPERIENCE* and American Visual Art Today." Ibid.: 117-26.]

---. Letter to the Editor. *Journal of Aesthetics and Art Criticism* 27 (1968): 461. [In reply to Donald Kuspit's "Dewey Critique of Art for Art's Sake." Ibid.: 93-98. Response by Kuspit, ibid.: 461.]

Rotigel, David E. "Back to Dewey Again: His Views on Teachers, Unions, and Strikes." *Changing Education* 2 (Fall 1967): 19-28.

Rucker, Darnell. *THE CHICAGO PRAGMATISTS*. Minneapolis: University of Minnesota Press, 1969.

---. "Dewey's Ethics." Part Two. In *GUIDE TO THE WORKS OF JOHN DEWEY*, edited by Jo Ann Boydston, pp. 112-30.

Rugg, Harold. "Representative Quotations from John Dewey's Written Statements on the Curriculum (1900-1926)." In *THE FOUNDATIONS AND TECHNIQUE OF CURRICULUM-CONSTRUCTION*. National Society for the Study of Education, Twenty-Sixth Yearbook, pt. 2, pp. 165-87. Bloomington, Ill.: Public School Publishing Co., 1926.

---. "Dewey and the Psychology of the Act." In his *FOUNDATIONS FOR AMERICAN EDUCATION*, pp. 99-121. Yonkers, N.Y.: World Book Co., 1947.

---. "Dewey and His Contemporaries." In *John Dewey in Perspective: Three Papers in Honor of John Dewey*, edited by A. Stafford Clayton, pp. 1-14.

---, and Shumaker, Ann. *THE CHILD-CENTERED SCHOOL, AN*

APPRAISAL OF THE NEW EDUCATION. Yonkers, N.Y.: World Book Co., 1928. [Dewey, passim.]

Runyon, Laura Louisa. "A Day with the New Education." *Chautauquan* 30 (1900): 589-92.

Ruppel, Robert W. "John Dewey and Piano Teaching." *Piano Teacher* 7 (May-June 1965): 2-4.

Rusk, Robert R. "Dewey." In his *THE DOCTRINES OF THE GREAT EDUCATORS*, pp. 284-303. New York: St. Martin's Press, 1965.

Russell, Bertrand. "Professor Dewey's *ESSAYS IN EXPERIMENTAL LOGIC.*" *Journal of Philosophy* 16 (1919): 5-26.

---. "Dewey's New *LOGIC.*" In *THE PHILOSOPHY OF JOHN DEWEY*, edited by Paul Schilpp, pp. 137-56. [Reprinted in part in *PRAGMATIC PHILOSOPHY*, edited by Amelie Rorty, pp. 315-27.]

---. *AN INQUIRY INTO MEANING AND TRUTH.* New York: W. W. Norton and Co., 1940. [Dewey, pp. 400-410.]

---. "John Dewey." In his *A HISTORY OF WESTERN PHILOSOPHY AND ITS CONNECTION WITH POLITICAL AND SOCIAL CIRCUMSTANCES FROM THE EARLIEST TIMES TO THE PRESENT DAY*, pp. 819-28. New York: Simon and Schuster, 1945.

---. *MY PHILOSOPHICAL DEVELOPMENT.* New York: Simon and Schuster, 1959. [Dewey, passim.]

Russell, John Dale, and Judd, Charles Hubbard. *THE AMERICAN EDUCATIONAL SYSTEM.* Boston: Houghton Mifflin Co., 1940. [Dewey, passim.]

Russell, John Edward. "Objective Idealism and Revised Empiricism." *Philosophical Review* 15 (1906): 627-33. [Reply to Dewey's "Experience and Objective Idealism." Ibid.: 465-81.]

Russell, Kirk. *THE CONSERVATIVE MIND--FROM BURKE TO SANTAYANA.* Chicago: Henry Regnery Co., 1953. [Dewey, pp. 365-66.]

Russell, William Fletcher. "Introductory Remarks." *Teachers College Record* 51 (1949): 127-28. [At celebration of Dewey's ninetieth birthday, Teachers College, 20 October 1949.]

Sacksteder, William. "John Dewey and the Owl of Min-
erva." In *University of Colorado Studies*, Series in
Philosophy, no. 2, pp. 67-82. Boulder: University
of Colorado Press, 1961.

Sait, Una Bernard. "Studying under John Dewey."
Claremont Quarterly 11 (1964): 15-22.

Salter, Paul, and Librome, Jack. "Dewey, Russell and
Cohen: Why They Are Anti-Communist." *New Masses*, 17
July 1934, pp. 24-27; 24 July 1934, pp. 22-23.

Sanchez, Ramon. "John Dewey's THE SCHOOL AND SOCIETY--
Perspectives 1969." *History of Education Quarterly*
10 (1970): 78-83.

Sanders, William Joseph. "The Logical Unity of John
Dewey's Educational Philosophy." *Ethics* 50 (1940):
424-40. [From his doctoral dissertation, "The
Hegelian Dialectic in the Educational Philosophy of
John Dewey." Yale University, 1935.]

Santayana, George. "Dewey's Naturalistic Metaphysics."
Journal of Philosophy 22 (1925): 673-88. [Reply by
Dewey, "Half-Hearted Naturalism." Ibid. 24 (1927):
57-64.] [Santayana's article reprinted in *THE PHI-
LOSOPHY OF JOHN DEWEY*, edited by Paul Schilpp, pp.
243-62.]

---. "Three American Philosophers." *American Scholar*
22 (1953): 281-84. [Dewey, James, and Santayana.]

Santee, Joseph Frederic, and Givens, Willard Earl.
"John Dewey, Educational Philosopher." *Phi Delta
Kappan* 34 (1952): 9-10.

Sarkar, Benoy Kumar. *THE POLITICAL PHILOSOPHIES SINCE
1905.* Madras: B. G. Paul and Co., 1928. [Dewey,
pp. 303-4.]

Saturday Review of Literature. "Critic of John Dewey."
Saturday Review of Literature, 3 December 1949, pp.
25-26. [Letters from Alan Reynolds Thompson and
William S. Tacey on the John Dewey issue, 22 October
1949.]

---. "John Dewey--Pro and Con." *Saturday Review of
Literature*, 4 January 1950, p. 22. [Letters from
Haskell Fain, Frank Smoyer, and Anne Mowat in reply

to letter of Alan Reynolds Thompson, 3 December 1949.]

Saunders, T. Frank. "Art: Object, Language, and Judgment." In *PHILOSOPHY OF EDUCATION 1966: Proceedings of the Twenty-Second Annual Meeting of the Philosophy of Education Society*, pp. 119-24. Edwardsville, Ill.: Studies in Philosophy and Education, 1966. [Dewey, pp. 123-24.]

---. "Originality in American Philosophy: Educational Perspectives." In *CONTEMPORARY ISSUES IN AMERICAN EDUCATION*, edited by F. Robert Paulsen, pp. 81-88. Tucson: University of Arizona Press, 1967.

Savage, Willinda. "John Dewey and 'Thought News' at the University of Michigan." *Michigan Alumnus Quarterly Review* 56 (1950): 204-9. [Reprinted in *STUDIES IN THE HISTORY OF HIGHER EDUCATION IN MICHIGAN*, edited by Claude Eggertson, pp. 12-17. Ann Arbor: Ann Arbor Publishers, 1950.]

Savan, David B. "John Dewey's Conception of Nature." *University of Toronto Quarterly* 17 (1947-48): 18-28.

---. "John Dewey, 1859-1952." *Canadian Forum* 32 (1952): 103-5.

Savery, William. "The Significance of Dewey's Philosophy." In *THE PHILOSOPHY OF JOHN DEWEY*, edited by Paul Schilpp, pp. 479-514.

Sayers, E. V. "Two of Dewey's Conceptions that Have Most Affected School Practice." *Hawaii Educational Review* 18 (1929): 35, 46-50.

---, and Madden, Ward. *EDUCATION AND THE DEMOCRATIC FAITH*. New York: Appleton-Century-Crofts, 1959. [Dewey, passim.]

Schack, William. *ART AND ARGYROL: THE LIFE AND CAREER OF DR. ALBERT C. BARNES*. New York: Thomas Yoseloff, 1960. [Dewey, pp. 100-108, 239-43, and passim.]

Schaub, Edward Leroy. "Dewey's Interpretation of Religion." In *THE PHILOSOPHY OF JOHN DEWEY*, edited by Paul Schilpp, pp. 391-416.

Scheffler, Israel. "Educational Liberalism and Dewey's

Philosophy." *Harvard Educational Review* 26 (1956):
190-98.

---. "Is the Dewey-like Notion of Desirability Absurd?"
Journal of Philosophy 51 (1954): 577-82.

---. "Comments on Professor Geiger's Paper." In *EDU-
CATION IN TRANSITION*, edited by Frederick C. Gruber,
pp. 256-59. Philadelphia: University of Pennsylvania Press, 1960. [In response to George Geiger,
"John Dewey's Social Philosophy." Ibid., pp. 243-
55.]

Schiller, F. C. S. "Thought and Immediacy." *Journal
of Philosophy* 3 (1906): 234-37. [On Dewey's "Immediate Empiricism." Ibid. 2 (1905): 597-99.]

---. "Aristotle and the Practical Syllogism." *Journal
of Philosophy* 14 (1917): 645-53.

Schilpp, Paul Arthur. "John Dewey, America's Typical
Voice at the Philosophical Round-Table." In his
COMMEMORATIVE ESSAYS, 1859-1929, pp. 41-47. Stock-
ton, Cal.: Privately published, 1930.

---. "John Dewey: American Citizen No. 1." *Educational Trends* 7 (November-December 1939): 23-25.

---. "The Impact of John Dewey's Philosophy upon
American Education." *Chicago Review* 14 (1960):
97-108.

---. "The Faith of John Dewey." In *HORIZONS OF A PHI-
LOSOPHER: ESSAYS IN HONOR OF DAVID BAUMGARDT*, edited
by Joseph Frank, Helmut Minkowski, and Ernest J.
Sternglass, pp. 371-77. Leiden: E. J. Brill, 1963.

---, ed. *THE PHILOSOPHY OF JOHN DEWEY*. The Library of
Living Philosophers, vol. 1. Evanston, Ill.: Northwestern University Press, 1939. [Reprinted, with
the bibliography extended to 1950 by Muriel Murray.
New York: Tudor Publishing Co., 1951.] [Reprinted
again, La Salle, Ill.: Open Court Publishing Co.,
1970.]

Schinz, Albert. "Professor Dewey's Pragmatism." *Journal of Philosophy* 5 (1908): 617-28. [Reprinted as
"Le Cas Dewey." In his *ANTI-PRAGMATISME: EXAMEN DES*

*DROITS RESPECTIFS DE L'ARISTOCRATIE INTELLECTUELLE
ET LA DÉMOCRATIE SOCIALE*, pp. 72-93. Paris: Felix
Alcan, 1909. English translation, "The Dewey Case."
In his *ANTI-PRAGMATISM: AN EXAMINATION INTO THE
RESPECTIVE RIGHTS OF INTELLECTUAL ARISTOCRACY AND
SOCIAL DEMOCRACY*, pp. 88-109. Boston: Small, May-
nard and Co., 1909.]

Schipper, Edith Watson. "Existence and Common Sense."
Journal of Philosophy 41 (1944): 298-302.

Schmuller, Allen M., and Thorpe, Louis P. "Problem
Solving: Dewey's View of Learning as Experience."
In their *CONTEMPORARY THEORIES OF LEARNING WITH AP-
PLICATION TO EDUCATION AND PSYCHOLOGY*, pp. 362-83.
New York: Ronald Press, 1954.

Schneider, Herbert Wallace. "John Dewey and His Influence." *New Era* 2 (1921): 136-40.

---. "He Modernized Our Schools." *New York Herald
Tribune*, 13 October 1929. [Reprinted in "Some Pop-
ular Appraisals of John Dewey," edited by Clyde R.
Miller, pp. 215-18.]

---. "The Prospect for Empirical Philosophy." In
JOHN DEWEY: THE MAN AND HIS PHILOSOPHY. Addresses
Delivered in New York in Celebration of His Seven-
tieth Birthday, pp. 106-34. Cambridge: Harvard Uni-
versity Press, 1930. [Reprinted as "Pan, the Logos
and John Dewey: A Legend of the Green Mountains."
In *Pan, the Logos and John Dewey*, edited by Mercedes
Irene Moritz Randall, pp. 7-15.]

---. "Dewey's Eighth Decade." In *A BIBLIOGRAPHY OF
JOHN DEWEY 1882-1939*, edited by Milton Halsey
Thomas, pp. ix-xviii.

---. "Moral Obligation." *Ethics* 50 (1939): 45-56.

---. "A Note on Dewey's Theory of Valuation." *Journal
of Philosophy* 36 (1939): 490-95.

---. *A HISTORY OF AMERICAN PHILOSOPHY*. Columbia
Studies in American Culture, no. 18. New York: Columbia University Press, 1946. [Dewey, passim.]

---. "Speaker Says UVM Helped Shape Dewey Ideas."

Vermont Alumni News 30 (December 1949): 20-21.

---. "Laity and Prelacy in American Democracy." In *JOHN DEWEY: PHILOSOPHER OF SCIENCE AND FREEDOM*, edited by Sidney Hook, pp. 177-83.

---. "John Dewey As My Teacher." *Progressive Education* 30 (1952): 11-13.

---. "Biographical Memoir: John Dewey (1859-1952)." In American Philosophical Society, *Yearbook, 1952*, pp. 311-15. Philadelphia: American Philosophical Society, 1953.

---. "Recollections of John Dewey." *Claremont Quarterly* 11 (Winter 1964): 23-31.

---. *SOURCES OF CONTEMPORARY PHILOSOPHICAL REALISM IN AMERICA*. New York: Bobbs-Merrill Co., 1964. [Dewey, passim.]

---. Review of Gérard Deledalle's *L'IDÉE D'EXPÉRIENCE DANS LA PHILOSOPHIE DE JOHN DEWEY*. *Journal of the History of Philosophy* 5 (1967): 300-301.

---. "Introduction to John Dewey's *PSYCHOLOGY*." In *The Early Works of John Dewey, 1882-1898*, edited by Jo Ann Boydston, vol. 2, pp. xxiii-xxvi.

---. "Dewey's Psychology." In *GUIDE TO THE WORKS OF JOHN DEWEY*, edited by Jo Ann Boydston, pp. 1-14.

---. "Dewey's Ethics." Part One. In *GUIDE TO THE WORKS OF JOHN DEWEY*, edited by Jo Ann Boydston, pp. 99-111.

---. "John Dewey's Empiricism." In *A BIBLIOGRAPHY OF JOHN DEWEY*, edited by Milton Halsey Thomas and Herbert Wallace Schneider, pp. ix-xxi. New York: Columbia University Press, 1929.

Schneider, Samuel. "On Some Criticisms of 'Experimentalism' in Education from the Moral Point of View." *Educational Theory* 10 (1960): 262-73.

Schoenchen, Gustav G. *THE ACTIVITY SCHOOL: A BASIC PHILOSOPHY FOR TEACHERS*. New York: Longmans, Green and Co., 1940. [Dewey, pp. 200-221, 284-94,

319-23, and passim.]

Scholastic Teacher. "Dewey Centennial." *Scholastic Teacher* 75 (1959): 1T.

School and Society. "Quotations: Tributes to John Dewey." [From *New York Times* and *New York Herald Tribune.*] *School and Society* 30 (1929): 577-79.

———. "A Publication in Honor of John Dewey's Eightieth Birthday." *School and Society* 50 (1939): 400-401.

———. "Meetings in Celebration of John Dewey's Eightieth Birthday." *School and Society* 50 (1939): 491-92.

———. "Wayne University Lecture Series on John Dewey." *School and Society* 70 (1949): 250.

School Executives Magazine. "Doctor John Dewey, Educator, Philosopher, and Exponent of Social Progress." *School Executives Magazine* 49 (1929): 172-74.

School Journal. "Pedagogy in the University of Chicago." *School Journal* 55 (1897): 210-11.

———. "The Fetich of Primary Education." *School Journal* 56 (1898): 629-30. [Editorial comment on Dewey's "The Primary Education Fetich." *Forum* 25 (1898): 315-28 (*Early Works of John Dewey* 5: 254-69.)]

———. "What They Think of Our Dewey." *School Journal* 71 (1905): 322. [Quotations from articles by E. A. Riley, Australia, and Alice Ravenhill, England.]

Schrader, Kristin. "Dewey on Science and Religion." *Thomist* 36 (1972): 658-70.

Schrag, Peter. "Teachers College: John Dewey with a Hard Nose." *Saturday Review*, 16 December 1967, pp. 62-64, 75-76.

Schultz, Frederick M. "'Intelligence' and 'Community' as Concepts in the Philosophy of John Dewey." *Educational Theory* 21 (1971): 81-89. [A response to Walter Feinberg's "The Conflict between Intelligence and Community in Dewey's Educational Philosophy."

Ibid. 19 (1969): 236-48. Reply by Feinberg, "Reply to Professor Schultz." Ibid. 21 (1971): 90-92.]

---. "Community as a Pedagogical Enterprise and the Functions of Schooling within It in the Philosophy of John Dewey." *Educational Theory* 21 (1971): 320-27.

Schwab, Joseph Jackson. "John Dewey: The Creature as Creative." *Journal of General Education* 7 (1953): 109-21.

---. "The 'Impossible' Role of the Teacher in Progressive Education." *School Review* 67 (1959): 139-59.

Schwartz, Benjamin. *CHINESE COMMUNISM AND THE RISE OF MAO*. Cambridge: Harvard University Press, 1951. [Dewey, pp. 19-23.]

Schwartz, Robert, and Atherton, Margaret. "Practice, Purpose, and Pedagogy." *Studies in Philosophy and Education* 7 (1970): 158-61.

Scott, Fred Newton. "John Dewey." *Castalian* 6 (1891): 23-29.

Scott, J. J. "Parker Called Originator of the School of Education." *New York Times*, 24 November 1929, p. 5. [Reply to Irwin Edman, "Our Foremost Philosopher at Seventy." *New York Times Magazine*, 13 October 1929, pp. 3, 23.]

Search-Light [Pseudonym for Waldo Frank]. "The Man Who Made Us What We Are." *New Yorker*, 22 May 1926, pp. 15-16. [Reprinted in *TIME EXPOSURES* (by Search-Light), pp. 121-27. New York: Boni and Liveright, 1926.]

Searles, Herbert Leon. "John Dewey and the New Liberalism." *Personalist* 28 (1947): 161-72.

---. "Pragmatism Today." *Personalist* 32 (1951): 137-52.

Sears, Laurence. *RESPONSIBILITY: ITS DEVELOPMENT THROUGH PUNISHMENT AND REWARD*. New York: Columbia University Press, 1932. [Dewey, pp. 59-67, 172-79, and passim.]

---, and Muelder, Walter George, eds. *THE DEVELOPMENT OF AMERICAN PHILOSOPHY: A BOOK OF READINGS*. Boston: Houghton Mifflin Co., 1940. [Dewey, pp. 315-16, and passim.]

Seasholes, Henry Craig. "Dewey or Marx?" *Ohio Schools* 26 (1948): 309.

Seigle, Kalman. "World Cheers Dewey at Lively 90; 1,500 Hear Educator Extolled." *New York Times*, 21 October 1949, p. 1.

Sellars, Roy Wood. "The Status of Epistemology." *Journal of Philosophy* 14 (1917): 673-80.

---. "Dewey on Materialism." *Philosophy and Phenomenological Research* 3 (1943): 381-92. [Abstracted in *Journal of Philosophy* 38 (1941): 684-85.]

---. "Is Naturalism Enough?" *Journal of Philosophy* 41 (1944): 533-44.

---; McGill, V. J.; and Farber, Marvin, eds. *PHILOSOPHY FOR THE FUTURE: THE QUEST FOR MODERN MATERIALISM*. New York: Macmillan Co., 1949. [Dewey, pp. 522-42, 604-10, and passim.]

Sellars, Wilfrid. "Language, Rules and Behavior." In *JOHN DEWEY: PHILOSOPHER OF SCIENCE AND FREEDOM*, edited by Sidney Hook, pp. 289-315.

Selsam, Howard. *PHILOSOPHY IN REVOLUTION*. New York: International Publishers, 1957. [Dewey, passim.]

---, and Lamont, Corliss. "Materialism and John Dewey." *New Masses*, 25 February 1947, pp. 17-23.

---. "'Philosophy in Revolution': A Discussion." *Science and Society* 22 (1958): 56-68. [Lamont's review, pp. 56-62; Selsam's reply, pp. 62-68.]

Sen, Krishna. "A Comparative Study of the Concept of Faith of Walter Terence Stace, Dewey, Søren Kierkegaard, and St. Thomas Aquinas." *Philosophical Quarterly* [India.] 19 (1956-57): 69-74.

Sesonske, Alexander, and Cavell, Stanley. "Logical Empiricism and Pragmatism in Ethics." *Journal of*

Philosophy 48 (1951): 5-17. [Reprinted in *PRAGMATIC PHILOSOPHY*, edited by Amelie Rorty, pp. 382-95.]

Seymour, Charles. Statement on Dewey in "Pragmatism in Education," by Boyd H. Bode. *New Republic*, 17 October 1949, p. 16.

Shamsuddin, Shri. "John Dewey's Philosophy of Education." *Aryan Path* 33 (1962): 262-65.

Shane, Harold Gray, ed. *THE AMERICAN ELEMENTARY SCHOOL.* Thirteenth Yearbook of the John Dewey Society. New York: Harper and Brothers, 1953. [Dewey, pp. 10-23, and passim.]

---. "An Interpretation of John Dewey's Basic Ideas and Their Influence on Classroom Practices." *Kent State University Bulletin*, College of Education Semicentennial Addresses, May 1960, pp. 7-17.

Shapiro, Phyllis P. "The Language of Poetry." *Elementary School Journal* 70 (1969): 130-34.

Shaw, Wilfred Byron, ed. *THE UNIVERSITY OF MICHIGAN: AN ENCYCLOPEDIC SURVEY.* 4 vols. Ann Arbor: University of Michigan Press, 1951. [See DeWitt Henry Parker and Charles B. Vibbert, "The Department of Philosophy," vol. 2, pp. 668-79; Walter Bowers Pillsbury, "The Department of Psychology," vol. 2, pp. 708-14; and Robert Cooley Angell, "The Department of Sociology," vol. 2, pp. 725-30.]

Shearer, Edna Aston. "Dewey's Esthetic Theory, Parts I and II." *Journal of Philosophy* 32 (1935): 617-27, 650-64.

Sheeks, Wayne. "The Concept of Truth in Certain Writings of Dewey, Santayana, and Royce." *Murray State University Review* 42 (1967): 53-64.

---. "The Role of Principles in Moral Judgment in the Philosophy of John Dewey." *Murray State University Review* 42 (1969): 119-24.

Sheerin, John B. "John Dewey and Christmas, 1950." *Catholic World* 172 (1950): 161-65.

---. "What Was the Question at Pasadena?" In *PUBLIC*

EDUCATION UNDER CRITICISM, edited by C. Winfield
Scott and Clyde M. Hill, pp. 94-98. Englewood
Cliffs, N.J.: Prentice-Hall, 1954.

Sheldon, Wilmon Henry. "Professor Dewey, The Protagonist of Democracy." *Journal of Philosophy* 18
(1921): 309-20.

---. *AMERICA'S PROGRESSIVE PHILOSOPHY*. New Haven:
Yale University Press, 1942. [Dewey, passim.]

---. "Critique of Naturalism." *Journal of Philosophy*
42 (1945): 253-70. [Reply by Dewey, with Sidney
Hook and Ernest Nagel, "Are Naturalists Materialists?" Ibid.: 515-30. Response by Sheldon, ibid.
43 (1946): 197-209.]

---. "The Conquest of Dualism." *New Republic*, 17 October 1949, pp. 29-32.

Shipka, Thomas A. "Dewey and the Functionalists."
Journal of Human Relations 18 (1970): 1177-1189.

---. "Conflict in Dewey's Philosophy." Proceedings
of the Ohio Philosophical Association Annual Meeting, University of Akron, 11 April 1970, pp. 34-44.
Mimeographed.

Shoemaker, Francis. *AESTHETIC EXPERIENCE AND THE HU-
MANITIES*. New York: Columbia University Press,
1943. [Dewey, pp. 86-92, and passim.]

Shoen, Harriet H., ed. "Conference to Celebrate John
Dewey's Eightieth Birthday." *School and Society* 50
(1939): 633-35. [Excerpts from papers read at the
conference of the Progressive Education Association,
New York City, 20 and 21 October 1939.]

Shotwell, James Thomson "Divergent Paths to Peace."
New Republic, 28 March 1928, p. 194. [In response
to Dewey's "As an Example to Other Nations." Ibid.,
7 March 1928, pp. 88-89.]

Shouse, James Blaine. "John Dewey: Giovanni Gentile."
Educational Forum 1 (1936): 74-80.

---. "The Educational Philosophy of John Dewey--
'Changing the World Through Action'." *Educational
Forum* 11 (1947): 223-31.

---. "The Educational Philosophy of John Dewey--

'Changing the Self in Emotion and Idea'." *Educational Forum* 11 (1947): 429-36.

Shumaker, Ann, and Rugg, Harold. *THE CHILD-CENTERED SCHOOL, AN APPRAISAL OF THE NEW EDUCATION.* Yonkers, N.Y.: World Book Co., 1928. [Dewey, passim.]

Sichel, Betty A. "Comments on Arthur M. Wheeler's 'Creativity in Plato's States'." *Educational Theory* 21 (1971): 208-18. [Dewey, p. 211.]

Silberman, Charles E. *CRISIS IN THE CLASSROOM: THE REMAKING OF AMERICAN EDUCATION.* New York: Random House, 1970. [Dewey, passim.]

Simec, Sophie M. "Human Nature According to John Dewey." In *PROCEEDINGS OF THE AMERICAN CATHOLIC PHILOSOPHICAL ASSOCIATION*, vol. 29, pp. 225-34. Washington, D.C.: Catholic University of America, 1955.

Simonson, Rebecca M. "The Making of Free, Responsible Citizens. I. Without Lock-Step." *Saturday Review of Literature*, 22 October 1949, p. 13.

---. "Teachers and Students of America Pay Tribute." In *JOHN DEWEY AT NINETY*, edited by Harry W. Laidler, pp. 25-26.

Simpson, George. Discussion of Theodore Brameld's review of *INTRODUCTION TO DIALECTICAL MATERIALISM* by August Thalheimer. *Marxist Quarterly* 1 (1937): 148-50. [Brameld's review, pp. 144-48.] ·

Sinclair, Upton. *THE AUTOBIOGRAPHY OF UPTON SINCLAIR.* New York: Harcourt, Brace and World, 1962. [Dewey, pp. 132-33, and passim.]

Singer, Marcus George. "Formal Logic and Dewey's Logic." *Philosophical Review* 60 (1951): 375-85.

---; Hay, William H.; and Murphy, Arthur E., eds. *REASON AND THE COMMON GOOD.* Englewood Cliffs, N.J.: Prentice-Hall, 1963. [Dewey, passim.]

Sisson, Edward O. "The Significance of John Dewey." *Hawaii Educational Review* 18 (1929): 29-32, 38-41.

Sizer, Nancy F. "John Dewey's Ideas in China, 1919 to

1921." *Comparative Education Review* 19 (1966): 390-403.

Skeeles, Arthur G. "The Parent and the Pedagogue *on Dewey*." *Ohio Schools* 25 (1947): 360-61.

Skilbeck, Malcolm. Introduction to *JOHN DEWEY*, edited by Malcolm Skilbeck. Educational Thinkers Series. London: Macmillan and Co., 1970.

Sleeper, Ralph William. "Being and Value in the Axiology of John Dewey." In *PROCEEDINGS OF THE AMERICAN CATHOLIC PHILOSOPHICAL ASSOCIATION*, vol. 33, pp. 83-96. Washington, D.C.: Catholic University of America, 1959.

---. "John Dewey's Empiricism and the Christian Experience." *Cross Currents* 9 (1959): 367-78.

---. "Dewey's Metaphysical Perspective: A Note on White, Geiger, and the Problem of Obligation." *Journal of Philosophy* 57 (1960): 100-115. [Reply to *SOCIAL THOUGHT IN AMERICA*, by Morton G. White, and *JOHN DEWEY IN PERSPECTIVE*, by George Geiger.]

---. "Pragmatism, Religion, and 'Experiencable Difference'." In *AMERICAN PHILOSOPHY AND THE FUTURE: ESSAYS FOR A NEW GENERATION*, edited by Michael Novak. New York: Charles Scribner's Sons, 1968. [Dewey, pp. 273-77, 298-307, and passim in Sleeper's essay.]

Sloan, Paul W. "Some Essentials of John Dewey's Progressivism." *Educational Administration and Supervision* 36 (1950): 501-4.

Slochower, Harry. "John Dewey: Philosopher of the Possible." *Sewanee Review* 52 (1944): 151-68. [Reprinted in his *NO VOICE IS WHOLLY LOST*, pp. 43-56. New York: Creative Age Press, 1945.]

---. "John Dewey and Morris R. Cohen." *Thinker* 4 (September 1931): 33-41.

Slosson, Edwin Emery. "John Dewey: Teacher of Teachers." *Independent*, 26 March 1917, pp. 541-44. [Reprinted in his *SIX MAJOR PROPHETS*, pp. 234-75. Boston: Little, Brown and Co., 1917.]

Smart, Harold Robert. "The Unit of Discourse."

Philosophical Review 50 (1941): 268-88.

---. "The Alleged Predicament of Logic." *Journal of Philosophy* 41 (1944): 598-604.

Smith, B. Othanel, and Ennis, Robert H., eds. *LANGUAGE AND CONCEPTS IN EDUCATION*. Chicago: Rand McNally and Co., 1961. [Dewey, passim.]

Smith, C. M. "The Aesthetics of John Dewey and Aesthetic Education." *Educational Theory* 21 (1971): 131-45. [Reply by Ernest E. Bayles, "Did Dewey Flub One?" Ibid.: 455-57. Response by Smith, ibid.: 458. See also Lawrence J. Dennis, "Dewey's Debt to Albert Coombs Barnes." Ibid. 22 (1972): 325-33.]

Smith, Ferrer. "A Thomistic Appraisal of the Philosophy of John Dewey." *Thomist* 18 (1955): 127-85.

Smith, James Ward. "Pragmatism, Realism, and Positivism in the United States." *Mind* 61 (1952): 190-208.

Smith, John Edwin. *ROYCE'S SOCIAL INFINITE*. New York: Liberal Arts Press, 1950. [Dewey, passim.]

---. "The Course of American Philosophy." *Review of Metaphysics* 11 (1957-58): 279-303. [Dewey, passim.]

---. "John Dewey: Philosopher of Experience." *Review of Metaphysics* 13 (1959): 60-78. [Reply by Richard Bernstein, "Dewey's Naturalism." Ibid.: 340-53.] [Also published in *JOHN DEWEY AND THE EXPERIMENTAL SPIRIT IN PHILOSOPHY*, edited by Charles W. Hendel, pp. 93-119. Reprinted in *REASON AND GOD* by John E. Smith, pp. 92-114. New Haven: Yale University Press, 1961. Also reprinted in *THE SPIRIT OF AMERICAN PHILOSOPHY* by John E. Smith, pp. 115-60. New York: Oxford University Press, 1963.]

---. *EXPERIENCE AND GOD*. New York: Oxford University Press, 1968. [Dewey, passim.]

---. *THEMES IN AMERICAN PHILOSOPHY: PURPOSE, EXPERIENCE AND COMMUNITY*. New York: Harper and Row, 1970. [Dewey, passim.]

Smith, John Milton. "John Dewey and Plato: The Foundations of Their Educational Philosophies." *Progressive Education* 27 (1949): 33-37.

---. "A Critical Estimate of Plato's and Dewey's Educational Philosophies." *Educational Theory* 9 (1959): 109-15.

Smith, Martin J. *JOHN DEWEY AND MORAL EDUCATION.* Washington, D.C.: Guthrie Lithograph Co., 1939. [Doctoral dissertation, University of Munich.]

Smith, Philip G. "Some Comments on Dewey's Theory of Valuation." Proceedings of the Philosophy of Education Society 16th Annual Meeting, 1960, pp. 69-71. Mimeographed.

---. "Going Beyond Experimentalism." *Educational Theory* 10 (1960): 78-82.

---. "Dimensions of Analysis and Recognized Meanings." *Educational Theory* 13 (1963): 183-88.

---. *PHILOSOPHY OF EDUCATION.* New York: Harper and Row, 1964. [Dewey, passim.]

---. "Valuations and the Uses of Language." In *PHILOSOPHY OF EDUCATION 1966: Proceedings of the Twenty-Second Annual Meeting of the Philosophy of Education Society*, pp. 145-56. Edwardsville, Ill.: Studies in Philosophy and Education, 1966. [Response by William Gruen, "Emotion, Imagination, and Logic in the Process of Thought." In ibid., pp. 157-60.]

---. "*HOW WE THINK*: A Re-examination." *Educational Forum* 31 (1967): 411-20.

Smith, Ralph A. "The Mass Media and John Dewey's Liberalism." *Educational Theory* 15 (1965): 83-93, 120.

Smith, S. L. "A First-Order Analysis of 'Education'." *Educational Theory* 20 (1970): 387-98.

Smith, Thomas Vernor. "Dewey's Theory of Value." *Monist* 32 (1922): 339-54.

---. "The Promise of American Politics." In *Resources for Building America*, Progressive Education Booklet, no. 15, pp. 5-19. Columbus, Ohio: Progressive Education Association, 1939.

---. "The Social Way of Life with John Dewey as Guide."
In his *THE PHILOSOPHIC WAY OF LIFE IN AMERICA*, pp.
81-104. 2d ed. New York: F. S. Crofts and Co., 1943.

---. "A Discussion of the Theory of International Re-
lations." *Journal of Philosophy* 42 (1945): 477-97.
[A discussion by several philosophers of two para-
graphs of Dewey's Introduction to Jane Addams, *PEACE
AND BREAD IN TIME OF WAR*. New York: King's Crown
Press, 1945.] [Smith, pp. 478-79. Other philoso-
phers: E. A. Burtt, Joseph P. Chamberlain, William
Ernest Hocking, Sidney Hook, Arthur O. Lovejoy,
Glenn R. Morrow, and Jerome Nathanson.]

Smith, Vincent Edward. "Dewey's Discovery of the Instrument." In his *IDEA-MEN OF TODAY*, pp. 25-54.
Milwaukee: Bruce Publishing Co., 1950.

---. "John Dewey (1859-1952): An Editorial." *New
Scholasticism* 26 (1952): 391-92.

Smith, William A. *JOHN DEWEY, ON HIS WRITINGS AND
IDEAS*. New York: Barrister Publishing Co., 1966.

Smuts, Jan Christian. Statement on Dewey in "The Influence of a First-Hand Mind," by Ralph Barton
Perry. *New Republic*, 17 October 1949, p. 13.

Snoddy, Elmer Ellsworth. "John Dewey and Pragmatism."
College of the Bible Quarterly 18 (1941): 4-32.

Snook, I. A. "The Concept of Indoctrination." *Studies
in Philosophy and Education* 7 (1970): 65-108.

Social Frontier. Editorial remarks. *Social Frontier*
3 (1936): 134-35. [On Dewey's "Rationality in Education." Ibid.: 71-73.]

Soderbergh, Peter A. "The Guilt of John Dewey: The
View from the Radical Right." *Educational Forum* 32
(1968): 315-22.

---. "Charles A. Beard in Chicago, 1896." *Journal of
the Illinois State Historical Society* 63 (1970):
125, 127.

Somjee, Abdulkarim H. *THE POLITICAL THEORY OF JOHN
DEWEY*. New York: Teachers College Press, 1968.

Sontag, Frederick. "Science and Evolution in Education: Dewey's Dream and Reality." *Journal of General Education* 17 (1965): 91-100.

Spain, Charles L. "Practical Aspects of John Dewey's
Philosophy." *Platoon School* 3 (1929): 149.

Spaulding, Edward Gleason. "Realism: A Reply to Professor Dewey and an Exposition." *Journal of Philosophy* 8 (1911): 63-77. [In response to Dewey's "The
Short-Cut to Realism Examined." Ibid. 7 (1910):
553-57.]

---. "A Reply to Professor Dewey's Rejoinder."
Journal of Philosophy 8 (1911): 566-74. [In re-
sponse to Dewey's "Rejoinder to Dr. Spaulding."
Ibid.: 77-79.]

---. "Joint Discussion with Articles of Agreement and
Disagreement: Professor Dewey and Dr. Spaulding."
Journal of Philosophy 8 (1911): 574-79.

Spitz, David. *ESSAYS IN THE LIBERAL IDEA OF FREEDOM.*
Tucson: University of Arizona Press, 1964. [Dewey,
passim.]

Spitzer, David D. "John Dewey: His Aesthetics Considered as a Contemporary Theory in Teaching the Humanities." *Art Education* 18 (November 1965): 8-12.

Spitzer, S. C. "A Liberal Has An Open Mind." *New
Masses* 7 (June 1931): 11.

Spivey, Ludd M. "What John Dewey Means by Habit." In
*Some Interpretations of John Dewey's Educational
Philosophy.* Bulletin of Florida Southern College,
vol. 67, pp. 28-31. Lakeland: Florida Southern
College, 1951.

Springfield [Mass.] *Union and Republican.* "John Dewey,
70 Today: Honored as America's Foremost Thinker."
Springfield Union and Republican, 20 October 1929.
[Reprinted in "Some Popular Appraisals of John
Dewey," edited by Clyde R. Miller, pp. 208-11.]

Stack, George J. "Critique of Dewey's Concept of the
Self." *Philosophical Quarterly* [India.] 39 (1966):
109-17.

Stanley, William O., and Benne, Kenneth D., eds. *Essays for John Dewey's Ninetieth Birthday*. Urbana: Bureau of Research and Service, College of Education, University of Illinois, 1950.

Stanwyck, Douglas J.; Felker, Donald W.; and Van Mondfrans, Adrian P. "An Examination of the Learning Consequences of One Kind of Civil Disobedience." *Educational Theory* 21 (1971): 146-54. [Dewey, pp. 146, 148-49.]

Starr, Isidore. "John Dewey, My Son, and Education for Human Freedom." *School Review* 62 (1954): 204-12.

Starr, Mark. "The Philosopher as a Man of Action." *Saturday Review of Literature*, 22 October 1949, p. 18. [Editorial.]

---. "Organized Labor and the Dewey Philosophy." In *JOHN DEWEY: PHILOSOPHER OF SCIENCE AND FREEDOM*, edited by Sidney Hook, pp. 184-93.

---. "John Dewey Attacked by the Communists." *Progressive Education* 29 (1951): 58-59.

Steibel, Gerald Lee. "John Dewey and the Belief in Communication." *Antioch Review* 15 (1955): 286-99.

---. "John Dewey, the Pragmatic Protagonist." *School Executive* 76 (1956): 53-64.

Steinberg, Ira S. *RALPH BARTON PERRY ON EDUCATION FOR DEMOCRACY*. Studies in Educational Theory of the John Dewey Society, no. 7. Columbus: Ohio State University Press, 1970. [Dewey, pp. 43-46, and passim.]

Steinberg, Julien, ed. *VERDICT OF THREE DECADES*. New York: Duell, Sloan and Pearce, 1950. [Leon Trotsky, "Why Stalin Triumphed," pp. 314-27, with Dewey on pp. 318-19; and Louis Fischer, "The Moscow Trials and Confessions," pp. 328-57, with Dewey on p. 347.]

Sternsher, Bernard. *REXFORD TUGWELL AND THE NEW DEAL*. New Brunswick, N.J.: Rutgers University Press, 1964. [Dewey, passim.]

Stevenson, Charles Leslie. *ETHICS AND LANGUAGE*. New

Haven: Yale University Press, 1944. [Dewey, pp. 253-64, and passim.]

---. "Reflections on John Dewey's Ethics." *Proceedings of the Aristotelian Society* n.s. 62 (1961-62): 77-98. [Reprinted in his *FACTS AND VALUES*, pp. 94-116. New Haven: Yale University Press, 1963.]

Stewart, David A. "Naturalism and the Problem of Value." *Queen's Quarterly* [Canada.] 56 (1949): 15-29.

Stiernotte, Alfred. "Dewey, Wieman, and Marx." *Christian Register* 124 (February 1945): 49-51.

Stine, William D. "Dewey's Conception of Logic." *Michigan Academician* 4 (1971): 101-13.

Stoddard, George Dinsmore. "On the Denigration of John Dewey." Princeton Unitarian Pulpit. Princeton, N.J.: Unitarian Church of Princeton, 1959. Mimeographed.

Stolberg, Benjamin. "Degradation of American Psychology." *Nation*, 15 October 1930, pp. 395-98.

Storey, M. L. "Dewey and Niebuhr: A Brief Juxtaposition." *Educational Theory* 3 (1953): 182-84.

---. "Learning by Thinking." *Science Education* 37 (1953): 331-35.

Storr, Richard J. *HARPER'S UNIVERSITY: THE BEGINNINGS*. Chicago: University of Chicago Press, 1966. [Dewey, pp. 124, 131, 296-302, and 339-41.]

Straight, Wood C. "Dewey and Our Inefficient Schools." *Brooklyn Daily Eagle*, 15 June 1922.

Strain, John Paul. "An Answer to the Misconceptions of John Dewey's Philosophy of Education." *Educational Theory* 8 (1958): 269-74.

Stratton, George M. "A Psychological Test of Virtue." *International Journal of Ethics* 11 (1901): 201-13. [On Dewey's *THE STUDY OF ETHICS: A SYLLABUS*.]

Strauss, Anselm. Introduction to *GEORGE HERBERT MEAD*

ON SOCIAL PSYCHOLOGY, edited by Anselm Strauss. Rev. ed. Chicago and London: University of Chicago Press, 1964. [Also passim.]

Stroh, Guy W. "John Dewey, Naturalism and Instrumentalism." In his *AMERICAN PHILOSOPHY FROM EDWARDS TO DEWEY*, pp. 237-76. Princeton, N.J.: D. Van Nostrand Co., 1968. [Also passim.]

Strong, Edward William. "Metaphors and Metaphysics." *International Journal of Ethics* 47 (1937): 461-71.

---. "John Dewey's Humanism: Man Making Himself. Part I: Man and Nature. Part II: Historical Humanism." *Humanist* 10 (1950): 203-7, 257-60.

Strout, Cushing. *THE PRAGMATIC REVOLT IN AMERICAN HISTORY: CARL BECKER AND CHARLES BEARD*. New Haven: Yale University Press, 1958. [Dewey, passim.]

---. "Pragmatism in Retrospect: The Legacy of James and Dewey." *Virginia Quarterly Review* 43 (1967): 123-34. [Reprinted in his *INTELLECTUAL HISTORY IN AMERICA FROM DARWIN TO NIEBUHR*, vol. 2, pp. 73-82. New York: Harper and Row, 1968.]

Stuart, Henry Waldgrave. "Dewey's Ethical Theory." In *THE PHILOSOPHY OF JOHN DEWEY*, edited by Paul Schilpp, pp. 291-334.

Sugitani, Masafumi. "Main Problems of Philosophy of Education in Japan Today." *Education in Japan* 1 (1966): 83-93. [Dewey, pp. 85-86.]

Suits, Bernard Herbert. "Naturalism: Half-Hearted or Broken-Backed?" *Journal of Philosophy* 58 (1961): 169-79.

Sullivan, Phyllis. "John Dewey's Philosophy of Education." *High School Journal* 49 (1966): 391-96.

Summerscales, William. *AFFIRMATION AND DISSENT: COLUMBIA'S RESPONSE TO THE CRISIS OF WORLD WAR I*. New York: Teachers College Press, 1970. [Dewey, passim.]

Sun, H. C. "Chinese Philosophy Since the Seventeenth Century." *Educational Theory* 14 (1964): 54-64.

---. "Open Classroom: A Critique." *High School Journal* 56 (1972): 134-41. [Condensed in *Education Digest* 38 (March 1933): 32-34.]

Suppan, A. A. "The Making of Free, Responsible Citizens. 3: Participants in Life." *Saturday Review of Literature*, 22 October 1949, p. 14.

Survey. "John Dewey in Russia." *Survey* 61 (1928): 348-49.

---. "John Dewey Looks Ahead." *Survey* 75 (1939): 344.

---. "John Dewey at 85." *Survey* 80 (1944): 323.

---. "Among Ourselves." *Survey* 85 (1949): 506. [Dewey's Ninetieth Birthday Celebration.]

Susky, John E. "How Would Dewey Answer Critics of 'Deweyism'?" *Phi Delta Kappan* 40 (1958): 24-27.

Suttell, Lloyd. "Intelligence in the Modern World (John Dewey: 1859-1952)." *Pedagogia* 1 (1953): 70-84.

---. "Dewey's Theory of Judgment." *Pedagogia* 3 (1955): 25-31.

Sweeney, Florence. "The Making of Free, Responsible Citizens. 2: Learning by Doing." *Saturday Review of Literature*, 22 October 1949, pp. 13-14.

Sylwester, Robert, and Bowers, C. A. "John Dewey: Our Man in Chicago and Woodstock." *Instructor* 80 (1970): 83-85.

Tagliacozo, Giorgio. "The Tree of Knowledge." *American Behavioral Scientist* 4 (1960): 6-12.

Takeda, Kazuo. "An Examination of Post-War Japanese Education Based on John Dewey's Theory." *Educational Forum* 26 (1961): 53-61.

Tamme, Anne Mary. *A CRITIQUE OF JOHN DEWEY'S THEORY OF FINE ART IN THE LIGHT OF THE PRINCIPLES OF THOMISM.* Washington, D.C.: Catholic University of America, 1956. [Doctoral dissertation.]

Tate, Allen. "The Aesthetic Emotion as Useful." *This Quarter* 5 (1932): 292-303.

Taylor, George Edward, and Michael, Franz Henry. *THE FAR EAST IN THE MODERN WORLD.* Rev. ed. New York: Henry Holt and Co., 1964. [Dewey's visit to China, pp. 229, 232, 234-35, and 715.]

Taylor, Harold. Statement on Dewey in "The Conquest of

Dualism," by Wilmon Henry Sheldon. *New Republic*, 17 October 1949, p. 31.

---. "Modern Education and the Progressive Movement." *Antioch Review* 15 (1955): 272-85.

Taylor, John E. *PRAGMATISM AND INSTRUMENTAL EXPERI-MENTALISM*. Ottawa: Editorial de l'Université, 1942. [Dewey, passim.]

Taylor, Richard Wirth, ed. *LIFE, LANGUAGE, LAW: ESSAYS IN HONOR OF ARTHUR F. BENTLEY*. Yellow Springs, Ohio: Antioch Press, 1957. [Dewey, passim.]

Templin, Ralph. "Dewey, Gandhi and the Community in Education." *Journal of Human Relations* 1 (Autumn 1952): 55-61.

Tenenbaum, Samuel. *WILLIAM HEARD KILPATRICK: TRAIL BLAZER IN EDUCATION*. New York: Harper and Brothers, 1951. [Dewey, passim.]

Tesconi, Charles A., Jr. "John Dewey's Theory of Meaning." *Educational Theory* 19 (1969): 156-70.

Thayer, Horace Standish. "Two Theories of Truth: The Relation between the Theories of John Dewey and Bertrand Russell." *Journal of Philosophy* 44 (1947): 516-27. [Taken from his Master's thesis, of the same title, Columbia University, 1947.]

---. "Critical Notes on Dewey's Theory of Propositions." *Journal of Philosophy* 48 (1951): 607-13. [Apropos of Dewey's "Propositions, Warranted Assertibility and Truth." Ibid. 38 (1941): 169-86.]

---. *THE LOGIC OF PRAGMATISM: AN EXAMINATION OF JOHN DEWEY'S LOGIC*. New York: Humanities Press, 1952. [Doctoral dissertation, Columbia University.]

---. "Pragmatism." In *A CRITICAL HISTORY OF WESTERN PHILOSOPHY*, edited by D. J. O'Connor, pp. 437-62. New York: Free Press, 1964.

---. *MEANING AND ACTION: A CRITICAL HISTORY OF PRAG-MATISM*. Indianapolis: Bobbs-Merrill Co., 1968. [Dewey, pp. 165-204, 460-87, and passim.]

---. Introduction to *PRAGMATISM: THE CLASSIC WRITINGS*,

edited by Horace Standish Thayer, pp. 253-61. New
York: New American Library, 1970.

Thayer, Vivian Trow. "John Dewey's Seventieth Anniversary." *Journal of Educational Research* 20 (1929):
373-75.

---. *RELIGION IN PUBLIC EDUCATION.* New York: Viking
Press, 1947. [Dewey, passim.]

Thilly, Frank. "Contemporary American Philosophy."
Philosophical Review 35 (1926): 522-38.

Thomas, Dana Lee, and Henry. "John Dewey--The Architect of a Better World." In their *LIVING ADVENTURES
IN PHILOSOPHY*, pp. 301-12. Garden City, N.Y.: Han-
over House, 1954.

Thomas, George F. "Naturalistic Humanism: Feuerbach
and Dewey." In his *RELIGIOUS PHILOSOPHIES OF THE
WEST*, pp. 339-51. New York: Charles Scribner's
Sons, 1965.

Thomas, Henry. "Dewey, John." In his *BIOGRAPHICAL
ENCYCLOPEDIA OF PHILOSOPHY*, pp. 71-74. New York:
Doubleday and Co., 1965.

---, and Dana Lee. "John Dewey--The Architect of a
Better World." In their *LIVING ADVENTURES IN PHI-
LOSOPHY*, pp. 301-12.

Thomas, Lawrence G. "Implications of Transaction Theory." *Educational Forum* 32 (1968): 145-55.

Thomas, Milton Halsey. *A BIBLIOGRAPHY OF JOHN DEWEY,
1882-1939.* Introd. by Herbert W. Schneider. New
York: Columbia University Press, 1939.

---. *JOHN DEWEY: A CENTENNIAL BIBLIOGRAPHY.* Chicago:
University of Chicago Press, 1962.

---, and Schneider, Herbert Wallace. *A BIBLIOGRAPHY OF
JOHN DEWEY.* New York: Columbia University Press,
1929.

Thomas, Wendell Marshall. *A DEMOCRATIC PHILOSOPHY.*
New York: Correlated Enterprises, 1938. [Dewey, pp.
11-37, and passim.]

---. "Reflections on Dewey's Philosophy." *Journal of Adult Education* 12 (1940): 23-25.

---. "Anglo-American Views: Dewey; Lloyd Morgan." In his *ON THE RESOLUTION OF SCIENCE AND FAITH*, pp. 72-81. New York: Island Press, 1946. [Also passim.]

Thompson, Dorothy. "The Statement of Dr. John Dewey." *New York Herald Tribune*, 27 December 1937. [On Dewey's interview with Agnes E. Meyer, *Washington Post*, 19 December 1937.]

Thorpe, Louis P., and Schmuller, Allen M. "Problem Solving: Dewey's View of Learning as Experience." In their *CONTEMPORARY THEORIES OF LEARNING WITH AP-PLICATIONS TO EDUCATION AND PSYCHOLOGY*, pp. 362-83. New York: Ronald Press Co., 1954.

Threlkeld, Archie Lloyd. "Dr. Dewey's Philosophy and the Curriculum." *Curriculum Journal* 8 (1937): 164-66.

Thut, I. N. "The Status of John Dewey's Philosophical Position Today." *Educational Theory* 10 (1960): 26-31, 56.

Tibbetts, Paul. "Some Recent Philosophical Contribu-tions to the Problem of Consciousness." Parts 1 and 2. *Philosophy Today* 14 (1970): 3-22, 23-32. [Dewey: 14-15, 30-31.]

---. "John Dewey and Contemporary Phenomenology on Experience and the Subject-Object Relation." *Phi-losophy Today* 15 (1971): 250-75.

Time. "To Moscow." *Time*, 4 June 1928, pp. 16-17.

---. "Trotsky's Trial." *Time*, 17 May 1937, p. 20.

---. "One Wonders." *Time*, 20 February 1939, pp. 56-57.

---. "Dewey at 80." *Time*, 30 October 1939, pp. 38-40. [Reprinted in *CONTEMPORARY AMERICAN BIOGRAPHY*, ed-ited by John A. Beckwith and Geoffrey G. Coope, pp. 171-73. New York: Harper and Brothers, 1941.]

---. "Mission II and I." *Time*, 17 May 1943, pp. 19-20.

---. "Dewey Unchanged." *Time*, 24 June 1946, pp. 45-46, 48.

---. "Perpetual Arriver." *Time*, 31 October 1949, pp. 35-36.

---. "Mortimer Adler: Fusilier." *Time*, 17 March 1952, pp. 76-84. [Dewey, pp. 76-77.]

---. "Account Rendered." *Time*, 9 June 1952, pp. 47-48.

---. "Let Us Get On . . ." *Time*, 12 October 1953, pp. 89-90.

---. "The Long Shadow of John Dewey." *Time*, 31 March 1958, p. 44.

Times (London). "Dr. John Dewey's 90th Birthday." *Times*, 22 October 1949, p. 3.

Times Literary Supplement (London). "Humanism Revisited." *Times Literary Supplement*, 20 January 1961, p. 41.

To, Cho-Yee. "John Dewey's View of the School as a Democratic Community." *Education and Psychology Review* 8 (1968): 3-13.

---. "The Method of Intelligence in Dewey's Philosophy of Education." *Malaysian Journal of Education* 5 (1968): 121-39.

Townsend, Harvey Gates. *PHILOSOPHICAL IDEAS IN THE UNITED STATES*. New York: American Book Co., 1934. [Dewey, pp. 233-50, and passim.]

Trembath, Margaret. "John Dewey, Philosopher and Educator." *Australian Pre-School Quarterly and Aboriginal Gazette* 7 (1966): 20-23.

Trotsky, Leon. "Trotsky Sees Trial As Reply to Dewey." *New York Times*, 3 March 1938, p. 15.

Troutner, Leroy F. "What Can the Educator Learn from the Existential Philosopher?" In *PHILOSOPHY OF EDUCATION 1966: Proceedings of the Twenty-Second Annual Meeting of the Philosophy of Education Society*, pp. 98-105. Edwardsville, Ill.: Studies in Philosophy

and Education, 1966. [Response by Victor Kestenbaum, "Phenomenology and Dewey's Empiricism: A Response to Leroy Troutner." *Educational Theory* 22
(1972): 99-108.]

---. "Dewey and the Individual Existent." *Personalist*
48 (1967): 281-96.

---. "John Dewey, the Individual Existent, and Education." In *PHILOSOPHY OF EDUCATION, 1967: Proceedings of the Twenty-Third Annual Meeting of the Philosophy of Education Society*, pp. 84-96. Edwardsville, Ill.: Studies in Philosophy and Education,
1967.

---. "The Confrontation Between Experimentalism and
Existentialism--From Dewey Through Heidegger and
Beyond." In *PHILOSOPHY OF EDUCATION, 1968: Proceedings of the Twenty-Fourth Annual Meeting of the Philosophy of Education Society*, pp. 186-94. Edwardsville, Ill.: Studies in Philosophy and Education,
1968. [Revised and expanded in *Harvard Educational
Review* 39 (1969): 124-54.]

Troy Record. Editorial comment. *Troy Record*, 27 December 1930. [On Dewey's letter to Senator George
William Norris in *New York Times*, 26 December 1930,
p. 1.]

Tugwell, Rexford G. *THE BRAINS TRUST*. New York:
Viking Press, 1968. [Dewey, passim.]

Turner, Joseph. "Irony Compounded." *Science* 133
(1961): 301.

Tyack, David B., ed. *TURNING POINTS OF AMERICAN EDU-
CATIONAL HISTORY*. Waltham, Mass.: Blaisdell Publishing Co., 1967. [Dewey, pp. 314-23, 359-62, and
passim.]

Ulich, Robert. "John Dewey." In his *HISTORY OF EDU-
CATIONAL THOUGHT*, pp. 315-36. New York: American
Book Co., 1945.

---. "Contemplations on the Philosophy of John Dewey."
Comparative Education 3 (1967): 79-84.

---. "Dewey 1859-1952." In *THREE THOUSAND YEARS OF*

EDUCATIONAL WISDOM. Selections from Great Documents,
edited by Robert Ulich, pp. 615-17. 2d enl. ed.
Cambridge: Harvard University Press, 1954. [Intro-
duction to Dewey reprints.]

University [of Michigan] *Record.* Announcement of
"Thought News." *University Record* 2 (1892): 22.

Ushenko, Andrew. "Inquiry and Discourse." *Journal of
Philosophy* 37 (1940): 484-91.

Valentine, Willard L., and Wickens, Delos D. *EXPERI-
MENTAL FOUNDATIONS OF GENERAL PSYCHOLOGY.* 3d ed.
New York: Rinehart and Co., 1949. [Dewey, pp.
390-94, and passim.]

Vandenberg, Donald. "Experimentalism in the Anesthetic
Society: Existential Education." *Harvard Educational Review* 32 (1962): 155-87.

Van Dusen, Henry Pitney. "The Faith of John Dewey."
Religion in Life 4 (1935): 123-32. [Reply by Marion
John Bradshaw, "A Comment on Van Dusen's Dismissal
of Dewey." *Review of Religion* 3 (1938): 97-100.]

*VANITY FAIR. SELECTIONS FROM AMERICA'S MOST MEMORABLE
MAGAZINE.* New York: Viking Press, 1960. ["John
Dewey," p. 187.]

Van Liew, Charles Cecil. Discussion of Dewey's "Interpretation of the Culture-Epoch Theory." *Public
School Journal* 15 (1896): 546. [Dewey's article,
ibid.: 233-36 (*Early Works of John Dewey* 5: 247-53.)]

Van Patten, James. "Camus, Dewey and Relevance."
Journal of Thought 3 (1968): 48-60.

Van Til, William A. "John Dewey's Disciples." *Educational Leadership* 7 (1949): 201-2.

Van Wesep, Henry B. *SEVEN SAGES. THE STORY OF AMER-
ICAN PHILOSOPHY: FRANKLIN, EMERSON, JAMES, DEWEY,
SANTAYANA, PEIRCE, WHITEHEAD.* New York: Longmans,
Green and Co., 1960. [Dewey, pp. 182-247.]

Veazie, Walter B. "John Dewey and the Revival of Greek
Philosophy." In *University of Colorado Studies,*
Series in Philosophy, no. 2, pp. 1-10. Boulder:

University of Colorado Press, 1961.

Vermont Alumni News. "Campus Extends Cheering Welcome to One of Its Most Distinguished Alumni." *Vermont Alumni News* 30 (1949): 20.

Vermont Cynic. "A Day in the Life of John Dewey"; "Professor H. W. Schneider Delivers Lecture"; "Noon-time Reception for John Dewey"; Letter to the Editor. *Vermont Cynic*, 2 November 1949.

Viator, Britannicus. "Representative Men: VI--John Dewey." *English Review* 62 (1936): 644-46.

Villemain, Francis Trowbridge. "Dewey and the Critical Faculty." *Saturday Review*, 21 November 1959, pp. 26, 52.

---, and Champlin, Nathaniel. "Frontiers for an Experimentalist Philosophy of Education." *Antioch Review* 19 (1959): 345-59.

---, eds. "Dewey and Creative Education." *Saturday Review*, 21 November 1959, pp. 19-25. [Manifesto signed by Joe Burnett, Hobert W. Burns, Nathaniel Champlin, Otto Krash, Frederick C. Neff, and Francis T. Villemain.]

Virtue, Charles F. Sawhill. "General Philosophy and Philosophy of Education: A Word from an Academic Philosopher." *Educational Theory* 8 (1958): 203-12.

Visalberghi, Aldo. "Remarks on Dewey's Conception of Ends and Means." *Journal of Philosophy* 50 (1953): 737-53.

Vivas, Eliseo. "A Definition of the Esthetic Experience." *Journal of Philosophy* 34 (1937): 628-34.

---. "A Note on the Emotion in Mr. Dewey's Theory of Art." *Philosophical Review* 47 (1938): 527-31. [Reprinted in his *CREATION AND DISCOVERY: ESSAYS IN CRITICISM AND AESTHETICS*, pp. 223-28. New York: Noonday Press, 1955.]

---. "John Dewey's Achievement." *Partisan Review* 6 (1939): 79-91.

---. "The Instrumentalist Moral Theory." In his *THE*

MORAL LIFE AND THE ETHICAL LIFE, pp. 100-137. Chicago: University of Chicago Press, 1950.

Wade, Francis C. "The Child-Centered School--Dogma or Heresy?" *National Catholic Education Association Bulletin* 52 (1955): 200-209. [Also printed in *PROCEEDINGS OF THE AMERICAN CATHOLIC PHILOSOPHICAL ASSOCIATION*, vol. 29, pp. 263-74. Washington, D.C.: Catholic University of America, 1955.]

Walcott, Fred George. "Dewey's Theory of Social Progress." *Education* 80 (1960): 319.

Waldman, Joseph. Letter on John Dewey and Albert Coombs Barnes, in response to Sidney Hook's "Some Memories of John Dewey". *Commentary* 14 (1952): 503-4. [Hook's article, ibid.: 245-53. His reply to Waldman, ibid.: 504.]

Walker, Leslie J. *THEORIES OF KNOWLEDGE: ABSOLUTISM, PRAGMATISM, REALISM*. Stonyhurst Philosophical Series. London: Longmans, Green and Co., 1910. [Master's thesis, University of London.] [Dewey, passim.]

Walling, William English. *THE LARGER ASPECTS OF SOCIALISM*. New York: Macmillan Co., 1913. [Dewey, pp. 9-27, 34-40, 263-86, and passim.]

Walton, John. "Professor Jargon: A Remedy." *Peabody Journal of Education* 30 (1952): 161-65.

Wang, Tsi C. *THE YOUTH MOVEMENT IN CHINA*. New York: New Republic, 1927. [Dewey, passim.]

Warbeke, John M. "Form in Evolutionary Theories of Art." *Journal of Philosophy* 38 (1941): 293-300. [Abstracted with the title "Esthetic Form and Criteria in Croce and Dewey," in ibid. 36 (1939): 679.]

Ward, Leo Richard. *PHILOSOPHY OF VALUE: AN ESSAY IN CONSTRUCTIVE CRITICISM*. New York: Macmillan Co., 1930. [Doctoral dissertation, Catholic University of America, 1929.] [Dewey, passim.]

---. *VALUES AND REALITY*. London: Sheed and Ward, 1935. [Dewey, passim.]

---. "John Dewey in Search of Himself." *Review of*

Politics [University of Notre Dame.] 19 (1957): 205-13.

---. "Dewey's Learning by Doing." In his *NEW LIFE IN CATHOLIC SCHOOLS*, pp. 101-21. St. Louis: B. Herder Book Co., 1958.

Ward, Paul William. "The Doctrine of the Situation and the Method of Social Science." *Social Forces* 9 (1930): 49-54.

Warde, William F. "John Dewey's Theories of Education." *International Socialist Review* 21 (1960): 5-8.

---. "The Fate of Dewey's Theories." *International Socialist Review* 21 (1960): 54-57.

Wardwell, Mary Spargo. "College Youth Better Mannered." *Vermont Alumnus* 18 (1939): 196-97. [Interview.]

Warnock, Mary. *ETHICS SINCE 1900*. 2d ed. London: Oxford University Press, Galaxy Books, 1966. [Dewey, pp. 107-13, 115.]

Warren, William Preston. "The Limits of Instrumentalism, or John Dewey's Replies to His Critics." *Furman Bulletin* 22 (April 1940): 41-54.

---. "Experimentalism Plus." *Philosophy and Phenomenological Research* 33 (1972): 149-62.

Watson, Goodwin. "John Dewey as a Pioneer in Social Psychology." *Teachers College Record* 51 (1949): 139-43.

Webb, John Nye. "Three Score and Ten: Interview with John Dewey." *Columbia Varsity* 11 (1929): 3-4.

Weber, C. A. "A Reply to Critics of 'Progressive' Methods in Education." *Educational Administration and Supervision* 31 (1945): 79-86.

Wegener, Frank C. "Some Differences between the Organic Philosophy of Education and John Dewey's Experimentalism." *Educational Theory* 8 (1958): 239-48.

Wehrwein, Austin C. "Universities Tied to Bad Education." *New York Times*, 29 October 1957, p. 28.

[Dr. Lawrence A. Kimpton on "distortion" of Dewey's philosophy.]

---. "Massive Revision of History Urged." *New York Times*, 29 December 1959, p. 9. [Lawrence A. Cremin defends Dewey's theories against proponents of "tougher education."]

Weinstock, Henry R. "Dewey's Views on a Science of Education." *Educational Forum* 30 (1965): 491-96.

Wellman, Robert R. "Dewey's Theory of Inquiry: The Impossibility of Its Statement." *Educational Theory* 14 (1964): 103-10. [Reply by Philip Eddy, "On the Statability of Dewey's Theory of Inquiry." Ibid. 15 (1965): 321-26. Response by Wellman, "Further Notes on Dewey's Logic: A Response." Ibid. 15 (1965): 327-29.]

Wells, Harry K. *PRAGMATISM: PHILOSOPHY OF IMPERIALISM*. New York: International Publishers, 1954. [A Marxist critique of Charles S. Peirce, John Fiske, Oliver Wendell Holmes, William James, and John Dewey.]

Welsh, Paul. "Judgment and Propositions in Dewey's *LOGIC*." *Methodos* 7 (1955): 107-14.

---. "Means and Ends in Dewey's Ethical Theory." *Journal of Philosophy* 56 (1959): 960-66.

---. "Some Metaphysical Assumptions in Dewey's Philosophy." *Journal of Philosophy* 51 (1954): 861-67.

Wenley, Robert Mark. *THE LIFE AND WORK OF GEORGE SYLVESTER MORRIS*. New York: Macmillan Co., 1917. [Dewey, pp. 312-21, and passim.]

Werkmeister, William Henry. "The Experimentalism of John Dewey." In his *A HISTORY OF PHILOSOPHICAL IDEAS IN AMERICA*, pp. 541-61. New York: Ronald Press Co., 1949.

West, C. P. "Pragmatism: The Logic of Capitalism." *New Essays* [United Workers Party, Chicago.] 6 (1943): 61-79.

Whalen, Willis L. "A Fifth Column in Catholic Education?" *Homiletic and Pastoral Review* 51 (1951): 708-12.

Wheeler, Arthur M. "God and Myth." *Hibbert Journal* 62 (1964): 170-73.

---. "Niebuhr, Dewey, and God." *Journal of Religious Thought* 25 (1968-69): 42-48.

Wheeler, James E. "Education and the Aristoi." *Educational Theory* 1 (1951): 41-46, 62. [Dewey, pp. 45-46, 62.]

---. "John Dewey's DEMOCRACY AND EDUCATION." *Social Education* 16 (1952): 100-102.

---. "The Thought of John Dewey in its Historical Setting." *Educational Theory* 4 (1954): 87-94.

White, Carl Milton. "The Bearing of John Dewey's Philosophy of Education on Problems Confronting Librarians." *School and Society* 45 (1937): 516-17.

White, Edward A. "Naturalism versus Supernaturalism: John Dewey." In his *SCIENCE AND RELIGION IN AMERICAN THOUGHT: THE IMPACT OF NATURALISM.* Stanford University Publications, Series in History, Economics, and Political Science, vol. 8, pp. 90-109. Stanford, Cal.: Stanford University Press, 1952.

White, Howard Burton. "The Political Faith of John Dewey." *Journal of Politics* 20 (1958): 353-67.

White, Lucia, and Morton Gabriel. "The Plea for Community: Robert Park and John Dewey." In their *THE INTELLECTUAL VERSUS THE CITY*, pp. 155-78. Cambridge: Harvard University Press, 1962.

White, Morton Gabriel. *THE ORIGIN OF DEWEY'S INSTRUMENTALISM.* Columbia Studies in Philosophy, no. 4. New York: Columbia University Press, 1943. [Doctoral dissertation, 1942.]

---. "IV. Dewey on the Genetic Method." *Journal of Philosophy* 42 (1945): 328-31.

---. "The Revolt Against Formalism in Americal Social Thought of the Twentieth Century." *Journal of the History of Ideas* 8 (1947): 131-52.

---. *SOCIAL THOUGHT IN AMERICA: THE REVOLT AGAINST FORMALISM.* New York: Viking Press, 1949. [2d ed., with new preface and an epilogue, "Original Sin, Natural Law, and Politics," defending Dewey against Reinhold Niebuhr and Walter Lippmann. Boston: Beacon Press, 1957.] [Response by Ralph William Sleeper, "Dewey's Metaphysical Perspective." *Journal of Philosophy* 57 (1960): 100-115.]

---. "Value and Obligation in Dewey and [Clarence Irving] Lewis." *Philosophical Review* 58 (1949): 321-29. [Reprinted in *READINGS IN ETHICAL THEORY*, edited by Wilfrid Stalker Sellars and John Hospers, pp. 332-39. New York: Appleton-Century-Crofts, 1952.] [Later revised in *PRAGMATISM AND THE AMERICAN MIND* by Morton G. White, pp. 155-67. New York: Oxford University Press, 1973.]

---. "The Analytic and the Synthetic: An Untenable Dualism." In *JOHN DEWEY: PHILOSOPHER OF SCIENCE AND FREEDOM*, edited by Sidney Hook, pp. 316-30.

---. "Science and Morals: John Dewey (1859-1952)." In his *THE AGE OF ANALYSIS: TWENTIETH CENTURY PHILOSOPHERS.* The Great Ages of Western Philosophy, vol. 6. Boston: Houghton Mifflin Co., 1955; New York: New American Library of World Literature, 1955. [Extract from *THE QUEST FOR CERTAINTY*, with White's discussion of Dewey's ethical views on pp. 173-78. Also Dewey, passim.]

---. "Experiment and Necessity in Dewey's Philosophy." *Antioch Review* 19 (1959): 329-44. [From a paper delivered at Brandeis University, April 1959, in the series "John Dewey in the Light of Recent Philosophy."] [Revised version in *SIDNEY HOOK AND THE CONTEMPORARY WORLD*, edited by Paul Kurtz, pp. 392-406.] [Later revised version in *PRAGMATISM AND THE AMERICAN MIND* by Morton G. White, pp. 138-54. New York: Oxford University Press, 1973.]

---. "John Dewey: Rebel Against Dualism." In his *SCIENCE AND SENTIMENT IN AMERICA. PHILOSOPHICAL THOUGHT FROM JONATHAN EDWARDS TO JOHN DEWEY*, pp. 266-89. New York: Oxford University Press, 1972.

---. "Social Darwinism and Dewey's Pragmatism." In his *PRAGMATISM AND THE AMERICAN MIND*, pp. 194-99. New York: Oxford University Press, 1973. [A revised version of his review of Richard Hofstadter's *SOCIAL DARWINISM IN AMERICAN THOUGHT, 1860-1915*. *Journal of the History of Ideas* 6 (1945): 119-22.]

---. "John Dewey: A Great Philosopher of Education." In his *PRAGMATISM AND THE AMERICAN MIND*, pp. 244-47. [First printed as a review of *JOHN DEWEY: LECTURES IN THE PHILOSOPHY OF EDUCATION: 1899*, edited by Reginald D. Archambault. *New York Times Book Review*, 24 July 1966, pp. 11-12.]

---. ed, *DOCUMENTS IN THE HISTORY OF AMERICAN PHILOSOPHY, FROM JONATHAN EDWARDS TO JOHN DEWEY*. New York: Oxford University Press, 1972. [Introduction to several Dewey reprints, pp. 443-46.]

---, and Lucia. "The Plea for Community: Robert Park and John Dewey." In their *THE INTELLECTUAL VERSUS THE CITY*, pp. 155-78.

White, Stephen Solomon. *A COMPARISON OF THE PHILOSOPHIES OF F. C. S. SCHILLER AND JOHN DEWEY*. Chicago, 1940. [Reproduced from typewritten copy, "Private edition, distributed by the University of Chicago Libraries, Chicago, Illinois."] [Doctoral dissertation, 1938.]

Whitehead, Alfred North. Remarks on Dewey's "Whitehead's Philosophy." *Philosophical Review* 46 (1937): 178-86. [Dewey's article, ibid.: 170-77.]

---. "John Dewey and His Influence." In *THE PHILOSOPHY OF JOHN DEWEY*, edited by Paul Schilpp, pp. 477-78. [Reprinted in Whitehead's *ESSAYS IN SCIENCE AND PHILOSOPHY*, pp. 120-21. New York: Philosophical Library, 1947.]

Whitman, Howard. "Progressive Education--Which Way Forward?" *Collier's*, 14 May 1954, pp. 32-36.

Whittemore, Robert Clifton. "Learning as Living: John Dewey." In his *MAKERS OF THE AMERICAN MIND*, pp. 440-59. New York: William Morrow and Co., 1964.

Wickens, Delos D., and Valentine, Willard L. *EXPERIMENTAL FOUNDATIONS OF GENERAL PSYCHOLOGY*. 3d ed. New York: Rinehart and Co., 1949. [Dewey, pp. 389-94, and passim.]

Wickham, Harvey. "The Winnowing Fan." In his *THE UNREALISTS: JAMES, BERGSON, SANTAYANA, EINSTEIN,*

BERTRAND RUSSELL, JOHN DEWEY, ALEXANDER AND WHITE-HEAD, pp. 196-218. New York: Lincoln MacVeagh, Dial Press, 1930.

Wielenga, G. "Didactics and a Philosophy of Life (John Dewey)." *Free University Quarterly* [Amsterdam.] 2 (1953): 236-50.

Wieman, Henry Nelson. "Religion in Dewey's *EXPERIENCE AND NATURE*." *Journal of Religion* 5 (1925): 519-42.

---. "Religion in John Dewey's Philosophy." *Journal of Religion* 11 (1931): 1-19. [Abridged in *Divinity Student* 8 (1931): 1-16.]

---. "John Dewey's Common Faith." *Christian Century* 51 (1934): 1450-52. [Reply by Edwin Ewart Aubrey, "Is John Dewey a Theist?" Ibid.: 1550. Wieman's response, ibid.: 1550-51. Dewey's reply, ibid.: 1551-52. Wieman's response, ibid.: 1552-53.]

---. "Dewey and Buckham on Religion." *Journal of Religion* 15 (1935): 10-21.

---. "Philosophers' Dean: The Dual Dewey." *Christian Register* 128 (November 1949): 22-24.

---, and Macintosh, Douglas Clyde. "Mr. Wieman and Mr. Macintosh 'Converse' with Mr. Dewey." *Christian Century* 50 (1933): 299-302. [In response to Dewey's "A God or The God?" Ibid.: 193-96. Rejoinder by Dewey, "Dr. Dewey Replies." Ibid.: 394-95.]

Wiener, Philip Paul. *EVOLUTION AND THE FOUNDERS OF PRAGMATISM*. Cambridge: Harvard University Press, 1949. [Dewey, passim.]

Wienpahl, Paul De Velin. "Dewey's Theory of Language and Meaning." In *JOHN DEWEY: PHILOSOPHER OF SCIENCE AND FREEDOM*, edited by Sidney Hook, pp. 271-88.

Wiggins, Forrest Oran. "William James and John Dewey." *Personalist* 23 (1942): 182-98.

Wild, John Daniel, ed. *THE RETURN TO REASON: ESSAYS IN REALISTIC PHILOSOPHY*. Chicago: Henry Regnery Co., 1953. [Dewey, passim.]

Wilkins, Burleigh Taylor. "James, Dewey, and Hegelian

Idealism." *Journal of the History of Ideas* 17
(1956): 332-46.

---. "Pragmatism as a Theory of Historical Knowledge:
John Dewey on the Nature of Historical Inquiry."
American Historical Review 64 (1959): 878-90.

Williams, Chester Sidney. *HOW PROGRESSIVE IS JOHN
DEWEY'S PHILOSOPHY OF EDUCATION?* University of
Wichita Studies, no. 43, pp. 3-10. Wichita, Kans.:
University of Wichita, 1959.

Williams, Donald Cary. "Mr. John Dewey on Problems and
Men." *Harvard Educational Review* 16 (1946): 297-
308.

---. *PRINCIPLES OF EMPIRICAL REALISM*, edited by Harry
Ruja. American Lecture Series, edited by Marvin
Farber, no. 615. Springfield, Ill.: Charles C.
Thomas, 1966. [Dewey, passim.]

Williams, Jay. "Dewey and the Idea of a Science of
Education." *School Review* 67 (1959): 186-94.

Williams, Lloyd P. "The Experimentalist's Conception
of Authority." *Educational Theory* 3 (1953): 208-11.

---. "The Experimentalist's Conception of Freedom."
Educational Theory 4 (1954): 105-12.

---. "A Note on John Dewey's View of History." *Southwestern Social Science Quarterly* 38 (1957): 228-35.

---. "A Liberal's Perspective on the Dismal Science:
John Dewey's View of Economic Theory and Practice."
Educational Theory 20 (1970): 177-88.

Williams, Robert Bruce. "John Dewey and Oil City."
Peabody Journal of Education 46 (1969): 223-26.

Willing, Matthew H. "John Dewey and Education." In
IN HONOR OF JOHN DEWEY ON HIS NINETIETH BIRTHDAY,
pp. 24-28. Madison: University of Wisconsin, 1951.

Wilson, Francis Graham. "The Foremost Philosopher of
the Age." *Modern Age* 2 (1957-58): 54-62.

Winetrout, Kenneth. "Must Pragmatists Disagree? Dewey

and Schiller." *Educational Theory* 10 (1960): 57-65.

---. *F. C. S. SCHILLER AND THE DIMENSIONS OF PRAGMA-TISM.* Studies in Educational Theory of the John Dewey Society, no. 5. Columbus: Ohio State University Press, 1967. [Dewey, passim.]

---. "Adlerian Psychology and Pragmatism." *Journal of Individual Psychology* 24 (1968): 5-24.

Winkelmann, Roy R. "Revolution Within an Evolution." *Christian Century* 86 (1969): 1577-80.

Winn, Ralph B. *AMERICAN PHILOSOPHY.* New York: Philosophical Library, 1955. [Dewey, pp. 288-90.]

Winterrle, John F. "John Dewey and the League of Nations." *North Dakota Quarterly* 34 (1966): 75-88.

Wirth, Arthur G. *JOHN DEWEY AS EDUCATOR: HIS DESIGN FOR WORK IN EDUCATION (1894-1904).* New York: John Wiley and Sons, 1966. [Reprinted, New Delhi: Wiley Eastern, 1969.]

---. "Reply to George Dykhuizen." *Studies in Philosophy and Education* 6 (1968): 23. [In response to Dykhuizen's review of *JOHN DEWEY AS EDUCATOR.* Ibid.: 14-22.]

---. "Psychological Theory for Experimentation in Education at John Dewey's Laboratory School, the University of Chicago, 1898-1904." *Educational Theory* 18 (1968): 871-80.

---. "John Dewey's Design for American Education: An Analysis of Aspects of His Work at the University of Chicago, 1894-1904." *History of Education Quarterly* 4 (1964): 83-105.

---. "John Dewey in Transition from Religious Idealism to the Social Ethic of Democracy." *History of Education Quarterly* 5 (1965): 264-68.

---. "The Deweyan Tradition Revisted." *Teachers College Record* 69 (1967): 263-69. [Revised and expanded in *Washington University Magazine* 38 (1968): 46-51.] [Abstracted in *Education Digest* 33 (April 1968): 28-31.]

---. "The Vocational-Liberal Studies Controversy between John Dewey and Others (1900-1917)." Washington, D.C.: U.S. Department of Health, Education and
Welfare, 1970. [For an article based on this study,
see his "John Dewey's Philosophical Opposition to
Smith-Hughes Type Vocational Education." *Educational
Theory* 22 (1972): 69-77.] [This study, with modifi-
cations, published as *EDUCATION IN THE TECHNOLOGICAL
SOCIETY: The Vocational-Liberal Studies Controversy
in the Early Twentieth Century*. Scranton: Intext
Educational Publishers, 1972.]

---. "John Dewey *vs*. the Social Efficiency Philosophers." *Man/Society/Technology* 6 (1972): 170-72.

---, and Bewig, Carl. "John Dewey on School Architecture." *Journal of Aesthetic Education* 2 (1968):
79-86.

Wisconsin, University of. *IN HONOR OF JOHN DEWEY ON
HIS NINETIETH BIRTHDAY* . . . Madison: University of
Wisconsin, The School of Education and the Depart-
ment of Philosophy, 1951. [Papers by Max Otto,
Matthew Willing, Frederick Logan, Fred Clarenbach,
Leonard Huskins, and Horace Fries.]

Woll, Matthew. Reply to Dewey's "Labor Politics and
Labor Education". *New Republic*, 20 February 1929,
pp. 19-20. [Dewey's article, ibid., 9 January 1929,
pp. 211-14. Rejoinder by Dewey, ibid., 20 February
1929, p. 20.]

Wolstein, Benjamin. "A Transaction with Mr. Kahn."
Journal of Philosophy 44 (1947): 663-66. [Reply to
Sholom J. Kahn, "Transaction vs. Interaction."
Ibid.: 660-63.]

---. "Science and Esthetic Experience." *Columbia
Review* 28 (February 1948): 20-27.

---. *EXPERIENCE AND VALUATION: A STUDY IN JOHN DEWEY'S
NATURALISM*. New York: Privately Printed, 1949.
[Doctoral dissertation, Columbia University.]

---. "Addison Webster Moore: Defender of Instrumentalism." *Journal of the History of Ideas* 10 (1949):
539-66.

---. "Dewey's Theory of Human Nature." *Psychiatry*

12 (1949): 77-85.

---. "The Meaning of Power in Scientific Inference." *Philosophy and Phenomenological Research* 10 (1950): 420-25.

---. "A Note on the Functional Theory of Habit." *Journal of the History of Ideas* 11 (1950): 490-92.

---. *TRANSFERENCE: ITS STRUCTURE AND FUNCTION IN PSYCHOANALYTIC THERAPY*. 2d ed. New York: Grune and Stratton, 1964. [Dewey, passim.]

Wood, Charles W. "Professor Dewey of Columbia on War's Social Results." *New York World*, 29 July 1917. [Interview.]

---. "Professor John Dewey on the Hysteria Which Holds Teaching in Check." *New York World*, 27 August 1922. [Interview.]

Woodbridge, Frederick James Eugene. "Of What Sort Is Cognitive Experience?" *Journal of Philosophy* 2 (1905): 573-76. [In response to Dewey's "The Postulate of Immediate Empiricism." Ibid.: 393-99.]

---. "The Promise of Pragmatism." *Journal of Philosophy* 26 (1929): 541-52.

---. "Experience and Dialectic." *Journal of Philosophy* 27 (1930): 264-71. [Reprinted in his *NATURE AND MIND*, pp. 230-39. 1937. New York: Columbia University Press, 1964.] [Response by Dewey, "In Reply to Some Criticisms." *Journal of Philosophy* 27 (1930): 271-77.]

Woodmansee, R. E. "Dr. Dewey and the I.L.P." *New Republic*, 27 February 1929, p. 46.

Woodring, Paul. "The Shadow of John Dewey." In his *LET'S TALK SENSE ABOUT OUR SCHOOLS*, pp. 27-48. New York: McGraw-Hill Book Co., 1953. [Also passim.]

---. "A Pragmatic Point." *Nation*, 31 July 1954, p. 99. [In reply to James Campbell Bay, "Our Public Schools: Are They Failing?" Ibid., 26 June 1954, pp. 539-41.]

---. *A FOURTH OF A NATION*. New York: McGraw-Hill

Book Co., 1957. [Dewey, passim.]

Woody, Susan Minot. "The Theory of Sovereignty: Dewey Versus Austin." *Ethics* 78 (1968): 313-18.

Woolf, S. J. "John Dewey Surveys the Nation's Ills." *New York Times*, 10 July 1932, p. 9. [Interview.]

---. "A Philosopher's Philosophy." *New York Times*, 15 October 1939, pp. 5, 17. [Interview.]

Woolverton, John Frederick. "William Augustus Muhlenberg and the Founding of St. Paul's College." *Historical Magazine of the Protestant Episcopal Church* 29 (1960): 192-218.

World Tomorrow. "Education in Action: The Story of John Dewey." *World Tomorrow* 14 (1931): 106-9.

World's Work. "A Philosopher on Broadway." *World's Work* 59 (April 1930): 36. [Editorial.]

Wright, Henry Wilkes. "Ethics and Social Philosophy." In *PHILOSOPHY TODAY*, edited by Edward Leroy Schaub, pp. 87-104. Chicago: Open Court Publishing Co., 1928.

Wu Han Lih. "Professor Dewey's Second Visit to China." *China Weekly Review*, 4 April 1931, pp. 176-77.

Wynne, John Peter. "Mind and Education from the Standpoint of John Dewey and George Herbert Mead." *Educational Theory* 2 (1952): 129-40.

Yarros, Victor S. "Empiricism and Philosophic Method: Professor Dewey's Views." *Open Court* 39 (1925): 586-92.

---. "Metaphysics, Psychology, and Philosophy: Professor Dewey's Views." *Open Court* 39 (1925): 669-75.

---. "The Province and Issues of Philosophy: Professor Dewey's Views." *Open Court* 39 (1925): 755-66.

---. "Social Science, Subjectivism, and the Art of Thinking." *Open Court* 40 (1926): 537-46.

Yengo, Carmine A. "John Dewey and the Cult of Efficiency." *Harvard Educational Review* 34 (1964): 33-53.

Yocum, Albert Duncan. "Dr. Dewey's 'Liberalism' in Government and in Public Education." *School and Society* 44 (1936): 1-5.

Young, Elizabeth L. "Dewey and Bruner: A Common Ground?" *Educational Theory* 22 (1972): 58-68, 77. [Apropos of June Fox, "Epistemology, Psychology and Their Relevance for Education in Bruner and Dewey." Ibid. 19 (1969): 58-75.]

Young, Ella Flagg. "The Philosophy of Education, 1895-1902, John Dewey." In her *SOME TYPES OF MODERN EDUCATIONAL THEORY*. University of Chicago Contributions to Education, no. 6, pp. 53-67. Chicago: University of Chicago Press, 1902.

Young, Warren Cameron. "The Influence of John Dewey in Religious Education." Typewritten. Chicago, Ill.: Published by the Author, 1949.

Younker, Donna Lee. "Structures For Society: A Comparison of B. F. Skinner and John Dewey." In *PHILOSOPHY OF EDUCATION, 1969: Proceedings of the Twenty-Fourth Annual Meeting of the Philosophy of Education Society*, pp. 149-55. Edwardsville, Ill.: Studies in Philosophy and Education, 1969.

Zedler, Beatrice Hope. "John Dewey in Context." In *SOME PHILOSOPHIES OF EDUCATION: Papers Concerning the Doctrines of Augustine, Aristotle, Aquinas, and Dewey*, edited by Donald A. Gallagher, pp. 1-25. Milwaukee: Marquette University Press, 1956.

---. "Dewey's Theory of Knowledge." In *JOHN DEWEY: HIS THOUGHT AND INFLUENCE*, edited by John Blewett, pp. 59-84.

Zeno, Mary. "Stoicism in Education--Dewey and Brameld." *Social Justice Review* 53 (1961): 298-300.

Zepper, John T. "Krupskaya on Dewey's Educational Thought." *School and Society* 100 (1972): 19-21.

Zink, Sidney. "Warranted Judgments in Dewey's Theory of Valuation." *Philosophical Review* 51 (1942): 502-8.

---. "The Concept of Continuity in Dewey's Theory of
Esthetics." *Philosophical Review* 52 (1943):
392-400.

Zinman, Meyer E. "John Dewey's Philosophy and the
Classroom Teacher." *High Points* [New York City
Board of Education] 14 (November 1932): 31-36.

Zuidema, S. U. "Contemporary Situationism in John
Dewey and Martin Heidegger: A Comparison." In his
COMMUNICATION AND CONFRONTATION, pp. 190-214.
Netherlands: Royal Van Gorcum, 1972.

UNPUBLISHED WORKS ABOUT DEWEY

Ackley, Sheldon Carmer. "John Dewey's Conception of Shared Experience as Religious." Doctoral dissertation, Boston University, 1948.

Adams, Eugene Taylor. "The Epistemology of John Dewey." Doctoral dissertation, Yale University, 1934.

Aeschliman, Adrian Rene. "Exposition and Criticism of Dewey's Theory of Knowledge." Master's thesis, Washington University, 1932.

Ahern, Alvin A. "The Significance of the Views of John Dewey and William Ernest Hocking for Moral Education." Master's thesis, New York University, 1939.

Aichele, Ronald Guy. "John Dewey's DEMOCRACY AND EDUCATION: From a Logical Point of View." Doctoral dissertation, University of Missouri, 1971.

Alamshah, William H. "John Dewey's Ethical Theory." Doctoral dissertation, University of Southern California, 1955.

Allen, Bernard L. "Dewey's Writings on War in Peace." Master's thesis, Southern Illinois University, 1964.

---. "John Dewey's Views on History, 1859-1952." Doctoral dissertation, West Virginia University, 1971.

Allen, Harold. "Dewey's Criticism of the British Empiricists." Master's thesis, Columbia University, 1951.

Ames, Edward Scribner. "Religious Implications of John

Dewey's Philosophy." N.d. [Dewey Collection,
Morris Library, Southern Illinois University.]

Anderberg, Clifford W. "The Impact of Evolution on
Dewey's Theory of Knowledge and the Critics of
Dewey." Doctoral dissertation, University of Wis-
consin, 1953.

Anderson, Emerald Balboa. "Semantic Problems in Dewey's Logic." Doctoral dissertation, Syracuse University, 1966.

Anderson, Frederick Mitchell. "John Dewey's Critique
of Philosophies." Doctoral dissertation, Harvard
University, 1961.

Anderson, John Melchoir. "Education for an Optimum
Community: A Study of Community Type and Significance in John Dewey's Philosophy." Doctoral dissertation, University of Wisconsin, 1972.

Appell, Morris Lionel. "John Dewey--Pattern for Adven-
turing." Master's thesis, Ohio State University,
1941.

Armstrong, Philip J. "The Role of Language in John
Dewey's Philosophy of Man." Master's thesis, Catholic University of America, 1962.

Aronovitz, Alfred. "The Foundations of John Dewey's
Political Theory." Typewritten manuscript submitted
for the Bennett Prize, Harvard University, 1950.

Arscott, John Robert. "Moral Freedom and the Educative
Process; A Study in the Educational Philosophy of
William Torrey Harris." Doctoral dissertation, New
York University, 1948. [Dewey, pp. 97-143.]

Aschener, Mary Jane. "A Study of John Dewey's Conception of the Improvement of Thinking." Master's
thesis, University of Illinois, 1953.

Augur, Sherwood. "Functionalism--The Chicago School."
In "E. L. Thorndike's Educational Psychology and
the American Educational Program of 1890-1915," pp.
24-39. Doctoral dissertation, University of Michigan, 1961.

Austin, Avel. "Symbol and Existence in Locke and

Dewey." Master's thesis, Columbia University, 1953.

Austin, Ernest Hampton, Jr. "John Dewey's Application of History: The Relation of Past Events to Contemporary Problems as Presented by the Experimental Philosophy of History." Doctoral dissertation, University of Florida, 1965.

Aveilhe, Clyde C. "Pragmatism and American Education: A Philosophical Examination of Four Crucial Issues." Master's thesis, Howard University, 1966. [Dewey, passim.]

Avent, George Jacob. "The Logic of Evaluation in the Philosophy of John Dewey." Master's thesis, Emory University, 1948.

Bahn, Lorene Anna. "Principles of Educational Administration Based upon the Writings of John Dewey." Doctoral dissertation, Washington University, 1963.

Baird, Robert Malcolm. "John Dewey and Richard Brandt: A Study in the Justification of Ethical Principles." Doctoral dissertation, Emory University, 1967.

Baird, Ronald J. "The Application of John Dewey's Philosophy to Industrial Arts Teacher Education." Doctoral dissertation, Michigan State University, 1960.

Bal, Amarjit Singh. "A Comparative Study of the Educational Objectives of John Dewey and Mahatma Gandhi and an Examination of Basic Education in Punjab, India." Doctoral dissertation, University of California at Berkeley, 1970.

Baldauf, Violet Miriam. "The Religious Implications of the Philosophy of John Dewey." Master's thesis, New York University, 1938.

Bales, James David. "The Instrumentalism of John Dewey." In "A History of Pragmatism in American Educational Philosophy," pp. 90-129. Doctoral dissertation, University of California at Los Angeles, 1946. [Also passim.]

Barcewicz, Regina. "Thomas Edward Shields and John Dewey: A Comparative Study." Master's thesis, University of Detroit, 1955.

Barr, Helen A. "The Ethics of John Dewey." Master's thesis, University of Wisconsin, 1932.

Barske, Charlotte. "Social Studies Program Based on John Dewey's Theories." Master's thesis, University of Bridgeport, 195--.

Bassano, Helen J. "The Ideas of Jean Jacques Rousseau and John Dewey on Discipline in Education." Master's thesis, East Texas State University, 1967.

Battle, John J. "The Metaphysical Presuppositions of the Philosophy of John Dewey." Doctoral dissertation, Fribourg, 1951.

Baum, Maurice James. "A Comparative Study of the Philosophies of William James and John Dewey." Doctoral dissertation, University of Chicago, 1928.

Beard, John S. "The Religious Implications of John Dewey's Philosophy of Experimentalism." Bachelor's thesis, Duke University, 1944.

Beck, Robert Holmes. "American Progressive Education, 1875-1930." Doctoral dissertation, Yale University, 1942.

Bednar, Charles S. "John Dewey's Rationale for a Democratic Society." Doctoral dissertation, Columbia University, 1960.

Beebe, Walter Scott. "Are Scientific Propositions concerning Ethics Possible? Moritz Schlick and John Dewey." Master's thesis, University of Colorado, 1952.

Beeson, Richard W. "Cultural Determinants in British Philosophy; Support for a Deweyan Hypothesis." Master's thesis, University of New Mexico, 1964.

Bell, James William. "A Comparative Analysis of the Normative Philosophies of Plato, Rousseau, and Dewey as Applied to Physical Education." Doctoral dissertation, Ohio State University, 1971.

Belth, Marc. "The Concept of Democracy in Dewey's Theory of Education." Doctoral dissertation, Columbia University, 1956.

Bennett, Philip W. "John Dewey's Theory of Value in the Light of Contemporary Ethical Theory." Bachelor's thesis, Rutgers University, 1964.

Benson, Stephen Eric. "A Critique of John Dewey's Philosophical Method in the Light of an Examination of His Belief in the Continuity of Nature." Doctoral dissertation, University of Colorado, 1970.

Benster, Ada Roe. "Unrealistic Aspects of Dewey's Social Philosophy." Master's thesis, University of Colorado, 1949.

Berleant, Arnold. "Logic and Social Doctrine: Dewey's Methodological Approach to Social Philosophy." Doctoral dissertation, University of Buffalo, 1962.

Berliner, Michael S. "John Dewey's View of Free-Will." Doctoral dissertation, Boston University, 1971.

Bernstein, Richard Jacob. "John Dewey's Metaphysics of Experience." Doctoral dissertation, Yale University, 1958.

Berry, Cornelius Oliver. "The Concept of the Self in John Dewey and John Macmurray: A Summary Critique." Doctoral dissertation, Columbia University, 1971.

Betts, Eugenia S. "A Study of the Progressive Education Movement in the United States." Master's thesis, University of Texas, 1952. [Dewey, passim.]

Billings, Anne. "The Idea of Scientific Method in Dewey's *LOGIC, THE THEORY OF INQUIRY*." Bachelor's thesis, Reed College, 1958.

Bilstad, Ingeborg Warne. "Aspects of Dewey's *THE PUBLIC AND ITS PROBLEMS* as Reflected in Selected Secondary Textbooks." Master's thesis, University of Wisconsin, 1946.

Bingham, William Eugene, Jr. "A Study of Sense-Imagery Conditioning the Aims of Education of John Dewey and Rabindranath Tagore." Master's thesis, University of Southern California, 1941.

Bixhorn, Seymour W. "Implications of the Writings of John Dewey for Educational Administration." Doctoral dissertation, University of Connecticut, 1963.

Black, Hugh C. "The Learning-Product and Learning-Process Theories of Education--An Attempted Synthesis." Doctoral dissertation, University of Texas, 1949.

Black, Penny Merle. "The Moral Bias of John Dewey's Liberalism." Honors thesis, Harvard University, 1964.

Blake, William Northrup. "John Dewey's Concept of Work and Educational Implications." Master's thesis, University of Alberta, 1964.

Blankenship, Earl Scott. "Some Implications of Dewey's Theory of Knowledge for the Study of Economics." Doctoral dissertation, Ohio State University, 1955.

Blewett, John. "The Origins and Early Mutations of John Dewey's Ethical Theory (1884-1904)." Doctoral dissertation, St. Louis University, 1959.

Blockman, Betty Ray. "A Critique of Four of the Philosophies of Education." Master's thesis, Memphis State University, 1960. [Dewey, pp. 40-44, and passim.]

Boardman, William Giles. "A Study in Dewey's Theory of Knowledge." Master's thesis, Columbia University, 1936.

Bock, Daniel Raymond. "The Viewpoints of John Dewey on Selected Questions from Curriculum Theory." Doctoral dissertation, Northwestern University, 1960.

Bögholt, Carl M. "John Dewey's Views on Philosophic Method in His Early Writings, 1882-1903." Doctoral dissertation, University of Wisconsin, 1933.

Bonar, W. F. "Dewey's Philosophy of Democracy in Education." Master's thesis, University of Akron, 1934.

Boor, John G. "A Validation of Brubacher's Interpretation of Progressive Education Based on the Writings of John Dewey." Master's thesis, St. Louis University, 1957.

Bordeau, Edward J. "The Practical Idealism of John
    Dewey's Political Philosophy: An Answer to Some
    Critics." Doctoral dissertation, Fordham University,
    1969.

Bourdeaux, Robert M. "The Influence of the Theory of
    Evolution on John Dewey's Concept of Self." Mas-
    ter's thesis, University of North Carolina, 1968.

Bowman, Jimmie A. "A Study of John Dewey's Educational
    Philosophy as Related to the Current Teaching of
    Poetry in American Secondary School English Classes."
    Master's thesis, Arizona State University, 1965.

Bradford, Alvin Priestly. "An Approach to the Philos-
    ophy of Adjustment; a Consideration of Organic Cate-
    gories and the Sociology of Knowledge with Reference
    to Correlativity as a Category of Integration."
    Master's thesis, University of Texas, 1941.

Brady, Mary L. "John Dewey: Philosophy as a Methodol-
    ogy." Doctoral dissertation, Fordham University,
    1945.

Brantl, George E. "The Meaning of Pragmatism." Mas-
    ter's thesis, Fordham University, 1951.

Braun, John T. "John Dewey: Systematic Theologian."
    Master's thesis, Reed College, 1954.

Bretscher, T. A. "Subjectivism and Objectivism as Seen
    from the Point of View of the Instrumentalogic of
    John Dewey and Rudolf Eucken." Master's thesis,
    University of Cincinnati, 1929.

Brod, Carol. "Dewey and Heidegger: The Problem of
    Knowledge." Master's thesis, Hunter College, 1966.

Brodbeck, May. "The Theory of Propositions in John
    Dewey's Logic." Master's thesis, University of
    Iowa, 1945.

---. "A Critical Examination of John Dewey's *LOGIC:
    THE THEORY OF INQUIRY*." Doctoral dissertation, Uni-
    versity of Iowa, 1947.

Brodhead, Bickley Burns. "A Comparison of the Ethics
    of John Dewey and Frederick Nietzsche." Doctoral

dissertation, Temple University, 1956.

Brodsky, Garrett Martin. "John Dewey's Theory of Inquiry." Doctoral dissertation, Yale University,
1960.

Brosio, Richard Anthony. "The Relationship of Dewey's
Pedagogy to His Concept of Community." Doctoral
dissertation, University of Michigan, 1972.

Brown, Bob B. "The Relationship of Experimentalism to
Classroom Practice." Doctoral dissertation, University of Wisconsin, 1963.

Brown, James Good. "The Evolutionary Concept in John
Dewey's Philosophy and Its Implications for Religious Education." Doctoral dissertation, Yale University, 1936.

Brown, Marcus. "The Question of Ontology in Dewey's
Philosophy." Master's thesis, New York University,
1954.

Brown, Patricia Babcock. "An Analysis of the Theories
of John Dewey and Alfred North Whitehead on the
Qualitative Aspect of Experience and the Relation of
These Theories to Education." Doctoral dissertation, New York University, 1962.

Browning, Robert W. "Reason in Ethics and Morals, with
Special Reference to the Contribution of Hume and
Dewey." Doctoral dissertation, University of Cali-
fornia, 1947.

Brownson, William Earl. "John Dewey's Concept of Habit
and the Dynamics of Growth." Doctoral dissertation,
Stanford University, 1970.

Bruce, Lee. "John Dewey's Theory of Experience."
Master's thesis, University of Chicago, 1932.

Buchcik, Anthony Alfred. "The Concept of Morals in the
Philosophies of St. Augustine and John Dewey." Doctoral dissertation, University of Chicago, 1955.

Bucher, Raymond John. "The Current Academic Crisis:
Toward a Solution According to John Dewey's Notion
of the Public." Doctoral dissertation, Fordham

University, 1970.

Burnside, Houston M. "Philosophic Foundations of John
Dewey's Teaching Method." Master's thesis, Claremont Graduate School, 1963.

---. "John Dewey and Martin Buber: A Comparative
Study." Doctoral dissertation, Claremont Graduate
School, 1969.

Burr, John Roy. "Three Dimensions of Philosophic Intelligence: Private, Public, and Visional, in the
Philosophies of Warner Fite, John Dewey, and George
Santayana." Doctoral dissertation, Columbia University, 1959.

Burton, Thomas H. "A Critique of Pragmatism in Education." Master's thesis, Marquette University, 1956.

Buswell, James Oliver, Jr. "The Empirical Method of Frederick Robert Tennant." Doctoral dissertation, New
York University, 1949.

Cahan, Ruth. "The Implementation of the John Dewey
Philosophy of Education in the University Elementary
School, U.C.L.A." Master's thesis, University of
California at Los Angeles, 1958.

Callahan, John C. "De-humanization of Man in John
Dewey's Philosophy." Master's thesis, Boston College, 1950.

Callison, Edwin Ray. "Plato and Dewey in Education."
Master's thesis, Washington University, 1940.

Campochiaro, Joseph N. "John Dewey's Theory of Work
Activity to Modern Education." Master's thesis,
Southern Connecticut State College, 1965.

Canoy, Mary Zeno. "Dewey: Stoic Socialism Parallels
Sociological Naturalism." In "Stoicism in Modern
Educational Theory and Practice," pp. 86-96. Mas-
ter's thesis, St. Louis University, 1957.

Carlin, Joseph E. "A Comparative Study of the Educational and Related Theories of Professor John Dewey
and Professor William Hocking." Doctoral dissertation, New York University, 1942.

Carew, George Benjamin. "John Dewey's Philosophy of
    State." Master's thesis, Howard University, 1968.

Carlisi, Joseph. "Dewey's Conception of Philosophy as
    Experimental." Master's thesis, Hunter College,
    1966.

Carloye, Jack Cloyd. "Bradley and Dewey: On Objective
    Knowledge." Master's thesis, University of Chicago,
    1953.

---. "Reason as a Natural Function in the Philosophy
    of John Dewey." Doctoral dissertation, University
    of Illinois, 1960.

Carpenter, Sandra Witt. "Mead, Dewey, and Wheelright
    on Scientific and Expressive Language." Doctoral
    dissertation, Claremont Graduate School, 1970.

Cartozian, Bruce K. "The Role of the Inferential Func-
    tion in Dewey's Theory of Knowledge." Bachelor's
    thesis, Reed College, 1950.

Case, Matthew H. "The Ethics of John Dewey Compared
    with the Moral Teachings of Jesus." Master's the-
    sis, Eastern Washington College of Education, 1955.

Casteel, Charles E. "John Dewey's Pupil Participation
    Concept and Its Implication for Religious Education."
    Doctoral dissertation, Iliff School of Theology,
    Denver, Colo., 1960.

Chamberlain, O. H. "A Study of John Dewey's Logical
    Reconstruction." Doctoral dissertation, University
    of North Carolina, 1931.

Champlin, Nathaniel Lewis. "Controls in Qualitative
    Thought." Doctoral dissertation, Teachers College,
    Columbia University, 1952.

Chan, Sion S. "A Comparative Study of Selected Aspects
    of the Educational Philosophies of Confucius and
    John Dewey." Master's thesis, Tennessee Technolog-
    ical University, 1969.

Chandler, Charles Clarence. "Veblen and Dewey." In
    "Institutionalism and Education: An Inquiry into the
    Implications of the Philosophy of Thorstein Veblen,"
    pp. 173-82. Doctoral dissertation, Michigan State
    University, 1959.

Chandler, Robert Woodward. "Ethical Relativism in the Light of Contemporary American Theories." Doctoral dissertation, Columbia University, 1953.

Chang, Chieh-Min. "The Utilitarian Theory of Jeremy Bentham Defended from Certain Criticism of John Stuart Mill and John Dewey." Master's thesis, Columbia University, 1925.

Chang, George W. "The Individual and Society in the Philosophy of John Dewey." Master's thesis, University of Hawaii, 1966.

Chang, Yin-Lin. "A Comparative Study of the Ethical Theories of G. E. Moore and John Dewey." Master's thesis, Stanford University, 1932.

Chao, Chen. "An Account of John Dewey's Conception of the Three Logical 'Laws of Thought'." Master's thesis, Columbia University, 1950.

Chartier, Thora. "A Study of the Progressive Education Movement in the United States." Master's thesis, Kansas State Teachers College, 1941.

Chavis, James Simon. "An Evaluation of John Dewey's Views on Human Nature and Their Appropriateness for Adult Christian Education." Doctoral dissertation, New Orleans Baptist Theological Seminary, 1970.

Cheleden, Algerdas Nicodemus. "Some Misconceptions concerning the Pragmatism of John Dewey." Master's thesis, University of California at Los Angeles, 1945.

Chen, Te. "Dewey's Concept of Moral Good." Doctoral dissertation, Southern Illinois University, 1969.

Chiang, Joanna M. Tse-Yu. "A Philosophy of Social Education According to John Henry Newman and John Dewey." Master's thesis, Manhattanville College of the Sacred Heart, 1955.

Clarke, Marion. "Contrasts of Method in Certain Contemporary Aesthetic Theories." Master's thesis, Smith College, 1939. [George Santayana, John Dewey, Vernon Lee, D. W. Prall.]

Clayton, Frank L. "Variant Philosophies and Their Significance to Education." Doctoral dissertation,

New York University, 1936.

Clohesy, William. "From Reason to Inquiry." Master's thesis, Southern Illinois University, 1971.

Clopton, Robert W. "A Critical Examination and Appraisal of Some Educational Values in the Philosophy of Instrumentalism." Master's thesis, University of Hawaii, 1940.

Coffin, Peter R. "Philosophy, Education, and Value: A Philosophic Study." Doctoral dissertation, Brown University, 1960.

Cohen, Beatrice M. "The Continuity of Means-ends in John Dewey's Reconstruction of Philosophy." Bachelor's thesis, Reed College, 1956.

Coit, John Knox. "A Criticism of Moritz Schlick's Ethics in the Light of Dewey's Naturalism." Master's thesis, Columbia University, 1945.

Collins, Maurice A. "The Implications of John Dewey's Theory of Teaching Method for Educational Practice." Doctoral dissertation, Southern Illinois University, 1971.

Collins, Russell J. "The Metaphysical Foundations of John Dewey's Theory of Knowledge." Master's thesis, Catholic University of America, 1945.

Collins, Verna Anne. "John Dewey: Man and His Ends." Master's thesis, University of Montreal, 1956.

Colquhoun, Norman W. "The Meaning of 'Good' in Three Representative Theories of Ethics." Bachelor's thesis, Amherst College, 1943. [G. E. Moore, Nicolai Hartmann, John Dewey.]

Comfort, Eunice Nicholas. "The Bearing of John Dewey's Philosophy upon Christianity." Master's thesis, Union Theological Seminary, 1923.

Condon, William Stephens. "John Dewey's Anti-dualism." Master's thesis, University of Pittsburgh, 1956.

Connor, Alice Mary. "A Comparative Study of the Social Theories of Education of Otto Willmann and John Dewey." Doctoral dissertation, New York University, 1944.

Conwell, Patricia G. "A Comparative Analysis of the Educational Theories of John Dewey and Robert Maynard Hutchins." Master's thesis, Claremont Graduate School, 1941.

Cooper, Ted Lincoln. "The Concepts of Knowledge of Peirce and Dewey: The Relation to Education." Doctoral dissertation, Stanford University, 1970.

Corn, Homer Yates. "John Dewey's Concept of History." Master's thesis, University of Iowa, 1969.

Coughlan, Neil Patrick. "Dewey and the University." Doctoral dissertation, University of Wisconsin, 1970.

Craver, Samuel Mock. "Individuality and Education: A Comparative Study of the Philosophies of John Dewey and Jean-Paul Sartre." Doctoral dissertation, University of North Carolina, 1971.

Creel, Richard. "Dewey's Theory of Common Good." Doctoral dissertation, Southern Illinois University, 1969.

Crockett, Campbell. "The Problem of the Given in Instrumentalism." Master's thesis, University of Cincinnati, 1941.

Crosby, Joseph Wallace. "A Comparative Analysis of the Educational Philosophies of John Dewey and Robert Hutchins." Master's thesis, University of Southern California, 1949.

Cua, Antonio S. "A Study of Dewey's Conception of Problematic Situation." Master's thesis, University of California, 1954.

Culliton, Joseph Thomas. "The Cosmic Visions of John Dewey and Teilhard de Chardin: A Comparative Study." Doctoral dissertation, Fordham University, 1972.

Cushing, Helen Isabel. "Dewey's Theory of Sense Perception." Master's thesis, University of Illinois, 1914.

Damico, Alfonso J. "Individuality and Community: The Social and Political Ideas of John Dewey." Doctoral dissertation, Ohio State University, 1971.

D'Amour, O'Neil C. "The Concept of the Universal and

Its Relation to the Experimental Trend in Modern Educational Philosophy." Master's thesis, Catholic University of America, 1950.

Danilowicz, Richard D. "Absolutes in the Philosophy of John Dewey." Master's thesis, Catholic University of America, 1951.

Danin, Elizabeth Lucy. "The Social Philosophy of John Dewey." Master's thesis, New York University, 1942.

Danneker, Carl J. "The Concept of Religion as Held by Recent Non-Catholic Educational Writers." Master's thesis, Catholic University of America, 1950.

Dasgupta, Debendra Chandra. "The Rise of the Theory of Sense-Training from John Locke to John Dewey." Master's thesis, University of California, 1928.

Davenport, Frances Littlefield. "The Education of John Dewey." Doctoral dissertation, University of California at Los Angeles, 1946.

Davis, Audie May. "The Religious Problem in the Writings of John Dewey." Master's thesis, University of Oklahoma, 1961.

Davis, Sydney Charles. "Theories of Education for the Development of Freedom and Responsibility." Doctoral dissertation, Teachers College, Columbia University, 1953.

Day, John L. "John Dewey's Objections to Realism in Education." Master's thesis, Claremont Graduate School, 1959.

De Andrea, Joseph. "Philosophy of Man According to Karl Marx and John Dewey: A Comparative Study." Master's thesis, Catholic University of America, 1957.

de Auer, Stephen Leslie. "A Study of Dewey's Theory of Valuation." Master's thesis, University of New Brunswick, 1969.

De Camargo, Candido Procopio Ferrera. "Social Relativism and the Philosophy of John Dewey." Master's thesis, Columbia University, 1956.

Deeves, Evelyn Irene. "The Implications of the Dewey-

Bruner Philosophies for Curriculum Planning." Doctoral dissertation, Florida State University, 1968.

Deininger, Whitaker Thompson. "John Dewey's Theory of Valuation Appraised." Master's thesis, Columbia University, 1948.

Dennis, Lawrence J. "The Implications of Dewey's Esthetics for the Teaching of Music." Doctoral dissertation, Southern Illinois University, 1967.

Desjardins, Pit Urban. "Social Change in the Social Philosophy of John Dewey." Master's thesis, University of British Columbia, 1961.

Dewey, Charles Sherman. "Some Concepts of Vocational Education and Guidance in England from 1600-1760." Doctoral dissertation, Stanford University, 1944.

Dhami, Sadhu Singh. "Philosophy of John Dewey in the Light of Oriental Philosophy." Master's thesis, University of Alberta, 1934.

---. "The Philosophy of John Dewey: Its Bearing on India." Doctoral dissertation, University of Toronto, 1937.

Dicker, Georges. "Knowing and Coming-to-Know in Dewey's Theory of Knowledge." Doctoral dissertation, University of Wisconsin, 1969.

Dickey, Thomas Wilson. "The Genesis of Dewey's Ethical Method." Master's thesis, Columbia University, 1933.

Dickinson, Henry B. "The Philosophy of John Dewey." Bachelor's thesis, Reed College, 1930.

Dickinson, Mary Coope. "The Implications of Dewey's Philosophy Found in Current Theories Regarding the Teaching of Literature." Master's thesis, Ohio State University, 1931.

Dickson, David B., III. "The Contributions of John Dewey to the Philosophy of Religion." Master's thesis, Florida Southern College, 1950.

Diggins, John P. "Freedom and Authority in Education."

Master's thesis, Catholic University of America, 1936.

Dillick, Sidney. "The Political Philosophy of John Dewey." Doctoral dissertation, University of Toronto, 1942.

Dimmick, Olive Heiser. "The Progressive Education Movement: Its History and Philosophy with Special Reference to Secondary Education in the United States." Master's thesis, University of Delaware, 1941. [Dewey, pp. 14-15, 17.]

Di Muccio, Mary-Jo. "A Relevant Concept of Individual Freedom and Responsibility in Contemporary Democratic Society in Relation to the Thinking of John Dewey." Doctoral dissertation, United States International University, 1970.

Doll, William Elder, Jr. "An Analysis of John Dewey's Educational Writings Interpreted with Reference to His Concept of Change." Doctoral dissertation, The Johns Hopkins University, 1972.

Dommeyer, Frederick Charles. "Four Pragmatic Theories of Meaning." Doctoral dissertation, Brown University, 1937. [Dewey, Peirce, James, C. I. Lewis.]

Donoso, Anton. "The Relation between Commonsense and Science According to John Dewey." Doctoral dissertation, University of Toronto, 1960.

Dreiling, Donald Dean. "Cartesian Dualism and Its Relevance to the Naturalism of Dewey." Master's thesis, St. Mary's College, Winona, Minn., 1964.

Drossos, Nicholas Christ. "John Dewey's Scientific Theory and the Moral Good." Master's thesis, Guilford College, Greensboro, N.C., 1949.

Du Chemin, Roderic Clark. "Aspects of the Philosophies of John Dewey and Bertrand Russell and Their Relation to Education." Doctoral dissertation, Ohio State University, 1953.

Dufrain, Viola Maude. "Implications for Religion in John Dewey's Philosophy." Master's thesis, University of Chicago, 1933.

Dunn, Dorothy Ann. "The Problem of Dualism in John Dewey." Doctoral dissertation, St. Louis University, 1966.

Duplisea, Eric A. "Creativity and the Progressive Education Movement." Master's thesis, Kent State University, 1965. [Dewey, passim.]

Eagleton, Clifford J. "An Inquiry into Contemporary Philosophers of Education in Regard to a Basic Philosophical Dichotomy." Master's thesis, Northern Illinois University, 1964. [Frederick S. Breed, Herman H. Horne, Robert Maynard Hutchins, John Childs, William H. Kilpatrick, and John Dewey.]

Eames, Elizabeth R. "A Discussion of the Issues in the Theory of Knowledge Involved in the Controversy between John Dewey and Bertrand Russell." Doctoral dissertation, Bryn Mawr College, 1951.

Eames, Ivan Lee. "The Theories of Social Change of John Dewey and Karl Mannheim: A Comparative Analysis." Master's thesis, University of Maryland, 1965.

Eames, S. Morris. "Some Methodological Problems in John Dewey's Theory of Valuation." Doctoral dissertation, University of Chicago, 1958.

---. "Experience and Philosophical Method in John Dewey." Typewritten. 1972. Dewey Collection, Southern Illinois University, Carbondale, Illinois.

Eastman, George Herbert. "John Dewey on Education: The Formative Years." Doctoral dissertation, Harvard University, 1963.

Eckmans, Christian. "Limitations of the Educational Theory of John Dewey in the Light of Christian Principles." Doctoral dissertation, Fordham University, 1965.

Eddy, Lyle Krenzien. "The Challenge of Dewey's Philosophy to Its Critics." Master's thesis, University of Chicago, 1948.

Edel, Abraham. "Human Nature in Ethical Theory." Paper read at Middle Atlantic States Philosophy of

Education Society meeting in honor of the "Centennial of the Birth of John Dewey", 14 November 1959. Mimeographed.

Eder, James M. "The Development of the Concept of Responsibility in John Stuart Mill and in John Dewey, and the Relation of the Notion of Freedom to These Concepts." Master's thesis, City College of the City University of New York, 1963.

Ehrenreich, Isaac. "The Idea of God in Dewey and Whitehead." Master's thesis, Columbia University, 1942.

Ehrlich, Reva. "An Image of Progressive Education as Revealed in Adverse Criticism in Lay Periodical Literature in the United States from 1929 to 1958." Master's thesis, Brooklyn College, 1960. [Dewey, passim.]

Ellis, Matt Locke. "John Dewey's Theory of Value." Doctoral dissertation, Yale University, 1933.

Elseroad, John Kenny. "A Comparative Study of the Educational Ideas of Michel de Montaigne and John Dewey." Master's thesis, University of Maryland, 1967.

Emmons, Douglas Lloyd. "The Early Development of the Conceptions of Social Psychology and the Social Organism in the Philosophy of John Dewey." Master's thesis, University of Oklahoma, 1968.

---. "The Paradox of Man in the Philosophy of John Dewey." Doctoral dissertation, University of Oklahoma, 1970.

Ensley, Francis G. "The Naturalistic Interpretation of Religion by John Dewey." Doctoral dissertation, Brown University, 1938.

Estrada, Josefa Presbiteo. "A Critical Comparison of the Educational Philosophies of John Dewey and William Heard Kilpatrick." Doctoral dissertation, Fordham University, 1929.

Etzel, Raymond A. "A Thomistic Criticism of John Dewey's Criterion of Truth." Master's thesis,

Catholic University of America, 1946.

Ewing, Raymond. "Dewey's Conception of Philosophy."
Master's thesis, Columbia University, 1951.

Ezorsky, Gertrude. "Truth as a Warranted Performance;
A Synthesis of John Dewey's and P. F. Strawson's
Concepts of Truth." Doctoral dissertation, New York
University, 1961.

Fain, Haskell. "A Comparison of the Theories of Logic
of John Dewey and Charles Sanders Peirce." Master's
thesis, University of Illinois, 1949.

Fawcett, Donald Franklin. "Analysis of John Dewey's
Theory of Experience: Implication for Physical Education Methodology." Master's thesis, University
of Southern California, 1966.

Featherstone, Joseph Luke. "John Dewey: An American
as Reformer." Honors thesis, Harvard University,
1962.

Feinberg, Walter. "A Comparative Study of the Social
Philosophies of John Dewey and Bernard Bosanquet."
Doctoral dissertation, Boston University, 1966.

Feldman, William Taft. "The Fundamental Motivations in
the Philosophy of John Dewey." Doctoral dissertation, The Johns Hopkins University, 1932.

Fendrich, Roger Paul. "Experience and Explanation:
Dewey's Metaphysics and Theory of Inquiry." Doctoral dissertation, University of Texas, 1971.

Fish, William C. "A Comparison of the Political
Thought of John Dewey and Reinhold Niebuhr." Bachelor's thesis, Amherst College, 1956.

Flay, Joseph Charles. "Hegel and Dewey and the Problem
of Freedom." Doctoral dissertation, University of
Southern California, 1965.

Fletcher, Thomas Joseph. "John Dewey's Philosophy of
Education." Master's thesis, Guilford College,
Greensboro, N.C., 1963.

Fleury, Bernard J., Jr. "A Comparative Study of the

Philosophies of Education of John Dewey and Jacques
Maritain." Master's thesis, University of Massachusetts, 1956.

Floyd, Samuel A., Jr. "The Implications of John Dew-
ey's Theory of Appreciation for the Teaching of
Music Appreciation." Doctoral dissertation,
Southern Illinois University, 1969.

Francis, Luther Edgar. "What is the Philosophy of John
Dewey." Master's thesis, Guilford College, Greensboro., N.C., 1929.

Francis, Richard Patrick. "Ultimate Constants in the
Metaphysics of John Dewey." Master's thesis, University of Colorado, 1958.

---. "The Doctrine of Natural Selection in John Dewey's Value Theory." Doctoral dissertation, University of Notre Dame, 1964.

Francisco, Felix, Jr. "A Critical Comparison of the
Social and Political Theories of Karl Marx and John
Dewey." Master's thesis, University of Missouri,
1950.

---. "The Concepts of Instinct, Habit and Mind in the
Educational Philosophies of William James and John
Dewey." Doctoral dissertation, University of Mis-
souri, 1957.

Fries, Horace Snyder. "The Development of John Dewey's
Utilitarianism." Doctoral dissertation, University
of Wisconsin, 1934.

Fuller, Howard Raymond. "An Implication for Religion
in John Dewey's Philosophy: Faith." Master's thesis, Wheaton College, Wheaton, Ill., 1943.

Fullerton, Dwain Nash. "Dewey and Bradley: A Study in
Esthetics." Master's thesis, Stanford University,
1960.

Gale, Richard Milton. "Dewey and the Problem of the
Alleged Futurity of Yesterday." Master's thesis,
New York University, 1958.

---. "Experience in the Philosophies of Art of Imman-

UNPUBLISHED WORKS					213

uel Kant and John Dewey." Honors Paper, Ohio Wesleyan University, 1954.

Gant, Dorothy. "John Dewey's Theory of Value." Master's thesis, Vassar College, 1940.

Garretson, Susan. "Intrinsic Value in the Aesthetics
of John Dewey." Senior essay in philosophy, Wells
College, 1960.

Garrett, Roland W. "Dewey's Metaphysics." Doctoral
dissertation, Columbia University, 1970.

Garvin, Thomas Robert. "The Individual and Society in
John Dewey." Doctoral dissertation, St. Louis University, 1971.

Gebre-Hiwet, Mengesha. "Contrasting Philosophies of
Education: Nunn and Dewey." Doctoral dissertation,
Ohio State University, 1958.

Gelsomino, Joseph. "The Dewey-Croce Controversy in
Aesthetic Theory." Master's thesis, State University of New York at Buffalo, 1964.

Gensemer, Bruce Lee. "The Unification of Inquiry in
John Dewey and a Reinterpretation of Economic Methodology." Honors paper, Ohio Wesleyan University,
1961.

George, Samuel S. "The Influence of Pragmatism upon
American Religion." Doctoral dissertation, Temple
University, 1939.

Gerber, Marvin. "American Pragmatism: A Historical
Analysis." Master's thesis, Newark State College,
1964. [Dewey, pp. 8-13, 121-23.]

Gerrity, Benignus. "John Dewey's Theory of Ethics."
Master's thesis, Fordham University, 1933.

Gettys, Joseph Miller. "The Philosophy of Life Con-
tained in the Fourth Gospel Compared with the Philosophies of Plato and Dewey." Doctoral dissertation, New York University, 1938.

Geyer, Denton Loring. "The Pragmatic Theory of Truth
as Developed by Peirce, James, and Dewey." Doctoral

dissertation, University of Illinois, 1914.

Gifford, Ruth V. "A Comparative Study of Certain
Phases of the Educational Theories of Plato and John
Dewey." Master's thesis, Syracuse University, 1931.

Giles, Charles Stanton. "The Contributions of John
Dewey to Art Education on the College Level." Master's thesis, Florida Southern College, 1949.

Glatt, Charles A. "Interaction and Transaction. An
Experience in Deweyology." [Typewritten class paper,
University of New Mexico, 1961.] [Copy at Dewey
Center.]

Glenn, Gary Dean. "An Essay on John Dewey's Human Nature and Conduct." Master's thesis, University of
Chicago, 1963.

Goehegen, Grace. "The Educational Theories of Rousseau
and Dewey." Master's thesis, Birmingham Southern
College, 1933.

Goldman, Carl Allen. "Notes on the Political Philosophy of John Dewey; Experimentalism as a Method of
Politics." Honors thesis, Harvard University, 1955.

Goldstein, Eli Whitney. "Liberalism in the U.S.A. as
Exemplified by Thomas Jefferson, John Dewey, and
Walter Lippmann." Master's thesis, University of
Pittsburgh, 1955.

Goodman, Frederick Lewis. "The Critics of John Dewey."
Doctoral dissertation, University of Michigan, 1961.

Goodman, Ruth Paula Weiss. "Ideals of Life and Man and
the Common School Theories of Moral Education for
the Public Schools from Horace Mann to John Dewey."
Doctoral dissertation, Washington University, 1969.

Goodwin, John B. "Differences in the Meaning of Religion for Two American Pragmatists: William James
and John Dewey." Doctoral dissertation, Temple
University, 1970.

Goodwin, Sarah Hall. "Values in John Dewey's Philosophy of Education for Evangelical Christian Education." Master's thesis, Asbury Theological Seminary,

Wilmore, Ky., 1948.

Goran, Morris Herbert. "The Nature of Science for
    Dewey and Einstein and Certain Educational Implica-
    tions of These Views." Doctoral dissertation, Uni-
    versity of Chicago, 1957.

Gorospe, Vitaliano R. "Moral Obligation in John Dew-
    ey's Ethical Naturalism." Doctoral dissertation,
    St. Louis University, 1962.

Gouinlock, James. "Metaphysics and Value Theory: Study
    in the Moral Philosophy of John Dewey." Doctoral
    dissertation, Columbia University, 1969.

Gould, James Adams. "The Independent Origin of Prag-
    matism in France, Germany, and the United States."
    Doctoral dissertation, University of Michigan, 1954.

Grad, Eli. "Ideology and Education; an Investigation
    of the Relationship between Ideology, Educational
    Theory, and Educational Practice." Doctoral disser-
    tation, Wayne State University, 1965. [Dewey, pp.
    153-57.]

Graham, Edna Jeanne. "John Dewey's Philosophy of Re-
    ligion." Master's thesis, University of Nebraska,
    1938.

Grant, James L. "The Ethics of Pluralism: A Study of
    William James and John Dewey." Master's thesis,
    University of Chicago, 1965.

Greene, James Peter. "The Relation of Science to
    Common Sense in the Philosophy of John Dewey."
    Doctoral dissertation, University of Notre Dame,
    1971.

Greenleaf, Lillian Snow. "A Philosophy of Democracy as
    Worked out by John Dewey." Master's thesis, Univer-
    sity of Chicago, 1919.

Griffin, Richard M. "The Nature and Role of Subject
    Matter in John Dewey's Philosophy of Education."
    Master's thesis, Washington State University, 1967.

Griffin, Robert Lewis. "Misconceptions of John Dewey's
    Educational Philosophy by Contemporary Critics."

Doctoral dissertation, Oklahoma State University, 1965.

Griffiths, Nellie Lucy. "A History of the Organization of the Laboratory School of the University of Chicago." Master's thesis, University of Chicago, 1927.

Grossman, Althea Somerville. "The Reality of Values: A Critical Study of the Theories of Dewey and White-Head." Master's thesis, University of Missouri, 1940.

Grunewald, Robert Nichol. "An Exposition of John Dewey's Concept of the Problematic Situation and An Appraisal of That Concept from the Standpoint of the Ames Demonstrations in Perception." Doctoral dissertation, Claremont Graduate School, 1964.

Guth, Hans Paul. "Threat as the Basis of Beauty: Pragmatist Elements in the Aesthetics of Richards, Dewey, and Burke." Doctoral dissertation, University of Michigan, 1957.

Gutzke, Manford George. "Some Implications for Education in Religion in John Dewey's Conception of Intelligence." Doctoral dissertation, Columbia University, 1954.

Guy, George V. "An Analysis of Selected Influential Concepts of Experience and Their Bearing upon a Theory of Education." Doctoral dissertation, University of Illinois, 1957.

Hagyard, Romoyne A. "The Application of the Dewey Philosophy of Education in the Music Teaching Methods of James Mursell as Reflected in the *Music For Living Series*, Grades I through VI." Master's thesis, University of Maryland, 1964.

Halbert, Anna E. "The Problem of Self-Activity in Modern Educational Theory, with Special Reference to Rousseau, Harris, Dewey and Montessori." Doctoral dissertation, New York University, 1925.

Halbur, Mary N. "A Comparative Study of the Principle of Self-Activity in the Learning Process According to the Theories of Dewey and Montessori." Master's thesis, Marquette University, 1965.

Halferty, Brian Joseph. "John Dewey and the Religious Elements of Experience." Master's thesis, University of St. Michael's College, 1969.

Hall, Jessie M. "John Dewey: Philosopher, Educator." Master's thesis, Western Connecticut State College, 1963.

Halsey, John Easton. "John Dewey's Conception of Philosophic Method." Doctoral dissertation, Columbia University, 1970.

Hamada, Ikujiro. "Ethical Implication of Two Contrasted Philosophies of Life, Illustrated in John Dewey and Bertrand Russell." Master's thesis, Columbia University, 1919.

Hamilton, James T. "The Philosophy of John Dewey in Relation to American Education." Master's thesis, University of Oregon, 1933.

Hamm, William Conrad. "Applications of Dewey's Philosophy of Education to College Education." Master's thesis, Yale University, 1932.

Hammond, John Luther. "Perry, Dewey, C. I. Lewis, and Critics of Ethical Naturalism." Doctoral dissertation, Stanford University, 1965.

Handford, Donald William. "A Comparison of the Philosophies of Education of John Dewey and Jacques Maritain." Master's thesis, University of Western Ontario, 1957.

Haney, John Clifford, Jr. "A Critical Comparison of the Educational Philosophies of John Dewey and George Albert Coe." Doctoral dissertation, Boston University, 1959.

Harada, Michael Francis Mitsun. "A Comparative Study of Some Aspects of the Pragmatism of Sir Francis Bacon and John Dewey." Master's thesis, Occidental College, Los Angeles, Cal., 1957.

Hardin, William J. "Free Will, Determinism, and the Nature of Education: The Philosophical Viewpoints of

Benedict Spinoza and John Dewey." Doctoral dissertation, St. Louis University, 1971.

Harlow, Rex Francis. "The Educational Implications of
the Theories of Value of Nicolai Hartmann and John
Dewey." Master's thesis, University of Texas, 1935.

Harmon, Frances Bolles. "The Social Philosophy of the
St. Louis Hegelians." Doctoral dissertation, Columbia University, 1943. [Dewey, passim.]

Harris, Patricia. "A Comparison of the Linguistic For-
mulations of Alfred K. Korzybski and the Pragmatism
of John Dewey." Master's thesis, Arizona State College, 1954.

Hartman, Donald George. "The Application of a Personal
Philosophy of Education in the Field of the Social
Studies." Master's thesis, Ohio State University,
1936.

Haworth, Lawrence Lindley. "The Practical Philosophies
of John Dewey and Elijah Jordan." Doctoral dissertation, University of Illinois, 1952.

Heller, Benjamin Theodore. "John Dewey, Educator." In
his "Theories of Knowledge and Their Relation to
Higher Education," pp. 57-69. Senior Project, Social Studies Division, Bard College, 1948.

Hendershot, Vernon Edwards. "A Comparative Study of
the Educational Philosophies of Plato and Dewey."
Master's thesis, University of Southern California,
1927.

Henderson, Anna Louise. "The Recognition of Individual
Differences as Expressed in the Educational Philos-
ophies of Certain Educators from Plato to Dewey.
Master's thesis, University of Utah, 1937.

Herbert, Rose. "The American School." Master's thesis, Clark University, 1925. [Dewey, passim.]

Hermann, Robert M. "The Relevance of Recent Educational Criticism to the Thought of John Dewey."
Doctoral dissertation, University of Pittsburgh,
1962.

Herzstein, Robert Erwin. "Pascal and Dewey: The Quest

for Certainty and the Naturalistic Imperative."
Honors thesis, Harvard University, 1952.

Heslep, Robert D. "The Philosophical Views of Thomas
Jefferson and John Dewey as Basis for Clarifying the
Role of Education in an American Democracy." Doc-
toral dissertation, University of Chicago, 1963.

Hetenyi, Laszlo Joseph. "Outline of a Philosophic
Position and Its Application to an Introductory
Music Program in General Education." Doctoral dissertation, Michigan State University, 1956. [Dewey,
pp. 50-65, and passim.]

Heumann, Audrey Miriam. "The Education Theories of
John Dewey as Seen in a Framework of Tradition,
Evolution, and Transition." Senior project paper,
Bard College, 1948.

Hill, Knox Calvin. "Philosophic Method and Theory of
Art in Croce and Dewey." Doctoral dissertation,
University of Chicago, 1954.

Hill, Walker H. "Peirce and Dewey and the Spectator
Theory of Knowledge." Doctoral dissertation, University of Wisconsin, 1938.

Hilty, Everett Jay. "An Examination of the Structure
of the Objects of Sense Perception in the Philosophy
of John Dewey." Master's thesis, University of
Colorado, 1967.

Hinkel, Eva J. "Philosophy of Art Education for the
Culturally Deprived High School Student Based on
the Aesthetics of John Dewey." Master's thesis,
Adelphi University, 1967.

Hodges, Donald Clark. "Dewey's Theory of Political
Conflict." Master's thesis, Columbia University,
1949.

Holmes, Robert Lawrence. "John Dewey's Ethics in the
Light of Contemporary Metaethical Theory: An Analysis and Interpretation of His Account of the Nature
of Moral Judgments." Doctoral dissertation, University of Michigan, 1961.

———. "Creativity in John Dewey's Social Ethics."
Paper presented at the annual meeting of the Western

Division of the Society for a Philosophy of Creativity. St. Louis, 2 May 1968.

Hopkins, Raymond Frederick. "Faith and Religion as Found in the Philosophies of Søren Kierkegaard and John Dewey." Honors paper, Ohio Wesleyan University, 1960.

Horne, James Robert. "Dewey's Concept of Desire. Analysis and Criticism." Master's thesis, University of Western Ontario, 1958.

Horridge, Frederick. "A Comparison of Dewey's *DEMOCRACY AND EDUCATION*, [Ernest Carroll] Moore's *WHAT IS EDUCATION?*, and [James] Welton's *WHAT DO YOU MEAN BY EDUCATION?*." Master's thesis, University of California, 1917.

Horvath, Walter Julius. "The Inadequacy of Representative Government as Reviewed by Mill, Lippmann and Dewey." Master's thesis, Columbia University, 1932.

Horwitz, Robert Henry. "The Political Philosophy of Civic Education." Doctoral dissertation, University of Chicago, 1954.

Howlett, Charles F. "John Dewey's Pacifism in Relation to the Coming of the Second World War." Master's thesis, State University of New York at Albany, 1969.

---. "John Dewey and the Outlawry of War During the 1920's." Doctoral dissertation, State University of New York at Albany, 1971.

Huddleston, Nancy. "Dewey's Logic in Relation to His Theory of Religious Quality." Master's thesis, University of Chicago, 1947.

Huebsch, Arthur. "Jean-Jacques Rousseau and John Dewey: A Comparative Study and a Critical Estimate of Their Philosophies and Their Educational and Related Theories and Practices." Doctoral dissertation, New York University, 1930.

Hunt, Thomas Chapman. "A Critical Analysis of John Dewey's Concept of Growth as the Aim of Education." Doctoral dissertation, University of Southern California, 1952.

Hutchinson, James M. "A Common Faith: Elements in the Philosophy of Religion of John Dewey." Bachelor's thesis, Tufts University, 1946.

Ibrahim, Naguib I. "Theories of Learning as Viewed from the Pragmatic Philosophy Standpoint." Master's thesis, Kent State University, 1952. [Dewey, passim.]

Igoe, Charles John. "A Critical History of the Philosophy of Change and Educational Policy." Doctoral dissertation, Pennsylvania State University, 1971. [Discusses the philosophical inquiries as to the nature of change of the following: Thales, Anaximander, Heraclitus, Socrates, Plato, Aristotle, Augustine, Aquinas, Bergson, Dewey, Marx, and Engels.]

Iida, Teruaki. "The Problem of Time in the Philosophy of William James." Master's thesis, University of New Mexico, 1959. [Dewey, pp. 66-75.]

Isaac, John R. "A Discussion of Dewey's Philosophy of Individual Freedom." Bachelor's thesis, Reed College, 1961.

Itzkoff, Seymour William. "Cultural Pluralism and American Education; A Reinterpretation through the Philosophy of Ernst Cassirer." Doctoral dissertation, Teachers College, Columbia University, 1965. [Dewey, passim.]

Jaeger, Gertrude Ottilie. "John Dewey's Theory of Valuation: A Critical Statement." Master's thesis, University of Chicago, 1947.

James, Keith Warren. "Dewey's Application of the Logic of Inquiry to Ethical Theory." Master's thesis, Duke University, 1949.

Jamison, Howard Louis. "The Methodology of Scientific Social Practice: J. S. Mill and John Dewey." Doctoral dissertation, Harvard University, 1950.

Jenks, Esther Newton. "The Function of Adult Education in a Democracy." Master's thesis, Indiana State University, 1939. [Dewey, passim.]

Johnson, Frank Wagner. "An Analysis of Bertrand Rus-

sell's, Brand Blanshard's, and John Dewey's Views on
Causality." Master's thesis, Columbia University,
1947.

Johnson, John Prescott. "The Pragmatic Concept of
Truth." Master's thesis, Kansas State College of
Pittsburg, 1948. [Dewey, passim.]

Johnson, Richard Carl. "The Need for a Moral Absolute;
Kant, Dewey and Ross." Master's thesis, University
of Colorado, 1962.

Johnson, Robert W. "Experience in the American Tradi-
tion of John Dewey as Culminated in the Work of
Robert O. Johann, S. J." Master's thesis, St.
Mary's College, Winona, Minn., 1965.

Jones, Ralph O. "John Dewey: A Study of His Concept of
Education." Master's thesis, University of Detroit,
1959.

Jordan, James Augustus, Jr. "John Dewey's Theory of
Knowing and the Christian Teacher." Master's thesis, Emory University, 1956.

---. "A Concept of Self and Value from Whitehead and
Its Implications for Education." Doctoral dissertation, Emory University, 1958. [Contains a chapter
comparing Whitehead and Dewey.]

Kalodner, P. P. "Dewey, Santayana, and the American,
1951: A Study in Temperament." Bachelor's thesis,
Amherst College, 1951.

Kane, William J. "A Critique of the Concept of Nature
in the Philosophy of John Dewey According to Thomistic Principles of Being." Master's thesis, Catholic University of America, 1950.

Kaplan, J. M. "Ethics as a Method of Inquiry." Bachelor's thesis, Amherst College, 1950.

Keenan, Barry Campbell. "John Dewey in China: His
Visit and the Reception of His Ideas." Doctoral
dissertation, Claremont Graduate School, 1969.

Keenan, Kevin Brendan. "Toward Philosophic Reconstruction: Comments on the Philosophy of John Dewey."

Master's thesis, Columbia University, 1946.

Kennick, William Elmer. "A Methodological Approach to Metaphysics, with Special Reference to the Philosophies of Aristotle, Hume, Dewey, and Whitehead." Doctoral dissertation, Cornell University, 1952.

Kent, William Phelps. "The Political Philosophy of John Dewey." Doctoral dissertation, University of Chicago, 1950.

Kerby-Miller, Sinclair. "The Early Development of Dewey's Logical Theory." Master's thesis, Columbia University, 1921.

Kestenbaum, Victor. "An Interpretation of Dewey's Notion of Habit from the Perspective of Merleau-Ponty's Phenomenology of the Habitual Body." Doctoral dissertation, Rutgers University, 1972.

Kiernan, Vincent. "An Analysis of the Theory of Experience in the Educational Philosophy of John Dewey." Master's thesis, Central Connecticut State College, 1966.

Kilbridge, John Thomas. "The Concept of Habit in the Philosophy of John Dewey." Doctoral dissertation, University of Chicago, 1949.

Kim, Dong Hwan. "Carnap, Russell, and Dewey: A Critique of Their Conceptions of Philosophy." Master's thesis, University of Florida, 1959.

Kindred, Ray E. "A Critical Analysis of Those Aspects of John Dewey's Philosophy Which Give Evidence of a Metaphysics." Doctoral dissertation, Claremont Graduate School, 1959.

Kinrade, A. Dorothy. "Discipline and Freedom in Education: A Comparison of Theories of John Dewey and Bertrand Russell." Doctoral dissertation, University of Toronto, 1963.

Kircher, George Hallock. "A Critique of *THE QUEST FOR CERTAINTY* by John Dewey." Master's thesis, Bob Jones University, 1944.

Kirsch, Myron R. "A Philosophical Analysis of Intel-

lectual Freedom in American Public High Schools
Based upon Certain Education Viewpoints of Robert
Ulich and John Dewey." Doctoral dissertation,
Claremont Graduate School, 1966.

Kittrell, Jean McCarty. "Objectivity in John Dewey's
Moral Theory." Master's thesis, University of Chicago, 1952.

Kline, William Eugene. "A Critique of Carl Rogers'
Therapeutic Conditions: An Examination from the
Knowledge Views of Dewey and Bentley." Doctoral
dissertation, University of Denver, 1965.

Kobayashi, Victor Nobuo. "Some Implications of Dewey's
Esthetic Theory for Mathematics Education." Master's thesis, University of Hawaii, 1960.

Koch, Donald F. "Dewey's Psychology of Ethics." Doctoral dissertation, Claremont Graduate School, 1967.

Kolb, Jonathan Robert. "The Idea of Community in the
Writings of Park, Addams, and Dewey." Master's thesis, University of Iowa, 1967.

Kopp, Joyce Goforth. "Dewey's Criticism of the Platonic
'Absolute'." Master's thesis, University of Chicago,
1948.

Kowalski, Adalbert N. "Contributions of Certain Edu-
cators to the Development of Selected Aspects of
Sensory Education." Master's thesis, St. Johns Uni-
versity, 1942. [Comenius, Montaigne, Rabelais,
Froebel, Herbart, Ratke, Bacon, Pestalozzi, and
Dewey.]

Kozlowski, Leo J. "Thomistic Concept of the Common
Good Contrasted with That of John Dewey." Master's
thesis, Catholic University of America, 1957.

Krause, James Lance. "Intelligence as a Common Faith:
An Analysis and Commentary on John Dewey's Method
of Intelligence." Senior Project paper, Bard College, 1969.

Kuenzli, Alfred Eugene. "Organismic Conceptions of the
Educative Process: A Study of the Functional and
Configurational Psychologies of John Dewey and Kurt

Lewin." Master's thesis, Indiana University, 1953.

Kuo, David D. "The Impact of Science on Dewey's Ethics." Doctoral dissertation, Southern Illinois University, 1969.

La Dow, Charles R. "Presuppositions of a Social Philosophy; A Study of the Pragmatism of William James and John Dewey." Master's thesis, Claremont Graduate School, 1939.

Laine, Iver. "The 'Activity' Principle in the Educational Theories of Froebel and Dewey." Master's thesis, Clark University, 1937.

Lakin, Robert Dean. "An Introduction to Dewey's Philosophy of Liberalism." Master's thesis, University of Illinois, 1959.

Lambdin, Henry Lyle. "Current Instrumentalism: Dewey-Russell-Lippmann." In "A Christian Critique of Representative Philosophies of Blessedness," pp. 176-97. Doctoral dissertation, Drew University, 1935.

Lamont, Margaret Hayes. "Dewey's Conception of Intelligence and the International Mind." Master's thesis, Columbia University, 1928.

Lampman, Patricia A. "Adaptation to an Elementary Art Program of a Synthesis of Educational Philosophies of John Herbart and John Dewey." Master's thesis, Bradley University, 1953.

Landesman, Charles S., Jr. "The Concept of Form in Four Philosophies of Logic." Doctoral dissertation, Yale University, 1959.

Lapoint, George Melvin. "Reconstruction of Experience; John Dewey's Philosophy of Education." Master's thesis, Tufts University, 1941.

Larkin, Richard Anderson. "The Influence of John Dewey on Physical Education." Master's thesis, Ohio State University, 1936.

Larson, Gunnar John. "Some Aspects of the Problem of Fact and Value in the Philosophies of Ralph Barton

Perry, John Dewey, and Wilbur Marshall Urban." Master's thesis, University of Southern California, 1948.

Law, David Albert. "The Naturalistic Approach to Religion in the Philosophy of Eric Fromm, John Dewey and Paul Tillich." Master's thesis, University of Western Ontario, 1966.

Lawrence, Gordon Dwight. "John Dewey's Curriculum Theory." Doctoral dissertation, Claremont Graduate School, 1967.

Lawson, David. "Changing Modes of Thought in Moral Education." Doctoral dissertation, Teachers College, Columbia University, 1959.

Lee, John S. "Transaction in Experience: The Key to John Dewey's Epistemology." Master's thesis, University of Hawaii, 1964.

Leinhardt, Walter. "John Dewey and the New Program of Progressive Education in New York City." Bachelor's thesis, Amherst College, 1953.

Leonard, Linda Schierse. "Some Uses of a Novel in Ethical Investigation." Master's thesis, University of Colorado, 1963. [*MAN'S FATE* by André Malraux is studied in connection with the ethical theories of Aristotle, Kant, and Dewey.]

Levinson, Joseph David. "The Problem of Freedom in the Political Philosophy of John Dewey." Master's thesis, Ohio State University, 1954.

Levitt, Morton. "Freud and Dewey: A Comparative Study of Their Psychological Systems." Doctoral dissertation, University of Michigan, 1956.

Lewis, Hal Graham. "Occupations in John Dewey's Educational Theory." Doctoral dissertation, Rutgers University, 1971.

Lewis, Lula W. "Certain Major Tenets of John Dewey: Their Status in Contemporary Educational Criticism." Master's thesis, Southwestern Louisiana Institute, 1959.

Liedtke, J. H., II. "Scepticism: A Study of Religion

and the Limits of Knowledge in the Philosophies of Hume, Santayana, and Dewey." Bachelor's thesis, Amherst College, 1942.

Lieurance, William Berry. "Certain Implications of John Dewey's Theory of Habit for Social Studies Teachers." Master's thesis, Ohio State University, 1950.

Lindel, Bertha Neola. "A Study of the Poems of Robert Browning with the Object of Finding Ideas Contributory to the Educational Theory of John Dewey." Master's thesis, University of Southern California, 1933.

Linehan, Mary St. Paul. "The Thomistic Theory of Knowledge Contrasted with That of John Dewey." Master's thesis, St. Louis University, 1957.

Linn, A. M. "Experience and Knowledge in the Philosophy of John Dewey." Bachelor's thesis, Amherst College, 1949.

Linzmeyer, Robert A. "An Appraisal of the Five-Step Thought Method of John Dewey in the Light of Some Thomistic Principles." Master's thesis, Catholic University of America, 1956.

List, Davida Norma. "A Comparative Study of John Dewey's Concept of Learning and Its Conditions with Those of Some Modern Secondary Schools." Master's thesis, New York University, 1954.

Liu, Kwoh C. "John Dewey's Logical Theory." Master's thesis, University of Wisconsin, 1932.

Liu, Margaret. "John Dewey's Conceptions of the Child and the Curriculum." Master's thesis, University of Rochester, 1949.

Long, Jerome B. "Dewey and Pragmatism: Towards a True Conception of Values in Process." Doctoral dissertation, Fordham University, 1962.

Long, Marcus. "The Relation between the Logical Theories of Lotze, Bosanquet, and Dewey: A Study in the Morphology of Knowledge." Doctoral dissertation, University of Toronto, 1940.

Lorenz, Gilbert. "A Semantic Analysis of Dewey's *LOGIC: THE THEORY OF INQUIRY*." Master's thesis, University of Illinois, 1961.

Lu, Henry Chung-Ming. "John Dewey's Philosophy and Education." Doctoral dissertation, University of Alberta, 1968.

Lucitt, M. John. "Historical Analysis of American Educational Thought on the Treatment of Controversial Issues in the Classroom." Doctoral dissertation, Boston College, 1963.

Lugton, Robert Cameron. "Three Concepts of Contemporary Logic: An Exposition for College Teachers of English." Doctoral dissertation, Teachers College, Columbia University, 1966. [Discusses the logic of Bertrand Russell, P. F. Strawson, and John Dewey.]

Luther, Leroy. "The Metaphysical Pre-Suppositions of John Dewey as Compared with Harvey Cox and Their Implications for the Theistic Administrator." Doctoral dissertation, University of Tulsa, 1971.

Lutton, Bertram L. "A Contrasting Study of Idealism and Biological Pragmatism as Developed in the Writings of Herman Harrell Horn and John Dewey." Master's thesis, Temple University, 1930.

McAvin, Martha Woodbridge. "The Political Philosophy of John Dewey." Master's thesis, University of Nebraska, 1949.

McClintock, James A. "The Instrumentalism or Experimentalism of John Dewey and the Idea of God." In "The Pragmatic Spirit in Modern English and American Theism," vol. 1, pp. 40-64. Doctoral dissertation, Drew University, 1934-35. [Dewey, vol. 2, passim.]

McCormack, Eric David. "Frederick Matthias Alexander and John Dewey: A Neglected Influence." Doctoral dissertation, University of Toronto, 1959.

McDermott, John Donovan. "John Dewey: Ethical Inquiry and the Psychological Standpoint." Doctoral dissertation, University of Notre Dame, 1969.

McDermott, John J. "Experience Is Pedagogical: The

Genesis and Essence of the American Nineteenth Century Notion of Experience." Doctoral dissertation, Fordham University, 1959.

McGrane, Joan. "Leslie Stephen and John Dewey: The Relation of Scientific Method to the Problems of Men." Doctoral dissertation, Columbia University, 1950.

McKemie, Augustus Keaton. "The Philosophy of John Dewey in Its Implications for Education as Found in the Publications of 1897-1918." Master's thesis, University of Cincinnati, 1931.

McKenney, John L. "The Problem of a Science of Ethics in the Philosophies of John Dewey and Bertrand Russell." Doctoral dissertation, Ohio State University, 1952.

McMahon, Edwin M. "A Study of John Dewey and Experimentalism in Relation to the Contemporary Problem of Re-evaluation of Education in Our Democracy." Master's thesis, Gonzaga University, 1958.

McMullen, Robert Johnston. "A Comparative Study of the Ethics of Confucius and John Dewey." Master's thesis, Union Theological Seminary, 1936.

McMurray, Gudelia Abarcar. "The Pragmatic Theory of Meaning as a Potential Resource for Educational Theory." Doctoral dissertation, University of Illinois, 1969.

McNeil, Genna Rae. "An Examination of the Social Philosophy of John Dewey from 1919-1939." Master's thesis, Kalamazoo College, 1969.

McNitt, Harold Austin. "John Dewey's Democratic Liberalism: Its Philosophical Foundations." Doctoral dissertation, University of Michigan, 1957.

McVeigh, Ronald J. "An Inquiry into the Life, Thoughts, and Influences of John Dewey." Master's thesis, Southern Connecticut State College, 1962.

Magee, Harry A. "John Dewey and the Mind of America." Master's thesis, University of Florida, 1969.

Magruder, James. "Dewey's Treatment of Quality." Master's thesis, Southern Illinois University, 1968.

Maguire, James Francis. "The Ethical Principles Underlying John Dewey's Educational System." Master's
thesis, St. Louis University, 1930.

Mahedy, William P. "God in the Philosophy of John
Dewey." Master's thesis, Villanova University,
1966.

Mannison, Donald Sherwood. "The Function of Impulse
in Dewey's Theory." Master's thesis, University of
Illinois, 1957.

Marion, David Jeffrey. "A Comparison of John Dewey's
and Ludwig von Bertalanffy's Conception of Human
Development: Its Educational Implications." Doctoral dissertation, Boston University, 1971.

Market, John C. "A Critical Study of the Educational
Tenets of Jean-Jacques Rousseau and John Dewey in
the Light of Catholic Doctrine on Original Sin and
the Supernatural Destiny of Man." Master's thesis,
Catholic University of America, 1950.

Marshall, Charles. "The Instrumentalism of John Dewey." Master's thesis, Jacksonville State University, 1960.

Marshall, George N. "The Basic Considerations for a
Metaphysics of Pragmatic Empiricism." Master's
thesis, Tufts University, 1943. [Dewey, passim.]

Martin, Clyde Vincent. "A Comparative Study of the
Concept of Interest in the Educational Philosophies
of Johann Friedrich Herbart and John Dewey." Doctoral dissertation, University of Southern California, 1952.

Martland, Thomas Rodolphe. "Some Evidence for Congruent
Ontology in Religion and Philosophy." Doctoral dissertation, Columbia University, 1959.

Mathur, Dinesh Chandra. "The Significance of 'Qualitative Thought' in Dewey's Philosophy of Art." Doctoral dissertation, Columbia University, 1955.

Mayer, Henry Charles. "The Theory of a State in the

Philosophy of John Dewey." Master's thesis, University of Notre Dame, 1957.

Mayeroff, Milton. "An Examination of Some Criticisms of John Dewey's *LOGIC: THE THEORY OF INQUIRY*." Master's thesis, New York University, 1950.

---. "John Dewey's Concept of the Unification of the Self; An Exposition and Critique." Doctoral dissertation, Columbia University, 1961.

Mayers, Ronald Burton. "The Problem, Meaning and Function of 'Transcendence' in a Social Ethic with Particular Reference to the Social Ethics of John Dewey and Reinhold Niebuhr." Doctoral dissertation, Syracuse University, 1972.

Mead, Hunter. "A Critique of the Pragmatic Concept of Experience." Master's thesis, Claremont Graduate School, 1933. [Dewey, pp. 32-49, 50-67.]

Meihofer, Susan Stevens. "The Individual and Social in John Dewey's Philosophy of Education." Senior essay in philosophy, Wells College, 1960.

Meiklejohn, Donald Waldron. "The Relation between Ethical and Intellectual Judgments in the Philosophy of John Dewey." Doctoral dissertation, Harvard University, 1936.

Melchert, Norman Paul. "Hume, Dewey, and Stevenson; A Comparative Enquiry into Ethical Theories." Master's thesis, University of Pennsylvania, 1959.

Mengis, Regina M. "John Dewey and Joseph Fletcher, A Presentation of the Concept of Morality." Master's thesis, University of Dayton, 1969.

Mercieca, Charles. "An Investigation into the Applicability of Dewey's Methodology in all American Schools, Public and Private." Doctoral dissertation, University of Kansas, 1966.

Mesthene, Emmanuel George. "Some Views About the Nature of Intelligibility." Doctoral dissertation, Columbia University, 1964.

Metz, Joseph G. "A Critical Analysis of the Theory of

Democracy in the Philosophy of John Dewey." Doctoral dissertation, Catholic University of America, 1966.

Mikula, Donald Max. "John Dewey's Treatment of Greek Philosophy." Master's thesis, Washington University, 1964.

---. "The Concept of the Moral Self in Dewey's Ethical Theory." Doctoral dissertation, Southern Illinois University, 1967.

Miles, Edith I. "A Search for Romantic Elements in Some Aspects of John Dewey's Educational Theory." Doctoral dissertation, Rutgers University, 1967.

Miller, Edward R. L. "Pragmatism and John Dewey." Master's thesis, State University of New York at Buffalo, 1951.

Miller, Mabrey L. "Experience-Centered Learning Activities and Attitudes toward School and People." Doctoral dissertation, University of Nebraska Teachers' College, 1960. [Dewey, pp. 14-16.]

Miller, Margaret Mary. "The Prevalence of Confusion among Educators with Regard to Democratic Concepts." Master's thesis, San Francisco College for Women, 1961.

Mills, Frederick Buckingham. "Critical Thinking and Education, a Survey." Master's thesis, Cornell University, 1952.

Mims, Katherine H. "An Analysis of Some Presuppositions concerning the Nature of Men in the Ethical Theories of John Dewey and Reinhold Niebuhr." Master's thesis, University of North Carolina, 1952.

Minkiel, Stephen J. "The General Ethics of John Dewey in the Light of Thomism." Dissertatio ad lauream in facultate philosophica apud Pontificium Athenaeum "Angelicum" de urbe, Rome, 1959.

Minogue, William John Desmond. "The Educational Philosophies of John Dewey and Alfred North Whitehead." Doctoral dissertation, Ohio State University, 1950.

Mohr, Robert L. "The Relation of John Dewey's Educational Theory to His Metaphysics." Master's thesis, Lehigh University, 1928.

Montgomery, Leroy Jeremiah. "Comparison of the Theism of the American Personalists with the Naturalism of John Dewey." Master's thesis, Union Theological Seminary, 1930.

Moore, Harold Francis. "Instrumentalism and the Assessment of Social Importance." Doctoral dissertation, Fordham University, 1971.

Moore, Lea Bevan. "The Significance of the Work of Colonel Francis Wayland Parker in the Progressive Educational Movement, with Special Reference to His Influence on John Dewey." Master's thesis, University of the Pacific, Covell College, 1937.

Moran, James A. "Martin Buber's 'I and Thou': An Interpretive Study." Doctoral dissertation, Fordham University, 1971.

Morris, Leonard C. "A Comparison of the Value Theories of DeWitt Parker and John Dewey." Master's thesis, University of Utah, 1957.

Morton, Joseph. "Education for Democracy: The Problems Involved and John Dewey's Proposed Solutions." Bachelor's thesis, Amherst College, 1959.

Mowat, Harold Glen. "The Concept of God in John Dewey's Thought." Master's thesis, McMaster University, 1968.

Mullen, Edward John. "John Dewey's Concept of Mind." Master's thesis, St. Louis University, 1970.

Murie, Martin L. "Art as the Expression of Meaning: A Study in John Dewey's Philosophy of Art." Bachelor's thesis, Reed College, 1950.

Muschinske, David James. "Social Ideas and the Social Studies: Relationships between Social Thought and Proposals for Social Science Education in American Public Schools as Revealed in the Writings of John Dewey, G. Stanley Hall, Harold Rugg, Charles McMurry, Frank McMurry, Charles DeGarmo, and the American Historical Association's Committees on the Study and Teaching of History in Elementary and

Secondary Schools." Doctoral dissertation, Boston University, 1971.

Myvett, Hartfield E. "A Critical Analysis of the Mexican Educational Philosophy in Relationship to the Theories of Professor John Dewey." Master's thesis, Catholic University of America, 1964.

Najarian, Pergrouhi Haroutun. "The Educational Frontiers in Lebanon; and John Dewey's Philosophy of Education." Master's thesis, Cornell University, 1950.

Neff, Frederick C. "A Pragmatic Interpretation of Freedom and Its Meaning for Education: A Study of the Writings of John Dewey and Boyd H. Bode." Doctoral dissertation, University of California at Los Angeles, 1950.

Nelson, Thomas W. "A. J. Ayer and John Dewey: Two Theories of Knowledge from the Perspective of Education." Master's thesis, Fresno State College, 1966.

Nelson, William Edward. "Art and Education in John Dewey's Philosophy." Master's thesis, Claremont Graduate School, 1952.

Newbury, Dorothy June. "The Idea of Freedom in Dewey and Some Consequences of the Idea for Educational Practice." Master's thesis, University of Chicago, 1949.

---. "A Theory of Discipline Developed from Dewey's Theory of Growth in Explicit Relationship to His Theory of Inquiry." Doctoral dissertation, University of Chicago, 1953.

Newcomb, Muriel Cecil. "A Brief Discussion of the Educational Ideals of John Dewey and Jean-Jacques Rousseau." Master's thesis, University of Rochester, 1945.

Neyhouse, Dorothy Ayahr. "A Comparison of the Theory of Education Found in the Philosophical Dictionary of Voltaire and the Modern Theory of Education." Master's thesis, Indiana State University, 1935. [Dewey, passim.]

Nielsen, Charles Merritt. "The Meaning of Morals in

John Dewey's Philosophy." Bachelor's thesis, Reed College, 1949.

Nnamonu, Silas C. "John Dewey's Philosophy of Education: A Nigerian Critique." Master's thesis, Dalhousie University, 1965.

Noonan, Joseph Francis. "The Practical Significance of Dewey's Educational Ideals." Master's thesis, New York University, 1925.

Nutter, Glen L. "John Dewey and the *New Republic* 1914-1930." In "Education and Politics in the *New Republic* Magazine 1914-1928," pp. 110-33. Doctoral dissertation, George Peabody College for Teachers, 1968.

O'Connor, John Joseph. "Dewey's Logical Theory; Some Clarifications and Criticisms." Doctoral dissertation, Columbia University, 1952.

O'Connor, Patrick D. "Human Nature, Pragmatism and Democracy: An Interpretation of John Dewey." Doctoral dissertation, United States International University, 1972.

O'Farrell, John J. "A Thomistic Evaluation of the Epistemological and Ontological Bases of John Dewey's Instrumentalist Philosophy." Doctoral dissertation, Fordham University, 1951.

O'Grady, Francis Thomas. "The Theory of Good in the Philosophy of John Dewey." Doctoral dissertation, University of Ottawa, 1950.

Okada, Gosaku. "The Significance of Dr. John Dewey's Philosophy for Religion." Master's thesis, New York University, 1931.

O'Kelly, Jarrell A. "The Morality of Art: A Comparison of the Methods of John Dewey and Yvor Winters." Master's thesis, University of Denver, 1958.

Olds, James. "The Possibility of Science in Morals." Bachelor's thesis, Amherst College, 1947.

O'Leary, Joseph Mary. "The Educational Philosophy of John Dewey." Master's thesis, St. Louis University, 1929.

Olguin, Manuel. "The Problem of the Criteria of Truth in John Dewey." In his "The Contribution of Pragmatism to Epistemology," pp. 60-75. Master's thesis, Oberlin College, 1942.

Olsen, Stanley L. "The Educational Philosophy of Dr. John Dewey: Exposition and Evaluation." Master's thesis, New York University, 1933.

O'Reilly, Francis Joseph. "A Presentation and Criticism of John Dewey's Moral Reconstruction." Master's thesis, St. Louis University, 1933.

Ortinez, James. "A Comparison between St. Joseph Calasanctius and John Dewey." Master's thesis, Immaculate Heart College, 1958.

Osora, Ann M. "An Evaluation of John Dewey's Instrumentalism Stressing Application to a Personal Classroom Philosophy." Master's thesis, Central Connecticut State College, 1964.

Oswalt, Howard Crane. "Process and Product in Art and Education with Special Emphasis on the Philosophy of John Dewey." Doctoral dissertation, University of Southern California, 1960.

Otterness, Omar Gordon. "Human Nature as Interpreted by John Dewey and Reinhold Niebuhr." Master's thesis, University of Illinois, 1944.

Ouyang, Tze-Hsiang. "John Dewey's Concept of Experience in Its Relation to Education." Doctoral dissertation, University of Toronto, 1942.

Paelian, Garabed H. "Nicholas Roerich's Contribution to Modern Life and Education." Doctoral dissertation, New York University, 1936. [Dewey, passim.]

Palmer, David James. "An Analysis of John Dewey's Conception of Democracy." Master's thesis, University of Illinois, 1953.

Palmer, Lewis C. "A Study of John Dewey's Application of Scientific Method to Social Problems." Master's thesis, University of Wisconsin, 1934.

Pan, Cedric. "Dewey on Valuation Propositions." Master's thesis, Southern Illinois University, 1969.

Panaro, Arthur Williams. "The Choice-Making Process in the Ethics of John Dewey and St. Thomas Aquinas." Master's thesis, University of Delaware, 1970.

Pape, Leslie Manock. "The Naturalistic Ethics of John Dewey." Doctoral dissertation, University of Chicago, 1930.

Park, Bong Mok. "An Analysis of the Ideas of John Dewey and Reinhold Niebuhr on Social Justice and the Implications of these Ideas for Korean Education." Doctoral dissertation, New York University, 1968.

Parkins, Ivan W. "John Dewey; Freedom as Intellectual Participation." Doctoral dissertation, University of Chicago, 1955.

Pass, Frederic. "A Survey of the Logic of Kant and Dewey: A Study in Contrasts." Undergraduate research paper, Honors in Philosophy, Albion College, Albion, Mich., 1960.

Paul, George Case. "A Comparison of the Educational Philosophies of Plato and John Dewey." Master's thesis, Temple University, 1929.

Pauson, Marian La Garde. "A Study of the Sublime." Doctoral dissertation, Tulane University, 1965.

Pavela, Gary. "John Dewey, Hu Shih and the Failure of Experimentalism in China." Master's thesis, Connecticut Wesleyan University, 1970.

———. "The Failure of John Dewey's Experimentalism in China and Its Implications for the Black Revolution in America." Project paper, University of Wisconsin, 1971.

Pedram, Manouchehr. "A Critical Comparison of the Educational Theories and Practices of John Amos Comenius with John Dewey's Concept of Experience." Doctoral dissertation, University of Kansas, 1963.

Peel, James Claudius. "A Comparative Study of the Educational Theories of Lester F. Ward and John

Dewey." Doctoral dissertation, New York University, 1943.

Pell, Orlie Anna Haggerty. "Value-Theory and Criticism." Doctoral dissertation, Columbia University, 1930. [The value-theories of Prall, Perry, and Dewey.]

Perlmutter, Oscar William. "Some Aspects of the Political Philosophy of John Dewey." Master's thesis, University of Chicago, 1949.

Peroaswamy, Asirvatham. "School and Society According to John Dewey and Mahatma Gandhi: A Retrospective Critique." Master's thesis, Loyola University, 1969.

Perrius, Lenore Ruth. "An Inquiry into the Philosophy of Elementary Education." Senior independent study paper, College of Wooster, Wooster, Ohio, 1970.

Pfuntner, Carl Herman. "An Examination of the Extent of Philosophical Dependence, Methodological and Metaphysical, of John Dewey on Charles Peirce." Doctoral dissertation, Georgetown University, 1967.

Phillips, Alice Nadine. "The Concept of Contingency in the Writings of John Dewey." Master's thesis, Washington University, 1945.

Pine, Mona Roberta. "Education and Democracy: A Study of Educational Theory and Practice in Relation to American Society." Senior project paper, Bard College, 1948.

Pingel, Martha Mary. "The Relation of Morality and Politics to Art as Discussed by Taine, Guyau, Tolstoi, Santayana, and John Dewey." Master's thesis, Columbia University, 1945.

Pizzo, Antonia. "The Logical Implications of Dewey's Educational Theory." Master's thesis, Smith College, 1922.

Podeschi, Ronald Lee. "John Dewey: Education, Educators, and Social Change." Doctoral dissertation, Northwestern University, 1968.

Pool, Maurice Glen. "The Metaphysical Foundation of

John Dewey's Theory of Education." Master's thesis, University of Oklahoma, 1961.

Power, Robert Joseph. "The Bases of Political Rights in the Philosophy of John Dewey." Doctoral dissertation, Emory University, 1964.

Price, John David. "A Comparison of Three Philosophies of Science and Religion and Their Implications for Science Education." Doctoral dissertation, Claremont Graduate School, 1968. [John Dewey, Alfred North Whitehead, and William Temple.]

Prince, Robert Graham. "Dewey on Intrinsic Value." Master's thesis, University of California at Los Angeles, 1966.

Pulham, John Donald. "The Pragmatism of William James Contrasted with the Instrumentalism of John Dewey." Master's thesis, University of Illinois, 1960.

Quick, Harold Edward. "The Theory of Man in the Thought of John Dewey and Reinhold Niebuhr." Master's thesis, Washington University, 1963.

Radlow, Sydney S. "Contrasting Conceptions of the Social Function of the Public Schools in the Period between the Two World Wars." Doctoral dissertation, Teachers College, Columbia University, 1948.

Raimendo, Dolores. "A Comparative Analysis of the Aims and Problems of Education in a Democracy According to John Dewey and Paul Goodman." Master's thesis, Jersey City State College, 1967.

Ramsey, Katherine Holbrook. "A Comparative Study of the Educational Theories of Rousseau and John Dewey." Master's thesis, Texas Technological College, 1931.

Rapton, Avra. "A Naturalist Esthetics. (A study in the esthetics of Leo Tolstoy, I. A. Richards, and John Dewey.)" Master's thesis, New York University, 1953.

Read, Waldemer Pickett. "John Dewey's Conception of Intelligent Social Action." Doctoral dissertation, University of Chicago, 1947.

Reed, Gerald Douglas. "Epistemology: Cybernetics and Uncertainty: Philosophical Observations on the Work of Warren McCulloch and John Dewey." Master's thesis, Simon Fraser University, 1968.

Reese, Hobart Lawrence. "A Methodological Examination of the Ethical Writings of John Stuart Mill and John Dewey." Master's thesis, Ohio State University, 1949.

Reiger, Anthony Elton. "John Dewey and the Total Learner." Doctoral dissertation, United States International University, 1971.

Reynolds, Joanne Rieta. "Choice Making; Its Educational Significance." Doctoral dissertation, Teachers College, Columbia University, 1965.

Rhodes, William Stacy. "John Dewey's Philosophic Method and Contemporary Republicanism." Honors thesis, Occidental College, Los Angeles, Cal., 1966.

Rich, John Martin. "Aspects of the Social Philosophies of John Dewey and Reinhold Niebuhr as They Relate to Education." Doctoral dissertation, Ohio State University, 1958.

Rieman, Timothy Wayne. "A Comparative Study of the Understanding of Man in the Writings of Reinhold Niebuhr and John Dewey and Some Implications for Education." Doctoral dissertation, Northwestern University, 1959.

Ringuette, Adrien L. "The Status of Individual Rights in a Sovereign Society." Bachelor's thesis, Amherst College, 1948.

Ripley, Edward Franklin. "John Dewey's Philosophy of Religion." Master's thesis, Columbia University, 1953.

Rislov, Sigurd Ingvald. "John Dewey's Concept of the Function of Philosophy in Our Civilization." Master's thesis, University of Iowa, 1941.

Robertson, Robert E. "The Concept of the Given in New Realism and Pragmatism." Doctoral dissertation, University of Texas, 1953.

Robinson, Edgar Stern. "John Dewey's Political Thought." Doctoral dissertation, Columbia University, 1952.

Robinson, Gertrude Joch. "The Relationship between the Theories of Truth and Verification in the Philosophies of Russell and Dewey." Master's thesis, University of Chicago, 1952.

Robinson, Joseph A. "A Comparison of the Educational Philosophy of John Dewey with That of Scholasticism." Doctoral dissertation, Boston University, 1944.

Robinson, Mary Alice. "A Critical Comparison of the Philosophies of Religion of John Dewey and George Santayana." Undergraduate tutorial in philosophy, Chatham College, Pittsburgh, Pa., 1961.

Robischon, Thomas Gregory. "The Historical Development of John Dewey's Ethical Theory." Master's thesis, Columbia University, 1952.

Roche, Lawrence Anthony. "A Comparative Study of the Idea of the Science of Education in the Works of John Dewey and Edward L. Thorndike." Doctoral dissertation, Case Western Reserve University, 1969.

Roe, Chungil Yhan. "The True Function of Education in Social Adjustment; a Comparative Estimate and Criticism of the Educational Teachings of Confucius and the Philosophy of John Dewey with a View to Evolving a Project for a System of National Education which will meet the Needs of Korea." Doctoral dissertation, University of Nebraska, 1927.

Rogers, Carolyn Grace Aiken. "John Dewey's Educational Philosophy." Master's thesis, Stanford University, 1956.

Rohrberg, C. Richard. "James' and Dewey's Methodologies in Relation to Their Conception of Mind." Doctoral dissertation, Columbia University, 1970.

Rosenfeld, Isaac Louis. "The Conception of Animal Nature in the Philosophy of John Dewey." Master's thesis, University of Chicago, 1941.

Rosenstrater, John. "The Philosophy of John Dewey and

Religious Values." Master's thesis, University of
Denver, 1931.

Ross, Stephen David. "The Philosophy of Experience; An
Analysis of the Concept of Experience in the Philosophy of John Dewey." Doctoral dissertation, Columbia University, 1961.

Roth, Robert J. "The Conditions for Self-Realization
in the Philosophy of John Dewey." Doctoral dissertation, Fordham University, 1961.

Rothman, Robert. "The Place of Knowledge in Valuation:
A Comparative Study of John Dewey's Philosophy of
Value." Doctoral dissertation, University of Mich-
igan, 1936.

Rott, Robert Kenneth. "Toward John Dewey's Theory of
Communication." Doctoral dissertation, State University of New York at Buffalo, 1966.

Rudner, Richard Samuel. "Four Studies of the Esthetic
Object." Doctoral dissertation, University of
Pennsylvania, 1949.

Ruhlen, Ralph L. "The Relationship of the Economic
Order to the Moral Ideal in the Thought of Maritain,
Brunner, Dewey, and Temple." Doctoral dissertation,
Boston University, 1959.

Russell, Charlotte Ann. "A Study in Christian Educa-
tion: The Appropriation of Hebraic Time through
Dewey and Bushnell." Master's thesis, Pacific
School of Religion, 1972.

Salesses, William Edward, Jr. "A Comparative Study of
Two Ethical Theories in Education." Master's thesis,
Claremont Graduate School, 1963. [Jacques Maritain
and John Dewey.]

---. "A Statement of the Ethical Theories of Pragmatism and Thomism as Expressed by John Dewey and
Jacques Maritain, and a Critical Analysis of Pragmatic Theories as They Apply to the Modern School
From the Thomistic Point of View." Doctoral dissertation, Claremont Graduate School, 1968.

Salzman, Samuel. "A Comparison of the Educational
Theories of John Dewey and Bertrand Russell." Master's thesis, New York University, 1930.

Sanchez, Ray. "John Dewey, Jean-Paul Sartre and the
Modern Metaphysics of Value." Doctoral dissertation,

Teachers College, Columbia University, 1961.

Sanders, William Joseph. "Evidences of the Hegelian Dialectic in the Educational Philosophy of John Dewey." Doctoral dissertation, Yale University, 1935.

Santulli, Michael. "The Character of the Natural: A Study of John Dewey's Philosophy of Science." Doctoral dissertation, Pennsylvania State University, 1970.

Sarkar, Sisirbindu. "A Pragmatic Interpretation of Self and Knowledge." Master's thesis, Claremont Graduate School, 1967.

Savage, Rosa Tiampo. "Nature and Naturalism in John Dewey." Doctoral dissertation, St. Louis University, 1967.

Savage, Willinda Hortense. "The Evolution of John Dewey's Philosophy of Experimentalism as Developed at the University of Michigan." Doctoral dissertation, University of Michigan, 1950.

Schenker, Nathan. "Dewey's Philosophy of Education." Master's thesis, New York University, 1962.

Schermerhorn, Roger L. "The Metaphysical Basis of Value for John Dewey." Master's thesis, San Diego State College, 1969.

Schipper, Gerrit J. "The Empirical Naturalism of John Dewey." Doctoral dissertation, Harvard University, 1942.

Schneider, Herbert Wallace. "John Dewey." A talk delivered by Professor Schneider at the Dewey ninetieth birthday celebration, University of Vermont, 26 October 1949. [Dewey Collection, Morris Library, Southern Illinois University.]

---. "Last Words from John Dewey." November, 1964. [Dewey Collection, Morris Library, Southern Illinois University.]

---. "Reminiscences about John Dewey at Columbia, 1913-1960." June, 1966. [Dewey Collection, Morris

Library, Southern Illinois University.]

Schoenchen, Gustav G. "Eduard Burger and John Dewey:
A Comparative Study of Burger's Arbeitsschule and
Contemporary American Activity Schools as Representative of Dewey's Educational Philosophy." Doctoral
dissertation, New York University, 1939.

Schoettinger, Robert Anthone. "John Dewey's Concept of
Philosophy." Master's thesis, St. Louis University,
1949.

Schultz, Frederick M. "The Concept of Community in
the Philosophy of John Dewey." Doctoral dissertation, Indiana University, 1969.

Schumacher, Patricia Anne. "The Principle of Continuity in John Dewey's Ethics." Master's thesis, Columbia University, 1947.

Schwartz, Nadine Shanler. "Beyond John Dewey: Paul
Goodman's Theory of Human Nature." Doctoral dissertation, Rutgers University, 1970.

Seegers, Arthur John. "A Comparative Study of the
Views of John Dewey and Martin Luther on Moral Education." Master's thesis, University of Nebraska,
1930.

Segal, Jerome. "John Dewey's Theory of Perception."
Doctoral dissertation, Northwestern University,
1972.

Segal, Sol. "Science and Values; A Comparative Study
of the Relations between Science and Values, partic-
ularly Ethical Values, in the Writings of John Dewey
and Frederick Engels." Doctoral dissertation, New
York University, 1961.

Seguel, Mary Louise. "The Shaping of a Field of Spe-
cialization, Curriculum Making; A Critical Study of
Selected Writings of Charles and Frank McMurry,
Franklin Bobbitt, W. W. Charters, Harold Rugg,
Hollis Caswell, and John Dewey." Doctoral disser-
tation, Teachers College, Columbia University, 1964.

Shah, Mian M. "A Comparative Analysis of the Philosophies of Education of John Dewey and H. S. Broudy."

Master's thesis, University of Illinois, 1967.

Shales, John Melville. "Study of the Use of Out of School Environment by Talks of Certain Small Rural Schools." Doctoral dissertation, Cornell University, 1928.

Shargel, Emanuel Israel. "Dewey's Dialectic." Doctoral dissertation, Cornell University, 1971.

Shaw, Marvin Cabrera. "Naturalism and the Divine: The Possibility of a Naturalistic Theism Based on the Philosophies of Santayana and Dewey." Doctoral dissertation, Columbia University, 1968.

Sheppard, David Irving. "A Study of the Resemblances between the Educational Ideas of John Dewey, and Those of Rousseau, Herbart, and Froebel." Master's thesis, University of California at Los Angeles, 1942.

Sheridan, Constance M. "William Heard Kilpatrick and Progressive Education." Master's thesis, Boston College, 1953. [Dewey, passim.]

Shermis, Sherwin Samuel. "Interaction in the Writings of John Dewey." Master's thesis, University of Kansas, 1960.

---. "John Dewey's Social and Political Philosophy: Its Implications for Social Studies Education." Doctoral dissertation, University of Kansas, 1962.

Shipka, Thomas A. "Social Conflict and Re-construction." Doctoral dissertation, Boston College, 1969.

Shkolnik, Don Gerald. "John Dewey's Social Philosophy; the Cultural Content of Democracy." Master's thesis, Ohio State University, 1966.

Sibley, William Maurice. "An Examination of Dewey's Theory of Knowledge." Doctoral dissertation, Brown University, 1943.

Simon, Robert Leonard. "Four Concepts of Equality." Doctoral dissertation, University of Pennsylvania, 1969. [Dewey, pp. 123-24, 147-57, and passim.]

Singer, Irving. "John Dewey's Theory of Value; A Critical Analysis." Honors thesis, Harvard University, 1948.

---. "The Role of Valuation in John Dewey's Theory of Value; A Critical Analysis." Francis Bowen Prize Essay, Harvard University, 1951.

Skilbeck, Malcolm. "Criticisms of Progressive Education, 1916-1930." Master's thesis, University of Illinois, 1958.

Skoglund, Henry Leonard. "John Dewey's Moral Theory." Master's thesis, University of Chicago, 1953.

Sleeper, Ralph William. "Metaphysics and the Value Theories of Urban, Dewey, and Perry." Doctoral dissertation, Columbia University, 1956.

Smith, Allen K. "The Concept of the Reflex Arc and George Herbert Mead's Theory of History." Master's thesis, Tulane University, 1971.

Smith, Clarence Arthur. "An Analysis of the Educational Philosophy of a Selected Group of Educators." Master's thesis, Washington University, 1929. [Plato, Quintilian, Montaigne, Comenius, Pestalozzi, Herbart, and Dewey.]

Smith, Ferrer. "A Thomistic Appraisal of the Philosophy of John Dewey." Doctoral dissertation submitted to the Pontifical Faculty of the Immaculate Conception, Washington, D.C., 1955.

Smith, James Ward. "Propaedeutic to Value Theory." Doctoral dissertation, Princeton University, 1942.

Smith, Joanmarie. "John Dewey and the Ideal Community." Doctoral dissertation, Fordham University, 1971.

Smith, John Milton. "A Comparison and Criticism of the Educational Philosophies of Plato and John Dewey." Doctoral dissertation, State University of Iowa, 1941.

Smith, Philip Lloyd. "The Development and Formulation of John Dewey's Theory of Mind." Doctoral dissertation, University of Michigan, 1972.

Snook, Ivan Augustus. "Indoctrination and the Teaching of Religion." Doctoral dissertation, University of Illinois, 1968. [Dewey, pp. 13-18, and passim.]

Snyder, Sam R. "John Dewey and Erich Fromm: Two Concepts of Freedom and Some Implications for Education." Master's thesis, University of Toledo, 1965.

Somjee, Abdulkarim. "Some Methodological Aspects of John Dewey's Political Philosophy." Doctoral dissertation, London School of Economics and Political Science, 1954.

Sommerfeld, Richard Edwin. "Nature of Man in the Philosophy of John Dewey." Bachelor's thesis, Concordia Seminary, St. Louis, Mo., 1954.

Sosensky, Irving. "John Dewey's Theory of Warranted Assertibility." Doctoral dissertation, Columbia University, 1955.

Spees, Emil Ray. "Philosophy: A Base for College Student Personnel Work." Doctoral dissertation, Claremont Graduate School, 1969. [Dewey, pp. 67-96.]

Spellman, Delma Lynne. "An Exploratory Review of Recent Research in Teaching Methodology in Relation to Contemporary Learning Theory." Master's thesis, Cornell University, 1967.

Spencer, Thomas Eugene. "Education and American Liberalism: A Comparison of the Views of Thomas Jefferson, Ralph Waldo Emerson, and John Dewey." Doctoral dissertation, University of Illinois, 1963.

Spielberg, Paul Jay. "Problems of an Empirical Theory of Valuation--A Consideration of John Dewey and Charles Stevenson." Master's thesis, Columbia University, 1949.

Staffelbach, Hubert W. "Some Historical Backgrounds of the Principles and Purposes of Progressive Education." Master's thesis, Stanford University, 1942. [Dewey, pp. 79-82, 305-23.]

Staley, J. R. "Dewey and the new-Thomists." Bachelor's thesis, Amherst College, 1952.

Stanford, Lincoln Cooper. "The Concepts of Knowledge

of Peirce and Dewey; The Relation to Education."
Doctoral dissertation, Stanford University, 1970.

Steibel, Gerald Lee. "John Dewey's Philosophy of Democracy Applied in a Critique of Classic Liberalism."
Doctoral dissertation, Columbia University, 1951.

Steinberg, Charles Side. "Contemporary Aesthetic Theory; the Philosophy of Art of John Dewey and George
Santayana." Master's thesis, New York University,
1939.

Steinert, Peter M. "Rickover, Dewey, and Education."
Master's thesis, Western Connecticut State College,
1963.

Sternfeld, Robert. "Contemporary Philosophies of Experience: Philosophic Method in Dewey, Bradley, and
Husserl." Doctoral dissertation, University of Chicago, 1948.

Stine, William D. "The *A Priori* in John Dewey's Theory
of Inquiry." Doctoral dissertation, Harvard University, 1969.

Suggs, William Albert. "The Comparative Influence of
Herbartism and Deweyism upon the Objectives of
Twentieth Century Education." Master's thesis,
Tennessee Agricultural and Industrial State Univer-
sity, 1957.

Suits, Bernard Herbert. "The Aesthetic Object in Santayana and Dewey." Doctoral dissertation, University of Illinois, 1958.

Süleyman, Zekiye. "A Study of the History and Development of Education in Turkey, with Special Emphasis
upon the Influence of Professor Dewey's Theories of
Education." Master's thesis, Smith College, 1934.

Swenson, John Vernon. "The Corrigibility of Value-
Judgments in C. I. Lewis." Master's thesis, University of Iowa, 1948.

Swick, Kevin J. "John Dewey's Concept of Morality and
Some of Its Implications for Modern Education."
Master's thesis, Bowling Green State University,
1967.

Swimmer, George Gershon. "A Comparison of the Intellectual Development of John Dewey and William H. Kilpatrick with Implications for Differences in Their Educational Theories." Doctoral dissertation, Northwestern University, 1957.

Sylvester, R. Peter. "Possible Approaches to a World Faith--A Critical Analysis." Bachelor's thesis, Amherst College, 1949.

Tabb, Annie Laurie. "From Pragmatism to the Instrumentalism of John Dewey in Contemporaneous Philosophy; the Course of Pragmatism." Master's thesis, University of Alabama, 1932.

Taylor, Albert J. "Dewey and Russell as Educational Theorists: A Comparative Analysis." Doctoral dissertation, Rutgers State University, 1966.

Taylor, John E. "An Essay on the Philosophy of John Dewey." Doctoral dissertation, University of Ottawa, 1942.

Terkel, Meyer. "John Dewey's Educational Principles and Contributions to Education in the United States." Master's thesis, College of the City of New York, 1928.

Thayer, Horace Standish. "Two Theories of Truth: The Relation between the Theories of John Dewey and Bertrand Russell." Master's thesis, Columbia University, 1947.

Thompson, Betty Ann. "Implications of Reflective Thinking to Physical Education. An Interpretation of Dewey and Pragmatism to the Field." Master's thesis, Ohio State University, 1953..

Tillman, Mary Joan. "John Dewey's Religious Experience." Master's thesis, St. Louis University, 1966.

Titus, James Emerson. "Studies in American Liberalism of the 1930s: John Dewey, Benjamin Cardozo and Thurman Arnold." Doctoral dissertation, University of Wisconsin, 1957.

To, Cho-Yee. "John Dewey's Conception of the Relation of Education to the Democratic Ideal." Doctoral dissertation, Southern Illinois University, 1968.

Tofield, Aaron J. "Dewey and Woodbridge on Tradition."
Master's thesis, Columbia University, 1937.

Toland, William Gipsy. "The Later Wittgenstein and
Classical Pragmatism: A Critical Appraisal." Doctoral dissertation, University of North Carolina,
1967.

Torres, José Arsenio. "Philosophic Reconstruction and
Social Reform in John Dewey and José Ortega y Gas-
set." Doctoral dissertation, University of Chicago,
1954.

Trageser, Gertrude A. "Criticism of John Dewey's *QUEST
FOR CERTAINTY*." Doctoral dissertation, Fordham University, 1934.

Triplett, Janet Clair-Marvel. "A Study of the Episte-
mologies of David Hume and John Dewey." Master's
thesis, University of Oklahoma, 1966.

---. "John Dewey--A Critical Analysis of the Interde-
pendence of Knowledge and Action." Doctoral dissertation, University of New Mexico, 1972.

Tromble, William Warner. "The American Intellectual
and Music: An Analysis of the Writings of Susanne
K. Langer, Paul Henry Lang, Jacques Barzun, John
Dewey, and Leonard Bernstein--with Implications for
Music Education at the College Level." Doctoral
dissertation, University of Michigan, 1968.

Troutner, Leroy F. "Educational Implications of Exis-
tentialism: An Analysis and Comparison of Martin
Heidegger and John Dewey." Doctoral dissertation,
Stanford University, 1962.

Trumbull, Edward. "The Aesthetics of John Dewey."
Master's thesis, New York University, 1959.

Trusso, Mary A. "A Study of the Educational Philosophy
of John Dewey as Shown in *DEMOCRACY AND EDUCATION*."
Master's thesis, Canisius College, 1959.

Tsurumi, Kazuko. "The Method of Instrumentalism and
Dewey's Social Philosophy." In "A Comparative Study

of Method in Historical Materialism and Instrumentalism," pp. 68-130. Master's thesis, Vassar College, 1941.

Tuohy, Walter Joseph. "John Dewey and the American Legal Realists." Master's thesis, St. Louis University, 1960.

Turner, Robert Yongue. "Dewey's and Kant's Classifications of the Arts." Master's thesis, University of Chicago, 1951.

Tuttle, Elbert Parr, Jr. "Individualism in Recent American Thought: William James, William Graham Sumner, and John Dewey." Bachelor's thesis, Princeton University, 1942.

Tuttle, Robert Eugene. "A Comparative Study of Basic Assumptions in the Philosophy of John Dewey." Master's thesis, Oberlin College, 1934.

Tyrell, Katherine. "The Influence of John Dewey upon the Progressive Education Movement." Master's thesis, Claremont Graduate School, 1931.

Ulbricht, Robert Emil. "A Study of John Dewey's Philosophy of Art." Master's thesis, University of Illinois, 1953.

Updegraff, Kathryn. "History in Dewey's Theory of Education: A Critical Analysis." Master's thesis, University of California, 1952.

Van Der Ross, Richard Ernst. "The Pragmatism of John Dewey and Its Relation to His Educational Philosophy." Doctoral dissertation, University of Cape Town, 1952.

Van De Water, Anne. "Dewey's Theory of Truth." Senior essay in philosophy, Wells College, 1967.

Villemain, Francis Trowbridge. "The Qualitative Character of Intelligence." Doctoral dissertation, Teachers College, Columbia University, 1952.

Vingol, Robert Henry. "F. H. Bradley and His Critique of Pragmatism." Doctoral dissertation, University of Toronto, 1953.

Waldman, Theodore. "Kantian and Instrumentalist Epis-
temologies Compared." Master's thesis, Washington
University, 1948.

Wall, Mary Elizabeth. "Progressive Educators and the
Planned Society." Master's thesis, Boston College,
1954.

Walsh, Frederick Michael. "John Dewey's *ART AS EXPE-
RIENCE*." Master's thesis, University of Guelph,
1970.

Walsh, Mary R. "Reverend Francis H. Drinkwater and
Progressive Education." Master's thesis, Boston
College, 1954.

Walsh, William Joseph. "John Dewey's Concept of Democracy." Master's thesis, Villanova University, 1949.

Ward, Charles D. "Transaction, Interaction and Situation in Dewey's Philosophy." Master's thesis,
Tulane University, 1971.

Warren, Guy H. M. "Some Misinterpretations of John
Dewey." Master's thesis, Wisconsin State College,
1953.

Wasson, Everett Lawrence. "Human Personality in the
Philosophy of John Dewey." Master's thesis, Union
Theological Seminary, 1933.

Watkins, Thomas Hamer, II. "Dewey: A Philosophy of
Total Integration." In "A Consideration of the
Aesthetic-Productive Process as Integration of Self
and Environment," pp. 261-96. Master's thesis,
University of New Mexico, 1948.

Watrous, Mary W. "A Comparative Study of John Dewey's
DEMOCRACY AND EDUCATION and *EXPERIENCE AND EDUCA-
TION*." Master's thesis, Gonzaga University, 1953.

Watson, Genevieve Margaret. "The Educational Philosophy of Froebel and Dewey Compared and Evaluated."
Doctoral dissertation, New York University, 1931.

Weatherstone, Richard A. "The Significance of Value
Judgments in the Philosophy of John Dewey." Master's
thesis, St. Mary's College, Winona, Minn., 1963.

Weaver, Earl J. "John Dewey: A Spokesman for Progressive Liberalism." Doctoral dissertation, Brown University, 1963.

Weber, Edward Lawrence. "The Beginnings of Progressive Education." Bachelor's thesis, Princeton University, 1956.

Weisner, John Joseph. "Habits in John Dewey's Theory of Ethics." Master's thesis, St. Louis University, 1968.

Welch, Cyril. "A Phenomenological Analysis of the Occurrence of Meaning in Experience." Doctoral dissertation, Pennsylvania State University, 1964. [Dewey, passim.]

Welch, Mary Stanislas. "The Contribution of John Dewey's Philosophy of Education to an Understanding of the Nature and Function of Authority." Master's thesis, Georgetown University, 1967.

Welch, Stuart. "John Dewey's Position Respecting the Role of the American School in Achieving Social Change." Doctoral dissertation, Rutgers University, 1971.

Weldon, Ward Wendell. "John Dewey's Temporal Criteria of Educative Experience." Doctoral dissertation, Northwestern University, 1971.

Welsh, Paul. "Dewey's Theory of Inquiry." Doctoral dissertation, Cornell University, 1947.

Wen, Lien Chung. "The Conception of Culture with Special Reference to the Educational Philosophy of John Dewey." Doctoral dissertation, Ohio State University, 1932.

Wentworth, Eva. "Three Advanced Educational Reformers." Doctoral dissertation, University of Southern California, 1931. [Sanderson of Great Britain, Tagore of India, and Dewey.]

Wetzel, Charles R. "A Critical Evaluation of John Dewey's Theory of Inquiry." Doctoral dissertation, University of Nebraska, 1962.

Whale, George J. K. "John Dewey and Pragmatism: Philosophy as Education: 'All Philosophy is Philosophy of Education'." Master's thesis, Simon Fraser University, 1969.

Wheeler, Arthur M. "Secular and Religious Approaches to Morality." Master's thesis, University of Chicago, 1953. [Dewey, pp. 5, 11-14, 16-17, 19-26, 30.]

---. "The Value Theory of John Dewey." In "The Concept of Rationality in the Ethics and Value Theory of Clarence Irving Lewis," pp. 23-40. Doctoral dissertation, University of Wisconsin, 1958.

Wheeler, James Erskine. "Confusions of Romantic Progressive Education with Dewey's Instrumentalism." Doctoral dissertation, Yale University, 1950.

Whitaker, Mildred E. "Reading in an Experience Program in Light of Recent Educational Research." Master's thesis, Indiana State University, 1941.

Whitehead, Eugene S. J. "Dewey's Educational Standards as Related to the Public Schools." Master's thesis, University of Texas, 1928.

Williams, Noah. "John Dewey and Rudolf Steiner, A Tentative Analysis from Limited References of a Theory of Inquiry as Viewed by John Dewey and a Theory of Knowledge as Viewed by Rudolf Steiner with Some Relations and Distinctions." Master's thesis, Adelphi University, 1950.

Williston, Frank Samuel. "A Comparative Analysis of John Dewey's Theory of Valuation." Doctoral dissertation, University of Minnesota, 1969.

Willower, Donald Jay. "John Dewey's Conception of Social Values." Master's thesis, State University of New York at Buffalo, 1951.

Wilson, Howard Woodrow. "Some Implications of Dewey's Philosophy for the Teaching of Speech." Master's thesis, University of Illinois, 1940.

Wilson, Netta White. "The Development of the Sociological Trend in John Dewey's Ethical Theory." Master's thesis, University of Minnesota, 1929.

Wilson, Patrick Seymour. "Educational Philosophy of
John Dewey." Doctoral dissertation, Victoria University of Wellington, 1947.

Wimmer, J. R. "An Analysis of Immanuel Kant and John
Dewey." Bachelor's thesis, Amherst College, 1950.

Winterrle, John F. "John Dewey: Instrumentalism and
Social Problems." Doctoral dissertation, University
of Oregon, 1963.

Wolfard, Helen M. "What Dewey Means by Experience:
Some Implications for Education." Master's thesis,
Reed College, 1954.

Workman, Rollin Wallace. "A Comparison of the Theories
of Meaning of John Dewey and Oxford Ordinary Language Philosophers with Some Attention to That of
F. C. S. Schiller." Doctoral dissertation, University of Michigan, 1958.

Wright, Donald Oswald. "A Comparative Study of the
Relative Works of John Dewey and Viktor Lowenfeld in
the Field of Art and Art Education." Master's thesis, University of Southern California, 1960.

Wright, Ward Wilbur. "The Psychology of John Dewey."
Master's thesis, Oberlin College, 1936.

Wu, Joseph Sen. "The Problem of Existential Import in
Dewey's Theory of Propositions." Doctoral dissertation, Southern Illinois University, 1967.

Wyckoff, D. Campbell. "Are John Dewey's Anti-Theistic
Views Biased?" Master's thesis, New York University,
1942.

Wyckoff, Harry W. "A Study of the Esthetics of John
Dewey." Master's thesis, Stanford University, 1936.

Wyn, Ronald. "The New Metaphysics." Bachelor's thesis,
Amherst College, 1955.

Yeager, Iver Franklin. "Personal-Social Values in John
Macmurray and John Dewey: A Basis for a Creative
Relationship between Religion and Higher Education."
Master's thesis, University of Chicago, 1948.

Yelle, Joseph Robert. "A Contextual Approach to the

Problem of the Relation of Dewey's Theories of Value, Inquiry, and Experience." Master's thesis, University of Chicago, 1950.

Yonemori, Yuji. "Dewey's Theory of Language and Meaning: Its Philosophical and Educational Implications." Doctoral dissertation, Ohio State University, 1960.

Young, Homer H. "Contributions of John Dewey to American Education." Master's thesis, Stanford University, 1937.

Young, Warren Cameron. "Nature and Naturalism in the Thought of Frederick J. E. Woodbridge and John Dewey." Doctoral dissertation, Boston University, 1947.

Yu, Yung-juin. "A Critical Examination of Dewey's Views on Human Nature, Human Behavior, and Morality." Doctoral dissertation, University of Illinois, 1959.

Zallys, Richard Paul. "Ideals or Experience--Santayana and Dewey." Master's thesis, University of Chicago, 1956.

Zau, Foo. "The Individual and Social Dimensions of John Dewey's Philosophy of Education." Doctoral dissertation, University of Colorado, 1949.

Zimmerman, Robert Lloyd. "John Dewey's Theory of Communication." Master's thesis, New York University, 1959.

Zink, Sidney. "A Critique of the Ethical Theory of John Dewey." Doctoral dissertation, University of Cincinnati, 1941.

ART AND EDUCATION. By John Dewey, Albert C. Barnes,
Laurence Buermeyer, Thomas Munro, Paul Guillaume,
Mary Mullen, and Violette de Mazia. Merion, Pa.:
Barnes Foundation Press, 1929. [2d ed., rev. and
enl. Merion, Pa.: Barnes Foundation Press, 1947.]

Reviewed in *Elementary School Journal* 30 (1930): 550-51
(W. G. Whitford); *Journal of Philosophy* 44 (1947):
558-59 (Helmut Kohn).

ART AS EXPERIENCE. New York: Minton Balch and Co.;
London: G. Allen and Unwin, 1934.

Reviewed in *A.L.A. Booklist* 30 (1934): 272; *American
Mercury* 33 (1934): 253-55 (Ernest Sutherland Bates);
Apollo 20 (1934): 337-38 (H. F.); *Boston Evening Trans-
cript*, 13 June 1934 (E. N.); *Burlington Magazine for
Connoisseurs* 66 (1935): 148-49 (Listowel); *Chicago
Tribune*, 25 August 1934 (Daniel C. Rich); *Christian
Century* 51 (1934): 1211-12 (Edwin Buehrer); *Christian
Science Monitor*, 25 April 1934, Mag. Sec. p. 11 (E.
C. S.); *Current History* 40 (1934): xii (A. H.); *Educa-
tional Administration and Supervision* 21 (1935):
235-36 (H. G. Hullfish); *Hibbert Journal* 33 (1934-35):
465-69 (J. M. Lloyd Thomas); *Journal of Aesthetics and
Art Criticism* 6 (1948): 203-7 (Benedetto Croce);
Journal of Philosophy 31 (1934): 275-76 (Irwin Edman);
London Mercury 31 (1935): 387-88 (I. Berlin); *More
Books* 9 (1934): 235; *Nation*, 20 June 1934, pp. 710-11
(Robert J. Goldwater); *New Era* 15 (1934): 256-57 (D. G.
Cleage); *New Republic*, 25 April 1934, pp. 315-16 (Ken-
neth Burke); *New York Herald Tribune Books*, 6 May 1934,
p. 8 (Horace Gregory); *New York Times Book Review*,

8 April 1934, pp. 2, 14 (Dino Ferrari); *Philosophical
Review* 44 (1935): 388-90 (David Wight Prall); *Social
Frontier* 2 (1936): 109-13 (John H. Randall, Jr.);
Spectator 153 (1934): sup. 6, 8 (Wyndham Lewis); *Studio*
(London) 112 (1936): 111-12 (Reginald Wilenski); *Times
Literary Supplement* (London), 24 January 1935, p. 43;
Yale Review 24 (1934): 188-89 (Samson Faison, Jr.).

THE BERTRAND RUSSELL CASE.   Edited by John Dewey and
     Horace M. Kallen.   New York: Viking Press, 1941.

Reviewed in *American Association of University Professors Bulletin* 27 (1941): 601-10 (P. A. Carmichael);
*Annals of the American Academy of Political and Social
Science* 219 (1942): 184 (Edgar Wallace Knight);
Clearing House 16 (1942): 434 (P. W. L. Cox); *Journal
of Philosophy* 38 (1941): 573-81 (Peter Archibald Carmichael); *Nation*, 6 June 1942, p. 664.

THE CASE OF LEON TROTSKY.   New York, London: Harper and
     Brothers, 1937.   [Stenographic report of hearings
     in Mexico City.]

Reviewed in *New Republic*, 24 November 1937, p. 79
(Bertram D. Wolfe); editorial comment in ibid., 22 December 1937, pp. 181-82.

CHARACTERS AND EVENTS.   Edited by Joseph Ratner.
     2 vols.   New York: Henry Holt and Co., 1929.   [Re-
     prints of articles published in various journals.]

Reviewed in *A.L.A. Booklist* 26 (1929): 8; *American
Mercury* 17 (1929): xiv, xviii; *Bookman* 70 (1929): iv,
vi; *Boston Evening Transcript*, 15 June 1929 (E. N.);
Chicago Tribune, 14 December 1929 (James Hayden Tufts);
Christian Science Monitor, 7 June 1930; *Expository
Times* (Edinburgh) 41 (1929-30): 115; *New York Evening
Post*, 18 May 1929 (John Herman Randall, Jr.); *New York
Times Book Review*, 14 July 1929, pp. 5, 17 (William
MacDonald); *New York World*, 20 October 1929 (Harry
Hansen); ibid., 27 October 1929 (C. Hartley Grattan);
Outlook 152 (1929): 187 (Gorham B. Munson); *Saturday
Review of Literature*, 26 October 1929, p. 310 (Ralph
Barton Perry); *Symposium* 1 (1930): 128-32 (Laurence
Buermeyer); *Times Literary Supplement* (London), 17 Oc-

tober 1929, p. 804; *World Tomorrow* 12 (1929): 472-73
(E. N.).

A COMMON FAITH. New Haven: Yale University Press;
London: Humphrey Milford, Oxford University Press,
1934.

Reviewed in *A.L.A. Booklist* 31 (1934): 50; *Anglican
Theological Review* 17 (1935): 44-45 (Frederick C.
Grant); *Boston Evening Transcript*, 1 September 1934
(E. N.); *Catholic World* 140 (1934): 240 (G. A. T.);
Christian Century 51 (1934): 1281 (Winifred E. Garri-
son); *Christian Register* 113 (1934): 787-89 (Andrew
Banning); *Concordia Theological Monthly* 6 (1935):
312-13 (J. T. Mueller); *Descant* 11 (Spring 1967):
25-32 (Harry M. Campbell); *International Journal of
Ethics* 45 (1935): 359-61 (Albert Eustace Haydon);
Journal of Philosophy 31 (1934): 584-85 (Robert Scoon);
Mental Hygiene 20 (1936): 493-95 (Eleanor H. Johnson);
Mind 44 (1935): 397-99 (F. C. S. Schiller); *Monist* 45
(1935): 309; *Nation*, 26 September 1934, pp. 358-59
(Reinhold Niebuhr); *New Masses*, 2 October 1934, pp.
38-39 (Corliss Lamont); *New Republic*, 20 February 1935,
p. 53 (Norbert Guterman); *New York Herald Tribune*, 20
September 1934 (Lewis Gannett); *New York Herald Tribune
Books*, 4 November 1934, p. 2 (John H. Holmes); *New York
Times Book Review*, 30 September 1934, p. 10; *Philosoph-
ical Review* 44 (1935): 496-97 (Max C. Otto); *Philosophy*
(London) 10 (1935): 235-36 (A. E. Elder); *Psychiatric
Quarterly* 9 (1935): 156 (Brown); *Saturday Review of
Literature*, 22 December 1934, p. 389 (Albert C. Wyck-
off); *School and Society* 41 (1935): 744-45 (W. McAn-
drew); *Social Frontier* 2 (1936): 109-13 (John Herman
Randall, Jr.); *Springfield Daily Republican*, 5 October
1934; *Survey Graphic* 24 (1935): 87-88 (Charles S.
Brown); *Thought* 11 (1936): 147-53 (L. E. Sullivan);
Times Literary Supplement (London), 15 November 1934,
p. 799; *Yale Review* 24 (1934): 166-68 (Henry Hazlitt).

CONSTRUCTION AND CRITICISM. New York: Columbia University Press, 1930.

Reviewed in *New Scholasticism* 6 (1932): 76-78 (Virgil
Michel); *United India and Indian States* (Delhi) 32
(1930): 624-25.

CONTEMPORARY AMERICAN PHILOSOPHY: PERSONAL STATEMENTS.
Edited by George P. Adams and William P. Montague.
2 vols. New York: Macmillan Co., 1930. [Dewey,
"From Absolutism to Experimentalism," vol. 2, pp.
13-27.]

Reviewed in *New York Times Book Review*, 13 July 1930,
p. 10 (Axton Clark).

CREATIVE INTELLIGENCE: ESSAYS IN THE PRAGMATIC ATTI-
TUDE. By John Dewey, Addison Webster Moore, Harold
Chapman Brown, George Herbert Mead, Boyd Henry
Bode, Henry Waldgrave Stuart, James Hayden Tufts,
and Horace Meyer Kallen. New York: Henry Holt and
Co., 1917. [Dewey, "The Need for a Recovery of
Philosophy," pp. 3-69.]

Reviewed in *A.L.A. Booklist* 13 (1917): 423; *Bookman* 45
(1917): 181-82 (Florence F. Kelly); *Catholic World* 105
(1917): 393; *Dial* 62 (1917): 348-52 (Max C. Otto);
Journal of Philosophy 14 (1917): 505-20 (Wendell T.
Bush); ibid. 15 (1918): 149-57 (Delton T. Howard);
Mind n.s. 26 (1917): 466-74 (F. C. S. Schiller); *New
York Times*, 15 April 1917, pp. 141-42; *Philosophical
Review* 28 (1919): 200-208 (Katherine E. Gilbert);
Springfield Daily Republican, 3 February 1917; ibid.,
19 August 1917; *Survey* 39 (1917): 326 (John Collier).

"Definition." With Arthur Fisher Bentley. *Journal of
Philosophy* 44 (1947): 281-306.

Reviewed in *Journal of Symbolic Logic* 12 (1947): 99
(Arthur F. Smullyan).

DEMOCRACY AND EDUCATION: AN INTRODUCTION TO THE PHI-
LOSOPHY OF EDUCATION. Text Book Series in Educa-
tion, edited by Paul Monroe. New York: Macmillan
Co., 1916.

Reviewed in *A.L.A. Booklist* 12 (1916): 404-5; *Boston
Evening Transcript*, 15 April 1916; *Dial* 61 (1916):
101-3 (Thomas Percival Beyer); *Elementary School
Journal* 17 (1916): 13-17; *Humanist* 7 (1947): 97 (John
H. Hershey); *Independent* 86 (1916): 401-2; *Interna-
tional Journal of Ethics* 26 (1916): 547-50 (Addison

Webster Moore); *Journal of Philosophy* 14 (1917):
384-89 (Ernest Carroll Moore); *Modern School* 3 (1917):
103-5 (Carl Zigrosser); *Nation*, 4 May 1916, pp. 480-81;
New Republic, 1 July 1916, p. 231 (Walter Lippmann);
New York Review of Books, 29 February 1968, pp. 25-29
(David Hawkins); *Philosophical Review* 25 (1916): 735-41
(James Edwin Creighton); *Springfield Daily Republican*,
23 April 1916; *Survey* 36 (1916): 541-42 (Frank A.
Manny).

DEWEY ON EDUCATION. Introd. and notes by Martin S.
Dworkin. Classics in Education, no. 3. New York:
Bureau of Publications, Teachers College, Columbia
University, 1959.

Reviewed in *Personalist* 42 (1961): 142 (Robert L.
Brackenbury).

DEWEY ON EXPERIENCE, NATURE, AND FREEDOM. Edited by
Richard J. Bernstein. New York: Liberal Arts
Press, 1960.

Reviewed in *Personalist* 42 (1961): 95 (Wilbur Long).

"Does Reality Possess Practical Character?" In ESSAYS,
PHILOSOPHICAL AND PSYCHOLOGICAL, in Honor of Wil-
liam James, Professor in Harvard University, by his
Colleagues at Columbia University, pp. 53-80. New
York: Longmans, Green, and Co., 1908.

Reviewed in *Mind* n.s. 19 (1910): 97-105 (Horace Meyer
Kallen).

EARLY ESSAYS AND *LEIBNIZ'S NEW ESSAYS CONCERNING THE
HUMAN UNDERSTANDING*. The Early Works of John
Dewey, 1882-1898. Vol. 1, 1882-1888. Edited by
Jo Ann Boydston. Carbondale: Southern Illinois
University Press, 1969.

Reviewed in *Booklist* 65 (1969): 1026; *Buffalo Courier-
Express*, 20 April 1969 (E. T.); *Choice* 6 (1969):
827-28; *Library Journal* 94 (1969): 1880 (Howard Ozmon);
Long Beach Press-Telegram, 7 May 1969; *Modern Schoolman*
47 (1970): 243-44 (James Collins); *New Scholasticism* 44

(1970): 309-12 (C. F. Delaney); *Philosophy and Phenomenological Research* 31 (1970): 140-41 (Y. H. Krikorian); *Review of Metaphysics* 22 (1969): 750 (R. J. B.); *Washington Sunday Star*, 15 February 1970.

EARLY ESSAYS AND *THE STUDY OF ETHICS: A SYLLABUS*. The Early Works of John Dewey, 1882-1898. Vol. 4, 1893-1894. Edited by Jo Ann Boydston. Carbondale: Southern Illinois University Press, 1971.

Reviewed in *Booklist* 68 (1972): 371; *Choice* 9 (1972): 69; *Long Beach Press-Telegram*, 20 October 1971; *Modern Schoolman* 49 (1972): 397 (James Collins); *New York Review of Books*, 2 September 1971, p. 15.

THE EDUCATIONAL FRONTIER. Edited by William Heard Kilpatrick. New York, London: Century Co., 1933. [Dewey, with John Lawrence Childs, "The Social Economic Situation and Education," and "The Underlying Philosophy of Education," pp. 32-72, 287-319.]

Reviewed in *New Republic*, 24 May 1933, pp. 49-50 (Sidney Hook).

"Education and the Social Order." New York: League for Industrial Democracy, 1934.

Reviewed in *High Points* 16 (October 1934): 64-65 (Isidore Dubnau).

EDUCATION TODAY. Edited, with foreword by Joseph Ratner. New York: G. P. Putnam's Sons, 1940. [Reprinted articles and sections of books.]

Reviewed in *A.L.A. Booklist* 37 (1940): 83; *Educational Trends* 9 (March-April 1941): 34-35 (E. V. Sayers); *Library Journal* 65 (1940): 761 (Grace O. Kelley); *More Books* 15 (1940): 383-84 (A. L. M.); *New Republic*, 23 December 1940, p. 877 (Theodore Brameld); *Philosophic Abstracts* 1 (Winter 1940): 5-6 (Lester E. Denonn); *School and Society* 53 (1941): 578 (D. Snedden); *School Executive* 60 (1941): 31 (W. H. Lemmel).

ELEMENTARY SCHOOL RECORD. Chicago: University of
Chicago Press, 1900. [A Series of Nine Monographs,
nos. 1-9, February-December 1900. John Dewey,
editor. Laura Louisa Runyon, managing editor.]

Reviewed in *Nation*, 26 July 1900, pp. 77-78.

"Emerson--The Philosopher of Democracy." *International
Journal of Ethics* 13 (1903): 405-13.

Reviewed in *Philosophical Review* 12 (1903): 574 (G. H.
Sabine).

ESSAYS AND *OUTLINES OF A CRITICAL THEORY OF ETHICS*.
The Early Works of John Dewey, 1882-1898. Vol. 3,
1889-1892. Edited by Jo Ann Boydston. Carbondale:
Southern Illinois University Press, 1969.

Reviewed in *Bibliography of Philosophy* 18 (1971): 134
(Ernest W. Dewey); *Choice* 7 (1970): 1238; *Philosophy
and Phenomenological Research* 32 (1971): 128-29 (Y. H.
Krikorian).

ESSAYS IN EXPERIMENTAL LOGIC. Chicago: University of
Chicago Press, 1916. Reprinted, New York: Dover
Publications, 1953.

Reviewed in *A.L.A. Booklist* 13 (1916): 102; *Boston
Evening Transcript*, 26 July 1916; *Dial* 62 (1917):
136-37 (Horace Meyer Kallen); *Journal of Philosophy* 14
(1917): 246-48 (Harold Chapman Brown); *Mind* n.s. 26
(1917): 217-22 (Alfred Sidgwick); *New Republic*, 2 September 1916, pp. 118-19 (Morris Raphael Cohen) [Re-
printed in Cohen's *PREFACE TO LOGIC* (1944): 196-202];
Philosophical Review 26 (1917): 421-30 (Reinhold F.
Alfred Hoernlé); *Philosophy of Science* 22 (1955):
168-69 (George R. Geiger); *School Review* 24 (1916):
775-76 (Max C. Otto); *Times Literary Supplement* (London), 11 January 1917, p. 20.

ETHICS. With James H. Tufts. New York: Henry Holt
and Co., 1908. London: G. Bell and Sons, 1909.

Reviewed in *American Journal of Psychology* 20 (1909):

151 (Evander Bradley McGilvary); *American Journal of Sociology* 14 (1909): 687-90 (Guy Allen Tawney); *American Journal of Theology* 13 (1909): 140-43 (Arthur Oncken Lovejoy); *Dial* 46 (1909): 146; *Economic Bulletin* 1 (1908): 335-36 (Charles Abram Ellwood); *Educational Review* 37 (1909): 210; ibid.: 413-16 (Walter Taylor Marvin); *Independent* 67 (1909): 310; *Journal of Philosophy* 5 (1908): 636-39 (Norman Wilde); *Monist* 20 (1910): 478; *Nation*, 5 November 1908, p. 438; *Outlook* 90 (1908): 595-96; *Philosophical Review* 18 (1909): 221-29 (William Caldwell); *Psychological Bulletin* 6 (1909): 14-22 (Evander Bradley McGilvary); *School Review* 17 (1909): 204-6 (Irving E. Miller); *Science* n.s. 30 (1909): 89-92 (Frank Thilly); *Survey* 22 (1909): 217-18 (Frank Addison Manny).

ETHICS. Rev. ed. With James H. Tufts. New York: Henry Holt and Co., 1932.

Reviewed in *American Journal of Psychology* 46 (1934): 693-94 (Eugene G. Bugg); *Boston Evening Transcript*, 14 December 1932 (E. N.); *Crozer Quarterly* 10 (1933): 125 (A. S. Woodburne); *International Journal of Ethics* 44 (1933): 155-60 (Frank Chapman Sharp); *Philosophical Review* 43 (1934): 523-25 (DeWitt Henry Parker); *University of California Chronicle* 35 (1933): 134-36 (David Rynin).

EXPERIENCE AND EDUCATION. New York: Macmillan Co., 1938.

Reviewed in *American Sociological Review* 3 (1938): 917-18 (Arthur Katuna); *California Schools* 9 (1938): 148-49 (I. R. Waterman); *Clearing House* 13 (1938): 56 (O. M. Clem); *Commonweal*, 22 April 1938, pp. 729-30 (Ruth Byrns); *Curriculum Journal* 10 (1939): 90-91 (Harold Alberty); *Department of Secondary School Principals Bulletin* 23 (1939): 42; *High Points* 21 (February 1939): 74-76 (F. Griffith); *International Education Review* 7 (1938): 379-81 (Kurt F. Leidecker); *Philosophy* 14 (1939): 482-83 (F. A. Cavenagh); *Progressive Education* 15 (1938): 572-73 (Joseph Kinmont Hart); *Religious Education* 34 (1939): 252 (A. J. W. Myers); *School Review* 46 (1938): 786-89 (Frank N. Freeman); *Social Frontier* 4 (1938): 269 (George E. Axtelle).

EXPERIENCE AND NATURE. Lectures upon the Paul Carus
Foundation, First Series. Chicago, London: Open
Court Publishing Co., 1925.

Reviewed in *A.L.A. Booklist* 21 (1925): 356; *American
Review of Reviews* 72 (1925): 560; *Anglican Theological
Review* 8 (1925-26): 277-78 (Robert Mark Wenley); *Australasian Journal of Psychology and Philosophy* 3
(1925): 230-31 (C. F. Salmond); *Boston Evening Transcript*, 9 May 1925 (E. N.); *Dial* 78 (1925): 429; *Forum*
76 (1926): 316 (Joseph Jastrow); *Hibbert Journal* 24
(1926): 370-73 (C. R. Morris); *Independent* 115 (1925):
396; *International Journal of Ethics* 36 (1926): 201-5
(George Plimpton Adams); *Journal of Religion* 5 (1925):
445; ibid.: 519-42 (Henry Nelson Wieman); ibid. 6
(1926): 89-91 (Roy Wood Sellars); *Mind* n.s. 34 (1925):
476-82 (John Laird); *Nation*, 14 October 1925, sup.
430-32 (Matthew T. McClure); *Nation and Athenaeum* 37
(1925): 682, 684 (C. E. M. Joad); *New Republic*, 25
March 1925, pp. 129-31 (Clarence E. Ayres); *New York
Herald Tribune Books*, 3 May 1925, pp. 1-2 (Irwin Edman); *New York Times*, 3 May 1925, p. 4 (Robert L. Duffus); *OBITER SCRIPTA: LECTURES, ESSAYS AND REVIEWS*, by
George Santayana. Edited by Justus Buchler and Benjamin Schwartz. New York: Charles Scribner's Sons,
1936, pp. 231-40; *Outlook* 140 (1925): 267-68; *Philosophical Review* 35 (1926): 64-68 (H. Wildon Carr);
Quarterly Journal of the University of North Dakota 15
(1925): 363-66 (Norborne H. Crowell); *Saturday Review
of Literature*, 4 July 1925, pp. 874-75 (Ralph Barton
Perry); *Sewanee Review* 33 (1925): 496-99 (Hugh W. San-
ford); *Social Forces* 5 (1927): 686-87 (M. O.); *Spectator* 135 (1925): 494, 497 (F. C. S. Schiller); *Springfield Daily Republican*, 20 September 1925 (George
Brown); *Survey* 54 (1925): 534; 55 (1925): 239-40, 377;
55 (1926): 509-10, 570, 697; 56 (1926): 103-4, 266,
387, 471, 551, 642-43 (Joseph Kinmont Hart); *Welfare
Magazine* 18 (1927): 1401-2 (Thomas D. Eliot); *World
Tomorrow* 8 (1925): 383 (Paul Jones).

EXPERIENCE AND NATURE. 2d ed. New York: W. W. Norton
and Co.; London: G. Allen and Unwin, 1929.

Reviewed in *Bookman* 69 (1929): iv; *Expository Times*
(Edinburgh) 40 (1929): 493; *Journal of Theological
Studies* 31 (1929): 82-86 (Herbert H. Farmer); *Mind*
n.s. 38 (1929): 527-28 (E. M. Whetnall); *Nation and*

Athenaeum 45 (1929): 832, 834 (C. E. M. Joad); *Nature*
126 (1930): 680; *New York World*, 27 October 1929 (C.
Hartley Grattan); *Times Literary Supplement* (London),
23 January 1930, p. 63.

FREEDOM AND CULTURE. New York: G. P. Putnam's Sons,
    1939.

Reviewed in *A.L.A. Booklist* 36 (1939): 126; *Christian
Century* 57 (1940): 178-79 (Edwin Theophil Buehrer);
Current History 51 (1939): 6 (Norman Cousins); *Journal
of Philosophy* 36 (1939): 688-90 (Herbert Wallace
Schneider); *Nation*, 2 December 1939, pp. 621-22 (Wil-
liam Gruen); *Nature* (London) 146 (1940): 815-17; *New
Republic*, 6 December 1939, pp. 206-7 (Paul Weiss); *New
Yorker*, 21 October 1939, p. 79; *New York Herald Tribune
Books*, 5 November 1939, p. 2 (Ernest Sutherland Bates);
New York Times Book Review, 5 November 1939, pp. 1, 27
(C. Hartley Grattan); ibid., 6 July 1941, p. 2 (James
D. Adams); *Philosophic Abstracts* 1 (Spring 1940): 7-9
(Albert Hofstadter); *Saturday Review of Literature*,
11 November 1939, pp. 12-13 (Robert Bierstedt); *Scien-
tific Monthly* 51 (1940): 278-79 (F. R. Moulton);
Springfield Daily Republican, 22 October 1939; *Yale
Review* 29 (1939): 388-90 (Homer Edwards Woodbridge).

GERMAN PHILOSOPHY AND POLITICS. New York: Henry Holt
    and Co., 1915.

Reviewed in *A.L.A. Booklist* 12 (1915): 6; *American Review of Reviews* 52 (1915): 248; *Independent* 83 (1915):
24-25; *International Journal of Ethics* 26 (1915):
131-33 (James H. Tufts); *Journal of Philosophy* 12
(1915): 645-49 (George Santayana); *Mind* n.s. 25 (1916):
250-55 (F. C. S. Schiller); *Nation*, 29 July 1915, pp.
152-53; *New Republic*, 17 July 1915, pp. 283-84 (Francis
Hackett); *New York Times*, 18 July 1915, p. 1; *Philosophical Review* 24 (1915): 540-45 (Frank Thilly);
Springfield Daily Republican, 10 June 1915.

GERMAN PHILOSOPHY AND POLITICS. 2d ed., with new fore-
    word and introd. New York: G. P. Putnam's Sons,
    1942.

Reviewed in *Psychological Abstracts* 17 (1943): 268

(H. L. Ansbacher).

HOW WE THINK. Boston: D. C. Heath and Co., 1910.

Reviewed in *A.L.A. Booklist* 6 (1910): 372; *Educational Review* 40 (1910): 97-98 (Frank A. Fitzpatrick); *Independent* 69 (1910): 246; *Journal of Philosophy* 8 (1911): 244-48 (Max Eastman); *Nation*, 5 May 1910, p. 464; *New York Times Book Review*, 5 November 1910, p. 617 (Henry Addington Bruce); *Philosophical Review* 20 (1911): 441-42 (Walter Bowers Pillsbury); *Quarterly Journal of the University of North Dakota* 1 (1911): 388-92 (L. G. Whitehead); *School Review* 18 (1910): 642-45 (Boyd H. Bode).

HOW WE THINK. Rev. ed. Boston: D. C. Heath and Co., 1933.

Reviewed in *A.L.A. Booklist* 29 (1933): 349; *American Journal of Psychology* 46 (1935): 528 (Eugene G. Bugg); *Australasian Journal of Psychology and Philosophy* 15 (1937): 224-30 (John Anderson); *Boston Evening Transcript*, 21 June 1933 (E. N.); *British Journal of Educational Psychology* 4 (1934): 323-24; *Educational Outlook* 8 (1933): 56-57 (T. H. Briggs); *High School Quarterly* 22 (1933): 42 (J. C. Meadows); *Junior-Senior High School Clearing House* 8 (1934): 319; *New Republic*, 21 March 1934, p. 165 (Sidney Hook); *Philosophical Review* 44 (1935): 75-76 (Sven Nilson); *Saturday Review of Literature*, 1 July 1933, p. 682; *School and Society* 38 (1933): 24 (W. McAndrew).

HUMAN NATURE AND CONDUCT. New York: Henry Holt and Co., 1922.

Reviewed in *American Review* 1 (1923): 360-64 (Morris Raphael Cohen); *Boston Evening Transcript*, 18 March 1922; *Dial* 72 (1922): 514-16 (James Harvey Robinson); *International Journal of Ethics* 33 (1922): 108-9 (C. F. T.); *Journal of Philosophy* 19 (1922): 469-75 (C. E. Ayres); ibid. 20 (1923): 596-603 (George Plimpton Adams); *Mind* n.s. 32 (1923): 79-86 (G. C. Field); *Nation*, 5 July 1922, pp. 20-21 (Matthew Thompson McClure); *New Republic*, 24 May 1922, pp. 379-82 (Horace Meyer Kallen); *New York Evening Post*

Literary Review, 3 June 1922, pp. 701-2 (Abraham Aaron
Roback); *New York Times Book Review*, 8 October 1922,
p. 5 (Austin Hay); *Open Court* 36 (1922): 586-93 (Victor
S. Yarros); *Philosophical Review* 32 (1923): 182-97
(James Seth); *Quarterly Journal of the University of
North Dakota* 15 (1924): 77-80 (John Morris Gillette);
St. Louis Public Library Monthly Bulletin n.s. 20
(1922): 204 (D. D.); *Survey* 48 (1922): 81 (Joseph Kinmont Hart); *Times Literary Supplement* (London), 15 June
1922, p. 398; *Wisconsin Library Bulletin* 18 (1922):
129; *Yale Review* 12 (1923): 407-10 (Harry Todd Costello).

HUMAN NATURE AND CONDUCT.   Reprinted with new introd.
New York: Modern Library, 1930.

Reviewed in *New York Herald Tribune*, 27 January 1931;
New York Times Book Review, 20 July 1930, p. 10.

IMPRESSIONS OF SOVIET RUSSIA AND THE REVOLUTIONARY
WORLD, MEXICO--CHINA--TURKEY.   New York: New Republic, 1929.

Reviewed in *A.L.A. Booklist* 25 (1929): 280; *American
Mercury* 17 (1929): xviii; *Bookman* 69 (1929): xiii;
Boston Evening Transcript, 3 April 1929; *Christian
Science Monitor*, 5 June 1929; *Nation*, 19 June 1929, p.
744 (Jessica Smith); *New York Herald Tribune Books*,
31 March 1929, p. 10; *New York Times Book Review*, 21
April 1929, p. 12; *New York World*, 3 March 1929 (Bernard Smith); *Saturday Review of Literature*, 4 May 1929,
p. 971 (Norah Meade); *School and Society* 30 (1929):
617; *World Tomorrow* 12 (1929): 236.

INDIVIDUALISM, OLD AND NEW.   New York: Minton, Balch
and Co., 1930.   London: G. Allen and Unwin, 1931.
[Reprinted articles from the *New Republic*, incor-
porating considerable new matter.]

Reviewed in *A.L.A. Booklist* 27 (1931): 188; *Crozer
Quarterly* 8 (1931): 128-29 (Stewart G. Cole); *Current
History* 33 (1931): xxii-xxiv (Sidney Hook); *English
Review* 53 (1931): 510-11 (Herbert Agar); *Expository
Times* (Edinburgh) 43 (1931): 17; *Mind* n.s. 41 (1932):
131-32 (F. C. S. Schiller); *Nation*, 22 October 1930,

p. 47 (Henry Hazlitt); *New York Herald Tribune Books*,
23 November 1930, pp. 1, 6 (André Maurois); *New York
Times Book Review*, 21 December 1930, p. 2 (John Cham-
berlain); *New York World*, 19 October 1930 (C. Hartley
Grattan); *World Unity* 7 (1930): 193-201 (John Herman
Randall, Jr.).

THE INFLUENCE OF DARWIN ON PHILOSOPHY AND OTHER ESSAYS
    IN CONTEMPORARY THOUGHT. New York: Henry Holt and
    Co.; London: G. Bell and Sons, 1910.

Reviewed in *A.L.A. Booklist* 7 (1910): 12-13; *Dial* 49
(1910): 183-84; *Journal of Philosophy* 7 (1910): 557-59
(Henry Sturt); *New York Times Book Review*, 28 May
1910, p. 309 (Joseph Jacobs); *Outlook* 95 (1910): 368;
Philosophical Review 20 (1911): 219-21 (James Edwin
Creighton).

THE INFLUENCE OF DARWIN ON PHILOSOPHY AND OTHER ESSAYS
    IN CONTEMPORARY THOUGHT. Bloomington: Indiana Uni-
    versity Press, Midland paperback, 1965.

Reviewed in *New York Review of Books*, 22 April 1965,
p. 16 (Henry D. Aiken).

INTELLIGENCE IN THE MODERN WORLD: JOHN DEWEY'S PHILOS-
    OPHY. Edited, with introd. by Joseph Ratner. New
    York: Modern Library, 1939.

Reviewed in *Canadian Forum* 19 (1939): 121-23 (Eric A.
Havelock); *Ethics* 50 (1940): 375-76 (William Henry
Werkmeister); *Journal of Philosophy* 36 (1939): 585-86
(Herbert Wallace Schneider); *Modern Schoolman* 20
(1943): 246-47 (G. V. Kennard); *New Republic*, 17 May
1939, pp. 51-52 (C. E. Ayres); ibid., 6 December 1939,
p. 206 (Paul Weiss); *New York Herald Tribune Books*,
19 February 1939, p. 21; *New York World-Telegram*, 15
February 1939 (Harry Hansen); *Philosophic Abstracts* 1
(Winter 1939-40): 8; *Survey Graphic* 28 (1939): 453
(Joseph Kinmont Hart).

JOHN DEWEY AND ARTHUR F. BENTLEY: A PHILOSOPHICAL COR-
    RESPONDENCE, 1932-1951. Edited by Sidney Ratner
    and Jules Altman. New Brunswick, N.J.: Rutgers

University Press, 1964.

Reviewed in *American Historical Review* 70 (1965): 1137
(David Noble); *American Political Science Review* 59
(1965): 468 (C. B. Hagan); *Annals of the American Acad-*
emy of Political and Social Science 360 (1965): 222
(L. S. Feuer); *Choice* 2 (1965): 482; *Man and World* 2
(1968): 310-13 (Reuben Abel); *New York Times Book Re-*
view, 4 October 1964, p. 6 (Brand Blanshard); *Saturday*
Review, 21 November 1964, p. 75; *Scientific American*
213 (1965): 270 (P. Morrison); *Studies in Philosophy*
and Education 4 (1965): 108-21 (Lyle Krenzien Eddy).

JOHN DEWEY: DICTIONARY OF EDUCATION. Edited by Ralph
    B. Winn. Foreword by John Herman Randall, Jr.
    New York: Philosophical Library, 1959.

Reviewed in *Adult Education* 10 (1960): 251 (K. F. Ar-
gue); *Childhood Education* 36 (1960): 390 (J. A. Smith);
Personalist 41 (1960): 563 (W. E. C.); *Quarterly*
Journal of Speech 46 (1960): 330-31 (Henry L. Mueller).

JOHN DEWEY: HIS CONTRIBUTION TO THE AMERICAN TRADITION.
    Edited by Irwin Edman. Makers of the American Tra-
    dition Series. Indianapolis: Bobbs-Merrill Co.,
    1955.

Reviewed in *A.L.A. Booklist* 52 (1955): 4; *Library*
Journal 80 (1955): 1591 (R. H. Heimanson); *Nation*, 10
December 1955, p. 518 (Abraham Edel); *New Leader*, 31
October 1955, pp. 23-24; *New Republic*, 29 August 1955,
p. 18 (Arthur Bestor); *New Yorker*, 27 August 1955, p.
104; *New York Herald Tribune Book Review*, 25 September
1955, p. 11; *New York Times Book Review*, 24 July 1955,
p. 3 (Sidney Hook); *San Francisco Chronicle*, 1 August
1955 (G. E. Arnstein); *Saturday Review*, 13 August 1955,
p. 9 (Brand Blanshard).

JOHN DEWEY: LECTURES IN THE PHILOSOPHY OF EDUCATION:
    1899. Edited with introd. by Reginald D. Archam-
    bault. New York: Random House, 1966.

Reviewed in *Harvard Educational Review* 36 (1966):
556-58 (Jo Ann Boydston and Joe R. Burnett); *New Yorker*,
28 August 1966, p. 128; *New York Times Book Review*, 24

July 1966, pp. 11-12 (Morton White) [Reprinted in
White's *PRAGMATISM AND THE AMERICAN MIND*, pp. 244-47.];
Wall Street Journal, 16 June 1966 (Edmund Fuller).

JOHN DEWEY ON EDUCATION, SELECTED WRITINGS. Edited by
    Reginald D. Archambault. New York: Modern Library,
    1964.

Reviewed in *Choice* 6 (1965): 180; *Saturday Review*, 17
April 1965, p. 81; *Teachers College Record* 67 (1966):
303, 305 (Nathaniel Champlin).

JOHN DEWEY: PHILOSOPHY, PSYCHOLOGY AND SOCIAL PRACTICE.
    Edited by Joseph Ratner. New York: G. P. Putnam's
    Sons, 1963.

Reviewed in *Studies in Philosophy and Education* 4
(1965): 95-104 (George Eastman).

JOHN DEWEY. SELECTED WRITINGS, WITH AN INTRODUCTION
    AND COMMENTARY. Edited by F. W. Garforth. London:
    Heinemann, 1966.

Reviewed in *New Zealand Journal of Educational Studies*
1 (1966): 87-88 (F. W. Mitchell).

KNOWING AND THE KNOWN. With Arthur F. Bentley.
    Boston: Beacon Press, 1949.

Reviewed in *American Journal of Sociology* 57 (1951):
200 (Anselm Strauss); *Annals of the American Academy of
Political and Social Science* 268 (1950): 224 (Charles
W. Morris); *Crozer Quarterly* 27 (1950): 182 (William K.
Wright); *Humanist* 10 (1950): 30 (Harold A. Larrabee);
Journal of Symbolic Logic 15 (1950): 156 (Paul Ziff);
Modern Schoolman 27 (1950): 322-26 (James Collins); *New
Scholasticism* 25 (1951): 230-32 (R. Harvey); *New Yorker*,
29 October 1949, p. 115 (Max Wertheimer); *Philosophic
Abstracts* 11 (Winter 1949): 106 (L. E. Denonn); *Philo-
sophical Review* 59 (1950): 269-70 (Max Black); *Philos-
ophy* (London) 27 (1952): 263-65 (W. Mays); *Saturday
Review of Literature*, 22 October 1949, p. 15 (Harold A.
Larrabee); *School and Society* 70 (1949): 336; *Scientific
Monthly* 72 (1951): 135-36 (Solomon Weinstock); *Social*

Research 17 (1950): 248-50 (Sidney Ratner); *United States Quarterly Book List* 6 (1950): 29.

LEIBNIZ'S NEW ESSAYS CONCERNING THE HUMAN UNDERSTAND-
ING: A CRITICAL EXPOSITION. Grigg's Philosophical
Classics, edited by George Sylvester Morris, no.
7. Chicago: S. C. Griggs and Co., 1888.

Reviewed in *Mind* 13 (1888): 612; *New Englander and Yale
Review* 50 (1889): 66-68 (George Trumbull Ladd); *Science*
12 (1888): 188-89.

LETTERS FROM CHINA AND JAPAN. With Alice Chipman
Dewey. Edited by Evelyn Dewey. New York: E. P.
Dutton and Co., 1920.

Reviewed in *A.L.A. Booklist* 16 (1920): 341-42; *Bookman*
51 (1920): 631-32 (Raymond M. Weaver); *Freeman*, 14 July
1920, pp. 429-30; *Nation*, 24 July 1920, pp. 103-4
(Irita Van Doren); *New York Evening Post Literary Review*, 5 June 1920 (J. W. Robertson Scott); *New York
Times Book Review*, 30 May 1920, p. 285 (Maurice F.
Egan); *Outlook* 125 (1920): 281.

LIBERALISM AND SOCIAL ACTION. New York: G. P. Putnam's
Sons, 1935.

Reviewed in *A.L.A. Booklist* 32 (1935): 32; *American
Mercury* 37 (1936): 108-9 (Albert Jay Nock); *American
Review of Reviews* 92 (1935): 2; *Christian Century* 52
(1935): 1210 (Edwin Theophil Buehrer); *Current History*
43 (1935): v-vi (John Chamberlain); *International
Journal of Ethics* 46 (1936): 229-36 (Frank Hyneman
Knight); *Nation*, 11 September 1935, pp. 303-4 (Reinhold
Niebuhr); *New Republic*, 4 March 1936, pp. 115-16 (Ken-
neth Burke), also in his *PHILOSOPHY OF LITERARY FORM*
(1941): 388-91; *New York Times*, 20 August 1935, p. 19
(John Chamberlain); *New York Times Book Review*, 1 Sep-
tember 1935, p. 9 (Henry Hazlitt); *People's Lobby Bulletin* 5 (1936): 1-2; *Saturday Review of Literature*, 13
December 1935, p. 7 (Horace Meyer Kallen); *Survey
Graphic* 24 (1935): 555-56 (Walter Lincoln Whittlesey).

LOGIC: THE THEORY OF INQUIRY. New York: Henry Holt
and Co., 1938.

Reviewed in *A.L.A. Booklist* 35 (1938): 91; *Boston Evening Transcript*, 21 January 1939 (Leonard Carmichael); *Communist* 18 (1939): 163-69 (Philip Carter); *Congregational Quarterly* 17 (1939): 377-78 (Robert S. Franks); *Current History* 49 (1939): 64; *Ethics* 50 (1939): 98-102 (William Henry Werkmeister); *Johns Hopkins Alumni Magazine* 27 (November 1938): 33 (Albert Lanphier Hammond); *Journal of Philosophy* 36 (1939): 561-84 (Evander Bradley McGilvary, G. Watts Cunningham, Clarence Irving Lewis, Ernest Nagel, Wendell M. Thomas); *Mind* n.s. 48 (1939): 527-36 (John Laird); *Nation*, 22 October 1938, pp. 426-27 (William Gruen); *Nature* 144 (1939): 880-81 (Karl Britton); *New Republic*, 23 November 1938, pp. 79-80 (Paul Weiss); *New York Herald Tribune Books*, 11 December 1938, p. 5 (Irwin Edman); *New York Times Book Review*, 20 November 1938, p. 16 (Clifford Barrett); *Philosophical Review* 49 (1940): 259-61 (William Ray Dennes); *Philosophy* (London) 14 (1939): 370-71 (W. Kneale); *Philosophy of Science* 6 (1939): 115-22 (Jerome Nathanson); *Saturday Review of Literature*, 19 November 1938, p. 18 (Eliseo Vivas); *Southern Review* 5 (1939): 105-20 (Lyle Hicks Lanier); *Survey Graphic* 27 (1938): 615-16 (Eduard C. Lindeman); *Times Literary Supplement* (London), 29 April 1939, p. 244.

MORAL PRINCIPLES IN EDUCATION. Riverside Educational
    Monographs, edited by Henry Suzzallo. Boston:
    Houghton Mifflin Co., 1909.

Reviewed in *A.L.A. Booklist* 6 (1909): 39; *Elementary School Teacher* 10 (1909): 204 (Frank Addison Manny); *Journal of Educational Psychology* 1 (1910): 117-18 (C. E. Seashore); *Proceedings of the Second International Moral Education Congress* (1912): 184-87.

"The Moral Significance of the Common School Studies."
    Northern Illinois Teachers' Association, *Topics for General Sessions: Moral and Religious Training in the Public Schools, November 5th and 6th, 1909, Elgin, Illinois*, Northern Illinois Teachers' Association, pp. 21-27.

Reviewed in *Journal of Educational Psychology* 1 (1910): 304-5 (William C. Bagley).

"The Motivation of Hobbes' Political Philosophy," in
Studies in the History of Ideas by the Department
of Philosophy of Columbia University, vol. 1, pp.
88-115. New York: Columbia University Press, 1918.

Reviewed in *Dial* 65 (1918): 218-19; *Philosophical Review* 28 (1919): 213-16 (Joseph Alexander Leighton).

NATURALISM AND THE HUMAN SPIRIT, edited by Yervant Hovhannes Krikorian. Columbia Studies in Philosophy,
no. 8. New York: Columbia University Press, 1944.
[Dewey, "Anti-Naturalism in Extremis," pp. 1-16.]

Reviewed in *Canadian Forum* 24 (1944): 217-18 (J. M.);
Journal of Philosophy 42 (1945): 400-417 (Arthur E.
Murphy), [Dewey, pp. 402-5.]; *Nation*, 30 December 1944,
p. 804 (Philip Blair Rice); *New Republic*, 20 November
1944, pp. 667-68 (Isaac Rosenfeld); *New York Times Book
Review*, 3 September 1944, p. 8 (Irwin Edman).

NEW YORK AND THE SEABURY INVESTIGATION. A Digest and
Interpretation of the Reports by Samuel Seabury
concerning the Government of New York City, prepared by a Committee of Educators and Civic Workers
under the Chairmanship of John Dewey. New York:
City Affairs Committee of New York, 1933.

Reviewed in *School and Society* 39 (1934): 152 (William
McAndrew).

OUTLINES OF A CRITICAL THEORY OF ETHICS. Ann Arbor:
Register Publishing Co., 1891.

Reviewed in *Andover Review* 16 (1891): 95-98 (James
Hervey Hyslop); *Educational Review* 2 (1891): 297-98
(James Hervey Hyslop); *International Journal of Ethics*
1 (1891): 503-5 (Josiah Royce); *Mind* 16 (1891): 424;
Monist 1 (1891): 600-601; *New Englander and Yale Review*
55 (1891): 275; *Philosophical Review* 1 (1892): 95-99
(Thomas Davidson).

OUTLINES OF A CRITICAL THEORY OF ETHICS. Reprinted,
New York: Hillary House, 1957.

Reviewed in *Personalist* 39 (1958): 171 (V. H. Ringer).

PHILOSOPHY AND CIVILIZATION. New York: Minton, Balch and Co., 1931. London: G. P. Putnam's Sons, 1933. [Reprints, with revisions, of previously published articles.]

Reviewed in *A.L.A. Booklist* 28 (1931): 90; *Annals of the American Academy of Political and Social Science* 159 (1932): 181 (L. M. Pape); *Boston Evening Transcript*, 31 October 1931 (E. N.); *Commonweal*, 16 March 1932, pp. 556-57 (Gerald B. Phelan); *International Journal of Ethics* 44 (1933-34): 269-70 (George P. Adams); *Journal of Philosophy* 29 (1932): 412-15 (Thomas Vernor Smith); *Manchester Guardian*, 27 April 1933 (Samuel Alexander); *Mind* n.s. 41 (1932): 265 (F. C. S. Schiller); *Monist* 43 (1933): 157; *More Books* 6 (1931): 342-43; *New Republic*, 4 November 1931, pp. 330-31 (Sidney Hook); *New York Evening Post*, 15 October 1931 (Rudolf Kagey); *New York Herald Tribune Books*, 8 November 1931, p. 17 (Ernest Sutherland Bates); *Outlook and Independent* 159 (1931): 218 (N. L. Rothman); *Philosophical Review* 41 (1932): 324 (G. Watts Cunningham); *Philosophy* (London) 8 (1933): 360-61 (B. M. Laing); *Springfield Daily Republican*, 23 October 1931; *Thinker* (December 1931): 82-84 (Horace Meyer Kallen); *Times Literary Supplement* (London), 9 March 1933, p. 160; *Wisconsin Library Bulletin* 28 (1932): 25.

THE PHILOSOPHY OF JOHN DEWEY. Edited by Joseph Ratner. New York: Henry Holt and Co., 1928. London: G. Allen and Unwin, 1929.

Reviewed in *A.L.A. Booklist* 25 (1928): 52; *Boston Evening Transcript*, 1 August 1928; *Catholic World* 128 (1929): 624 (F. S. S.); *Cleveland Open Shelf*, November 1929, p. 136; *Journal of Philosophy* 26 (1929): 407-9 (Mary Shaw Kuypers); *Nation*, 31 October 1928, pp. 457-58 (Eliseo Vivas); *New Scholasticism* 2 (1928): 387-88 (Virgil Michel); *New Statesman* 32 (1929): 612; *New York Herald Tribune Books*, 5 August 1928, p. 1 (Irwin Edman); *North American Review* 226 (1928): adv. sec.; *Philosophical Review* 40 (1931): 276-81 (Donald Ayres Piatt); *Pittsburgh Monthly Bulletin* 33 (1928): 435; *Survey* 61 (1929): 454-55 (Joseph Kinmont Hart); *Time*, 10 September 1928, p. 45.

"Postulations." With Arthur Fisher Bentley. *Journal of Philosophy* 42 (1945): 645-62.

Reviewed in *Journal of Symbolic Logic* 10 (1945): 132-33
(Alonzo Church).

PROBLEMS OF MEN. New York: Philosophical Library, 1946.
[Articles from various journals, reprinted, with a
new introd.]

Reviewed in *A.L.A. Booklist* 42 (1946): 311; *American
Sociological Review* 11 (1946): 645 (Roy Wood Sellars);
Clearing House 21 (1946): 183-85 (J. C. Duff); *Educa-
tional Forum* 11 (1947): 254; *Ethics* 57 (1946): 73-74
(Glenn Negley); *Harvard Educational Review* 16 (1946):
297-308 (D. C. Williams); *Humanist* 6 (1946): 147-48
(Edward Fiess); *Journal of Philosophy* 44 (1947): 189-91
(Max Carl Otto); *Kenyon Review* 8 (1946): 683-85 (D. W.
Gotshalk); *Library Journal* 71 (1946): 755 (Grace O.
Kelley); *Mind* n.s. 56 (1947): 257-65 (Karl Britton);
Modern Schoolman 27 (1950): 320-22 (James Collins);
Nation, 19 October 1946, pp. 447-49 (Hannah Arendt);
New Republic, 28 October 1946, pp. 562-64 (Jerome Na-
thanson); *New York Herald Tribune Books*, 1 September
1946, p. 10 (John Herman Randall, Jr.); *New York Times
Book Review*, 9 June 1946, p. 7 (Alvin Johnson); *Person-
alist* 28 (1947): 96-98 (Daniel Sommer Robinson); *Philo-
sophical Review* 56 (1947): 194-202 (Arthur E. Murphy);
Philosophy and Phenomenological Research 9 (1948):
134-39 (Rubin Gotesky); *Review of Politics* 9 (1947):
502-3 (Leo Richard Ward); *San Francisco Chronicle*, 18
August 1946; *Saturday Review of Literature*, 20 July
1946, pp. 14-15 (Ordway Tead); *School and Society* 63
(1946): 366; *School Review* 54 (1946): 493-95 (Carroll
D. Champlin); *Social Studies* 37 (1946): 327-28 (Charles
Peters); *Springfield Daily Republican*, 30 June 1946
(E. A. F.); *Survey Graphic* 35 (1946): 166-67 (Harry
Hansen); *Thought* 21 (1946): 733-34 (Martin J. Smith);
Time, 24 June 1946, pp. 45-46; *Western Review* 11 (1947):
59-71 (Eliseo Vivas); *Yale Review* n.s. 36 (1946): 156-59
(Raphael Demos).

PSYCHOLOGY. New York: Harper and Brothers, 1887.

Reviewed in *American Journal of Psychology* 1 (1887):
154-59 (G. Stanley Hall); *Andover Review* 9 (1888):
437-41 (H. A. P. Torrey); *Bibliotheca Sacra* 45 (1888):
381-83; *Mind* 12 (1887): 301-2 (George Croom Robertson);
Ibid.: 439-43 (George Croom Robertson); *New Englander
and Yale Review* 46 (1887): 387-90.

PSYCHOLOGY. The Early Works of John Dewey, 1882-1898.
Vol. 2, 1887. Edited by Jo Ann Boydston. Carbondale: Southern Illinois University Press, 1967.

Reviewed in *Choice* 4 (1968): 151; *Long Beach Press-
Telegram*, 7 February 1968; *Modern Schoolman* 46 (1968):
59-61 (James Collins); *News Letter* (Ohio State University, College of Education) 33 (March 1968): 2; *Religious Humanism* 3 (1969): 135-36 (H. S. Thayer); *Review
of Metaphysics* 21 (1968): 747-48 (Richard J. Bernstein);
School Review 76 (1968): 352-56 (Harold B. Dunkel);
South Bend Tribune, 3 March 1968; *Sunday Star-Bulletin
and Adviser* (Honolulu), 15 June 1969; *Worchester Sunday
Telegram*, 17 March 1968.

THE PSYCHOLOGY OF NUMBER AND ITS APPLICATIONS TO
METHODS OF TEACHING ARITHMETIC. With James A. Mc-
Lellan. International Education Series, vol. 33,
edited by William Torrey Harris. New York: D. Appleton and Co.; London: Edwin Arnold, 1895.

Reviewed in *American Journal of Psychology* 7 (1896):
300-301 (G. Stanley Hall); *Education* 16 (1895): 249;
Inland Educator 1 (1896): 320-21 (Robert J. Aley);
Mind n.s. 5 (1896): 275; *Nation*, 28 November 1895, p.
395; *Popular Science Monthly*, November 1895, pp.
132-33; *Psychological Review* 3 (1896): 434-37 (Alex-
ander Ziwet); *Public School Journal* 15 (1896): 182-85
(George P. Brown); *School Review* 4 (1896): 102-4
(David E. Smith); *Science* n.s. 3 (1896): 134-36 (Henry
Burchard Fine) [*Early Works* 5: xxiii-xxvii].

THE PUBLIC AND ITS PROBLEMS. New York: Henry Holt and
Co.; London: G. Allen and Unwin, 1927.

Reviewed in *American Journal of Sociology* 34 (1928):
1192-94 (Robert E. Park); *Boston Evening Transcript*,
12 November 1927; *Humanist* 7 (1947): 96-97 (Alfred
Stiernotte); *Journal of Philosophy* 26 (1929): 329-35
(William Ernest Hocking); *Mind* n.s. 37 (1928): 368-70
(O. de Selincourt); *Monist* 40 (1930): 640; *New Republic*,
24 August 1927, pp. 22-23 (Robert Morss Lovett); *New
Scholasticism* 2 (1928): 210-12 (Virgil Michel); *New
York Herald Tribune Books*, 27 November 1927, p. 4
(Sterling Power Lamprecht); *New York Times*, 23 October
1927, p. 15 (Robert Luther Duffus); *Philosophical Re-
view* 38 (1929): 177-80 (Thomas Vernor Smith); *Saturday*

Review of Literature, 15 October 1927, pp. 198-99
(Harold Joseph Laski); *Survey* 59 (1927): 162-63 (Henry
Neumann); *Yale Review* n.s. 17 (1928): 610-12 (William
Bennett Munro).

THE QUEST FOR CERTAINTY. New York: Minton, Balch and
    Co., 1929. London: George Allen and Unwin, 1930.

Reviewed in *A.L.A. Booklist* 26 (1930): 144; *American
Association of University Women Journal* 23 (1930): 103
(K. McHale); *Among Our Books* 35 (1930): 5; *Book Review
Digest* (1929): 248; *Boston Evening Transcript*, 16 No-
vember 1929 (E. N.); *Christian Century* 47 (1930): 48-49
(Ewart Edmund Turner); *Columbia Varsity* 12 (1930):
27-28 (J. G.); *Congregational Quarterly* 8 (1930): 508-9
(E. J. Price); *Contemporary Review* 138 (1930): 663-64
(J. S. L.); *Current History* 31 (1930): 821-22 (S. B.);
Ecclesiastical Review 84 (1931): 309-10 (Francis Augus-
tine Walsh); *Expository Times* (Edinburgh) 41 (1929-30):
542-43; *Harvard Theological Review* 23 (1930): 213-33
(Julius Seelye Bixler); *Hibbert Journal* 29 (1930-31):
174-81 (J. H. Muirhead); *International Journal of
Ethics* 40 (1930): 425-33 (Clarence Edwin Ayres);
Journal of Higher Education 1 (1930): 179-80 (Boyd H.
Bode); *Journal of Philosophical Studies* 5 (1930):
448-51 (H. H. Price); *Journal of Philosophy* 27 (1930):
14-25 (Clarence Irving Lewis); *Journal of Theological
Studies* 32 (1930): 81-84; *Mental Hygiene* 14 (1930):
472-75 (Thomas Vernor Smith); *Methodist Review* 113
(1930): 307-8 (Oscar L. Joseph); ibid.: 724-34 (John
Wright Buckham); *Mind* n.s. 39 (1930): 372-75 (F. C. S.
Schiller); *Monist* 40 (1930): 483; *Nation*, 22 January
1930, pp. 100-101 (Henry Hazlitt); *New Era* 11 (1930):
116 (G. Thomson); *New Republic*, 3 September 1930, pp.
77-79 (Kenneth Burke), also in his *PHILOSOPHY OF LIT-
ERARY FORM* (1941), pp. 382-88; *New Statesman* 34 (1930):
748; *New York Evening Post*, 19 October 1929 (Irwin Edman); *New York Herald Tribune Books*, 20 October 1929,
p. 3 (Joseph Wood Krutch); *New York Times Book Review*,
20 October 1929, pp. 5, 36 (Percy Hutchison); *New York
World*, 27 October 1929 (C. Hartley Grattan); *Open Court*
44 (1930): 499-501 (Victor S. Yarros); *Philosophical
Review* 40 (1931): 79-89 (Max Carl Otto); *Religious Education* 25 (1930): 71-73 (Thomas Vernor Smith), 74-76
(Edgar Sheffield Brightman), 76-79 (Frank N. Freeman);
Saturday Review of Literature, 21 December 1929, p.
585 (Ralph Barton Perry); *Spectator* 144 (1930): sup.
619 (C. E. M. Joad); *Symposium* 1 (1930): 263-68 (George

Boas); *Times Literary Supplement* (London), 17 April
1930, p. 328; *Wisconsin Library Bulletin* 26 (1930): 37;
World Tomorrow 13 (1930): 89-90 (Howard Y. Williams).

RECONSTRUCTION IN PHILOSOPHY. New York: Henry Holt and
    Co., 1920. London: University of London Press,
    1921.

Reviewed in *A.L.A. Booklist* 17 (1920): 92; *Bookman*
(London) 60 (1921): 141-42 (John Adams); *Dial* 70
(1921): 454-57 (Ralph Barton Perry); *Freeman* 3 (1921):
140-41 (Horace Meyer Kallen); *Grinnell Review* 16
(1921): 378 (Clara M. Smertenko); *Nation*, 8 December
1920, pp. 658, 660 (Boyd H. Bode); *New York Evening
Post Literary Review*, 13 November 1920, p. 7 (Arthur
S. McDowall); *Open Court* 37 (1923): 596-604 (Victor S.
Yarros); *Philosophical Review* 30 (1921): 519-23 (George
Plimpton Adams); *Springfield Daily Republican*, 20 Jan-
uary 1921; *Yale Review* 12 (1923): 407-10 (Harry Todd
Costello).

RECONSTRUCTION IN PHILOSOPHY. Enl. ed., with new
    introd. Boston: Beacon Press, 1948.

Reviewed in *Crozer Quarterly* 26 (1949): 263 (E. A.
Burtt); *Humanist* 9 (1949): 46 (Edwin H. Wilson); *New
Republic*, 27 June 1949, pp. 15-16 (Yervant Hovhannes
Krikorian); *Philosophical Review* 59 (1950): 270-71
(W. M. Sibley); *Philosophy and Phenomenological Re-
search* 10 (1949-50): 303-5 (Sholom J. Kahn); *Thomist* 12
(1949): 525-27.

THE SCHOOL AND SOCIETY. Chicago: University of Chicago
    Press, 1899. London: P. S. King and Son, 1900.

Reviewed in *Chautauquan* 30 (1900): 589-92 (Laura Louisa
Runyon); *Dial* 29 (1900): 97-98 (B. A. Hinsdale and A.
S. Whitney); *Educational Review* 20 (1900): 303-6 (William S. Sutton); *Review of Education* 7 (1901): 31 (Addison W. Moore); *Transactions of the Illinois Society
for Child-Study* 4 (1899): 100-101; *University* [of Chi-
cago] *Record* 5 (1900): 159-60.

THE SCHOOL AND SOCIETY. 2d ed. Chicago: University of
    Chicago Press, 1915.

Reviewed in *A.L.A. Booklist* 12 (1915): 97; *Boston Evening Transcript*, 25 August 1915; *Elementary School Journal* 16 (1915): 67-69.

SCHOOLS OF TOMORROW. With Evelyn Dewey. New York:
    E. P. Dutton and Co.; London: J. M. Dent and Sons,
    1915.

Reviewed in *A.L.A. Booklist* 12 (1915): 9; *American Review of Reviews* 52 (1915): 248-49; *Bookman* 42 (1915): 88-89 (Florence Finch Kelly); *Dial* 59 (1915): 109-11 (Thomas Percival Beyer); *Independent* 83 (1915): 198; *Literary Digest* 51 (1915): 537; *Nation*, 9 September 1915, pp. 326-27; *New Republic*, 26 June 1915, pp. 210-11; *New York Times Book Review*, 15 August 1915, p. 291; *Outlook* 110 (1915): 875; *Quarterly Journal of the University of North Dakota* 6 (1916): 272-75 (Adoniram J. Ladd); *Survey* 34 (1916): 438 (Ernest Carroll Moore); *Wisconsin Library Bulletin* 11 (1915): 367.

"Science as Subject-Matter and as Method." *Science*
    n.s. 31 (1910): 121-27.

Reviewed in *Journal of Educational Psychology* 1 (1910): 419 (William Chandler Bagley).

"A Search for Firm Names." With Arthur Fisher Bentley.
    Journal of Philosophy 42 (1945): 5-6.

Reviewed in *Journal of Symbolic Logic* 10 (1945): 132-33 (Alonzo Church).

"The 'Socratic Dialogues' of Plato." In STUDIES IN THE
    HISTORY OF IDEAS by the Department of Philosophy of
    Columbia University, vol. 2, pp. 1-23. New York:
    Columbia University Press, 1925.

Reviewed in *Journal of Philosophy* 23 (1926): 300-303 (George Plimpton Adams); *Spectator* 135 (1925): 494-97 (F. C. S. Schiller).

"Some Questions About Value." *Journal of Philosophy* 41
    (1944): 449-55.

Reviewed in *Psychological Abstracts* 19 (1945): 2 (R. H. Dotterer).

THE SOURCES OF A SCIENCE OF EDUCATION. New York: Horace Liveright, 1929.

Reviewed in *Boston Evening Transcript*, 30 November 1929; *Journal of Educational Sociology* 3 (1930): 438-39 (Herman Harrell Horne); *Nation*, 22 January 1930, pp. 100-101 (Henry Hazlitt); *New York World*, 27 October 1929 (C. Hartley Grattan); *Vocational Guidance Magazine* 8 (1930): 390-91 (A. M. Church).

STUDIES IN LOGICAL THEORY. University of Chicago, The Decennial Publications, Second Series, vol. 11. Chicago: University of Chicago Press, 1903.

Reviewed in *Dial* 36 (1904): 328-29 (Arthur K. Rogers); *Edinburgh Review* 209 (1909): 363-88 (Bertrand Russell); *Educational Review* 28 (1904): 310-13 (Edwin L. Norton); *Journal of Philosophy* 1 (1904): 100-105 (Wilmon H. Sheldon); *Mind* n.s. 13 (1904): 100-106 (F. C. S. Schiller); ibid. n.s. 20 (1911): 435 (Bernard Bosanquet); *Monist* 14 (1904): 312; *Nation*, 15 September 1904, pp. 219-20 (Charles S. Peirce); *Philosophical Review* 13 (1904): 666-77 (A. Seth Pringle-Pattison), also in his *THE PHILOSOPHICAL RADICALS AND OTHER ESSAYS* (1907): 178-94; *Psychological Bulletin* 1 (1904): 1-5 (William James).

THE STUDY OF ETHICS: A SYLLABUS. Ann Arbor: Register Publishing Co., 1894. [2d ed., Ann Arbor: George Wahr, 1897.]

Reviewed in *International Journal of Ethics* 6 (1895): 110-13 (Josiah Royce); ibid. 11 (1901): 200-213 (George M. Stratton); *Psychological Review* 2 (1895): 430-31 (Roger B. Johnson).

THE TEACHER AND SOCIETY. First Yearbook of the John Dewey Society. New York: D. Appleton-Century Co., 1937. [Dewey, with Goodwin Watson, "The Forward View: A Free Teacher in a Free Society," pp. 330-45.]

Reviewed in *Social Frontier* 4 (October 1937): 28-29
(Alonzo F. Myers).

"A Terminology for Knowings and Knowns." With Arthur
   Fisher Bentley. *Journal of Philosophy* 42 (1945):
   225-47.

Reviewed in *Journal of Symbolic Logic* 10 (1945): 132-33
(Alonzo Church).

THEORY OF VALUATION. International Encyclopedia of
   Unified Science, vol. 2, no. 4. Chicago: University of Chicago Press, 1939.

Reviewed in *American Journal of Sociology* 45 (1940):
942-43 (Frank H. Knight); *Journal of Philosophy* 36
(1939): 490-95 (Herbert W. Schneider); *Philosophic Abstracts* 1 (Spring 1940): 9 (Abraham Edel); *Philosophical Review* 50 (1941): 443-46 (D. Bidney); *Philosophy
of Science* 6 (1939): 490-91 (William M. Malisoff).

"Time and Individuality." In TIME AND ITS MYSTERIES,
   ser. 2, pp. 85-109. New York: University Press,
   1940.

Reviewed in *Journal of Philosophy* 39 (1942): 22-24
(Ernest Nagel); *Thought* 16 (1941): 387-88 (J. A. Mc-
Williams).

"Unity of Science as a Social Problem." In ENCYCLO-
   PEDIA AND UNIFIED SCIENCE. International Encyclo-
   pedia of Unified Science, vol. 1, no. 1, pp. 29-38.
   Chicago: University of Chicago Press, 1938.

Reviewed in *Nation*, 17 September 1938, pp. 275-76 (William Gruen); *Philosophical Review* 50 (1941): 433-34
(Henry Margenau).

THE WAY OUT OF EDUCATIONAL CONFUSION. Cambridge:
   Harvard University Press, 1931.

Reviewed in *Boston Evening Transcript*, 18 July 1931;
Cambridge Review 53 (1932): 193 (K. B.); *Educational*

Outlook 6 (1932): 250; *High Points* 15 (January 1933):
86-87 (A. H. Lass); *Junior-Senior High School Clearing
House* 6 (1932): 312 (P. W. L. Cox); ibid. 7 (1932): 127
(P. W. L. Cox); *New York Times Book Review*, 31 May
1931, p. 28; *School and Society* 34 (1931): 640 (W. Mc-
Andrew); *School Review* 40 (1932): 67-68 (H. C. Morrison);
Virginia Teacher 14 (1933): 62-63 (W. J. Gifford).

WHAT IS DEMOCRACY? ITS CONFLICTS, ENDS AND MEANS.
   With Boyd H. Bode, and T. V. Smith. Coöperative
   Books, ser. 1, no. 2. Norman, Okla.: Coöperative
   Books, 1939. [Dewey, "The Future of Liberalism,
   or The Democratic Way of Change," pp. 3-10.]

Reviewed in *Philosophic Abstracts* 1 (Winter 1939-40):
6 (V. J. McGill); *Philosophical Review* 49 (1940): 383
(George Holland Sabine); *Philosophy* (London) 14 (1939):
236 (B. M. Laing).

THE WIT AND WISDOM OF JOHN DEWEY. Edited with introd.
   by Allison Heartz Johnson. Boston: Beacon Press,
   1949.

Reviewed in *Christian Century* 67 (1950): 18-19 (W. E.
G.); *Hibbert Journal* 17 (1948): 100-102 (S. P. White-
house); *Humanist* 10 (1950): 30 (Harold A. Larrabee);
Saturday Review of Literature, 22 October 1949, p. 44
(Harold A. Larrabee).

REVIEWS OF WORKS ABOUT DEWEY

Baker, Melvin Charles. FOUNDATIONS OF JOHN DEWEY'S
EDUCATIONAL THEORY. New York: Atherton Press,
1966. [Paperback reprint.]

Reviewed in *History of Education Quarterly* 10 (1970):
113-26 (Thomas B. Colwell, Jr.).

Berkson, Isaac Baer. THE IDEAL AND THE COMMUNITY: A
PHILOSOPHY OF EDUCATION. New York: Harper and
Brothers, 1958.

Reviewed in *Adult Education* 9 (1959): 186-90 (Thomas
A. Van Sant); *College and University* 34 (1959): 223-25
(Joseph S. Probst); *Journal of Educational Sociology*
32 (1958): 133-40 (Henry Miller); *School Review* 66
(1958): 488-93 (Leonard Gardner).

Bernstein, Richard J., ed. JOHN DEWEY. New York:
Washington Square Press, 1966.

Reviewed in *American Political Science Review* 61
(1967): 502 (William Ebenstein); *Library Journal* 91
(1966): 2496-97 (Howard Ozmon).

Blewett, John J., ed. JOHN DEWEY: HIS THOUGHT AND IN-
FLUENCE. Orestes Brownson Series on Contemporary
Thought and Affairs, no. 2. New York: Fordham Uni-
versity Press, 1960.

Reviewed in *Catholic World* 192 (1960): 382-83 (R. W.
Rousseau); *Commonweal*, 7 October 1960, pp. 53-55 (J. J.

McDermott); *Library Journal* 85 (1960): 2795 (Robert H.
Donahugh); *School and Society* 88 (1960): 495-96 (William W. Brickman).

Boydston, Jo Ann, with Andresen, Robert L., eds. JOHN
   DEWEY, A CHECKLIST OF TRANSLATIONS, 1900-1967.
   Carbondale: Southern Illinois University Press,
   1969.

Reviewed in *Choice* 6 (1970): 1553; *Library Journal* 94
(1969): 3991 (Donald Empson).

Boydston, Jo Ann, ed. GUIDE TO THE WORKS OF JOHN
   DEWEY. Carbondale: Southern Illinois University
   Press, 1970.

Reviewed in *Bibliography of Philosophy* 18 (1971): 420
(Ernest W. Dewey); *Choice* 8 (1971): 1159; *Christian
Century* 87 (1970): 1488; *Educational Forum* 36 (1972):
418-19 (Christopher J. Lucas); *Educational Studies* 2
(1971): 59-60; *Illinois Education* 59 (1971): 139; *Im-
proving College and University Teaching* 19 (1971): 83;
International Philosophical Quarterly 12 (1972):
301-303 (Robert J. Roth); *Journal of Extension* 9
(Summer 1971): 67; *Library Journal* 96 (1971): 1250
(Thomas M. Bogie); *Modern Schoolman* 49 (1971): 84
(James Collins); *Philosophical Books* (Leicester, Eng-
land) 13 (October 1972): 10-12 (Wolfe Mays); *Philosophy
and Phenomenological Research* 32 (1971): 285-86 (Arnold
Berleant); *Review of Metaphysics* 25 (1971): 141-42
(Richard J. Bernstein).

Brickman, William W., and Lehrer, Stanley, eds. JOHN
   DEWEY: MASTER EDUCATOR. New York: Atherton Press,
   1966. [Paperback reprint.]

Reviewed in *History of Education Quarterly* 10 (1970):
113-26 (Thomas B. Colwell, Jr.).

Buswell, James Oliver, Jr. THE PHILOSOPHIES OF F. R.
   TENNANT AND JOHN DEWEY. New York: Philosophical
   Library, 1950. [From his doctoral dissertation,
   "The Empirical Method of F. R. Tennant." New
   York University, 1949.]

Reviewed in *Australasian Journal of Philosophy* 30
(1952): 65-67 (Henry Thornton); *Crozer Quarterly* 28
(1951): 249 (E. S. Brightman); *Modern Schoolman* 28
(1951): 318; *San Francisco Chronicle*, 18 February
1951 (R. G. C.).

Cohen, Morris Raphael. AMERICAN THOUGHT: A CRITICAL
    SKETCH. Glencoe, Ill.: Free Press, 1954.

Reviewed in *Philosophical Review* 65 (1956): 254-60
(Marcus George Singer).

Conkin, Paul K. PURITANS AND PRAGMATISTS: EIGHT EMI-
    NENT AMERICAN THINKERS. New York: Dodd, Mead and
    Co., 1968. ["John Dewey," pp. 345-402.]

Reviewed in *Journal of the History of Philosophy* 8
(1970): 112-14 (Herbert Schneider).

Crosser, Paul K. THE NIHILISM OF JOHN DEWEY. New
    York: Philosophical Library, 1955.

Reviewed in *Humanist* 16 (1956): 98 (Sidney Ratner);
Philosophical Review 65 (1956): 274-77 (George Dykhui-
zen); *Philosophical Quarterly* 6 (1956): 276-77 (J. W.
L. Adams).

Curti, Merle. SOCIAL IDEAS OF AMERICAN EDUCATORS.
    Report of the Commission on Social Studies, Amer-
    ican Historical Association, part 10. New York:
    Charles Scribner's Sons, 1935. ["John Dewey," pp.
    499-541.]

Reviewed in *Catholic Education Review* 34 (1936):
313-16 (Richard J. Purcell); *Educational Method* 15
(1935): 171; *Elementary School Journal* 36 (1936):
386-88 (Thomas Woody); *High Points* 18 (April 1936):
74-79 (Hyman Sorokoff); *Illinois Teacher* 24 (1936): 246
(Robert B. Browne); *Journal of Adult Education* 7
(1935): 297-99 (Hans Kohn); *School and Society* 41
(1935): 480-82; *School Review* 43 (1935): 628-30 (Harold
H. Punke); *Social Studies* 26 (1935): 489-90 (John S.
Brubacher).

Feldman, William Taft. THE PHILOSOPHY OF JOHN DEWEY:
A CRITICAL ANALYSIS. Baltimore: Johns Hopkins
Press, 1934. [Doctoral dissertation, Johns Hopkins
University.]

Reviewed in *Boston Evening Transcript*, 28 July 1934
(E. N.); *Journal of Philosophy* 31 (1934): 583-84 (Arthur E. Murphy).

Fisch, Max H., ed. CLASSIC AMERICAN PHILOSOPHERS:
PEIRCE, JAMES, ROYCE, SANTAYANA, DEWEY, WHITEHEAD.
New York: Appletcn-Century-Crofts, 1951.

Reviewed in *Journal of Philosophy* 48 (1951): 536-37
(J. L. B.); *Modern Schoolman* 29 (1952): 319-21 (James
Collins); *Philosophic Abstracts* 13 (Spring 1951): 35.

Geiger, George Raymond. JOHN DEWEY IN PERSPECTIVE.
New York: Oxford University Press, 1958.

Reviewed in *American Historical Review* 65 (1959-60):
644-45 (B. T. Wilkins); *Antioch Review* 19 (1959):
412-16 (Glenn Negley); *Educational Forum* 24 (1960):
373-74 (John L. Childs); *Humanist* 19 (1959): 54-55
(Sidney Ratner); *Journal of Higher Education* 30
(1959): 505-6 (David L. Miller); *Kirkus* 26 (1958): 728;
New Yorker, 8 November 1958, p. 214; *Saturday Review*,
14 February 1959, p. 56 (Ernest Nagel); *Social Education* 23 (1959): 136-38 (H. Harry Giles); *Times Educational Supplement* (London), 5 December 1958, p. 1743.

Handlin, Oscar. JOHN DEWEY'S CHALLENGE TO EDUCATION:
HISTORICAL PERSPECTIVES ON THE CULTURAL CONTEXT.
John Dewey Society Lectureship Series, no. 2. New
York: Harper and Brothers, 1959.

Reviewed in *Annals of the American Academy of Political and Social Science* 329 (May 1960): 195 (Theodore
Brameld); *Booklist* 56 (1960): 437; *Commonweal*, 5 February 1960, p. 527 (J. J. McDermott); *Education* 80
(1960): 407 (William P. Sears, Jr.); *Educational Research Bulletin* 40 (1961): 136-37 (Robert R. Wellman);
Junior College Journal 30 (1960): 272-73 (Luis M.
Morton, Jr.); *Library Journal* 84 (1959): 3770 (Jay W.
Stein); *Saturday Review*, 21 November 1959, p. 56

(David Adams); *Springfield Daily Republican*, 22 November 1959.

Hart, Joseph Kinmont. INSIDE EXPERIENCE: A NATURAL-
   ISTIC PHILOSOPHY OF LIFE AND THE MODERN WORLD.
   New York: Longmans, Green and Co., 1927.

Reviewed in *Journal of Philosophical Studies* 3 (1928):
116-18 (J. J. Findlay); *Journal of Philosophy* 26
(1929): 409-11 (Mary Shaw Kuypers); *New Scholasticism*
2 (1928): 179-80 (Virgil Michel).

Hook, Sidney. JOHN DEWEY: AN INTELLECTUAL PORTRAIT.
   New York: John Day Co., 1939.

Reviewed in *Journal of Higher Education* 11 (1940):
226-29 (Boyd H. Bode); *Journal of Philosophy* 36 (1939):
695 (Herbert Schneider); *Nation*, 6 January 1940, p. 22
(Eliseo Vivas); *New Republic*, 6 December 1939, p. 206
(Paul Weiss); *New York Herald Tribune Books*, 5 November
1939, p. 2 (Ernest Sutherland Bates); *Philosophical Review* 50 (1941): 86-87 (Everett Wesley Hall); *Saturday
Review of Literature*, 11 November 1939, p. 13 (Robert
Bierstedt).

Hook, Sidney, ed. JOHN DEWEY: PHILOSOPHER OF SCIENCE
   AND FREEDOM. A SYMPOSIUM. New York: Dial Press,
   1950.

Reviewed in *Ethics* 61 (1950): 89 (Alan Gewirth); *Hu-
manist* 10 (1950): 223 (Rubin Gotesky); *Journal of Phi-
losophy* 48 (1951): 192-95 (Harold A. Larrabee); *Journal
of Symbolic Logic* 16 (1951): 209 (Carl G. Hempel);
Modern Schoolman 47 (1969): 132-33 (Kenneth L. Becker);
New York Times Book Review, 23 April 1950, p. 6 (Thomas
Vernor Smith); *San Francisco Chronicle*, 6 August 1950;
Saturday Review of Literature, 19 August 1950, p. 35
(Robert Bierstedt).

Howard, Delton Thomas. JOHN DEWEY'S LOGICAL THEORY.
   New York: Longmans, Green and Co., 1918.

Reviewed in *Philosophical Review* 28 (1919): 424-26
(Evander Bradley McGilvary).

JOHN DEWEY: THE MAN AND HIS PHILOSOPHY. Addresses
Delivered in New York in Celebration of His Seven-
tieth Birthday. Cambridge: Harvard University
Press, 1930.

Reviewed in *Boston Evening Transcript*, 5 July 1930;
Education 51 (1930): 124; *International Journal of
Ethics* 41 (1931): 276 (L. M. Pape); *Journal of Philo-
sophical Studies* 6 (1931): 264-65 (H. H. Price); *Nature*
126 (1930): 537-38; *New Scholasticism* 6 (1932): 76-77
(Virgil Michel); *Outlook* 155 (1930): 227 (Edward T.
Devine); *Pittsburg Missouri Bulletin* 35 (October 1930):
67; *Progressive Education* 7 (1930): 93-97 (J. Milnor
Dorey); *School and Society* 32 (1930): 474 (William Mc-
Andrew); *Survey* 64 (1930): 359 (Bruce Bliven).

Leander, Folke. THE PHILOSOPHY OF JOHN DEWEY. A CRIT-
ICAL STUDY. Göteborg: Elanders Boktryckeri Aktie-
bolag, 1939.

Reviewed in *Journal of Philosophy* 36 (1939): 586-87
(Herbert Schneider), [Rejoinder by Leander, ibid. 37
(1940): 407-8.]; *Philosophical Review* 49 (1940): 262-64
(Max C. Otto); *Philosophy* (London) 14 (1939): 481-82
(John Laird).

Lepley, Ray, ed. VALUE: A COOPERATIVE INQUIRY. New
York: Columbia University Press, 1949.

Reviewed in *Hibbert Journal* 48 (1950): 396 (F. H.
Heinemann); *Journal of Philosophy* 48 (1951): 705-6
(Charles A. Baylis); *Library* 74 (1949): 1902-3 (Robert
W. Henderson); *Saturday Review of Literature*, 6 May
1950, p. 60 (R. B.); *Times Literary Supplement* (London),
23 June 1950, p. 393; *U.S. Quarterly Booklist* 6 (March
1950): 31.

Levitt, Morton. FREUD AND DEWEY ON THE NATURE OF MAN.
New York: Philosophical Library, 1960. [From his
doctoral dissertation "Freud and Dewey: A Comparative Study of Their Psychological Systems." University of Michigan, 1956.]

Reviewed in *Christian Century* 77 (1960): 513; *Social
Education* 25 (1961): 262-65 (Donald W. Robinson).

Mayhew, Katherine Camp, and Edwards, Anna Camp. THE
DEWEY SCHOOL: THE LABORATORY SCHOOL OF THE UNIVER-
SITY OF CHICAGO 1896-1903. New York: D. Appleton-
Century Co., 1936.

Reviewed in *American Sociological Review* 1 (1936):
542-43; *Childhood Education* 13 (1937): 381 (Alice Temple); *Curriculum Journal* 9 (1938): 137-39 (Clifford
Woody); *Educational Method* 16 (1936): 43-44; *Educa-
tional Research Bulletin* 16 (1937): 22-23 (H. G. Good);
Elementary School Journal 37 (1937): 711-12 (Howard Y.
McClusky); *History of Education Quarterly* 10 (1970):
113-26 [Review of the 1965 reprint by Atherton Press,
New York.]; *Journal of Educational Sociology* 15 (1941):
254; *Kadel Review* 15 (1936): 404-5 (E. I. F. Williams);
Progressive Education 14 (1937): 216-19 (Flora J.
Cooke).

McCluskey, Neil Gerard. PUBLIC SCHOOLS AND MORAL EDU-
CATION: THE INFLUENCE OF HORACE MANN, WILLIAM
TORREY HARRIS, AND JOHN DEWEY. New York: Columbia
University Press, 1958. [Doctoral dissertation,
Columbia University.]

Reviewed in *American Historical Review* 65 (1959): 189
(William H. Cartwright); *British Journal of Educational
Studies* 8 (1959): 74 (A. C. F. Beales); *Christian Cen-
tury* 76 (1959): 263 (Huber F. Klemme); *Cross Currents*
10 (1960): 145-80 (James Collins), [Dewey, pp. 151-52.];
Hibbert Journal 58 (1959): 91-93 (Harold Loukes); *Reli-
gious Education* 54 (1959): 186 (Paul H. Vieth);
Teachers College Record 61 (1959): 114-16 (Richard D.
Mosier).

Meiklejohn, Alexander. EDUCATION BETWEEN TWO WORLDS.
New York and London: Harper and Brothers, 1942.

Reviewed in *Humanist* 3 (1943): 81-83 (Ernest Nagel)
[Reply by Meiklejohn, ibid.: 120-22; rejoinder by
Nagel, ibid.: 122-23.].

Moore, Edward Carter. AMERICAN PRAGMATISM: PEIRCE,
JAMES, AND DEWEY. New York: Columbia University
Press, 1961.

Reviewed in *Dialogue* 1 (1962): 223-24 (W. M. Sibley);

Ethics 72 (1962): 146-47 (Richard M. Rorty); *Journal of Philosophy* 59 (1962): 272-74 (Richard J. Bernstein); *New England Quarterly* 34 (1961): 532-33 (Kenneth S. Lynn).

Nathanson, Jerome. FORERUNNERS OF FREEDOM: THE RECON-STRUCTION OF THE AMERICAN SPIRIT. Washington, D.C.: American Council on Public Affairs, 1941. [Dewey, pp. 116-54.]

Reviewed in *Annals of the American Academy of Political and Social Science* 217 (1941): 180-81 (Herman Hausheer); *Journal of Philosophy* 38 (1941): 474-75 (Herbert Schneider).

Nathanson, Jerome. JOHN DEWEY: THE RECONSTRUCTION OF THE DEMOCRATIC LIFE. Twentieth Century Library Series, edited by Hiram Hayden. New York: Charles Scribner's Sons, 1951.

Reviewed in *High Points* 34 (October 1952): 79 (Martin Wolfson); *Humanist* 12 (1952): 138 (Edward William Strong); *Journal of Philosophy* 49 (1952): 478-79 (George Dykhuizen); *Kirkus* 19 (1951): 461; *New York Herald Tribune Books*, 11 November 1951, p. 8 (Joseph L. Blau); *Saturday Review of Literature*, 5 January 1952, p. 16 (Brand Blanshard).

New Republic. "John Dewey: An Appraisal of His Contributions to Philosophy, Education, and the Affairs of Men. Presented on the Occasion of His Ninetieth Birthday." *New Republic*, 17 October 1949, pp. 10-39.

Reviewed in *Modern Schoolman* 27 (1950): 319-20 (James Collins).

Nissen, Lowell. JOHN DEWEY'S THEORY OF INQUIRY AND TRUTH. New York: Humanities Press, 1968. [Paperback reprint.]

Reviewed in *Review of Metaphysics* 22 (1968): 150-51 (M. B. M.).

Ratner, Sidney, ed. THE PHILOSOPHER OF THE COMMON MAN.
ESSAYS IN HONOR OF JOHN DEWEY TO CELEBRATE HIS
EIGHTIETH BIRTHDAY. New York: G. P. Putnam's Sons,
1940.

Reviewed in *Journal of Philosophy* 37 (1940): 332-34
(J. H. Tufts).

Rosenstock, Gershon George. F. A. TRENDELENBURG--
FORERUNNER TO JOHN DEWEY. Carbondale: Southern
Illinois University Press, 1964. [Dewey, pp.
112-24, and passim.]

Reviewed in *Journal of the History of Philosophy* 4
(1966): 265-66 (Herbert W. Schneider); *Modern Schoolman*
43 (1966): 290-91 (Robert A. Preston); *Review of Metaphysics* 19 (1966): 599 (C. T. W.).

Roth, Robert J. JOHN DEWEY AND SELF-REALIZATION.
Englewood Cliffs, N.J.: Prentice-Hall, 1963.

Reviewed in *Dialogue* (Canada) 3 (1964-65): 210-11
(J. Rutledge).

Rucker, Darnell. THE CHICAGO PRAGMATISTS. Minneapolis: University of Minnesota Press, 1969.

Reviewed in *Dialogue* (Canada) 8 (1969): 512-13 (Mil-
lard Schumaker); *Journal of the History of Philosophy*
8 (1970): 496-501 (Van Meter Ames); *Modern Schoolman*
47 (1970): 362-64 (James Collins); *Transactions of the
Charles S. Peirce Society* 6 (1970): 58-62 (Manley
Thompson).

Schilpp, Paul Arthur, ed. THE PHILOSOPHY OF JOHN
DEWEY. The Library of Living Philosophers, vol. 1.
Evanston, Ill.: Northwestern University Press,
1939. [Reprinted, with the bibliography extended
to 1950 by Muriel Murray. New York: Tudor Publishing Co., 1951.]

Reviewed in *Boston Evening Transcript*, 30 December 1939
(Albert Wohlstetter); *Christian Century* 57 (1940):
313-15 (Charles Hartshorne); *Christian Science Monitor*,
6 January 1940 (A. F. Gilmore); *Ethics* 50 (1940): 353-59.

(William Henry Werkmeister); *Frontiers of Democracy* 6 (1940): 221-22 (John R. Reid); *Journal of Higher Education* 11 (1940): 226-29 (Boyd H. Bode); *Journal of Philosophy* 36 (1939): 691-95 (Sterling Power Lamprecht); *New Republic*, 6 December 1939, p. 206 (Paul Weiss); *New York Herald Tribune Books*, 5 November 1939, p. 2 (Ernest Sutherland Bates); *Philosophical Review* 49 (1940): 69-74 (Gustavus Watts Cunningham); *Philosophy* 15 (1940): 207-8 (John Laird); *Religious Education* 35 (1940): 45-50 (George A. Coe); *Saturday Review of Literature*, 11 November 1939, pp. 12-13 (Robert Bierstedt); *Science and Society* 4 (1940): 120-25 (Howard Selsam).

Somjee, Abdulkarim H. THE POLITICAL THEORY OF JOHN DEWEY. New York: Teachers College Press, 1968.

Reviewed in *American Political Science Review* 64 (1970): 210-12 (Ronald J. Terchek); *Choice* 64 (1969): 68; *Educational Theory* 21 (1971): 117-25 (N. C. Bhattacharyya); *History of Education Quarterly* 10 (1970): 113-26 (Thomas B. Colwell, Jr.).

Thomas, Milton Halsey, and Schneider, Herbert Wallace. A BIBLIOGRAPHY OF JOHN DEWEY. New York: Columbia University Press, 1929.

Reviewed in *A.L.A. Booklist* 26 (1930): 259; *American Journal of Sociology* 36 (1930): 344; *International Journal of Ethics* 40 (1930): 456; *Nation*, 22 January 1930, pp. 100-101 (Henry Hazlitt); *Times Literary Supplement* (London), 17 April 1930, p. 328.

Thomas, Milton Halsey. A BIBLIOGRAPHY OF JOHN DEWEY, 1882-1939. Introd. by Herbert W. Schneider. New York: Columbia University Press, 1939.

Reviewed in *Journal of Religion* 20 (1940): 421 (W. C. Bower).

Thomas, Milton Halsey. JOHN DEWEY, A CENTENNIAL BIBLIOGRAPHY. Chicago: University of Chicago Press, 1962.

Reviewed in *American Quarterly* 15 (1963): 222 (Lawrence

A. Cremin); *Library Journal* 87 (1962): 2124-25 (Frederick Wezeman); *Papers of the Bibliographical Society of America* 57 (1963): 251-53 (Robert L. Perkins); *Review of Metaphysics* 16 (1963): 587-88 (R. J. B.).

Thomas, Wendell Marshall. A DEMOCRATIC PHILOSOPHY. New York: Correlated Enterprises, 1938. [Dewey, pp. 11-37, and passim.]

Reviewed in *Christian Century* 56 (1939): 25-26; *Churchman* 152 (1938): 34; *Crozer Quarterly* 16 (1939): 76 (E. W. Powell); *Ethics* 49 (1938): 122 (Theodore Brameld).

White, Morton Gabriel. THE ORIGIN OF DEWEY'S INSTRU-MENTALISM. Columbia Studies in Philosophy, no. 4. New York: Columbia University Press, 1943. [Doctoral dissertation, Columbia University, 1942.]

Reviewed in *Crozer Quarterly* 20 (1943): 170 (E. M. Austin); *Ethics* 54 (1944): 155-56 (Arthur E. Murphy); *Humanist* 3 (1943): 86-87 (Alfred Stiernotte); *Journal of Philosophy* 40 (1943): 250-52 (David F. Bowers); *Springfield Daily Republican*, 20 April 1943 (C. D. Kean).

Wirth, Arthur G. JOHN DEWEY AS EDUCATOR: HIS DESIGN FOR WORK IN EDUCATION (1894-1904). New York: John Wiley and Sons, 1966.

Reviewed in *Studies in Philosophy and Education* 6 (1968): 14-22 (George Dykhuizen).

ADDENDA

Baym, Max I. *A HISTORY OF LITERARY AESTHETICS IN AMER-
ICA*. New York: Frederick Ungar, 1973. [Dewey, pp.
191-207, and passim.]

Clopton, Robert W., and Ou, Tsuin-chen. Introduction
to *JOHN DEWEY LECTURES IN CHINA, 1919-1920*. Honolulu: University Press of Hawaii, 1973.

Doll, William E., Jr. "Methodology of Experience: The
Process of Inquiry." *Educational Theory* 23 (1973):
56-73.

Fontinell, Eugene. "Pragmatism, Process, and Religious
Education." *Religious Education* 68 (1973): 322-31.
[Dewey, pp. 323-25.]

Frazier, Gordon E. "Sundry Support of a Deweyan Learn-
ing-to-Learn Concept of Education." In *PHILOSOPHY
OF EDUCATION 1972: Proceedings of the Twenty-Eighth
Annual Meeting of the Philosophy of Education Soci-
ety*, pp. 377-85. Edwardsville, Ill.: Studies in
Philosophy and Education, 1972.

Gallant, Thomas F. "Dewey's Child-Centered Education
in Contemporary Academe: Free Universities Movement."
Educational Forum 37 (1973): 411-19.

Girvetz, Harry K. *BEYOND RIGHT AND WRONG, A Study in
Moral Theory*. New York: Macmillan Co., Free Press,
1973. [Dewey, pp. 127-39, and passim.]

Hickson, Mark. "Dewey's Reflex Arc and Reflective
Thought: A Comparison with Korzybski." *ETC: A Review of General Semantics* 30 (1973): 127-30.

Hook, Sidney. "The Relevance of John Dewey's Thought."
In *THE CHIEF GLORY OF EVERY PEOPLE*, edited by Matthew
J. Bruccoli, pp. 55-75. Carbondale: Southern Illi-
nois University Press, 1973.

Karier, Clarence J. "American Educational History."
Educational Forum 37 (1973): 293-302. [Dewey, pp.
298-99.]

McDermott, John J., ed.   Introduction to *THE PHILO-SOPHY OF JOHN DEWEY*. 2 vols. New York: G. P. Putnam's Sons, 1973.

Okolo, Chukwudum Barnabas. "Self and Individual in Dewey: A Philosophic Inquiry." Doctoral dissertation, Catholic University of America, 1973.

Ou, Tsuin-chen, and Clopton, Robert W.   Introduction to *JOHN DEWEY LECTURES IN CHINA, 1919-1920*. Honolulu: University Press of Hawaii, 1973.

Richardson, Charles. "Dewey's Political Method." Master's thesis, Southern Illinois University, 1973.

Rockefeller, Steven C.   "John Dewey's Ethical Idealism: An Essay in the Philosophy of Religion." Doctoral dissertation, Middlebury College, 1973.

Sanchez, Ramon. "Can Philosophy of Education Deal with Reality?" *Contemporary Education* 44 (1973): 201-4.

Stone, George C. "Implications of John Dewey's Philosophy of History for a Theory of Teaching History." Doctoral dissertation, Southern Illinois University, 1973.

Troutner, Leroy F. "The Dewey-Heidegger Comparison Revisited: A Perspectival Partnership for Education." In *PHILOSOPHY OF EDUCATION 1972: Proceedings of the Twenty-Eighth Annual Meeting of the Philosophy of Education Society*, pp. 28-44. Edwardsville, Ill.: Studies in Philosophy and Education, 1972.

Whitehouse, Peter George. "Dewey's *ART AS EXPERIENCE*: The Implications for Practical Work in School Music Resulting from the Concepts of the Functional Self and Music as Sound." Master's thesis, University of New Brunswick, 1973.

Reviews

Dykhuizen, George. THE LIFE AND MIND OF JOHN DEWEY. Carbondale: Southern Illinois University Press, 1973.

Reviewed in *America*, 15 September 1973, pp. 162-65
(John W. Donohue); *Chicago Sun Times*, 23 September
1973 (Alan Gewirth); *New Republic*, 27 October 1973,
pp. 28-29 (Sidney Hook).

EARLY ESSAYS. The Early Works of John Dewey, 1882-1898.
  Vol. 5, 1895-1898. Edited by Jo Ann Boydston. Carbondale: Southern Illinois University Press, 1972.

Reviewed in *Booklist*, 15 April 1973, p. 776; *Library
Journal*, 1 December 1972, p. 3892; *Long Beach Independent*, 16 November 1972; *Long Beach Press-Telegram*,
15 November 1972; *School Review* 81 (1973): 299-301
(Harold B. Dunkel).

The Early Works of John Dewey, 1882-1898. Vols. 1-5,
  edited by Jo Ann Boydston. Carbondale: Southern
  Illinois University Press, 1967-1972.

Reviewed in *Psychological Record* 23 (1973): 270-71
(Paul T. Mountjoy); *Philosophy and Phenomenological
Research* 34 (1973): 131-32 (James Gouinlock).

The essays listed below were received as the Checklist went to press, too late to be included in the
index. All appeared in *Tulane Studies in Philosophy*
22 (1973).

George, Francis E. "Dewey and Dialectic," pp. 22-37.

Jardine, John G. "Experience as Revelatory of Nature
  in Dewey's Metaphysical Methodology," pp. 38-50.

Lee, Harold N. "Dewey and the Behavioral Theory of
  Meaning," pp. 51-62.

Moran, Jon S. "Mead on the Self and Moral Situations."
  [Dewey, pp. 63-65.]

Smith, Allen K. "Dewey's Transition Piece: The *Reflex
  Arc* Paper," pp. 122-41.

AUTHOR INDEX

AUTHOR INDEX

TITLE INDEX

TITLE INDEX

History, 246
MEAD, GEORGE HERBERT
  ON SOCIAL PSYCHOLOGY, 169-70
  PHILOSOPHER OF SOCIAL INDIVIDUAL, 100
  SELECTED WRITINGS, 113
  SOCIAL DYNAMICS OF, 125
  SOCIAL PSYCHOLOGY OF, 113
Meaning
  and Existence, 70
  Assertion, and Proposal, 31
  Dewey's Theory of, 172
  Dewey's Theory of Language and, 185, 256
  Phenomenological Analysis of Occurrence of, in Experience, 253
  Pragmatic Theory of, 229
  Some Meanings of, in Dewey's EXPERIENCE AND NATURE, 70
  Study in Wittgenstein's Theory of, 95
  Theories of, 208
  Theories of, of Dewey and Oxford Ordinary Language Philosophers, 255
  Time, and Transcendence, 104
MEANING
  AND ACTION, 172
  AND TRUTH, INQUIRY INTO, 151
  DEFINITION OF, FOR AMERICAN EDUCATION, 70
Means-Ends
  Continuity of, 204
  Distinction in Dewey's Philosophy, 149
Memorial, Dewey, University of Vermont May Have, 29
Memorial Address by Dewey, AFT Convention, 83
Memories of Dewey, 79
MEN AND MOVEMENTS IN AMERICAN PHILOSOPHY, 17
Merleau-Ponty, Jacques, his Phenomenology of Habitual Body, 223
Metaethical Theory, Dewey's Ethics in Light of, 219
Metaphysic, Dewey's Rejection and Acceptance of, 111
Metaphysical Assumptions in Dewey's Philosophy, 49, 181

Metaphysical Basis of Value for Dewey, 243
Metaphysical Development of Dewey, 27, 111, 127
Metaphysical Foundation of Dewey's Theory of Education, 238-39
Metaphysical Perspective of Dewey, 163
Metaphysical Presuppositions of Dewey compared with Cox, 228
  of Dewey's Philosophy, 196
METAPHYSICAL PRESUPPOSITIONS OF PHILOSOPHY OF JOHN DEWEY, 10
Metaphysics
  and Value Theories of Urban, Dewey and Perry, 246
  and Value Theory, 215
  Another Note on Dewey's Development of, 27
  Concerning Abandonment of Certain Deweyan Conception of, 26-27
  Concerning Certain Deweyan Conception of, 76
  Dewey's, 211, 213
  Dewey's Educational Theory related to his, 232-33
  Dewey's Epistemology and, 122
  Dewey's Naturalistic, 152
  Evidence of, in Dewey's Philosophy, 223
  Experience and Existence in Dewey's Naturalistic, 87
  Metaphors and, 170
  Methodological Approach to, 223
  New, 255
  of Experience, Dewey's, 14
  of Pragmatic Empiricism, 230
  Pragmatism and, 120
  Psychology and Philosophy, 190
  Ultimate Constants in Dewey's, 212
METAPHYSICS
  LOGIC WITHOUT, 124
  OF JAMES AND DEWEY, 111
  OF PRAGMATISM, 78
Method
  Dewey and Concept of, 106